The Eagle and the Cross

PAUL SHORE

The Eagle and the Cross

Jesuits in Late Baroque Prague

Institute of Jesuit Sources
Saint Louis

No. 16 in Series 3: Original Studies Composed in English

Institute of Jesuit Sources
3601 Lindell Blvd.
St. Louis, MO. 63108
tel: [314] 977-7257
fax: [314] 977-7263
e-mail: IJS@SLU.EDU

Library of Congress Control Number: 2002109141
ISBN: 1-880810-46-8

To the members of the Society of Jesus
on both sides of the Atlantic
who aided in the development
of this book

Contents

Preface

The Society of Jesus has always aroused strong reactions in those who come into contact with it; likewise, it has posed special challenges for its historians. Any study of the eighteenth-century Society must take into account the special circumstances of the time and, in particular, the declining sense of security and the unstable political climate in which the Society carried on its works during the decades immediately preceding its suppression. Several of these circumstances affect anyone engaged in research on the Bohemian Society and have shaped the direction this book has taken. These should be explained at the outset.

The first of these has to do with the sources available. The past thirty years have witnessed a revolution in attitude toward using documentary evidence from institutional or semiofficial sources to arrive at a new understanding of social history. Court records, wills, coroners' reports, and sermons, *inter alia,* have been called into service to shed light on the experiences and values of groups traditionally excluded from the historical narrative. By utilizing such documents historians have been able to construct theories about the similarities and differences characterizing the institutions that generated the documents. The results have forever changed our view of the early modern period and offer new possibilities to all historians of the Society.

It was with these new approaches in mind that I began an exploration of materials relating to the Jesuits in Bohemia. I was cheered to discover, still surviving in the National Library in Prague, a solitary copy of the annual reports (the *Litteræ annuæ* or, as they are sometimes referred to, the *Annales*) sent to Rome from Bohemia during the decades before the suppression; moreover, I came upon an unedited manuscript in the Strahov Monastery in Prague dealing with the careers of former Jesuits from Bohemia. The records left behind by these eighteenth-century Jesuits are extensive and detailed; the Jesuits were meticulous in their record keeping and systematic in the organization of their reports.

Yet, while the *Litteræ annuæ* are a cornerstone of any documentary study of the pre-suppression Society, they also present the historian with a puzzle. Composed in a Baroque Latin that veers between the shockingly revelatory and the clichéd, they were written to be read by other Jesuits;

and their authors were far from objective when reporting on how well they had achieved the core aim of the Society, to bring men and women to God.[1] My preliminary research on Jesuit *Litteræ* written during the same period in the Austrian Province had led me to suspect that despite the great variety of physical and cultural settings in which the Society worked, those who recorded its activities were trained to produce documents of surprising uniformity. Nor is there an abundance of other contemporary material from Bohemia that might be used to complement a study relying so heavily on a single collection of sources. The absence of any significant body of corroborating documentation from governmental, public, or personal sources constrains the historian to constantly weigh how to regard the claims made or the observations offered in the *Litteræ*.

This is not to suggest that other contemporary sources had nothing to say about the Jesuits. Across the German-speaking world, the 1750s, '60s, and '70s produced a flurry of popular writing about the Society (most of it unflattering); but very few of these publications were produced in Bohemia or related to conditions prevailing in that land. The records generated by the Theresian bureaucracy on matters of taxation, land reform, health, and the like were largely silent on the topic of the Society until the suppression presented the Crown with an unexpected windfall of property falling into its hands. Even a detailed contemporary history of the Jews of Prague makes no explicit mention of their nearest neighbors, the Jesuits. The level of literacy among most of the peasants and townspeople with whom the Jesuits came into contact was not high enough to ensure that very many diaries or letters would survive; and, in fact, aside from František Vavák's[2] well-known *Paměti,* very few writings from nonofficial sources are known today. Secondary sources occasionally tantalize with references to diaries and memoirs produced by former Jesuits, but searching for such leads has proved to be akin to pursuing a phantom.[3]

---

[1] Only very rarely do the writers of the *Litteræ* step out of this ritualistic Latinity to reveal something of their own reactions to events. Once when discussing a gift made to the Jesuit church in Znojmo, the writer of the *Litteræ* exclaimed, alluding to Oedipus's legendary riddle-solving prowess and the occasional difficulty of explaining the meaning of certain phrases, "Oedipus sit, non ego, qui donum verbis strictim notatum clare explicat" (Národní Knihovna [hereafter abbreviated to NK], 23/19, *Litt. An. Boh. Prov. 1769,* folio 165r). But even here, as the anonymous writer gives vent to a personal reaction, he does so with a classical allusion.

[2] For a discussion of proper names as found in various languages in use during this period, see Appendix I below, pp. 219 f.

[3] Ernest Denis, for example, refers to the memoirs of an anonymous Bohemian Jesuit that were reported by A. Rezek in the *"Comptes rendus de l'Académie des sciences"* in 1881. No such publication has been identified.

All of this is by way of saying that the *Litteræ* must remain the single most significant primary source in a study of the eighteenth-century Bohemian Province, but as such their value is hard to determine. This brings us to the second circumstance with which we must deal. Despite the limitations of the *Litteræ,* I remained convinced that their story was worth telling if I could adduce other types of evidence with which to complement it. Presented with a large and fascinating body of materials not easily put in context, I have turned to the visual arts, to studies done on folk cultures, to clues buried in the careers of former Jesuits after 1773, and to studies conducted on the social history of Bohemia in the eighteenth century (which surprisingly had for the most part little new to say about the Jesuits).

These have provided some insights, and also pointed up additional questions. Those historical studies produced during the forty years of Soviet domination of Czechoslovakia illustrate another problem facing the historian of the Bohemian Society: the downplaying of the impact of religion in much of the literature written about eighteenth-century Bohemia. Long before Marxism became the only paradigm in which Czechs might discuss history, the anticlerical historians of the late nineteenth century sought to minimize or demonize the role of the Catholic Church in Bohemia. Catholic historians, on the defensive, responded in kind, producing a body of literature that for too long retained a polemical rather than a scholarly flavor.

Only during the past decade has Czech historiography begun to shake off this burdensome legacy, and the process is not yet over. Exaggerated nationalism, antagonisms between Protestants and Catholics, and persistent stereotypes of Jesuits as book-burning fanatics (and indignant and hasty denials of Jesuit wrongdoing) still hamper students of this topic. Moreover, the influence of ethnic rivalries complicates this study, as does the practice, common to so much of eastern-European history, of anachronistically attributing nationalist sentiments to people who lived long before such notions were current. The following monograph attempts to contribute balance to the existing literature on Bohemian Jesuits by constructing a preliminary picture that is neither an apologia nor an indictment, but strives to address the motivations and beliefs of this unusual band of men.

Another question that had to be addressed as this book took shape was, What are the boundaries of this study? Originally I had planned to limit the topic to "the Jesuits of Prague," but it soon became clear that defining this group in exclusive terms would be impossible. The high degree of mobility that has always characterized the Society resulted in men spending a year or two within the city, and then being sent as teachers, librarians, missionaries, and the like to remote corners of the Bohemian Province. Other Jesuits were born and educated in Prague, but spent their entire careers outside the city, or even beyond the boundaries of their province. The Austrian and Upper German Provinces could also claim Jesuits born in Prague who maintained contact with the city of their birth. Some Prague

Jesuits participated in the annual pilgrimages that led into the countryside and attracted thousands of followers along the way, while remaining committed to their assignments in the city. A few Jesuits spent all or most of their professional careers in schools outside Prague, but wrote works that were used in the schools and the university there; these also had a direct influence on the institutional culture of the Society in Prague.

Finally, even if arbitrary lines could be drawn that would include some Jesuits and exclude others, the *Litteræ* themselves are tantalizingly vague. Their accounts often fail to specify the location of and participants in many of the events recorded. So who were the "Jesuits of Prague" and what was their sphere of action? I decided to define the group broadly, as the Jesuits themselves would probably have been most comfortable doing. At the same time, a study of this scale cannot claim to be a survey of all the Jesuits of the Bohemian Province. Brno, Olomouc, and the pilgrimage shrines each deserves more concentrated attention, as do the Jesuits working in smaller communities and those who directed large agricultural operations.[4] The scattered *collegia* of the Society operated in their own cultural context. Finally, a figure such as Fr. Koniáš occupies a place in Czech cultural history too large to fit within the categories of urban versus rural; his story will be touched on later, but he was considerably more than a "Prague Jesuit."

Having said all this, we must inevitably focus this study upon Prague, the "matka měst" (mother of Bohemian cities). Here it was that the leading Jesuit intellectuals of the region did their research and wrote, here the most lavish and visible Jesuit drama and liturgy were offered to the public, here the largest number of students received training in the schools of the Society, and here the most prominent former Jesuits continued to work after 1773. Yet the hinterlands remain important, because Bohemian society in the eighteenth century possessed an overwhelmingly rural character, and the Jesuits made a very sizeable investment of time and effort working with the people of the countryside. One has only to look at the space devoted in the *Litteræ* to missions in the country, as opposed to the relatively brief attention paid to the universities and *collegia,* to grasp how central the rural mission and educational work was to the Society's understanding of itself. From the spires of the churches of Baroque Prague, the countryside was always visible, and throughout this book the same will also be true.

Since this project began to take shape in the fall of 1992, many individuals and institutions have contributed to its progress. At the outset, when I knew only a modest amount of Czech and was unfamiliar with the complexities of what was in those days known as the Czechoslovakian State Central Archives, Marie Černá and Michal Svatoš were extremely helpful. In

[4] The primary sources stored in the Zemský Archiv in Brno are cataloged in M. Švabenský, *Jesuité v Brně 1241–1773* (Brno: 1954).

the later stages of my research, Lilla Vekerdy, Robert Hohl, Matthew Mirow, Phil Gavitt, Martin Svatoš, Helga Robinson-Hammerstein, and Michael Maher, S.J., offered helpful insights. Frs. Claude Pavur, S.J., and John L. McCarthy, S.J., assisted in untangling passages of Baroque Latin. Professor Peter Jones was a constant source of intelligent criticism, wit, and optimism. Anthea Taylor made everything easier to do. Jill Crowley assisted with her painstaking and insightful editing. Saint Louis University provided a sabbatical year that was indispensable for the completion of this project, and this university's Department of History provided support for the arduous task of indexing. The Marchetti Jesuit Endowment enabled me to conduct research at the Harvard Divinity School, where I worked as a visiting scholar for one semester; and the Institute for Advanced Studies in the Humanities at the University of Edinburgh furnished the ideal environment of collegial stimulation in which to begin writing. Errors of fact and interpretation, of course, are traceable to me alone and do not reflect on these individuals and institutions.

Most of all, I would like to thank my wife Ilene, who was the sounding board for each new idea or interpretation, and always open to the idea that these eighteenth-century Jesuits were worth the time and effort to rediscover. My debt to her is the largest of all.

Cambridge, Mass.

May 2000

chapter one

INTRODUCTION

Bohemia can supply us.

—Prince Frederick von Schwarzenberg

The oppression of these poor people and the tyranny under which they suffer are known.

—Maria Thesesia to her son Ferdinand, February 1777

The second half of the eighteenth century was a period of momentous change for the lands of the Crown of Bohemia.[1] In 1750 this region was attempting to recover from the destruction and disruption of the War of Austrian Succession, and was vulnerable to renewed attack from Frederick II. Bohemia lacked a governmentally supported school system, any systematic approach to public health, or a modern infrastructure of roads. Its peasants labored under the hardships of the *robota* and the abuses of their lords, who resisted the imposition of any authority other than their own.[2] Its aristocracy, drawn to a significant degree from foreign supporters of the Habsburgs, were by and large unenlightened in their treatment of those over whom they ruled. Bohemia's agriculture was awaiting reform, its trade hampered by archaic tariffs, its industrial base, which would play such a pivotal role in the next century, scarcely even imagined. Some Bohemians feared that the "time of darkness,"

[1] Throughout this book, "Bohemia" and "Bohemian" will be used to denote the political and geographical entity known today in Czech as "Čechy." "Czech" will be used to describe the language and culture of the Slavic inhabitants of that land. During the seventeenth and eighteenth centuries, the word "Czech" or its cognates were rarely used except by a few writers when addressing Czech speakers.

[2] George J. Svoboda, "The Odd Alliance: The Underprivileged Population of Bohemia and the Habsburg Court, 1765–1790," in *The Czech and Slovak Experience: Selected Papers from the Fourth World Congress for Soviet and East European Studies, Harrogate, 1990,* ed. John Morison (New York: St. Martin's Press, 1992), 7–20.

as later Czech writers were to style it, would continue without relief or remedy.

This period of hardship had commenced with the defeat of the Bohemian forces at White Mountain more than a century before, and its effects still perdured. While populous and in some instances productive, Bohemia had been falling steadily behind other western-European lands in terms of culture and general prosperity. Prague, the cosmopolitan city that would welcome Mozart, was the exception (although some historians have written of its "inevitable decline"); the rest of the kingdom could claim neither cultural sophistication nor awareness of the ideals of the Enlightenment. The Baroque literary period, in both its Latin and Czech manifestations, had spent most of its force, while the revitalization of the Czech language was not yet a reality.[3] Although it was not a cultural backwater to the degree that Hungary had become, Bohemia presented a frequently distressing picture to travelers, including Maria Theresia's son and co-ruler, Joseph II.[4]

Four decades later, after 1750, profound changes had occurred in the culture of the Bohemian lands, changes that enabled this portion of the Habsburg domains to share in the broader European cultural and intellectual life of the coming century. These changes, while they overlapped and interacted with one another, may be summarized as follows:

1. The institutional reforms of the Habsburgs included the creation of a public-school system, the reduction of the number of monasteries and convents, the abolition of the *robota* or forced peasant labor, and the emancipation of the Jews. The popular term Josephinism is a less accurate characterization of this period of Habsburg rule, for the reign of Joseph's mother, Maria Theresia (1740–80), also witnessed numerous important reforms. Later sweeping changes accompanied, and in many instances paralleled, the centralizing and Germanizing programs of the reforming emperor Joseph II. These included, *inter alia,* reform of the judicial system and attempts at overhauling the internal bureaucracy of the region.[5]

---

[3] William E. Harkins, "The Periodization of Czech Literary History, 1774–1879," in *The Czech Literary Renaissance,* ed. Peter Brock and H. Gordon Skilling (Toronto: University of Toronto Press, 1970), 3 f.

[4] Derek Beales, *Joseph II: In the Shadow of Maria Theresia* (Cambridge: The University Press, 1987), 338–40. A remarkable extract from a letter written by Joseph in 1771 after a visit to Bohemia is found in *The Austrian Achievement, 1700–1800,* by Ernest Wangermann (London: Thames and Hudson, 1973), 99 f. In it Joseph criticizes (perhaps inaccurately) the Jesuits of Prague for turning away dying famine victims from their doors.

[5] Helen Liebel Weckowicz, "Auf der Suche nach neuer Autorität: Raison d'état in der Verwaltungs -und Rechtsreformer Maria Theresias und Josephs II," in *Österreich im Europa der Aufklärung* (Vienna: Verlag der Österreichischen Akademie der Wissenschaften, 1985), 362.

2. The rise in Czech national consciousness, culminating in the "National Awakening" that continued into the next century. This increased awareness manifested itself in a greater interest in Bohemian history and in the Czech language, and in a desire to reassert a claim to national identity that had been in large part snatched from them in the aftermath of the battle of White Mountain in 1620. Calls for independence or even for semiautonomy within the Habsburg state were still far in the future, but the issue of nationality would be present in virtually all literary debates of the coming century, and would deeply color the writing of Bohemian history.[6]

3. The suppression of the Society of Jesus by the papal brief *Dominus ac redemptor noster* in 1773, which remained in force, though with some important exceptions, until 1814.[7]

This last event was of worldwide significance, for not only were the Jesuits the most powerful religious order in the Catholic Church, but they also had unusually close ties to political leaders and had dominated the universities of the Catholic world for over a century. Large numbers of Jesuits served on foreign missions and came into contact with millions of Catholics and non-Catholics. The suppression of the Society, the largest and most centrally organized religious order in the history of Christianity, was not everywhere enforced with the same intensity and resulted in different consequences in different countries. The suppression has been the object of research on the part of scholars, many of them ardently partisan in their assessment of the Jesuits. In the last 150 years, no one has attempted a general history of the suppression itself; nor will the following study recount its story, either generally or specifically in a central-European context, a project that would extend far beyond the limitations of this book.[8] Instead, this volume will examine the experience of the Jesuits in a place where they had exercised extraordinary influence, Prague and the surrounding Bohemian countryside, during the final decades before the suppression put an end to their activities.

[6] Justin Prášek, *Dějiny Čech a Moravy na počátku národního znovuzrození* (Prague: Nakladatel I. L. Kober Knihupectví, 1903), vol. 7; György M. Vajda, *Wien und die Literaturen in der Donaumonarchie: Zur Kulturgeschichte Mitteleuropas* (Vienna: Böhlau Verlag, 1994), 79f.; in addition, see Josef Kočí, *Naše národní obrození* (Prague: Státní nakladatelesví politické literatury, 1960), although the last offers no documentation for its essentially Marxist analysis.

[7] The literature dealing with the suppression of the Society has tended to be partisan in interpretation, with the opponents of the Society exhibiting at least as much bias as its defenders. The best overall account of the events leading up to the issuance of *Dominus et redemptor noster* is still J. Crétineau-Joly, *Clement XIV et les Jésuites; ou, histoire de la destruction des Jésuites,* 6 vols. (Paris: Mellier Frères, 1848).

[8] An attempt to bring together the strands of Jesuit history in an eighteenth-century Habsburg context is found in László Szilás's essay "La Compagnia di Gesù e la politica ecclesiastica dell' Imperio Asburgo nei secoli xvii e xviii," in *I Gesuiti e gli Asburgo: Presenza della Compagnia di Gesù nell'area meridionale dell'Imperio Asburgo nei secoli xvii-xviii* (Trieste: Lint, 1995), 15–22.

This story is worth telling for several reasons. The members of the Society of Jesus who taught and ministered to the residents of Prague in the 1750s, '60s, and '70s inhabited two worlds. They were the direct heirs of the Counter-Reformation, which had first been felt in Bohemia at least two centuries earlier, and which had profoundly altered the course of that country's cultural development.[9] Their mission was to preserve and promote the doctrine of the Catholic Church in an environment that for several centuries had been largely hostile to these teachings.[10] Jesuits of the "fourth vow" had sworn obedience to the pope; and even those members of the Society who had not pronounced this fourth vow were trained and socialized within an international organization theoretically committed to a uniformity of institutional structure and educational principles that extended far beyond the geographical boundaries of the particular state in which they worked.

At the same time, Jesuits of the Bohemian Province were in almost every instance ethnic Czechs and Germans, and were natives of Bohemia. Unlike their fellows in many other parts of the world, the Bohemian Jesuits were not outsiders but natives intimately familiar with the society in which they worked. As speakers of either Czech, German, or both of those languages, they were influenced by the shifting patterns of language usage that took place during the eighteenth century.[11] They spoke the languages of the peoples with whom they interacted, understood intuitively the cultural patterns of Bohemian society, and perhaps felt some stirrings of what would

[9] This subject has understandably been the theme of many Czech historians, although an adequate treatment in English has yet to appear. See Robert J. Kerner, *Bohemia in the Eighteenth Century: A Study in Political, Economic and Social History with Special Reference to the Reign of Leopold II, 1790–1792* (New York: Macmillan, 1932); see also Ernest Sommer, *Into Exile: A History of the Counter-Reformation in Bohemia,* trans. Victor Grove (London: New Europe, 1943). Sommer touches on major themes without going into much detail. Contributions by Czech historians include Antonín Gindely, *Geschichte der Gegenreformation in Böhmen* (Leipzig: Duncker und Humblot, 1894); and Arnošt Klima, *Čechy v období temna* (Prague: Státní pedagogické nakladatelství, 1961); see also Ernest Denis, *La Bohême depuis la Montagne-Blanche,* 2 vols. (Paris: Ernest Leroux, 1930), a product of the pre–World War I movement for Czech independence; it lacks documentation in many instances.

[10] Enea Silvio presents an eyewitness account of some of the earliest documented cases of heresy in Bohemia in the fifteenth century in *Historia Bohemica* (Historie ceská), trans. Dana Martinková, Alena Hadraková, and Jiří Matl (Prague: KLP, 1998), 89–106.

[11] It has been shown conclusively that German was becoming the predominant language in increasingly extensive areas of Bohemia during the seventeenth century, and continued to spread in the eighteenth. This shift in balance not only complicated relations between the two language groups, but, because of the historic connection between the Czech language and the Hussite movement, altered the dynamic between Catholics and crypto-Protestants (Elizabeth Wiskemann, *Czechs and Germans: A Study of the Struggle in the Historic Provinces of Bohemia and Moravia* [Oxford: The University Press, 1938], 10 ff.; Danuše Krejcová, "Poznámka k jazykové hranici na mapách v tomto díle," in *Počátky českého Národního Obrození,* ed. Josef Petráň [Prague: Academia, 1990], 318).

later be identified as nationalist sentiment as they preached, taught, and administered the sacraments in either German or Czech.[12] That most shared many of the local attitudes and prejudices, especially an anti-Semitism born of religious belief rather than ethnic sentiment, is beyond dispute.[13] The Bohemian Jesuits were thus, on the one hand, representatives of an institution and idea that transcended national and dynastic boundaries, an institution that in its official records seldom spoke of the nationality of its members, in the modern sense of the term;[14] on the other hand, the Jesuits were also men with local roots, prejudices, and passions.

The Jesuits of Bohemia were also subjects of the House of Habsburg, a family that had always placed its survival and expansion above considerations of geographic identification.[15] Like the Society of Jesus, the Habsburgs were an international entity who regarded themselves as having a mission that might carry their commitments to remote corners of the world. The Austrian Habsburgs, formerly the cadet branch of the dynasty, had greatly expanded its territory in the first half of the eighteenth century, while the Spanish branch, which had been the senior partner in family undertakings for two centuries, had become extinct in 1700.[16] With this territorial expansion of the dynasty's domains had come a parallel expansion of the educational role of the Society in the eastern Habsburg realms, and a willingness on the part of the dynasty to make use of Jesuits in many capacities, including the diplomatic.[17] With the support of the Habsburgs, Jesuits had returned to Transylvania at the beginning of the eighteenth century and

---

[12] Seventeenth-century Jesuits were among the outstanding Czech poets of their time; and although this literary genre was neglected by Jesuits in the following century, many members of the Society continued to publish sermons and other theological and pastoral works in this language almost until the time of the suppression. Yet speaking as a former Jesuit and Enlightenment *literatus,* Josef Dobrovský pronounced a very negative judgment on these effusions (*Geschichte der böhmischen Sprache und Literatur* [Prague: 1792], 206 f.).

[13] A. Stein, *Die Geschichte der Juden in Böhmen* (Brünn: Jüdischer Buch- und Kunstverlag, 1904).

[14] The designation "Moravus," "Austriacus," or "Boemus" in records of the Society invariably refers to the place of birth, rather than native language or ethnic identity. For example, Moravský Zemský Archiv v Brně, Cerroniho sbírka, 2:345, folios 6r et passim.

[15] Brigitta Vacha, *Die Habsburger:* verfasst von Walter Pohl und Karel Vocelka (Graz: Verlag Styria, 1993). This expression of loyalty to the dynasty, traditionally denominated *Kaisertreue,* increasingly set internal politics within the Habsburg realms apart from the patterns of loyalty emerging in the nation states of Western Europe. The dependence of the dynasty on *Kaisertreue,* while ultimately a liability in the nineteenth century, was arguably still a source of strength in the eighteenth (Peter Sugar, "The Rise of Nationalism in the Habsburg Empire," *Austrian History Yearbook* 3 [1967]: 94).

[16] Oswald Redlich, *Das Werden einer Grossmacht: Österreich von 1700 bis 1740* (Baden bei Wien: Rudolf Rohrer, 1938).

[17] As early as 1680, the Habsburgs had utilized Fr. Dunod, an Austrian Jesuit, for diplomatic missions in the eastern reaches of their realms.

reopened schools and universities that they had lost during the previous century; they also solidified their school system in Royal Hungary.[18]

As the century wore on, despite the attacks on the Society being mounted on many fronts, the relationship between the Jesuits and their patrons the Habsburgs seemed to remain strong. The educational reforms undertaken by Maria Theresia in the 1750s and afterwards may be viewed today as warnings of the more serious challenges to the Jesuit educational hegemony that were to come; but it is difficult to be certain that the members of the Society understood them in such a way at the time.[19] In these years the Society was being systematically, and sometimes brutally, forced out of France, Spain, and the New World, a reality that could not have escaped the notice of any Jesuit. Yet the long-standing and complex relationship of mutual support and common goals between the Society and the dynasty no doubt cushioned the bad news from abroad and may have persuaded some Jesuits within the Austrian lands that they might escape the general destruction of their order. Ironically, it would be in Prussia, the greatest rival to the Habsburgs, where some Habsburg Jesuits would be able to continue their teaching after the suppression.[20]

The modern reader, knowing how the drama will play out, looks for signs that the Jesuits of Prague and other communities in Bohemia foresaw their fate, or recognized that their actions during the last ten years before the suppression betrayed an awareness that as individuals and as members of an organization they would have to reshape their identities. An examination of documents produced within the Society from this final decade reveals that while these men were doubtless aware of the forces that were threatening their organization at its highest levels and already eliminating it from

---

[18] Stefan Pascu, *Die Babeş-Bolyai Universität aus Cluj*, trans. Emma Maria Moiescu (Cluj: Dacia Verlag, 1972); Aurelian J. Hets, *A jezsuiták iskolái Magyarországon a 18. század közepen* (Pannonhalma: Pray Rent, 1938).

[19] For example, in 1769 Maria Theresia endowed a Faculty of Medicine at the Jesuit university of Trnava (Tyrnau, Nagyszombat), traditionally the training center for Jesuit educators throughout the eastern two-thirds of the Austrian Province. After the suppression this move was understood to be an implicit acknowledgement of the shortcomings of Jesuit education, which placed little emphasis on medical training; but in the short run the addition of a medical faculty might have been seen as strengthening the university overall, thus enhancing Jesuit prestige (Johann Christian von Engel, *Geschichte des Ungrischen Reichs*, 5 vols. [Vienna: In der Camesinaschen Buchhandlung, 1814], 4:334).

[20] Frederick forbade the publication of the papal brief, and the Prussian state did not begin to manage all the former Jesuit properties until 1800 (Franciscus Hanus, *Church and State in Silesia under Frederick II, 1740–1786* [Washington: Texts, Documents and Studies in Medieval and Modern Church History, 1944], 343). Frederick's position is set forth in a letter from Antonio Eugenio Visconti, the papal nuncio in Vienna, dated October 28, 1773 (*Der Schriftverkehr zwischen dem päpstlichen Staatsekretariät und dem Nuncio am Kaiserhof Antonio Eugenio Visconti 1767–1774*, no. 2684, ASV, Reg. Nunziatura Vienna 175 [Vienna: Hermann Böhlaus Nachfolger, 1970], 227 f.).

every other major European land by 1769, still, they did not exhibit any signs that they understood how close the end was in the Habsburg world. Jesuits went about their work with unabated commitment, and talented young men continued to be recruited into the Society. Indeed, one of the most brilliant of the Bohemian Jesuits, Josef Dobrovský, entered the Society less than a year before its suppression.[21]

The Jesuit opposition to change and reform in the eighteenth century has typically been a *leitmotiv* of studies in the final years of the Society before the suppression, and certainly of most studies of the history of education during the eighteenth century. The gradual surrender of what had been an almost complete control of schools in many regions evidently produced resistance on the part of Jesuits. When these reactions are coupled with ample evidence of Jesuit obscurantism, they create a picture of a recalcitrant and reactionary Society that refused to adjust to changing times. The truth, however, is somewhat more complicated. Hugo Hantsch has pointed out that "it was not the spirit of the Enlightenment that the Jesuits resisted, but rather the new formulation of education, summed up in Maria Theresia's words, 'The school is and remains a *Publicum*.' "[22]

Understandably, the Jesuits did not want to give up the system that they had created and that they believed was an integral part of their missions to care for souls and bring men "to the knowledge and love of our Creator and Redeemer."[23] To conceive of such a project as the property of the state, even a Catholic state, they found almost impossible. Moreover, they were engaged in professional rivalries with other Catholic teaching orders, especially the Piarists. And certainly personal rivalries and jealousies between individuals both within and beyond the ranks of the Jesuits had been present since the founding of the Society. All these factors poisoned the rancorous atmosphere enveloping the Jesuits and their activities in the 1760s.

But the pre-suppression Society needs to be viewed in the context of the other Jesuit activities that were not such bones of contention between Catholic religious orders. It will help us to understand more clearly how the Jesuits of the Habsburg realms, especially of Bohemia, were functioning before 1773 if we take care not to conjecture their techniques and their relationship to the Holy See in light of the anachronistic stereotypes that sprang up and were solidified in the nineteenth century. The rigid educational formalism into which the Society lapsed after its resurrection in 1814 has encouraged historians to project these traits onto the enterprises of

---

[21] Dobrovský entered the Society on October 1, 1772 (Franz Martin Pelzel, *Gelehrte und Schriftsteller aus dem Orden der Jesuiten* [Prague, 1786], 294).

[22] Quoted in Hans Leo Mikoletzky, *Österreich: Das grosse Jahrhundert* (Vienna: Austria-Edition, 1967), 259 (my translation).

[23] *The* Ratio studiorum *of 1599*, 1.

eighteenth-century Jesuits.[24] But the relationship of the pre-suppression Society to the currents of thought of the Enlightenment was more complex than simply one of unreasoning opposition or calculated accommodation.

This volume will endeavor to explore (1) how the Society confronted the challenges to its prescientific curricula and modes of inquiry that grew in strength throughout the century, and how the individual Jesuit and the Society as a whole played a crucial role during the last years of the Society before the suppression; (2) how individual members of the province of Bohemia responded to the Enlightenment and the Baroque; (3) how the Jesuit undertaking was carried out by means of the various apostolates of the Society. We will study as well (4) the apprehensive relationships between the Jesuits and the Jews, (5) the Jesuits' influence on the better-known educational institutions in Bohemia, (6) the Jesuits of Prague, and (7) the rebuilding of the Society after the suppression.

In reality, the Society in Bohemia presented a much less united front than many of its supporters or detractors have been ready to acknowledge. This disunity or, if one wished to cast it in a more positive light, diversity is most apparent when the scientific and mission-related activities of these Jesuits are placed side by side, but it can also be detected in fissures within teaching faculties of the Prague university and even between individual Jesuit scholars and researchers. While this variety makes it much harder to draw general conclusions about the objectives, conscious or unconscious, of the Jesuits of Bohemia in the mid-eighteenth century, it also helps explain the many different directions that former Jesuits took following 1773, and even sheds light on why the Society was not able to mount a more effective defense in the years before the suppression.

In the administrative organization of the Society, there was no specific unit that corresponded to the city of Prague. Prague itself lay within the Province of Bohemia, which included all of Bohemia proper, Moravia, and, until 1754, Silesia. Because of the characteristic mobility of the Society, Jesuits of the Bohemian Province might reside in Prague for several years before being reassigned to a smaller city or sent overseas. A Jesuit might have an assignment that periodically took him outside the confines of the city of Prague proper, but still made him responsible for teaching or preaching within the city. In addition, some Jesuits working in Prague were not members of the Bohemian Province. Therefore, as we have already suggested, the boundaries of this study are somewhat elastic; they do not

---

[24] The author is indebted to Fr. John W. O'Malley, S.J., for calling attention to this point.

exactly match the administrative units of either the Society or the four towns that made up eighteenth-century Prague.[25]

The activities of the Society can be grouped into five categories, although, given the structure of the Society, some overlapping and shifting among these always existed. First, the educational mission of the Society was divided into teaching at universities and at *collegia,* as prescribed in the *Ratio studiorum.* The university of Prague was the center of Jesuit intellectual activities for all of Bohemia during the eighteenth century, as well as the focal point of the most acrimonious controversies that developed when the Society began to come under attack. The university community was divided, not just along disciplinary and professional lines, but also between those faculties that were historically the responsibility of the Society and those that were dominated by lay professional teachers. Thus, we cannot say that the university was simply one of the projects of the Society; rather it was, as we shall see, a complex, hybrid institution with conflicting traditions where the Jesuits were a dominant, but not absolutely dominating, element. The literature on the university of Prague is extensive, reflecting the role of the school as the leading institution of higher education in the lands of the Crown of St. Wenceslaus for six centuries.[26] This book will focus its attention on the relationship of the Society to the university, with particular emphasis on those aspects where the institutional culture and educational aims of the Society collided with new trends or policies.

The *collegia* are sometimes referred to as secondary schools, but this designation is misleading, as in many cases the education offered in them was not preparatory, but complete in itself. The curriculum of the *collegia* had been established in the sixteenth century, as the Jesuits founded schools across Europe, and had taken a definitive form in 1599 with the publication of the *Ratio studiorum.* These schools taught Latin and Greek authors, censoring passages felt to endanger the morals of the students. They placed great emphasis on the oral and written production of Latin; and students were expected to participate in plays, engage in debates, and declaim both poetry and prose of their own composition.[27] The instructors were expected

---

[25] These towns were the Old Town; the New Town; the Malá Strana (Small Side), on the west bank of the Vltava; and Hradčany, the hill overlooking the city, where the Castle and St. Vitus's Cathedral were located. Although in the eighteenth century they were still separate administrative units, for practical and economic purposes they had long functioned as one city.

[26] Wilhelm Erman and Ewald Horn, *Bibliographie der deutschen Universitäten,* 3 vols. (Leipzig/Berlin: Teubner, 1904–5), 2:832–59.

[27] The majority of the plays put on by the students of the Prague collegium are lost today, or at best known only by their titles. The traces of these plays that have survived are most suggestive of the values promoted by the Society. A synopsis of the 1738 play "Agnus inter hædos a cultro Abrahæ maculosus . . ." (Státní Úřední Archiv, Prague, JS, III-415, fasc. 3), published in Czech and Latin, reveals the tension between the anti-Semitic attitudes of the day and the desire on the part of the Society to portray the Jewish protagonist as a virtuous figure.

to be models of probity as well as examples of learning and religious orthodoxy.

Yet, during the first two centuries of their existence, it was not uncommon for the collegia to count many Protestants among their students. The curriculum and teaching methods of the collegia were widely admired and imitated, and the policy of the Society not to charge tuition made their schools more accessible than were many others; but by the eighteenth century the program of the collegia was increasingly viewed as outmoded, and the Enlightenment and Josephinist educational reformers who came into their own after the suppression did not turn to the *Ratio* for inspiration.[28] Jesuit education, in the eyes of nineteenth-century historians, even came to be the foil for practical state-run school systems, although the question remains whether the collegia in actual practice were as out of touch with more modern ideas as their detractors have claimed. This study will attempt to shed light on the problem of the Jesuit collegia within a limited but important area: it will examine those schools conducted in Prague and several of the surrounding communities.

The most difficult sphere of Jesuit activity to assess is the apostolic work other than education performed by the Society. The greatest difficulty stems from the nature of the source materials, the vast majority of which are reports, letters, and other documents prepared by the Jesuits themselves. As we have already noted, while the reporting protocols of the Society were precise, requiring each professed house, school, or university to enumerate conversions, apostolic missions undertaken, and other contacts with the community, it seems clear that reporting followed stereotyped patterns, with the same phrases or even narrative accounts appearing over and over, in different settings and at different times.[29] Beyond this problem is the thornier phenomenological question of just what the Jesuit missionaries sincerely believed they were encountering in their work. The researcher must therefore utilize these reports with caution, recognizing that while they are unlikely to have been fabricated entirely, the picture they paint fits an overall vision of the Jesuit apostolates held up as an ideal during Jesuit training, and does not necessarily correspond to the realities of a specific mission experience in the way a social scientist or a Jesuit might describe it today. Yet, even tentative conclusions regarding the nature of the Jesuit missions may prove helpful as we assess the impact of these missions on the communities involved, and study the effect the ongoing mission project exerted on the Society itself.

I wish to thank Dr. Martin Svatoš for calling this document to my attention.

[28] Maragret Friedrich, "Anfänge eines staatlich geförderten Schulwesen," *Das achtzehnte Jahrhundert und Österreich* 10 (1995): 38.

[29] I am grateful for conversations with Dr. István Monok that have helped clarify the significance of this pattern.

Yet another category of activity undertaken by the Jesuits of Bohemia can be designated "literary," in the sense that the word was used in the eighteenth century, that is, to encompass scientific, historical, and theological writing as well as belles-lettres. No pronouncement in the *Ratio* or the Constitutions of the Society required or even encouraged Jesuits to engage in literary controversies or to write histories, but these activities very early on became important aspects of the Society's work and played a significant role in shaping the reputation of the Society among both Catholics and Protestants. Throughout the period under consideration in this work, Bohemian Jesuits produced an unending stream of works on a wide range of topics, in some cases far removed from what might seem the original mission of the Society as envisioned by St. Ignatius, but which were consonant with the well-established reputation of the Jesuits as the intellectual elite of the Church. At many points these writings intersect with the trends leading to the Czech National Awakening, sometimes adding to the body of literature that would later be recognized as the precursor to the Awakening, while on other occasions presenting an ideological or methodological stance that would be viewed as regressive and hostile to Czech national identity. In either instance, these writings contributed to the cultural climate of the time and merit attention here.

Another function of the Jesuits, likewise not part of their explicitly stated role as campaigners for the Gospel, can be called the capacity of individual Jesuits to serve as "handymen" to the dynasty, the bureaucracy, or the community. We have already mentioned the role of Jesuits as diplomats; in Bohemia Jesuits also designed military fortifications, reported meteorological data, operated pharmacies, built and performed on musical instruments, and engaged in countless other "practical," seemingly secular tasks. Unlike cloistered orders, which even if committed to teaching were generally in some way at a distance from the outside world, the Society sought integration with many aspects of secular life. By doing so, individuals belonging to the Society, rather than the institution as a whole, not rarely had a significant if subtle influence on day-to-day life in Bohemia, in a sphere that was often less fraught with polemic and confrontation than were many of the other undertakings of the Society.

Finally, a reader of standard histories of the Society, both by Jesuits and non-Jesuits alike, might come away with only a vague sense of the role of *coadjutores temporales* (temporal helpers or lay brothers) of the Society. In fact, these men were a major component of the Bohemian Society, numbering in the hundreds and varying greatly in education, ethnicity, and experience. Their activities are among the least understood and the most scantily documented ministries undertaken by the Society in Bohemia. Frequently literate, these brothers were, however, not encouraged to engage in literary pursuits, and thus have left virtually nothing from their own pens. Often the only clues about their lives must be gleaned from the obituary notices that appeared in the *Litteræ*. The irregular and scarce documentation of their activities has made it necessary to report such details as were available, which in some cases has meant focusing on a community outside of Prague, or on the life of a temporal coadjutor whose exact whereabouts at different periods in his career we can no longer establish. The clues that are at hand suggest the versatility and accomplishments of this group of men. The exact extent of their impact on Bohemian society may never be known, but it was certainly great. For these reasons the temporal coadjutors are included in this study, but are dealt with in Appendix 3, since the data available are of such a different nature from those that form the basis of the chapters of this book.

The Bohemian Society at the middle of the eighteenth century, therefore, presents many different faces. To the peasant or small town burgher, the most familiar role of the fathers might have been as moral arbiters, seizing forbidden books, attempting to reconcile estranged couples, and casting out demons with the help of prayer and miraculous objects. To the city dweller, the Society was the purveyor of a well-known, if no longer innovative, educational program and the sponsor of popular sodalities that served important religious and social functions. To the university student, the Jesuits were teachers, enforcer of rules, perhaps even mentors; to an intellectual who dreamed of a Renaissance of Czech culture, the members of the Society might seem to be allies or enemies, depending upon the specific circumstances and the individual Jesuits involved. To an aristocrat the Society represented a link to the political and religious status quo established after 1620, whether this was seen as a source of strength or as an obstacle to be overcome.

What the Society, collectively and individually, meant to the masters of Bohemia, Maria Theresia and Joseph II, is hardest of all to determine. The Queen-Empress's connection to individual Jesuits was positive throughout her lifetime, although her commitment to the educational aims and theological positions of the Society is less clear and may have shifted over time. While no intellectual herself, Maria Theresia was shrewd and equipped with the instincts of a survivor that enabled her to make decisions about the roles and potential usefulness of the individual Jesuits rather than view them as a homogenized mass. Her son's pragmatism likewise caused him to balance his antipathy towards the outward forms of Baroque Catholicism with the realization that the Society represented a pool of talent that he could not afford to waste. In any case, at the time of the suppression, Joseph was still reined in by his mother; and despite his persistent writing of impatient memoranda, he cannot be regarded as having the final say about the Jesuits or any other matter of religion in the 1760s and early 1770s.

These, then, are the points of contact between the Bohemian Society of Jesus and the surrounding world that the following chapters will consider. But before each can be examined in turn, we must briefly review the earlier history of the Jesuits in Bohemia, and examine the evolving climate in which the Society was plunged at midcentury, as it attempted to carry on the work of those who had preceded them.

chapter two

From Victory to Crisis, 1556–1765

[Peter Canisius] visited and revisited Prague five times in the years 1555–56. The explanation is that he had begun there one of his great "poldering" operations, the foundations of a Jesuit college which was to be one of the principal instruments of Divine Providence in reclaiming Bohemia from Hussitism and Lutheranism and making it into a permanently Catholic country.

—James Brodrick, S.J., *Progress of the Jesuits*

The time of the Jesuits was for Bohemia a period of the deepest decay in national and scientific education.

—W. V. Tomek

By the beginning of the third decade of the reign of Maria Theresia, the Society of Jesus had, with only brief interruptions, been a presence in the kingdom of Bohemia for over two hundred years. At the invitation of the Habsburg Ferdinand I, the first Jesuits had arrived in Prague in 1556, only sixteen years after the foundation of the Society.[1] From his throne in Vienna, Ferdinand was less than confident in the fidelity of the territories of the Crown of St. Wenceslaus entrusted to him by his brother, Charles V.[2] Memories of the Hussite wars of the fifteenth century lingered in Bohemia, and Prague had been without a Catholic archbishop since 1422. Therefore Prague, third only to the much more securely Catholic Cologne and the imperial capital Vienna, was among the first cities in the empire in which Jesuits established schools, in the hope of strengthening the Catholic Church and winning converts. Twelve Jesuits, soon joined by an

---

[1] J. F. Hammerschmied gives April 24, 1556, as the date of their arrival (*Prodromus gloriæ Pragæ,* [Vetero-Praga (here and elsewhere the section of Prague known as "Old Town")], 86).

[2] Kenneth J. Dillon, *King and Estates in the Bohemian Lands, 1526–1564* (Brussels: Les Editions de la Librairie Encyclopédique, 1976).

additional eighteen, at once founded a school in a disused Dominican cloister and admitted boys of Lutheran and Hussite families, as well as those from Catholic backgrounds.[3] Despite the unsettled state of the Catholic Church in Prague, the school prospered almost from its first day. By 1562 Ferdinand had granted the Society the right to graduate students in the theological and philosophical faculties of their school, an important milestone in the institutional history of the Society in Prague.[4] Poor students were admitted to the school, although the Jesuits never ceased to devote attention to the sons of the most powerful families in the city.[5]

In the years that followed, the Society expanded its properties along the Vltava River, acquiring neighboring houses and erecting in 1578 the church of St. Savior. By the start of the sixteenth century, the Jesuits had made considerable progress in developing these holdings into the complex of the Clementinum. This was a vast structure enclosing five courtyards and covering two hectares, the second largest architectural complex in the kingdom after the Prague Castle, and a deliberate rival to the medieval Carolinum, the original Prague university that had been "tainted" by the Hussite heresy.[6] They also founded, with the support of the ambitious local bishop, Vilem Prusinovký z Vickova, a university in the Moravian city of Olomouc, another stronghold of Protestantism.[7] Throughout the first half of the seventeenth century, the network of Jesuit schools expanded steadily until it gained a virtual monopoly on secondary and postsecondary education in Bohemia, a position made even more secure by the Society's considerable political influence.[8]

The Jesuits, however, did more than merely found schools intended to spread the teachings of Catholicism. Bohemian Jesuits in the seventeenth and eighteenth centuries, like their confrères throughout the world, produced a wide range of works on theology, philosophy, mathematics, and

---

[3] John W. O'Malley, *The First Jesuits* (Cambridge: Harvard University Press, 1993), 61, 207.

[4] The "Grundungspriveleg Ferdinands I. für das Jesuitenkolleg bei St. Klemens zu Prag 1562" is reproduced in *Quellenbuch zur Geschichte der Sudentenländer,* ed. Wilhelm Weizäcker (Munich: Robert Lerche, 1960), 86–88.

[5] Klement Borový, *Antonín Brus, z Mohelnice, Arcibiskup Pražský* (Prague: Kn. arcib. Knihtiskárny, 1873), 146.

[6] The Carolinum had been founded in 1348 by Charles IV and, until White Mountain, remained a center of resistance to the Habsburgs and, to a lesser extent, to Catholic orthodoxy.

[7] Václav Nešpor, *Dějiny University Olomoucké* (Olomouc: Nákladem Národního výboru hlavního města Olomouc, 1947); Zdeněk Hojda and Ivana Čornejová, "Pražska univerzita a vzdělanost v Českých zemích v 17. a 18. století," in I. Čornejová, ed., *Dějiny Univerzity Karlovy,* 3 vols. (Prague: Univerzita Karlova, 1995–1998), 2:233.

[8] One historian has called this power a "straitjacket" imposed on the Bohemian people: R. W. Seton-Watson, *A History of the Czech and Slovak Peoples* (Hamden, Conn.: Archon, 1965), 150.

linguistics, as well as abundant apologetic materials aimed at nonbelievers.[9] They strengthened their relationship to the House of Habsburg, established when the Society was only a few years old, by publicly demonstrating their devotion; for example, following the death of Maximillan II in 1578, they produced a play celebrating the deceased Emperor's virtues.[10] An institutionally self-conscious company of reformers committed to the "care of souls," the Jesuits of the Habsburg realms kept extensive records of their own activities and eventually even produced a detailed history of their early work in Bohemia.[11]

The battle of White Mountain, fought on a hill west of Prague on November 8, 1620, is a watershed in Czech history. Two years earlier, the Defenestration of Prague had signaled the resistance of the Bohemian Estates to the religious and political hegemony of the Catholic Habsburgs, and brought about the beginning of the Thirty Years' War. Before being defeated in this war, the Bohemian Estates, dominated by nobles either openly Utraquist or at least sympathetic with Protestant movements, had called for the expulsion of the Jesuits.[12] Such a demand was far from unexpected, for there had been constant opposition to the Jesuits in some quarters ever since their arrival.[13] No Jesuits appear to have remained in the city when the Protestant "Winter King," Frederick, Elector Palatine and son-in-law of James I of England, arrived for his coronation in 1620. But at White Mountain, the forces of Ferdinand II, the Catholic Habsburg emperor, defeated Frederick, who then fled the country, never to return.[14]

Habsburg rule once again established, the Jesuits returned and quickly resumed control of their churches and schools throughout the

---

[9] The starting point for research into Jesuit literary activity is the *Bibliothèque de la Compagnie de Jésus,* by Carlos Sommervogel, S.J., 11 vols. (Brussels: O. Schepens; Paris: A. Picard, 1890–1932).

[10] Maximillian, far less intent on the spread of orthodox Catholicism than his father had been, was nevertheless the object of Jesuit encomiums (Howard Louthan, *The Quest for Compromise: Peacemakers in Counter-Reformation Vienna* [Cambridge: Cambridge University Press, 1997], 141).

[11] Joannes Schmidl, *Historia Provinciæ Bohemiæ S.J.*, 4 vols. (Prague, 1749–59). See also the incomplete study *Geschichte der Böhmischen Provinz der Gesellschaft Jesu,* by Alois Kroess, 2 vols. (Vienna: Ambr. Opitz, etc., 1938).

[12] Victor-Lucien Tapié, *The Rise and Fall of the Habsburg Monarchy,* trans. Stephen Hardman (London: Pall Mall Press, 1971), 88.

[13] The printer Sixtus Palma had published a collection of verses attacking the Jesuits in Prague, including one poem containing the line "Dear Prague, what ugly birds live in you." (The black-robed Jesuits were often referred to as "blackbirds.") See Bořivoj Benetka, *Jesuité v Čechách* (Prague: Nakladatelství Vyšehrad, 1941), 20.

[14] Ernest Denis, *La Bohême depuis la Montagne-Blanche,* 1:7–100.

kingdom.[15] The older Prague university, or Carolinum, immediately felt pressure to exhibit strict religious conformity and allegiance to the House of Habsburg. Meanwhile, the new masters of Prague, with the Jesuits in their train, wasted no time in reversing the pro-Protestant tendencies the Carolinum had exhibited since the middle of the fifteenth century. Judicial proceedings and public spectacle drove this point home. On June 21, 1621, Jan Jesenius, the university rector, and the university master, Valentin Kochan z Prachové, were executed as traitors a short distance from the Carolinum in the Old Town Square of Prague.[16] Many other university masters fled Bohemia, adding to a stream of refugees that included the educational reformer Jan Comenius and many of the oldest landed families. The Prague university was then subjected to two tense years of awaiting its fate while Ferdinand, whose fervent devotion to Catholicism and to the Society was legendary, considered how best to recast the school as a center of his efforts to re-Catholicize the errant province.[17]

Finally on November 14, 1622, the masters of the Carolinum were commanded to hand over the keys of the school to the Jesuits, who would also continue to teach at their own institution, the Clementinum. In effect, there was now one university in Prague, an uneasy fusion of the Hussite *studium generale,* whose curriculum derived from medieval models and whose history was tied to Bohemian national identity and resistance to the papacy, and the tripartite Jesuit school; both were now under the control of the Society of Jesus.[18]

The curriculum of the Jesuit Clementinum was based on the classical program detailed in the fundamental Jesuit educational document, the *Ratio studiorum,* published in its definitive form in 1599 and used as the model for Jesuit schools from Transylvania to Portugal.[19] This curriculum, greatly influenced by Ignatius's experiences at the university of Paris and by the success of the collegium that Jerónimo Nadal established in Messina in 1548, stressed classical languages, philosophy, and theology, and required strict theological conformity with the doctrine of its teachers. This pedagogical regimen, formulated in the late Renaissance, would remain at least formally in place in all schools of the Society for the next 150 years.

---

[15] Karl Jaromir Erben, *Die Primatoren der kön. Altstatdt Prag* (Prague: Gottlieb Haase Söhne, 1858), 68.

[16] Jesenius's tongue had been torn out sometime earlier (W. W. Tomek, *Geschichte der Prager Universität* [Osnabrück: Biblio Verlag, 1969], 247).

[17] I. Čornejová, "Správní a institutionální vývoj pražské univerzity," in *Dějiny,* 2:23–27.

[18] Tomek, *Geschichte,* 251–69.

[19] *The Jesuit* Ratio Studiorum *of 1599,* trans. A. P. Farrell, S.J. (Detroit: Conference of Major Superiors of Jesuits, 1970); A. P. Farrell, S.J., *The Jesuit Code of Liberal Education* (Milwaukee: Bruce Publishing Co., 1956), 338 f., 372; The text of the *Ratio* in the form used during this period may be found in *Ratio atque institutio studiorum Societatis Iesu* (Antwerp, 1685).

The *Ratio* prescribed that all students up to the age of thirteen (all of whom were male) receive instruction in grammar, humanities, and rhetoric.[20] Next, in the Faculty of Philosophy, for three years the students pursued courses in logic, physics, metaphysics, ethics, moral philosophy, and mathematics. This program placed special emphasis on the works of Aristotle in Latin translation, and on selections from Thomas Aquinas and the medieval commentator Peter Lombard.[21] On a more advanced level, devoted to theology, students took on Greek and even elements of Hebrew and other "oriental" languages, while also studying homiletics, polemics, and casuistry. A rector—who was appointed by the general of the Society, the provincial, or his representative—directed the university in accordance with the prescriptions of the *Ratio;* the rector might also serve as prefect of studies over the various faculties, thereby maintaining close control over the actual day-to-day management of the school.[22]

The *Ratio* made no explicit provisions for teaching either medicine or law, so the Society found that it would have to turn to other models for guidance in how to manage these faculties, or in some instances they simply commended it to others.[23] Whatever its limitations, the pedagogical models and concepts of the *Ratio* were phenomenally influential for several centuries, even in Protestant schools.[24] By the beginning of the eighteenth century, the Society could look back with pride on the generations of political and cultural leaders educated in its schools, as well as on the thousands of sons of middle-class families who had gained a classical education according to the system of the *Ratio*.

Ferdinand II's amalgamation of the hierarchically organized and staunchly Catholic Clementinum and the older Carolinum resulted in an institution known as the Universitas Pragensis or the Carlo-Ferdinandea Universitas.[25] The school was so named in order to legitimate the new

---

[20] *Ratio studiorum,* 128 f., 135.

[21] Alison Simmons, "Jesuit Aristotelian Education: The *De anima* Commentaries," in *The Jesuits: Cultures, Sciences, and the Arts 1540–1773,* ed. John W. O'Malley, Gauvin Alexander Bailey, Stephen J. Harris, and T. Frank Kennedy (Toronto: University of Toronto Press, 1999), 522–37.

[22] St. Ignatius of Loyola, *The Constitutions of the Society of Jesus,* trans. and ed. George Ganss, S.J. (St. Louis: The Institute of Jesuit Sources, 1970), 225 f.

[23] The Jesuits' generally unenthusiastic view of professional schools undoubtedly contributed to the perceived decline of their universities in the eighteenth century, when the study of medicine and law at the university gained much respectability (Robert Haas, *Die Geistliche Haltung der katholische Unversitäten Deutschlands im 18. Jahrhundert* [Freiburg: Herder, 1952]).

[24] Marc Raeff, *The Well-Ordered Police State: Social and Institutional Change through Law in the Germanies and Russia* (New Haven and London: Yale University Press, 1983), 138 n. 182.

[25] *Ratio et modus quo Carolina academia cum patrum Societatis Iesu academia uniri et incorporari potest, servata Caroli IV memoria.* This act of union was published March 4, 1654 (Tomek,

university by associating the reputation of the fourteenth-century founder of the Carolinum, Charles IV, Holy Roman Emperor and Bohemia's most illustrious king, with the passionately Catholic Ferdinand, who sought in various ways to tie his dynasty to the most ancient biblical and classical antecedents.[26] The Universitas Pragensis now included among its five faculties the Faculty of Languages of the Jesuit academy, even though this faculty really functioned as a preparatory program. The faculties of medicine and law continued to be housed at the Carolinum, the home of the original Prague university, while the faculties constituting the Jesuit academy remained where they had previously been located, at the Clementinum.

To what degree the Society directly controlled the academic life of the "secular" faculties during the seventeenth and eighteenth centuries is a question not easily resolved. While the faculty and students of these faculties included virtually no members of the Society, the dominance of the Jesuits over the intellectual life of the entire region doubtless had an inhibiting effect upon anyone daring to espouse any doctrine at odds with Church teachings as understood by the Society. On the other hand, the often repeated claim that the Jesuits "dominated" the entire university until the suppression is harder to document.[27]

The following year, 1623, the Society consolidated its undertakings in Bohemia, Moravia, and Silesia into the Province of Bohemia, created from elements previously pertaining to the Province of Austria.[28] The Society's position in Bohemia, thus supported by the ultra-Catholic Ferdinand, seemed strong and likely to grow stronger. Meanwhile, the Society weathered another serious challenge: the plague of 1625. Even though the Jesuit

Geschichte, 276). An account of the process that resulted in the unification of the Carolinum and the Clementinum is found in *Universitas Carolina*, by Jan Havránek, Josef Petráň, and Anna Skybová (Prague: Univerzita Karlova, 1986), 34–37. See also Tomek, *Geschichte*, 255–80.

[26] Despite his collisions with the papacy, Charles (ruled 1346–78), had been a personally devout ruler and had eagerly endowed convents and schools. He was thus an eminently appropriate figure to include in the mythology of origin being fashioned for the newly reconstituted university. For the larger issue of the Habsburg mythology of origins and its expression in the visual arts, see *The Last Descendant of Aeneas*, by Marie Tanner (New Haven: Yale University Press, 1992).

[27] The Czech historian Mikuláš Teich has, for example, asserted that a scientific society was established at the university by order of Maria Theresia, "but the society did not succeed, since university life was controlled by the Jesuits" ("The Royal Bohemian Society of Sciences and the First Phase of Organized Scientific Advance in Bohemia," *Historica* 2 [1960]: 168). Teich cites W. W. Tomek, the nineteenth-century historian of the university, but Tomek offers no documentation for this claim (*Geschichte*, 322). Independent documentation of this imperially sanctioned scientific society has likewise not been discovered.

[28] F. Winter, *Tabulæ exhibentes sedes antiquæ Societatis Jesu: Missionum stationes et collegia, 1556–1773, Provinciæ Bohemiæ et Silesiæ* (Vienna, 1899), 26; B. Duhr, *Geschichte der Jesuiten in den Ländern der deutschen Zunge in der ersten Hälfte des XVII. Jahrhunderts*, 2 vols. (Freiburg/Regensburg: Herder, 1913), 2:315–17.

schools in Prague had to suspend operations during this period, they were able to open their doors once again at a later date.[29] But the new archbishop of Prague, twenty-seven-year-old Arnošt Vojtěch Harrach, bridled at the Jesuit monopoly over higher education in Prague and resented the influence the newer and aggressively self-confident religious order was gaining in the city and in the surrounding countryside. Wishing to promote the seminary he had founded in Prague, Harrach, who was soon to become a cardinal, forbade the Jesuits to preach in churches other than their own, and engaged in a bitter struggle with them for control of the university. In 1624 he also forbade the Society to conduct graduations in the Carolinum; and when the fathers cheerfully ignored his command, he went on to ban them from conducting graduations anywhere in the city.

Ultimately, the Jesuit fathers, with the Emperor at their back, won this battle, but soon they had to confront a new threat—the army of the Elector of Saxony. The Saxon occupation of Prague in 1631–32, following the battle of Breitenfeld, resulted in the Jesuits' being expelled and the university's taking on a Protestant orientation for a brief period; moreover, about one-third of all the city's Protestant emigrants returned, in some cases reoccupying the city's churches.[30] Although the Society was soon able to return to Prague, only after the conclusion of the Thirty Years' War could it once again dominate the university in Prague and other leading schools throughout Bohemia.

By 1636 conflict between the archbishop and the Society had moved from the pulpits of local churches into the streets and taverns of the city, reaching a climax when, in a brawl that erupted in a Prague taproom, a student of the Jesuit academy was accused of trying to kill a student at Harrach's seminary. But when the Jesuits refused to hand over their culprit to the archbishop's court for trial, an enraged Harrach petitioned Rome to excommunicate the involved parties. Jeering students from the Jesuit university tore down the official proclamation of excommunication. Next, their fellow students violently accosted Harrach in his coach as he rode through the streets of Prague. The cardinal responded with scathing condemnations of Jesuit immorality and renewed his efforts to rein in their activities.

In the meantime, in Rome the recently created Congregation for the Propagation of the Faith, supporting the archbishop's claim that the Prague university had been established by the pope, not by the Bohemian king Charles IV, decreed in 1638 that the Carolinum must be allowed to reopen. Prague now had, at least in theory, three universities: the original Caroli-

---

[29] Iulius Cordara, *Historiæ Societatis Iesu pars sexta* (Rome: Ex Typ. Antonii de Rubeis, 1750), 360.

[30] Josef Janáček, ed., *Dějiny Prahy* (Prague: Nakladatelství politické literatury, 1961), 351.

num, established by papal bull in 1347, the Jesuit Clementinum, and the "university seminary" founded by the archbishop. Such a situation, bordering on the ludicrous, required an immediate remedy.[31] To complicate the picture, the Jesuits had meantime earned the jealousy of other members of the Catholic hierarchy, such as the influential abbot of Emauz, Jan Caramuel z Lobkovic.[32]

At this point, the monarch once more came to the aid of the Society. Ferdinand II's son and successor, Ferdinand III, issued a rescript on February 23, 1654, formally and permanently unifying the Carolinum and the Clementinum into a single entity under the direction of the Society.[33] Among other changes, the *studia* of the Jesuit Clementinum now became university *facultates,* with all the prestigious associations that this term, derived from the medieval university, implied.[34] Also under this arrangement, the king of Bohemia (who for the past century had been a Habsburg) held ultimate authority at the university. The rescript also created a new administrative position, that of superintendent. The Jesuits were put in firm control of the Faculties of Theology and Philosophy, although their control of the university as a whole was less than absolute. The Faculty of Law, which had been part of the Carolinum, and the Faculty of Medicine, which had almost become extinct in the sixteenth century and which since 1622 had been affiliated with the Clementinum, were now united with the Jesuit-controlled faculties into a cohesive whole whose organizational structure would last for more than a century.[35]

---

[31] See n. 25 above.

[32] Tomáš Bílek, "Reformace katolická v Čechách 1650–1781," *Časopis Musea Království Českého,* 55 (1881): 59–61. Hereafter this source will be abbreviated to *ČMKČ.*

[33] I. Čornejová, "Správní a institutionální vývoj," in Čornejová, *Dějiny 2,* 34 f.

[34] The term *facultas* was not used by all universities in the Middle Ages, and was particularly associated with the prestigious university of Paris (Astrik L. Gabriel, *Garlandia: Studies in the History of the Mediaeval University* [Notre Dame, Ind.: The Mediaeval Institute, The University of Notre Dame, 1969], 97–101).

[35] The Faculty of Medicine had been inactive for some years before the restructuring of the university in 1622, although lectures on anatomy had continued in the Faculty of Arts (Karel Beránek, "O počátcich pražské lékařské fakulty, 1348–1622," *Acta Universitatis Carolinæ Pragensis—Historia Universitatis Carolinæ* 9, no. 2 (1968): 62–69; hereafter this source will be abbreviated to *AUCP—HUC;* Ludmila Hlaváčková and Petr Svobodný, *Dějiny pražských lékařských fakult* (Prague: Univerzita Karlova, 1993), 16, 22. The Faculty of Law had not undergone such a complete eclipse, continuing to function during the years 1634 to 1638, when the Society controlled the university. In 1638 Ferdinand III appointed a protector over the faculty (Karel Kučera, "K akademickým volbám na pražské universitě v 17. a 18. století," *Acta Universitatis Carolinæ - Philosophica et Historica II - Vojtiskův sborník* [1959], 69 ff.). Jesuits taught neither in the Faculty of Law nor the Faculty of Medicine (Karel Beránek, "Teologická fakulta," in Čornejová, *Dějiny 2,* 138–43).

The unification of the university had other significant side effects. For example, the rectorate devolved by turn upon representatives of the four faculties, starting with the Faculty of Law and then passing to the Faculties of Theology, Medicine, and finally Philosophy. This arrangement left the Society with considerable influence, but far from a total dictatorship over the university.[36] The absolute religious orthodoxy imposed on the reconstituted university was initially reinforced by the terms of the Peace of Westphalia, which granted to the Habsburgs the right to preserve or restore Catholicism *(ius reformandi),* giving only a seven-year period for non-Catholics to emigrate.[37] Then, three years later, a new, much stricter policy was enacted for Bohemia, giving Protestants only six weeks "ad conversionem vel emigrationem."[38] Clearly no room for heterodoxy remained at the Prague university or at any other school in the land.

The structural changes in the organization of the university say a great deal about the difficulty of integrating two fundamentally different educational institutions. Also at this time, references to the "nations"—the broad geographical groupings of students that were a standard feature of the medieval university—are no longer found in university documents. Rather than functioning as a cosmopolitan school serving students from all over Europe, the newly reformed Prague university was to be a bastion of the Counter-Reformation dedicated to the education of Bohemians in the Catholic faith. Meanwhile, throughout Bohemia Jesuit schools and missions continued the work of reintroducing Catholicism, a task for which they were better prepared than were their rivals, the Piarists, who, unlike the Jesuits, usually had come there from Italy or other foreign lands and thus were seldom native speakers of Czech.[39]

Nevertheless, in this first phase of the Society's activities in Bohemia, many of the leading Jesuits had come there from other lands: Peter Canisius, the leader of the first band to reach Prague, was Dutch.[40] Rodrigo Arriaga (1592–1667), an outstanding theologian and dean of the Theological Faculty of the university of Prague, was Castilian; Andreas de Buisson (ca.

---

[36] Leopold I issued this decree on October 3, 1659 (Tomek, *Geschichte,* 284).

[37] In 1626 Ferdinand II had already issued an edict requiring heretics to embrace Catholicism or emigrate, although he graciously allowed them to sell their possessions before departing (*Ottův slovník naučný,* 28 vols. [Prague: Otto, 1894], 8:575).

[38] Derek Croxton, *Peacemaking in Early Modern Europe: Cardinal Mazarin and the Peace of Westphalia, 1643–1648* (Selinsgrove: Susquehanna University Press, 1999).

[39] I. Cornejová, "Správní a institutionální vývoj," in *Dějiny* 2:39. The Piarists, however, remained active in Bohemia for the next two hundred years, and ultimately took over some of the educational programs of the Society after its suppression.

[40] Joseph Lecler, "Die Kirchenfrömmigkeit des heiligen Petrus Canisius," in *Sentire cum Ecclesia: Das Bewusstsein von der Kirche als gestaltende Kraft der Frömmigkeit,* ed. Jean Danielou and Herbert Vorgrimler (Freiburg: Herder, 1961), 302.

1606–52), rector of the collegium in the Old Town of Prague was, like Canisius, from the Low Countries, as was Carolus de Grobendonecque (1600–1672), dean of both the Faculties of Theology and Philosophy. Edmund Campion, an early professor at the university and the first Jesuit to be put to death for his faith in Europe, was English; Peter Wading, chancellor of the Jesuit university before 1638, was Irish; and Joannes Bock, dean of the Faculty of Philosophy in 1678, was born in what is today Poland.[41]

The international character of these first Jesuit academics and preachers sent to work in Bohemia was typical of several provinces during the first century of the Society's existence. The question of the national identities and loyalties of the Jesuits of Bohemia is complex, and became even more important in the century and a half after White Mountain. On the one hand, because so many members of the Province of Bohemia, both Jesuit priests and brothers, were native-born, the character of the missionary activities of the Society in Bohemia was different from what it was in other parts of the Habsburg domains, where Jesuits were often perceived as outsiders with little understanding of local customs and culture. At the same time, the Society was far more centralized in its administration than were most of the other Catholic teaching orders, and the uniformity of educational experience fostered in the *Ratio* encouraged a transnational outlook among Jesuit educators, in contrast to the more local sense of identity that individual Jesuits might have felt. Both of these factors would play important roles in the way individual Jesuits would respond to the deepening crisis of the eighteenth century.

The second half of the seventeenth century and the first decades of the eighteenth have long been known to students of Czech literary history as the period of darkness *(doba temna).* The suppression and decline of the Czech language, the denial of religious liberty, and the domination of the entire land by an aristocracy made up of Habsburg favorites and supporters justify this designation. That the Society played an important role in this transformation cannot be denied.[42] A further symptom of this decline was the failure of Prague, in other respects an important administrative and commercial center, to figure more than marginally in the flowering of the

[41] An invaluable summary of biographical data on Jesuits connected with the Faculties of Theology and Philosophy is found in *Životopisný slovník pražské univerzity: Filosofická a teologická fakulta 1654–1773,* by I. Čornejová and A. Fechtnerová (Prague: Univerzita Karlova, 1986). See also A. Fechnerová, *Rectores collegiorum Societatis Iesu in Bohemia, Moravia, ac Silesia usque ad annum MDCCLXXIII iacentum,* 2 vols. (Prague: Národní Knihovna, 1993), 1:39–67.

[42] This was the judgment even of eighteenth-century Bohemians who knew and admired individual Jesuits. Franz Martin Pelzel, in his *Příhody Václava Vratislava z Mitrovic,* found fault with the Society's destruction of Czech-language books, a criticism echoed by Dobrovský (Hugh Le Caine Agnew, *Origins of the Czech National Renaissance* [Pittsburgh: University of Pittsburgh Press, 1993], 117).

Baroque that took place elsewhere in central Europe.[43] It is understandable, therefore, that virtually all Czech nationalist writers of the last 150 years have indicted the Society as a force profoundly detrimental to Czech culture, one that imposed a foreign and uncongenial language, culture, and religion on the Czechs.[44]

Yet the cliché of the sinister, scheming "black fathers" following behind the Habsburgs, crushing Czech cultural expression as they went, is far from accurate. Many of the most prominent Jesuits writing in the seventeenth century were themselves ethnic Czechs, and many others made use of the native language in their own preaching and teaching. The enlightened bureaucrats of the late eighteenth century did far more to force German on the Czechs than did the Society or other Catholic clergy of the previous century.[45] Nor were the Habsburgs urging the repression of local languages. Indeed, it is said that even Leopold I, almost a caricature of Habsburg religious intolerance and hostility to national aspirations, learned enough Czech to follow a sermon preached in that language. Two of the leading Czech poets of the seventeenth century, Felix Kadlinský (1613–75) and Bedřich Bridel (1619–80), were themselves Jesuits.[46] Fragmentary evidence indicates that a library of popular books in the Czech language was created in 1669, partly on the initiative of the Jesuits.[47]

The outstanding defender of Czech language and culture during this period was Bohoslav Balbín (1621–88), a Jesuit polymath, who taught rhetoric at the Prague university.[48] Balbín produced both a *Dissertatio apologetica pro lingua Slavonica,* which sang the praises of the Czech language, as well as *Bohemia docta,* a compendium of the intellectual accomplishments

---

[43] Philip Hofer, *Baroque Book Illustration* (Cambridge, Mass.: Harvard University Press, 1951), 19. A complete list of titles of works published in Bohemia in the Baroque era is found in *Knihopis Československých tisků od doby nejstarší až do konce xviii. století,* Díl. 2: Tisky z let 1501–1800 (Prague: V Komisi Knihkupectví F. Topice, 1967).

[44] Much twentieth-century historiography, including Robert Kerner's *Bohemia in the Eighteenth Century: A Study in Political, Economic, and Social History with Special Reference to the Reign of Leopold II, 1790–1792* (New York: Macmillan, 1932) has been influenced by Ernest Denis, who is consistently negative in his assessment of the Society's impact. More recent Czech historians, including Čornejová and Fechtnerová, have been far less critical.

[45] Jean Bérenger, "The Austrian Church," in *Church and Society in Catholic Europe of the Eighteenth Century,* ed. William J. Callahan and David Higgs (Cambridge: The University Press, 1979), 88.

[46] Brief biographies of Bridel and Kadlinský appear in Václav Černý ed., *Kéž hoři popel můj: Z poesie evropského baroka* (Prague: Mladá Fronta, 1967), 271, 275.

[47] *Dictionnaire d'historie et de géographie ecclésiastiques,* (Paris) s.v. "Bohême."

[48] H. Sturm, ed., *Biographisches Lexikon zur Geschichte der Böhmischen Länder,* 12 vols. (Munich: Oldenbourg, 1974–), vol. 1, fasc. 1, p. 43.

of the Czechs.[49] Although both these treatises remained unpublished until more than a century after Balbín's death, when they did appear they exerted a notable influence on the earliest generation of Czech nationalist writers. Balbín, who along with Jan Amos Komenský (Comenius), is regarded as the outstanding figure in seventeenth-century Czech cultural history, also wrote works on philosophy and history, and his support of the local culture typifies the complex loyalties many Bohemian Jesuits experienced.[50]

During the seventeenth and eighteenth centuries, the Society, which was originally transnational in its mission and vision, increasingly came to be identified with national groups. The history of the Jesuits transcended the concept of the Society as a monolithic organization, as it became entwined with the history of the nations in which they worked and developed significant relationships. In the case of Bohemia, the Jesuits became enmeshed in the special problems of defining a nation or people and establishing relationships between the people and higher political authority.

In 1694, at the height of the Baroque era, Bohemian Jesuit polemicists and preachers drew upon contemporary belief in the miraculous and on native anti-Semitism to launch a propaganda campaign that sought to promote their own program to convert the Jews and strengthen their own position. Through much of the seventeenth century, the reconstituted Prague university had maintained only marginal relations with the Jewish ghetto that lay in close proximity to the Clementinum. An exception was made for Jewish barber-surgeons, who did not attend university lectures but who sought authorization to exercise their trade, and for Jewish physicians who requested permission to treat Christian patients.[51] The Prague Jesuit community as a whole showed no more toleration for its Jewish neighbors than did other city residents.

The murder on February 2, 1694, of Shimon Abeles, a Jewish youth of Prague who had been receiving religious instruction from the Jesuits of the Clementinum, provided an occasion for the Society to launch a propaganda campaign of European proportions, especially because the crime was imputed to the boy's father and another Jew.[52] The reburial of the boy's

---

[49] Bohoslav Balbín, *Dissertatio apologetica pro lingua Slavonica, præcipue bohemica,* ed. F. M. Pelzel (Prague, 1777); id., *Bohemia docta: opus posthumum,* ed. R. Ungar (Prague, 1780). See also Josef Hanuš, "Bohuslava Balbína *Bohemia Docta,*" *Český Časopis Historický* 12 (1906): 137, and n. 7.

[50] Victor-Lucien Tapié considers Balbín influential but overrated, noting his limitations as a historian and his cumbersome style (*Rise and Fall of the Habsburg Monarchy,* 132).

[51] Guido Kisch, *Die Prager Universität und die Juden* (Amsterdam: B. R. Grüner, 1969), 151–54.

[52] Antonín Novotný, "Pražská sensace A. D. 1694," *Aventinský magazin* 4(1930), 10–17; P. Pekař, "Simon Abeles," *Kalendář česko-židovský* 23 (1912–1913): 92–94; Egon Erwin Kisch, *Prager Pitaval* (Berlin: Erich Reiss, 1931), 133–43; Tomáš Pěkný, *Historie Židů v Čechách a na Moravě*

miraculously preserved body a few weeks later brought forth a lavish public ceremony that included a parade of Jewish children converted by the Society. Shortly thereafter, the public execution of one of the accused murderers was enlivened by a conversion on the gallows, prompted by a Jesuit. An account of the murder, written by a Jesuit member of the Philosophical Faculty and replete with references to the miraculous, was widely circulated, and an oratorio on the same theme was published in Prague.[53] Subsequently Jesuit gymnasia produced the play mentioned in chapter 1, "Agnus inter hædos, Simon Abeles," supposedly based on the life and death of the boy martyr. Even though few Jews were converted by these undertakings, the net impact of the propaganda surrounding these events was to assure that receptive Catholics would view the Society as the proper guardians of the mysteries of the bodies of the saints, a role Bohemian Jesuits had taken on earlier with their promotion of St. Jan Nepomucký.[54]

Demonizing the Prague Jews implicated in the murder enabled the Jesuits to identify themselves still more persuasively as defenders of the true Catholic faith. By acknowledging that the not-yet-baptized Abeles had a soul, the Society implicitly conceded his humanity, which some non-Catholics seemed willing to deny. This frank acknowledgement signified a portentous development whose potential significance should not be underrated.[55] Relations between the Society and Jewish communities throughout Bohemia would remain complex, with Jesuits attempting, generally with little success, to convert the Children of Israel, and Jews for their part seeing the Jesuits as one of the most threatening elements of Christian society.[56] Unconverted Jews could not be admitted to candidacy for university degrees throughout

---

(Prague: Sefer, 1993), 179. The trial and executions are described in a contemporary publication, *Processus inquisitorius* . . . (Prague, 1728; reprinted 1696).

[53] Joannes Eder, *Virilis constantia pueri duodecennis Simonis Abeles in odium fidei a Judeo parente* . . . (Prague, 1694); in the Strahov library is also the manuscipt of an oratorio by Don Rotundo Christoforo Angelo, *Il neomartire di Boemia; o vero, la conversione e martirio di Simon Abeles discritto in due oratori, per musica* (Prague, 1695), sign. BP VI 5 i c. 80.

[54] Emanuel Vlček, *Sv. Jan Nepomucký: Jeho Život, umučení a slavné působení ve světle současné historie a antropologie* (Prague: Vesmír, 1993); Paul Shore, "The Society of Jesus and the Culture of the Late Baroque in Bohemia," *East European Quarterly* 34, no. 1 (2000): 8.

[55] As we shall argue in chap. 5, the Jesuits made a distinction between the adult male Jewish population, whom they saw as their opponent on a theological and perhaps scholarly ground, and Jewish women and children, who were potentially more readily "rescued" from Judaism. The Abeles case makes it clear who the Society believed could be educated and saved. See Paul Shore, "Loving the Souls, Hating the Bodies: Jesuit Jewish Relations in Bohemia during the Eighteenth Century," *Proceedings of the Fifth Biennial Conference on Christianity and the Holocaust*, October 18–19, 1998 (Princeton, N.J.), 21–30.

[56] The strangest episode in the relationship occurred when the Turkish Porte, concerned with the treatment of Jews of Prague after their expulsion from that city in 1744, offered them sanctuary in the Ottoman Empire (Karl A. Roider, Jr., *Austria's Eastern Question, 1700–1790* [Princeton: Princeton University Press, 1982], 97 f.).

the Habsburg lands until the requirement that the candidate take an oath affirming the Immaculate Conception was removed in 1782.[57]

For Enlightenment intellectuals and Czech nationalists alike, the Jesuit personification of this "time of darkness" was Fr. Antonín Koniáš (1690–1760), who has earned a permanent place in the folklore of Bohemia through his fanatical devotion to the Catholic Church. Koniáš, who died in the Clementinum, is best remembered for destroying tens of thousands of heretical books, many of them in Czech.[58] This fearsome father, who sometimes lectured about the terrors of hell while wearing an iron chain around his neck, also wrote a guide to heretical literature that went through several printings.[59] The fanaticism of Koniáš reflects a worldview largely alien to the twenty-first century: it is said that he learned French solely to be able to offer the last anointing to dying French soldiers at the siege of Prague. In recent years Koniáš, whose intense devotion to the Church was exceptional even by the overheated standards of the Counter-Reformation, has been the subject of renewed controversy as scholars seek to evaluate the role he played in suppressing Czech culture and destroying Czech-language books.[60]

Granted that it is unfair to consider Koniáš as representative of the Bohemian Jesuits of his day, his fanaticism made a considerable impression upon his Jesuit contemporaries, who commented favorably upon his activities. Koniáš has remained a figure of controversy among Czech historians, as debate continues about the role of the Catholic Church in the modern-day Czech Republic.[61] It is best to understand him as a Baroque personality, whose focus on the "unseen world" and the dangers facing one's immortal soul is akin to that of Cotton Mather or Abraham à Sancta Clara.[62] This worldview had not completely disappeared in the second half of the eighteenth century, when many educated people still believed in demonic possession and witchcraft.[63]

---

[57] *Československnká vlastivěda,* Díl 2: Dějiny svazek 1 (Prague: Orbis, 1963), 464.

[58] One of the first Czech *literati* of the National Awakening to comment on Koniáš's destruction of Czech-language books was Karel Ignac Thám, who, drawing upon Koniáš's own accounts (which may have been exaggerated), estimated the number of books burned at sixty thousand, more than all the volumes destroyed during the Thirty Years' War (K. I. Thám, *Neuestes, ausführliches und vollständinges böhmisch-deutsches . . . Nationallexikon oder Wörterbuch* [Prague: Franz Johann Scholl, 1805], xxxviii).

[59] Antonín Koniáš, *Clavis hæresim claudens at aperiens* (W Hradci Král, 1749). This work also appeared in Czech as *Kljč kacyřské bludy. . . .*

[60] E.g., Jiří Bilý, *Jezuita Antonín Koniáš: Osobnost a doba* (Prague: Vyšehrad, 1996).

[61] Martin Svatoš, "Misionář Antonín Koniáš T. J. - služebík Bozí či Dáblův?" *Dějiny a součastnost* 2 (1996): 15–19.

[62] Robert Kann, *A Study in Austrian Intellectual History* (New York: Prager,1960), 50–115.

[63] Although belief in witches and demonic possession was on the decline throughout the late seventeenth and eighteenth centuries, this belief died slowly, even among relatively well-

At the beginning of the eighteenth century, the Clementinum stood at the center of a network of schools and missions reaching into all corners of the Bohemian Crown lands. After almost fifty years of Jesuit domination, the university had declined in academic quality, but nevertheless still dominated intellectual life in Bohemia.[64] Both students and teachers generally came from the surrounding area, and the earlier cosmopolitan character of the institution had largely been lost. Outside the city, Jesuit pastoral work, now well established after several generations of contact with the rural population, occasionally included defense of the peasants, who were severely oppressed to the point of rebelling in 1680.[65] Yet when peasants on Jesuit-owned estates joined the uprising, they aroused no sympathy in the fathers, nor did later popular movements gain the Society's support.[66] Some have maintained that by 1680 the process of reconverting the entire region to the Catholic faith, vigorously pursued for six decades, was at least outwardly complete, although crypto-Protestant beliefs never died out, and constant missionary efforts were necessary. This activity, often carried out with aggressive determination, earned the Jesuits deep resentment in some quarters, a resentment still palpable among Protestants two centuries later.[67]

The poverty and illiteracy of the Bohemian peasants prevented them from leaving behind many records of this difficult relationship. The few examples that do exist, however, clearly convey hostility and resentment. A painting dating from the eighteenth century shows a priestly figure, presumably a Jesuit, looking on as a religious dissenter is tortured with flaming brands. An accompanying illustration features clerics, probably meant to be Jesuits, in birettas and cassocks, seated at a table gambling.[68]

---

educated Catholic prelates. As late as 1768, the bishop of Ypres would do no more than suggest gingerly that cases of possession were far less common than popularly supposed—but he would not deny their existence (Henry Charles Lea, *Materials towards a History of Witchcraft*, 3 vols. [Philadelphia: University of Pennsylvania Press, 1939], 3:1055). This conservatism contributed to a general climate of acceptance of the miraculous that, as we shall see, played such a significant role in the Jesuit missionary undertakings in Bohemia. It is noteworthy that Friederich von Spee, S.J., opposed witchcraft trials in his *Cautio criminalis*.

[64] Notker Hammerstein, *Aufläkrung und katholisches Reich: Untersuchungen zur Universitätsgeschichte und Politik katholischer Territorien des Heiligen Römischen Reichs deutscher Nation im 18. Jahrhundert* (Berlin: Duncker und Humblot, 1977), 230–231.

[65] Ludwig Koch, S.J., *Jesuiten-Lexikon* (Paderborn: Verlag Bonifacius-Druckerei, 1934), 222.

[66] In eighteenth-century Katovice, peasants sought the abolition of the *robota* on lands controlled by the Society, but without success (Jiří Svoboda, *Protifeudalní a socialní hnutí v Čechách na konci doby temna (1750–1774)*, Acta Universitatis Carolinæ, Philosophica et historica monographia 17 [Prague: Universita Karlova, 1967], 22).

[67] Hermann Daum, *Die Verfolgerungen der Evangelisten in Böhmen* (Darmstadt: Eduard Zernin, 1860).

[68] Reproduced without attribution in *Česká národní obrození*, by Josef Kočí (Prague: Nakladatelství Svoboda, 1978), fourth plate following 64. Kočí identifies these paintings on glass

The holy campaign of reconversion was fought on many fronts. The Society was deeply involved in promoting the cults of Mary and other saints, among them St. Roch for protection against the plague (which came once more to central Europe in 1713–14), and St. Rosalie for protection against toothache. Pilgrimage churches built or manned by Jesuits dotted the countryside, and Jesuit preachers were a prominent part of urban life in Prague. Yet one cannot conclude with confidence that these men, despite their good works, were accepted and welcomed in many of the communities in which they labored. Certainly, the fervor with which at least some members of the Society carried out the draconian repression of heresy of all kinds throughout the late seventeenth and eighteenth centuries did not endear them to many Czechs.[69]

A distinguished historian characterized the Jesuits of Counter-Reformation Austria as "zealous and deferential" to the ruling dynasty; the description is vivid, but not accurate in all cases.[70] The loyalty that most Bohemian Jesuits exhibited towards the Habsburgs and their minions was sincere, but the expression of *pietas Austriaca* was more complex than merely a manifestation of deference to a foreign conqueror.[71] Rather, it resulted from the role in which the Society found itself cast as interpreter of the dynasty to the people. As a political force and often as individuals, as in the case of Leopold I, the Habsburgs embodied the devotional ideals held by Baroque Catholics in many parts of Europe; and support for the dynasty, whether in polemic, homily, or architecture, was an endorsement of earthly distinction and posthumous glory that lay at the heart of the high-Baroque Catholic understanding of religious experience.[72]

---

as "anti-Jesuit." However, granted that these illustrations, part of a longer series that includes figures of the devil tempting humans, have also been dated from 1765 and interpreted as accompanying a now lost folk song, the anti-Jesuit character of these paintings is not self-evident. The entire series is reproduced in *Československá vlastivěda,* díl 2, dějiny svazek 1, 564–70.

[69] Hermann Münch, *Böhmische Tragödie: Das Schicksal Mitteleuropas im Lichte der tschechischen Frage* (Braunschweig: Georg Westermann, 1949), 123.

[70] R. J. W. Evans, "Introduction," in Charles W. Ingrao ed., *State and Society in Early Modern Austria* (West Lafayette, Ind.: Purdue University Press, 1994), 6.

[71] The subtleties of this idea are developed in Anna Coreth, *Pietas Austriaca* (Munich, Oldenbourg, 1959).

[72] Although much has been written on Baroque religious art, the subject of Jesuit architecture in Bohemia requires more investigation: a good survey of Jesuit art for the seventeenth century is *Baroque Art: The Jesuit Contribution,* ed. Rudolf Wittkower and Irma B. Jaffe (New York: Fordham University Press, 1972). More work is needed on the relationship between Habsburg dynastic identity and the Baroque aesthetic, particularly at the hands of the Jesuits. *Der schöne Tod: Zeremonialstrukturen des Wiener Hofes bis Tod und Begräbnis zwischen 1640 und 1740,* by Magdalena Hawlik-van de Water (Vienna: Herder, 1989), serves as a beginning.

This understanding was not content with an entirely spiritual conceptualization of the divine, but turned repeatedly to naturalistic and anthropomorphic elements in its portrayal of religious experience, or even of God himself.[73] Thus, it was often easy through artistic representation to link a sensuously accessible, anthropomorphic divinity with the mortal representatives of the House of Habsburg. Even in death, the Habsburgs were surrounded by symbolism that recalled both imperial Rome and the kingdom of heaven. The Jesuits, frequently confessors to the members of the imperial household, were in a position to draw connections between the duties of their earthly patrons and the majesty of their divine Master.

In Bohemia the Society also had a unique opportunity to dominate the artistic and intellectual tone of both town and country, resulting in part from the absence of other groups who might have played a major role in setting rival aesthetic standards. Yet the Baroque sensibility offered by the Society's late-Baroque artistic undertakings was not without internal contradictions. By the middle of the century, as R. Po-Chia Hsia has observed, Jesuit plays were exhibiting tension between the older Baroque theme of the "transience of life" and the more rationalist worldview of the Enlightenment.[74] As we shall see in subsequent chapters, similar tensions would emerge in the literary culture of the Jesuits of Bohemia, and perhaps in its artistic undertakings as well.

Down to the end of the eighteenth century, Bohemia suffered from a lack of educated gentry and burghers, resulting in part from the confiscations and persecutions that followed White Mountain and the subsequent exodus of Protestants.[75] Folk culture persisted, but the extreme poverty and degradation facing many peasants throughout the eighteenth century, even when harvests were relatively good, did nothing to help them preserve folk traditions.[76] Thus, the Jesuits were able to move into this cultural vacuum with particular ease; and controlling the universities and secondary schools as they did, they availed themselves of the opportunity to erect schools and churches in a flamboyant Baroque style. But over and above the simply

[73] This is nowhere more evident than in the images found on late-Baroque altars, whose ornamentation suggests the relationship between sensuous splendor drawing upon naturalistic themes (clouds, leaves, and so forth), and the intense and concrete individual experience of the saint commemorated (Wolf-Dieter Hamperl and P. Aquilas Rohner, *Böhmisch-oberpfälzische Akanthusaltäre* [München/Zürich: Schnell & Steiner, 1984]).

[74] R. Po-Chia Hsia, *Social Discipline in the Reformation: Central Europe, 1550–1750* (New York/London: Routledge, 1989), 95.

[75] T. Bílek, "Reformace katolická v Čechách 1650–1781," 56–72; Jaroslav Werstadt, "Politické dějepisectví XIX století a jeho čeští představatelé," *Český časopis Historický* 26 (1920): 3. Hereafter this source will be abbreviated to *ČČH*.

[76] Konrad Schunemann, *Österreichs Bevölkerungspolitik unter Maria Theresia* (Berlin: Deutsche Rundschau, ca. 1943), 59.

material, the Society accommodated itself to the peculiar manifestations of the Baroque found in eighteenth-century Bohemia.

Some of these manifestations had roots in the humblest level of society, as when peasants attributed magical powers to the Jesuits working in rural districts.[77] At other times, the Baroque expressed itself in more grandiose strivings after the remote and distant. This Baroque longing for what was far removed fit nicely with both the celebrated far-reaching missionary endeavors of Francis Xavier and other Jesuits and the historically remote, if not entirely mythical, origins of the Habsburg dynasty with whom the Society had allied itself. Whatever its other shortcomings, the dynasty deserved some credit for thwarting the Ottoman advance into Europe, and for providing the region with a modicum of stability.[78] Not surprisingly, the Habsburgs did not shy away from advertising this accomplishment, while also portraying themselves as defenders of the Church from heretics and as upholders of the special relationship between the Holy See and the phantom Holy Roman Empire. Thus the "triumph of the casa d'Austria" was an oft repeated theme among Jesuit historians laboring in the service of the dynasty.[79] The Society willingly supported this portrayal of the dynasty, a task no doubt made somewhat more difficult in Prague, where in 1742 the Estates and even the archbishop accepted as their ruler the Bavarian claimant to the imperial throne, Charles VII, thus rejecting Maria Theresia.[80] Ironically, the dynasty would eventually abandon its most fervent propagandists.

Conclusion

Midcentury found the Jesuits slipping from their position as the esteemed "schoolmasters of Europe" into an increasingly marginalized status in which their schools no longer represented pedagogical innovation, but

---

[77] The character in folktales of the Jesuit or Franciscan priest endowed with special powers to cure sick animals or weave spells has not yet been investigated sufficiently (Alois John, *Sitten und Brauch im deutschen Westböhmen* [Prague: G. G. Calve'sche K. k. Hof -u. Universitäts Buchhandlung, 1905], 286).

[78] Ivan Porev, *Habsburgs and the Ottomans between Vienna and Belgrade, 1683–1739* (Boulder: E. European Monographs, 1994).

[79] Anna Coreth, *Österreichische Geschichtsschreibung in der Barockzeit* (Vienna: A. Holzhausens, 1950), 83 f.

[80] Archbishop Ernst Moritz Manderscheid-Blankenburg, although he did not actually participate in a coronation ceremony for Charles VII, was banished from Prague for several years following the recapture of that city (Otakar Odlozik, "The Nobility of Bohemia, 1620–1740," *East European Quarterly* 7, no. 1 (1973): 26; P. G. M. Dickson, *Finance and Government under Maria Theresia, 1740–1780,* 2 vols. (Oxford: Clarendon Press, 1987), 1:64. But see the account of the resistance of many Bohemians, including the students in the Prague university, to the French-supported Charles, found in Tapié, *Rise and Fall of the Habsburg Monarchy,* 181 f.

instead were identified (sometimes inaccurately) with intolerance, censorship, and superstition, and as dispensing a body of knowledge whose value was being called into question. Even the Jesuits' sincere efforts at modernization seemed too little too late. When Jesuit education took up the teaching of Newtonian physics before the Theresian reforms, this innovation did not silence the Society's critics.[81] In the humanities Jesuits continued to offer the classical curriculum established in the *Ratio* almost two hundred years earlier, but their bowdlerizing of texts was now viewed less favorably in many quarters.[82] It is significant that Jesuits were entirely excluded from the debate of the century between the "ancients" and the moderns that absorbed so much attention of literary theorists.[83]

The fathers had also made enemies in more progressive circles in Vienna.[84] Within the Catholic Church, Febronianism, a movement calling for more religious toleration and even the possible reunion of Protestant churches with the Catholic Church, placed itself in opposition to the stated mission of the Society.[85] Probably too much has been made of the influence of the *philosophes* in bringing about the downfall of the Society, although the hostile attitude of Voltaire and the *encyclopédistes* added fuel to the Jesuit opponents' charges that the Society stifled intellectual freedom, was too wealthy, and could not be depended upon to support the political regimes under which it served. Above all, the opposition of the Bourbon monarchies played a major part in the events that led up to the suppression of the Society in 1773.[86]

---

[81] Domonkos Kosáry, "L'Éducation en Europe Centrale et Orientale a l'âge des Lumières," in *Les Lumières en Hongrie, en Europe Centrale et en Europe Orientale* (Budapest: Akadémia Kiadó, 1984), 218.

[82] Peter Gay, *The Enlightenment: An Interpretation,* 2 vols. (New York: Alfred A Knopf, 1969), 2:504. It should be acknowledged, however, that some variation in the rigidity of this censorship no doubt existed by midcentury. A curricular outline of classical authors taught in the Bohemian Province has survived, and although it is not possible to ascertain with complete certainty whether the authors listed were censored, the mere presence of Seneca's *Medea* and an (interlinear) Homer suggests that the content could not have been reduced to a bowdlerized pablum (*Auctorum triennalium in schola rhetorices per Provinciam Bohemiæ Societatis Jesu prælegendorum Quorum syllabum sequens pagella exhibet annus primus* [Prague, 1720]).

[83] Allan Megell, "Aesthetic Theory and Historical Consciousness in the Eighteenth Century," *History and Theory* 17 (1978): 29–62.

[84] Frank T. Brechka, *Gerhard van Swieten and His World, 1700–1772* (The Hague: Martinus Nijhoff, 1970), 123–36.

[85] Karl Otmar Freiherr von Aretin, *Heiliges Römisches Reich, 1776–1806: Reichsverfassung und Staatssouveränität,* 2 vols. (Wiesbaden: Franz Steiner Verlag, 1967), 1:42; John Roberts, *Revolution and Improvement: The Western World, 1775–1847* (Berkeley: University of California Press, 1976), 72 f.

[86] J. Crétineau-Joly, *Histoire religieuse, politique et littéraire de la Compagnie de Jésus,* 6 vols. (Paris: P. Mellier, 1845–46), vols. 5 and 6. Two scholastics, refugees from the French Province, arrived in Bohemia in 1762 (NK, 1287 MS XXIII C105/15, *An. Prov. Boh. 1762,* folio 255r).

Around the fringes of the debate, charges of Jesuit sexual immorality were also bruited about. In 1743 *Travels of the Jesuits into Various Parts of the World* appeared, a much shortened and expurgated version of the thirty-four-volume *Lettres édifiantes et curieuses, écrites des missions étrangères par quelques missionaires de la Compagnie de Jésus* . . . (1717–74). In this work were hints that Jesuits had engaged in homosexual practices in China.[87] Taken by itself, a book like this meant little, but the very appearance of such rumors shows how willing some readers were to accept the worst-possible tales about the Jesuits. While Jesuits increasingly came under fire in different parts of the world for their missionary activities and their alleged wealth, a different, more confined drama was being played out in Prague.

In 1752, not by coincidence, a major debate over the list of banned books was underway in the Jesuit-influenced *Zensurkommission* in Vienna; it resulted in the Habsburg bureaucrats' simultaneously taking over the function of censor. Simultaneously, a major reform of university education was announced in Vienna for all the Habsburg lands.[88] The Prague university underwent significant changes, including the reduction of the course of study in the Faculty of Philosophy from three years to two, and the appointment of directors of studies for the Faculties of Theology and Philosophy (followed by similar appointments in the Faculties of Medicine and Law two years later).[89] Non-Jesuit clergy were allowed to teach in the Faculty of Theology. More systematic and complete methods of academic bookkeeping were also introduced, making professors more accountable to outside authorities.[90] In 1754 the professors of the Faculty of Law for the first time were allowed to purchase books by non-Catholic authors, a development that would have been unthinkable in the heyday of Jesuit influence in the university.[91]

---

[87] Reported in G. S. Rousseau, *Perilous Enlightenment: Pre- and Post-Modern Discourses* (Manchester: Manchester University Press, 1991), 31.

[88] The original document, "Norma für die Studien unter Maria Theresia," is reproduced in *Geschichte des österreichischen Bildungswesens: Erziehung und Unterricht auf dem Boden Österreichs*, by Herbert Engelbrecht, 5 vols. (Vienna: Österreichischer Bundesverlag, 1984), 3:461–63.

[89] The appointment of Vilem MacNeven, an outstanding physician, as the director of studies for the Faculty of Medicine in 1754 confirmed the rising status of this faculty, which had long eluded the direct control of the Society (Ludmila Hlavácková, "Chudinské peče a zdravotnictví," in Petráň, *Počátky*, 129.

[90] Surviving lists of students enrolled in classes date from 1752; individual instructors may have kept records before this date, but the new policy required the professors to follow an established system of record keeping (I. Raková, *Katalogy posluchačů Pražské University, 1752–1882: Inventární seznam* [Prague: Universita Karlova, 1984]).

[91] Johann Anton Riegger, *Materialen zur alten u. neuen Statistik von Böhmen*, 12 vols. (Prague, Leipizg: Kaspar Widtmann, 1787), 2:399. Details of the implementation of these liberalizing reforms are in many cases lacking, since the *Akten des älteren Staatsrates* were destroyed in 1945 (Rudolf Neck, "The Haus-, Hof-, und Staatsarchiv: Its History, Holdings, and

The Society was losing ground on other fronts as well. When a Prague Jesuit preached a sermon on probabilism, an informant sent a copy to Vienna, while a local abbot spread the rumor that the Society had offered Maria Theresia a bribe of fifty thousand florins if she would grant them a continued monopoly on university education.[92] Meanwhile, the pace of change continued, and even accelerated. An unmistakable straw in the wind was the removal in 1762 of any reference to the Society in the title of the university of Olomouc. Nine years later, a non-Jesuit, Dr. Fr. Baron Šubír, became chancellor.[93] In 1763 a chair of *Bergwissenschaft* was established at the Prague university, a further evidence of the advance of the applied sciences and the contraction of the realm of abstract thought previously dominated by the Jesuits.[94] The same year a complementary token of the secular, empirical, and practical trends emerging in education appeared with the founding of the first mining college in the world in Banská Štiavnica (Aranyos Marot) in Hungary.[95]

The admission of an applied science to the curriculum of the Faculty of Philosophy had other implications as well. Jan Thadeus Peithner, who lectured on *Bergwissenschaft*, did so in German.[96] Although this novelty had been introduced some decades earlier in German Protestant universities, the use of a living language as a medium of instruction in a traditionally Jesuit-led institution was of pivotal importance. The *Ratio* had enthroned Latin as the language of both teacher and student, and as both a means of communication and a vehicle for discussing the moral and theological lessons of classical and patristic authors. The decline of Latin, which occurred without well-documented objections, suggests the degree to which the moral and didactic force of the *Ratio* had waned.[97] The legendary power of Jesuit rhetoric was also losing ground. Public quarrels between Jesuits from the Clementinum and the newly appointed Dominican and Augustinian profes-

Use," *Austrian History Yearbook* 6–7 [1970–71]: 3–16).

[92] Eduard Winter, *Der Josefinismus: Die Geschichte des österrreichischen Reformkatholizismus, 1740–1848* (Berlin: Rütten und Loening, 1962), 49.

[93] Václav Nešpor, *Dějiny University Olomoucké*, 68.

[94] Herbert Egglmaier, "Am Beispiel Österreich: Die Wissenschaftspolitik eines aufgeklärt-absolutischen Staates," *Mitteilungen der österreichischen Gesellschaft für Wissenschaftsgeschichte* 15 (1995): 101–26.

[95] Dr. Ondrej Pavlík, *The Development of the Czechoslovak School System with Regard to Slovakia* (Bratislava: Comenius University Institute for Studies in Teacher Education, 1969), 3.

[96] This was not because the science of mining lacked a Latin vocabulary; in fact, such a vocabulary was highly developed during the Renaissance. Rather what was at stake was the Latin-comprehension levels of students who sought carers in applied sciences.

[97] This shift in content and language is also evident in the publication of one of the most ambitious scholarly projects of any Bohemian Jesuit, František Pubitschka's *Chronologische Geschichte Böhmens unter den Slaven* (Leipzig, Prague, 1770), written in the vernacular.

sors in the Faculty of Theology were unseemly and tended to leave the Jesuits worse off than before.[98]

After 1767 Jesuits no longer served as confessors for the imperial family, a position they had enjoyed for over a century.[99] In the same year the monarchy initiated a fundamental change in its relationship with the Holy See. Henceforth, no bulls issued by the pope would have validity in the Habsburg lands without the express permission *(placet)* of the monarch. Thus, more than a decade before Joseph II became the sole ruler and, in some commentators' estimation, the "revolutionary emperor," the institutional influence of the Church in general, and of the Society in particular, was curbed.[100] The backgrounds of professors at the university was changing as well, as instructors shaped by Enlightenment ideas arrived. In 1768 Joseph Ignatius Butschek (Buček) was hired as a professor of *Kameristik*. Butschek, born in Prague in 1741, had studied in Vienna under Joseph von Sonnenfels; later he served as a professor in the Faculty of Law and was elevated to the nobility as Ritter von Heratice in 1810.[101]

Each of these innovations subtly, and frequently not so subtly, reduced the independence of the Jesuits at the very center of their Bohemian power base. Yet, although the Society was undermined abroad and encountered increased opposition even at the Habsburg court, many elements of the Bohemian Province to all outward appearances continued to flourish.[102] In 1759, while the Seven Years' War was raging (1757–63), there were 1,239 Jesuits in the Province of Bohemia, despite the loss of some of its territory. (Silesia, lost by the Habsburgs to Prussia a dozen years earlier, was separated from the Province of Bohemia and became the short-lived Province of Silesia.)[103] The material holdings of the Society, including estates in the countryside that provided income to the community in Prague, remained

---

[98] Winter, *Josefinismus,* 51–53.

[99] Although a Jesuit nominally held the position of confessor for a few more years, in practical terms the new confessor was Ignaz Müller, provost of the Monastery of St. Dorothea and a Jansenist (Peter Hersche, *Der Spätjansenismus in Österreich* [Vienna: Verlag der Österreichischen Akademie der Wissenschaften, 1977], 125 ff., 358 f.). Müller heard Maria Theresia's final confession shortly before her death and continued to be a visible figure in Vienna until his death on August 31, 1782 (E. Tomek, *Kirchengeschichte Österreichs,* 3 vols. [Innsbruck: Tyrolia, 1935–], 3:393).

[100] Kern, *Bohemia in the Eighteenth Century,* 313.

[101] Čornejová and Fechtnerová, *Slovník,* 404 f.

[102] The British diplomat Lord Stormont could write to the Duke of Grafton in 1765, "The Jesuits have been greatly favored in [Moravia]; they have several most magnificent Convents" (quoted in Dickson, *Finance and Government,* 1:392).

[103] Silesia is sometimes referred to in Jesuit documents of the period as a "vice-province," an acknowledgement of its small size, and perhaps also of the hopes of the Bohemian Society that it would someday be reunited with the Bohemian Province (NK, 1288 MX XXIII C105/15, *An. Prov. Boh. 1761*, folio 137r).

untouched.[104] In Prague alone, Jesuits controlled eight churches.[105] Moreover, on the verge of its suppression the Society had such a sizeable presence in Bohemia that a dozen years later bureaucrats could draw up a list of ninety-two former Jesuits still capable of serving in the care of souls.[106]

Did Jesuits, in Prague and elsewhere in Bohemia, grasp the gravity of the situation their Society faced in the 1750s and '60s? We find a clue of the growing awareness among the leadership of the Society that trouble was approaching in phrases that started to appear in official documents in the 1760s.[107] In all probability, most Bohemian Jesuit priests and brothers did not anticipate what a complete suppression would entail or even that the activities of the Society might be seriously restricted, even after France, Spain, and other countries had expelled all its members from their territories. The presence of a few exiled Jesuits in Prague seems to have made no significant impression upon the native-born members of the Society.[108] The financial situation of the Society vis-à-vis the Habsburg government was in fact quite favorable, at least at first glance, the Jesuits being major creditors of the government after 1747.[109] Especially those Jesuits not directly involved in the academic and theological controversies of the day experienced no great change in the climate of the Counter-Reformation in the countryside or in the smaller towns. The rhythms of preaching, teaching, and attending to the "care of souls" proceeded uninterrupted as the forces conspiring to suppress the Society gathered strength.[110] In Prague the

[104] Former Jesuit estates were tallied in 1775 at the time of the abolition of the *robota*. In Bohemia alone these totalled 265 villages (William E. Wright, *Serf, Seigneur, and Sovereign* [Minneapolis: University of Minnesota Press, 1966], 128).

[105] "Summarischer Extractus denen pro Anno 1778 eingelegten Rechnungen deren Exjesuiten im Königreich Böhmen," in Státní Úřední Archiv, České Gubernium 16 (exjesuitica), 710a f3/1 karton 96. Hereafter this archives will be abbreviated to SÚA.

[106] "Verzeichnis aller Exjesuiten . . . in Böhmen," in Exjesuiten Acten: Inventorium (undated, but probably after 1784), Hofkammer Archiv Roter Nr. 155, folio 340v.

[107] For instance, "Communes calamitates quæ ab aliquot annis universam Societatem haud medocri dolore affecerunt" (Prague, Novembris 27, 1760; Moravský zemský Archiv v Brně Cerroniho Sbírka II, 345, 9). Hereafter this source will be abbreviated to MZAB.

[108] For example, Father Augustine Barruel, a Jesuit prevented from following his vocation when the Society was banished from France in 1764, migrated to Prague, where he continued to perform priestly functions. Barruel is noteworthy, for after the fall of the Bastille he put forth the theory that other former Jesuits, after becoming Freemasons, had helped bring about the French Revolution (Daniel Lignou, "Jésuites et Francs-Maçons: A propos d'un article de R. P. Riquet," *Dix-huitième siècle* 8 [1976]: 273–85).

[109] Dickson, *Finance and Government,* 2:307.

[110] An alert observer would have recognized the danger implied in the attempts of the Bohemian provincial to withdraw funds held by the Society and left behind in Naples after the expulsion of the Jesuits from that kingdom (*Korrespondence Jesuitů Provincie České z let 1584–1770 z Archivu Musea Království Českého,* ed. Václav Schulz [Prague: Nákladem České akademie Cisáře Františka Josefa pro vědy, slovesnost a umění, 1900], 267).

tensions between the scientific undertakings of a few outstanding Jesuit intellectuals and the late-Baroque mentality of many other members of the Society continued unabated, and there is no clearly documented evidence of an awareness that the mission of the Society itself was in jeopardy.[111] But profound changes were coming to the Habsburg lands, of which the accession of the twenty-six-year-old Joseph II as its co-ruler was only one element. The Jesuits, who had won so many battles in Bohemia with the support of the dynasty, would soon find themselves on the losing side of a struggle that would transform education and formal religion in Bohemia.

---

[111] An indication of the difficulties facing the Society can be found in the *Litteræ annuæ* of 1772, the last year for which these documents survive. In this year entries for various categories of activities undertaken by the Society are truncated or missing completely (NK, 23/19, folios 415r–425v).

chapter three

The Jesuits and the Long Twilight of the Bohemian Baroque

In the baroque imagination as projected onto the vaults and ceilings of churches, saints and martyrs were seen to rise amidst clouds and angels to the heavens, where they might contemplate the Father, the Son, and the Holy Ghost in bliss eternal. . . . the whole of the baroque, after an initial denial, would be transfigured and allowed to rise to a new empyrean, whose gods would be represented in temples called museums.

—Remy Saisselin, *The Enlightenment against the Baroque*

What Is the Baroque?

There is a risk in introducing the term "baroque" to a historical study not primarily concerned with the arts or literature. While the label is convenient shorthand for a set of more or less contemporaneous trends in the arts, politics, music, and other fields, no less an authority on the cultural history of central Europe than Robert Kann has acknowledged that finding the common element among these activities is difficult, if not impossible.[1] But despite the very real problem of defining the essence of the Baroque in its broader sense, the fact remains that in the tension among various points of view and modes of expression found in the works of the eighteenth-century Jesuits of Bohemia, a unique and distinctive aesthetic is visible. Art historians examining the emergence of the visual Baroque have identified some of the elements making up this tension, which seem relevant to an investigation of the culture promoted by the Jesuits of the eighteenth-

[1] Kann, *Study in Austrian Intellectual History,* 1–4.

century Province of Bohemia.[2] Other components have been analyzed from the perspective of folk piety, although Baroque Bohemia itself has not yet been the subject of such a study.[3]

One of the important influences on the Baroque often cited by historians is the "new religious enthusiasm kindled by the Jesuits" in the late sixteenth and seventeenth centuries.[4] Yet merely to argue that a new aesthetic movement embodies renewed religious feelings does not tell us much about the new artistic style, let alone the religious feelings themselves and the intellectual climate associated with it. Nor can we be sure that these feelings and their expression, initially identified in Italy, can be designated by the same name when we speak of art and literature produced several centuries later in Bohemia. Only after examining the evidence of the Jesuit expression of the Baroque in Bohemia can we formulate the outline of a theory of its aesthetic and the philosophy behind it. Moreover, while much has been written about the flowering of the Baroque in this land, no one has yet adequately described the specific nature of the Jesuit contribution or delineated the relationship of the Jesuit contribution to non-Jesuit art and culture. This chapter will not profess to have eliminated all the ambiguity that surrounds the term "Baroque," but the following pages will attempt to advance the understanding of this aesthetic as it can be documented in Bohemia, with special attention to its manifestations during the second half of the eighteenth century.

The aesthetic that was promoted by the Jesuits in Bohemia is rife with seeming contradictions. It embodies a worldview that is at once mystical and nonmaterial, yet at the same time profoundly sensual: one in which hope and dread, fear and exaltation seem frequently intermixed, and where the miraculous, viewed with disdain by some contemporaneous French Jesuits who frequented the salons of the *philosophes* and disparaged the miracles and wonders claimed by the adherents of Jansenism, plays a central role.[5] This at-times-conflicted, composite worldview was a dominant element in the institutional culture of the Society in Bohemia, as well as a powerful force in

---

[2] Gauvin Alexander Bailey, " 'Le Style Jésuite n'existe pas': Jesuit Corporate Culture and the Visual Arts," in O'Malley, *Jesuits: Cultures, Sciences, and the Arts (1540–1773),* 38 f.

[3] German Baroque piety has received a thorough and fair discussion in *Kirche und Volksfrömmigkeit im Zeitlater des Barock,* by Ludwig Andreas Veit and Ludwig Lenhart (Freiburg: Herder, 1956).

[4] Heinrich Wölfflin, *Renaissance and Baroque,* trans. Kathrin Simon (Ithaca: Cornell University Press, 1964), 86.

[5] The Jesuit editors of the *Journal de Trévoux,* which combatted Jansenism with what often seems a stubborn Enlightenment rationality, sought to dispose of the miracles and prodigies of this movement, although they themselves were heirs to a Counter-Reformation ideology that put considerable stress on the cult of relics and the miracles associated with it (R. R. Palmer, *Catholics and Christians in Eighteenth Century France* [New York: Cooper Square Publishers, 1961], 93).

the lives of individual Jesuits; but the evidences of this worldview are not always easily identified at a distance of more than two centuries. These evidences must be sought in the writings of the Jesuits and in the works of art that the Society created or commissioned. Let us turn first to some of the characteristics of the visual arts that helped create the physical context in which the Jesuit Baroque developed in Bohemia. This will assist us to construct a vocabulary of the less concrete aspects of the Baroque.

The artistic movement known as the Baroque arrived in Prague at almost the same time as the pre-suppression Society of Jesus, and lingered even longer.[6] Both have their roots in the mid-sixteenth century, and both effectively came to an end during the reign of Maria Theresia. Commentators have noted how long lasting was the Baroque aesthetic in the Bohemian lands, and also how, after 1770, the severe neoclassicism of the Josephinian period quickly supplanted it. In Bohemia, however, as opposed to the Austrias, this rapid transition manifests only minimally the influence of the Rococo. This style seems to have made only minor inroads into outdoor visual art and had virtually no impact on painting and sculpture in Bohemia. In this chapter we will argue that the persistence of Baroque art, in both its more courtly and less sophisticated forms, paralleled the survival of a less easily defined but nevertheless real Baroque mentality among many (but not all) of the Jesuits working in Prague during the final decades before the suppression and, moreover, that this mentality contributed to a fundamental tension within the Society during these years.

The Baroque aesthetic, in Bohemia or elsewhere, is easier to identify and discuss in the visual arts than are its manifestations in the psychological or sociological realms. We could offer many examples of very late manifestations of the Baroque in visual arts in Prague, but we will briefly touch on just two here to suggest some similar elements that appear elsewhere in the Baroque. The first is an altar created in 1776 for the figure of the Infant Jesus housed in the church of S. Maria de Victoria in the Malá Strana of Prague.[7] Although Maria de Victoria was never a Jesuit church, and in any

[6] The church of St. Salvator, erected by the Society in 1578 at the Clementinum, is often considered the most outstanding early-Baroque building in Prague (Martin Briggs, "Introduction," in Plicka, *City of Baroque and Gothic,* vi). By the end of the second decade of the seventeenth century, Baroque had completely superseded the Renaissance style in the Malá Strana and on the Hradčany (Emanuel Poche-Zdeněk and Bohumir Kozak, *Hradčany a Malá Strana* [Prague: Orbis, 1964], 16 f.).

[7] The figure of the Infant Jesus was brought to Prague from Spain in the sixteenth century, and soon became an object of pilgrimages and special veneration. Its arrival in Protestant Prague from the bastion of Catholicism and Habsburg power is a fitting metaphor for the importation of the Baroque aesthetic into Bohemia. Representations of Shimon Abeles, who will be discussed at greater length later, portray him as being much younger, even though he was actually twelve when he died. Thus, he was often portrayed in such a way as to suggest the erect and richly robed, yet still very young, figure of the Infant Jesus. Tapié notes that

case by 1776 had to contend with reduced Habsburg support for public processions and other expressions of faith, its new altar still conveys the exuberant Baroque aesthetic characteristic of the ecclesiastical architecture of the Bohemian Society, observable, for example, in the interior of the church of St. Nicholas, only a short distance away.[8] A contemporary illustration of the interior of S. Maria de Victoria shows the altar richly ornamented, in the style of the late Baroque, and surmounted by figures standing on heavenly clouds.[9] The figure of the Infant Jesus, standing upright and clothed in stiff garments that conceal much of his body while drawing attention to him, is dwarfed by the scale of the entire altar and rendered remote to the viewer, who approaches the waxen figure from below, as one might a monarch. The altar offers multiple presentations of the human body in the figure of the Infant Jesus and the attendant putti. This illustrates the tendency of the Baroque to make use of the body in a completely different way, for example, as decoration rather than for edifying or didactic purposes.[10]

The overall effect of this altar is theatrical and designed to create a feeling of even greater size than is actually the case (monumentality being a hallmark of the Baroque); yet the soft curves and detail work of the altar keep it from becoming superhuman or completely inaccessible, for the visible glory of the Baroque was always meant to be shared, not to create a barrier between object and viewer. In the case of the Infant Jesus, as with many other Baroque set pieces, this accessibility is aided by the presence of strong light on the figures, enabling the viewer to discern more easily both the details and the ornamentation of the figures, and the relationship of the various parts to the whole.[11]

This relationship between what is seen and the viewer serves as a metaphor for much that can be found in the other manifestations of the Bohemian Baroque; for the elaborate and indirect phraseology of late-Baroque prose often contains a very human and accessible narrative intertwined with stock passages communicating the miraculous or recalling the victories of the Church, conveyed in a stiff literary framework that at first

---

while the dressing of statues in churches had been banned by the Josephinian reforms, an exception was made for the Infant, which appeared in different costumes throughout the liturgical year (Tapié, *Rise and Fall of the Habsburg Monarchy,* 222).

[8] The high altar of St. Nicholas cannot be dated with precision, but probably was completed shortly before 1770, as were other details of the interior of the church (Jan Burian, Dalibor Kusák, Vladimir Hyhúk, and Miroslav Krob, *Baroko v Čechách a na Moravě* [Prague: Polygraphia, 1993], 78 f.).

[9] Reproduced in Erich Bachman, "Plastik," in *Barock in Böhmen,* 161.

[10] Plate 97, "Das Prager Jesulein, Maria de Victoria," in Ferdinand Seibt, ed. *Bohemia sacra: Das Christentum in Böhmen (973–1973)* (Düsseldorf: Schwann, 1974).

[11] G. R. Cragg, *The Church and the Age of Reason, 1648–1789* (Harmonsworth: Penguin, 1960), 261. We shall return later to the metaphor of the need for strong light in the Baroque.

glance conceals the human origins of the text. This is especially true of some of the literary records created by Jesuits to memorialize their fellows, or in the triumphalist accounts of the Society's missionary efforts; but the same tendency can be seen in the epigraphs commemorating the Habsburgs or members of the aristocracy. Yet even in Bohemia, whose literary tradition was attenuated during the eighteenth century, this stiff literary framework could be bent, when the vernacular was used, to accommodate satire.[12]

Literary evidences of the late Baroque exist even after the suppression had silenced Jesuit preachers and historians. In the fall of 1779, six years after the suppression of the Society, František Vavák, a rural *rychtár* (magistrate) from the village of Mlčič, journeyed to Prague to observe the celebration of the fiftieth anniversary of the canonization of St. Jan Nepomucký, a saint especially revered in Bohemia.[13]

> That evening, before and after the ceremony, the spire of the main church [St. Vitus] was illuminated with many thousands of lamps, making it shine and sparkle. From the very top of the spire there was a display of artificial fire (which the Germans call *Feuerwerk*), which lit up the entire church and castle. Elsewhere in halls or in large windows at ground level were various beautifully clothed figures *[strojení]* portraying the life of St. Jan or illustrating him being cast into the water.[14]

Such a public celebration of religion, with its processions and vivid visual displays, was, in the words of a French historian, "the apotheosis of Catholicism," which took the message of the Church into the streets and confronted heretics with the power, beauty, and potency of its message.[15] The use of fireworks (which also were used to accompany celebrations of military victories of the house of Austria), and physical re-creations of historical moments in the saint's life reveal how conservative officially

[12] Even Baroque Catholic piety might on occasion be satirized. Valentin Bernard Jestrábský in his *Dissenting View of a Simple Peasant* (1710), recounted a tale of women who decided to go on a pilgrimage and to flagellate themselves as they went. In order to make the experience less unpleasant, they began to drink wine, and soon drank so much that they collapsed on the ground. Passersby thought the pilgrims were overcome with religious devotion, but Jestrábský's skeptical narrator tells us that he knew better (R. B. Pynsent, "The Baroque Continuum of Czech Literature," *The Slavonic and East European Review* 62 [1984]: 335 f.).

[13] Devotion to Nepomucký was not entirely localized, however. He was also honored in Bavaria, because the Queen whose confession he had refused to divulge had been a Wittelsbach (Thomas Da Costa Kaufmann, *Court, Cloister, and City: The Art and Culture of Central Europe, 1450–1800* [Chicago: University of Chicago Press, 1995], 378).

[14] Jindřich Skopec, ed. *Paměti Františka Vaváka souseda a rychtáře Milčického,* 5 vols. (Prague: Cyrillo-Methodějská Knihtiskárna V. Kotruba—Nákladem "Dědictví Sv. Jana Nepomuckého," 1907–), vol. 1, fasc. 1, p. 125: my translation).

[15] Louis Châtellier, *The Europe of the Devout: The Catholic Reformation and the Formation of a New Society,* trans. Jean Birell (Cambridge University Press, 1987), 196.

sanctioned religious expression still was on the eve of the Josephinian reforms, and how the concrete and dramatic elements still predominated in the presentation of religious knowledge.[16] This Baroque expression delights in the contrast between light and dark, and in the theatrical representation of dramatic set pieces involving human figures, designed to instruct the populace, while intermingling folk elements with more sophisticated aspects of Catholic theology, a characteristic of the Jesuit mission throughout the Habsburg lands. The expression of the Baroque aesthetic, occurring so late in this historical period, also reflects the sometimes ambiguous and equivocal nature of confessional politics in the Habsburg realms, a fact recognized by Robert Kann.[17] Thus, while the triumphant and uncontested position of the Church was presented in visual form to the residents of Prague and the peasants who had flocked to the celebrations from the countryside, religious dissidents continued to surface, and were often most apparent when peasants were rising against their masters.[18]

Also characteristic of the Bohemian Baroque is the tendency of its artists to retain its thematic and stylistic elements even after they had received training in Italy or elsewhere abroad, giving the Bohemian Baroque, along with its strongly regional elements, a distinctly cosmopolitan flavor.[19] Bohemian artists were also, not surprisingly, influenced by styles emanating from Vienna and elsewhere in the Habsburg lands.[20] Even when Bohemian artists who worked in the Baroque idiom received their training closer to home, their pieces created for public consumption reflected the international style of the Baroque. Such was the case with Felix Anton Scheffler, who arrived in Prague in 1732 and then moved on to Wrocław (Breslau) the same year, remaining there until 1747. Returning then to Prague, from 1747 until his death in 1760 Scheffler produced grand allegor-

---

[16] Eberhard Fahler, "Emblematische Feuerwerke," in *Emblem und Emblematikrezeption: Vergleichende Studien zur Wirkungsgeschichte vom 16. bis 20. Jahrhundert*, ed. Sibylle Penkert (Darmstadt: Wissenschaftliche Buchgesellschaft, 1978), 46–56. Fireworks were also used to celebrate the recovery of Maria Theresia from a serious illness in 1768 (NK, 23/19, *Lit. An. Prov. Boh., 1767*, folios 87r–87v).

[17] Kann, *Study in Austrian Intellectual History*, 22–25.

[18] The peasant rising of 1732 in the Opcenska region was related to demands for religious freedom (F. Bednář, *Tolarančí patent* [Hrádec Králové: Nakladatelství Nědení Besídky, 1931], 10). Heretics were punished as criminals under a patent of Charles VI issued in 1726 (Benetka, *Jesuité v Čechách*, 30).

[19] Pavel Preiss, "Malby Františka Karla Palka v klášterech doksanském a strahovském," *Bibliotheca Strahoviensis* 2 (1996): 145–66.

[20] Pavel Preiss, "Böhmen und die östereichische Malarei," in *Österreich im Europa der Aufklärung: Kontinuität und Zäsur zur Zeit Maria Theresias und Josephs II* (Vienna: Verlag der Österreichischen Akademie der Wissenschaften, 1985), 637–51.

ical art in the high-Baroque tradition for many of the Jesuit communities in Bohemia.[21]

In addition, the creators of visual art in Bohemia during most of the eighteenth century had not yet begun the process of gaining political autonomy. The century-long tranquility that the Peace of Westphalia finally brought to long-suffering Bohemia did not so much encourage artistic freedom as extend and solidify dynastic paternalism.[22] In other words, art—and in particular religious art—did not yet seem to exist independently of the external power politics of the Habsburg regime. Bohemia differed in this from some of the smaller German states of the empire, where art and politics, at least as some commentators saw it, were gaining some mutual independence.[23] This prolonged interaction of politics and creative expression might be attributed to the backward state of social development in Bohemia, but by their ambitions and pretensions the Habsburgs also played an important part in shaping the ways in which the Baroque manifested itself. To a degree not apparent in the German principalities, the political goals of the dynasty dovetailed with the ecclesiastical imagery and representation found in the Hereditary Lands and Bohemia.

While Baroque art strove for a degree of unity between viewer and object, Baroque culture was deeply divided, torn between vivid sensuality and violent asceticism, between expressions of national identity and transnational allegiances, between the systematic collecting and cataloging of information gained from the material, empirical world and a passionate belief in the spontaneous and unsystematic intrusion of the miraculous into that material world.[24] The Society made its own contributions to the devel-

---

[21] Jane ten Brink Goldsmith, J. Patrice Marandel, J. Patrick Donnelly, S.J., and J. B. Harley, *Jesuit Art in North American Collections* (Milwaukee: Patrick and Beatrice Haggerty Museum of Art, 1991), 58.

[22] Some Catholic historians have tended not to see this as a disadvantage, emphasizing instead the "optimism and vitality" that the long period of political stability engendered (Götz Fehr, "Höhepunkte der Kunst im Kernland Europas," in *Tausend Jahre Bistum Prag (973–1973)* [Munich: Ackermann Gemeinde, 1974], 155).

[23] Maiken Umbach, ed., "Visual Culture, Scientific Images, and German Small-State Politics in the Enlightenment," *Past and Present* 158 (1998): 110 f.

[24] This miraculous, nonempirical vision was not limited to the works accomplished by the relics of saints. Jesuit pharmacopeias of the eighteenth century still stocked magical ingredients that would have been found among a medieval alchemist's supplies. When Austrian bureaucrats confiscated and inventoried the contents of the pharmacy in Olomouc, they discovered the following "Medicamenta": "Spiritus cornus cervi, Spiritus unicornum fossile, Mummia, Millepedes, Axungia humana, Axungia ursi" (Hofkammer Archiv Wien, Acta S. J., Fasc. 3, Roter Nummer 28, no. 23, December 12, 1773). These "medicines" involved such ingredients as a distillation of deer's horn and fossilized unicorns, mummy, millepedes, and grease rendered from humans and bears.

opment of the Baroque as an artistic style in a number of regions, including neighboring Hungary.[25]

The question is further complicated by the shift in the orientation of the Habsburg dynasty: from an affiliation with the predominantly German Holy Roman Empire, it went on to consolidate its own territorial holdings, a process that continued throughout the eighteenth century. The transnational Baroque that appeared throughout the empire was superseded by an equally non-national Baroque whose unifying element was the glorification of Catholicism and the Habsburgs.[26] In neither instance is it easy to assess the relationship of these styles to the specifics of local artistic traditions, elements of which were often incorporated into the larger scheme of the Baroque. In fact the tension between the local and the universal is a characteristic of the Baroque aesthetic, as the grand vistas of the theatrical and monarchical Baroque counterbalanced the narrow range of vision of the ordinary person. In Bohemia, as elsewhere, this vision, despite the advances in science and the continuing exploration of remote corners of the globe, remained extremely localized; and even at midcentury rural and village people looked to their local lords for direction and justice, rather than to the distant monarch and the bureaucracy of the capital.[27]

The Jesuits neither challenged this modus vivendi nor emphasized the transnational elements of the Baroque in their mission work, choosing instead to operate within the framework of the culture in which they found themselves.[28] Meanwhile, the distant monarch, struggling to bring rationality to the patchwork of lands under her scepter, was still insisting in 1766 on

---

[25] Johann Kapossy, "Stellung des ungarländischen Barock in der europäischen Kunstentwicklung," *Ungarische Jahrbücher* 11 (1951): 38–55.

[26] Joachim Whaley points out that despite the development of an entire Baroque culture in the Habsburg lands that lay within the empire (for example, the Austrias, Tyrol, Carinthia, Carniola, and the Bohemian lands), this culture never constituted a "national" identity ("Austria, 'Germany,' and the Dissolution of the Holy Roman Empire," in *The Habsburg Legacy: National Identity in Historical Perspective,* ed. Ritchie Robertson and Edward Timms [Edinburgh: Edinburgh University Press, 1994], 5). Moreover, by the middle of the eighteenth century, Hungary and Transylvania possessed examples of this Baroque culture, although these regions had a national (and to an extent religious) identity that was at odds with the agenda of the Habsburgs. Note, too, that while this process was underway, among the more sophisticated there was also a transformation of revealed religion into natural religion. This process cannot be attributed exclusively to the influence of Josephinism.

[27] Wright, *Serf,* 30. See also James Van Horn Melton, "Introduction," in *State and Society in Early Modern Austria,* ed. Charles W. Ingrao (West Lafayette, Ind.: Purdue University Press, 1994), 233 ff.

[28] The "time-rhythm" of rural life was in close relationship to popular religious expression and ecclesiastical ritual, a point not lost on Jesuit missionaries and pastors (Hermann Hörger, "Organizational Forms of Popular Piety in Rural Old Bavaria," in *Religion and Society in Early Modern Europe, 1500–1800,* ed. Kaspar von Greyerz [London: Allen and Unwin, 1984], 218).

the promulgation of additional laws to deal with reports of demon possession in Austria and Bohemia.[29] Herein lies yet another contradiction: the Baroque lived on in communities where such supernatural and irrational goings-on seemed possible, yet these events did not seem to contradict grand mechanical systems of the universe whose metaphor, the clock, was drawn upon repeatedly by Baroque writers.[30]

The intensity with which the metaphysical elements of the Baroque were retained in Catholic Europe helps explain why we may speak of "two Enlightenments" whose goals and characteristics overlapped at times, while remaining distinct in many features. The first of these enlightenments rebelled against the continental Catholicism that was so closely associated with the divided, emotional, and hierarchic Baroque expressions of religious experience. The other enlightenment, more sympathetic to a rational examination of religious questions and less stridently anticlerical, grew up in the British Isles, where the sensuous and tortured Baroque aesthetic had never made much headway and where rationalism and empiricism had already gained a head start among the followers of Sir Francis Bacon.[31]

In Bohemia, however, this second enlightenment was known only to a handful of the best educated and most widely traveled, and for a long time played only a marginal role in the intellectual life of the country. Instead, the debate concerning enlightenment revolved around its relationship to Baroque Catholicism, regarded as an ideology and as a social institution. The drastic steps taken by Joseph II against organized religion directed from Rome may be seen as a reaction against this pervasive Baroque aesthetic, which by the last years of his reign was finally in retreat throughout the Habsburg domains. Yet the reforms labeled Josephinism, especially in their earliest form, during the 1750s and '60s, were not a protest against the expressions of the Baroque found in the pastoral and proselytizing work of the Jesuits in Prague and smaller communities. Indeed, when the Society through its missions promoted loyalty to the dynasty, the Habsburgs warmly welcomed its contributions. The tendencies towards institutional centralization and educational standardization fostered by the Habsburgs drew upon existing elements of Jesuit culture, although in their refusal to acknowledge local cultural traditions, these reforms stand in sharp contrast to the values of the Bohemian Jesuits.

---

[29] Josef Kočí, *Čarodějnické procesy* (Prague: Horizont, 1973), 155 f. See also the discussion in chap. 6 below.

[30] Otto Mayr, *Authority, Liberty, and Automatic Machinery in Early Modern Europe* (Baltimore: Johns Hopkins University Press, 1986).

[31] Conor Cruise O'Brien, *On the Eve of the Millennium* (Concord, Ont.: House of Anansi Press, 1994), 107–10.

Modern-day visitors are overwhelmed by many of the architectural monuments erected by Baroque monarchs and churchmen, but the sheer scale of these buildings conceals the insecurity that helped bring them into existence. The use of the theatrical at the Baroque court was not derived from an overriding sense of security and superiority, as might be supposed, but from quite the opposite state of mind. The Baroque princes of central Europe, still surrounded with some of the survivals of a more culturally primitive era, felt insecure and behind the times.[32] Political power and the social hierarchy had to be expressed again and again through ceremonies, festivals, symbols, and the visual arts.[33] Though every ruling dynasty, from the petty princes of the empire to the Bourbons and Romanovs, made use of pageants and monuments, the Habsburgs were particularly concerned to promote dynastic legitimacy. Within the Habsburg lands a *Bauwut* or building frenzy also gripped the highest level of aristocrats, who proceeded to build palaces that were neither functional as residences nor of much use as centers of administration.[34] The Church itself, in the words of R. J. W. Evans, had entered an age of frenzied ostentation, building and rebuilding with unexampled haste throughout the monarchy, its myriad calvaries and pilgrimage churches, votive altars, and statuary creating a dense ecclesiastical landscape in country as well as town.[35]

For the less exalted, the pilgrimages and processions associated with sodalities sponsored by the Society were expressions not merely of piety but of the relation of the participants to the existing social hierarchy. When illustrious personages belonged to sodalities and took a visible role in their activities, the more humble members could bask a little in the reflected glory of their betters. The tens of thousands of pilgrims who converged on the "Sacro-Montana," near Příbam, dedicated to the Virgin were participating in an activity that mixed elements of devotion with the excitement of a fair and the security derived from a status quo that too often was missing from their lives.[36] The private devotion to relics that surged in popularity once again in

[32] As late as 1765, buffoons and dwarfs, who no longer performed in the Stuart courts of Britain, still entertained in the court of the Elector of Bavaria (Adrien Fouchier-Magnan, *The Small German Courts in the Eighteenth Century*, trans. Mervyn Savil [London: Methuen, 1958], 62).

[33] James J. Sheehan, *German History, 1770–1866* (Oxford: Oxford University Press, 1989), 150.

[34] Robert A Kann, "Aristocracy in the Eighteenth-Century Habsburg Empire," *East European Quarterly* 7, no. 1 (1973): 12.

[35] R. J. W. Evans, *The Making of the Habsburg Monarchy, 1550–1700* (Oxford: Clarendon Press, 1979), 445.

[36] No fewer than 20,000 people visited the Sacred Mountain in 1766 alone, according to Jesuit sources *(Annales Prov. Boh. S.J. ad annum 1766,* NK, 2L 23/15f, folio 438 v). In 1762 the number of communicants at the Sacred Mountain approached 120,000, or more than the number taking Communion throughout the year at the church of St. Clement in Prague (NK, 1287 MS XXIII C105/15, *An. Prov. Boh. 1762,* folio 256v).

the late-Baroque period reflected an interest in a more personal interaction with the divine that complemented rather than competed with the more public and collective manifestations of piety such as pilgrimages and processions.[37] The Society of Jesus valued and fostered each of these, viewing both as legitimate avenues to spirituality (provided the objects venerated did not fall into the category of inappropriate devotion).

The Violent Baroque

A discussion of the Baroque, however brief, cannot be considered balanced if it fails to mention the brutal side of the culture. Baroque culture, like those of many other periods and places, shared a taste for sanctioned public violence.[38] This violence was most widely observed and recorded when it was ritualized; sometimes it took the form of public executions, such as that of accused murderer Loebel Kurtzhandl, whom we will encounter once again later in this book. It could also show itself in entertainments involving the brutal treatment of animals, a sport that is equally incomprehensible to modern sensibilities. It was not merely urban ruffians and the rural peasantry who attended these entertainments; individuals as well from a wide range of backgrounds flocked to them. In early-eighteenth-century Vienna, home of sophisticated opera and imposing architecture, one could still witness a pack of trained dogs released to harass an ox that had been set on fire.[39]

The evolution of more enlightened attitudes towards other living creatures human or otherwise, as well as the appearance of the "man of sensibility" later in the century, would spell the decline of such vicious entertainments; but we should not pass over these activities without trying to place them in the context of Baroque culture. This culture, preoccupied as it was with death and the nature of the flesh, was naturally drawn to spectacles designed to publicly display both death and the utmost extremities to which the flesh might be subjected. More than simple voyeurism (if voyeurism is ever simple) was at work here.

It may be argued that the tolerance that all levels of society displayed toward public violence was generally greater several hundred years ago. But

---

[37] No comprehensive study of relics and reliquaries from the Baroque period has yet been conducted. Instructive examples of eighteenth-century reliquaries are found in *Zwischen Andacht und Andenken: Kleinodien religiöser Kunst und Wallfahrtsandenken aus Trierer Sammlung: Ein Katalog zur Gemeinschaftsausstellung des bischöflichen Dom- und Diözesanmuseums Trier und des Städtischen Museums Simeonstift Trier vom 16. Oktober 1992 bis 17. Januar 1993* (Trier, 1992), 167, 168, et passim.

[38] The author acknowledges the contributions to this section derived from discussions with the members of the East-West Seminar, "Progress and Violence," Berlin, July 1997.

[39] Sheehan, *German History*, 147.

the public display of violence was not simply the result of a high degree of tolerance or indifference, for displaying or destroying the body also possessed a moral dimension. One need only inspect the illustrations accompanying Mathias Tanner's history of the martyrs of the Society of Jesus to grasp the importance placed on a graphic depiction of a Baroque martyr's death.[40] The Society's missionaries in the field exploited the association of pain with holiness. Often Jesuits campaigning for conversions in the countryside turned to more lurid ways of conveying their message through violence and pain. In Jülich in the Upper Palatinate, Jesuits conducting a mission in 1715 scourged themselves with whips, and one priest even held his hand within a burning torch longer than it took to recite an Our Father.[41] These activities were admittedly shock tactics intended to bring about emotional conversions; but they can also be seen as shrewdly planned theatrical undertakings that took into account both the popular appetite for violence and suffering, and the general awareness among the population of the violent elements found in both the Bible and the widely repeated stories of saints and martyrs. In addition, these acts, which involved violence to the body and public demonstrations of faith, may also be viewed as sincere expressions of religious belief in the context of a culture fascinated with violence.

By the middle of the eighteenth century, there were signs that the appeal of graphic violence in Catholic Baroque culture was waning. Popular culture never lost its fascination with violence and crime, and the decrease in the number of public executions within the Habsburg realms cannot be taken as evidence that the public was less interested in these spectacles;[42] rather, it demonstrated that the central government was starting to take a different view of public displays of physical punishment. What had changed was the sense of simultaneous distancing and identification with the sufferer that had characterized the Baroque encounter with violence. The distancing had originally made it possible to view animal baiting, or even the execution of a criminal, without the on-lookers experiencing any stirrings of empathy toward the sufferers, but curiosity or pleasure instead. Yet the pious Catholic also identified with the sufferings of saint or martyr because of the different moral context in which the torments were inflicted. Suffering of ordinary mortals or of saints, like the suffering of Jesus, could produce

[40] Mathias Tanner, *Societas Jesu usque ad sanguinis et vitæ profusionem militans* . . . (Prague, 1678). This work, later issued in German, was widely known in pre-suppression Bohemia.

[41] Trevor Johnson, "Blood, Tears, and Xavier-Water: Jesuit Missionaries and Popular Religion in the Eighteenth-Century Upper Palatinate," in *Popular Religion in Germany and Central Europe, 1400–1800,* ed. Bob Scribner and Trevor Johnson (Basingstoke: Macmillan, 1996), 187.

[42] The Kriminal-Museum in Vienna displays examples of widely publicized crimes of the eighteenth century and the execution of the criminals involved.

positive results for the sufferer or for others.[43] Suffering blocked out the less important day-to-day world, and a meditation on denial and suffering invited the participant to enter another world where closeness to God was the reward for the act of distancing oneself from the material. The promoters of the Enlightenment did not share this view, but were much more concerned with the possibilities of happiness being achieved through less painful and non-supernatural means.

The breakdown of this seeming fusion of what appear to be polar opposites, empathy and distancing, was further fostered by a more dispassionate and analytical view of the body, in particular, the human body. The anatomical *Wachsenpräparaten* created in the 1780s for the Josephinum, the surgical institute established in Vienna by Joseph II, are the clearest demonstration of the break with the Baroque in the Habsburg world.[44] Although their postures and the tasseled pillows on which some of them are displayed are reminiscent of the waxen figures in Baroque reliquaries, these figures are guardians of a mystery with no theological or moral implications. They are instead aids to instruction at a state-supported school that teaches a practical skill imparted by a scientist rather than a priest, where no clergy are employed and whose every detail bears the mark of enlightened despotism.

The relationship of the Society of Jesus to these expressions of violence, both public and private, concrete and imagined, had at least three components. First, the Society identified with and sought to bring its recruits into closer communion with both the Lord's passion and the physical suffering of the saints, including Ignatius of Loyola, whose journey towards the spiritual life had begun while recuperating from a serious wound received on the battlefield. This communion could be achieved through acts of self-mortification such as had been practiced throughout the history of Christianity, and also through study, prayer, and meditation upon the physical sufferings of others. These latter practices were stimulated by both visual imagery and by the lessons older Jesuits taught to younger ones. The physical suffering experienced by the living human being was often compensated for by both a spiritual victory and a triumph over normal physical processes after death.

Abeles and Nepomucký were not the only objects of veneration whose bodies, or parts thereof, miraculously defied corruption; the body of one of

[43] Note also the related, but not identical, promotion of the devotion to the Sacred Heart of Jesus undertaken by the Jesuits in the seventeenth and eighteenth centuries (Gertrude Schiller, *Iconography of Christian Art: The Passion of Jesus Christ,* 2 vols. [London: Lund Humphries, 1972], 2:194).

[44] Helmuth Wyklicky, *Das Josephinum* (Vienna/Munich: Christian Brandstetter, 1985), 49, 52, 53.

the greatest early Jesuits, Francis Xavier, after his death in the Far East, was regularly displayed, even after the suppression, to a reverent public who noted that his tongue(!) remained supple and uncorrupted.[45] The mysteries of inner and outward signs of grace as elucidated in the writings of the major spiritual figures of the Baroque provided the explanatory language for the wonders attending bodies and body parts. Bohemian Jesuits investigating the sciences had already found this language inadequate, revealing how great was the tension between the varying views of the world espoused by members of the Society. An additional, if less obvious, tension likewise existed between the Latinity of the Jesuits recording the miraculous and the heretical that they encountered in their missions, and the actual experience of the lay people. Reading these reports, the modern researcher is left with the strong impression that the Jesuits who recorded these events saw divine grace operating to bring about the miraculous events described. Yet the experience and responses of the laypersons involved remains obscured.

A second component in the relationship of the Jesuits to public demonstrations of violence and suffering is the tradition within the Society of individuals testing their own physical and spiritual limits as men committed to Christ. Too much has been made of the supposedly military character of the Society, and we should resist the temptation to interpret all the actions of the Jesuits as the battles of "soldiers of Christ," motivated by attitudes of exaggerated masculinity. Yet as an all-male order, unconfined to a cloister and operating with considerable freedom of action in a turbulent, violent world, the Society of Jesus undoubtedly attracted many individuals more comfortable with expressions of spirituality that demonstrated their fortitude and courage, their skills and strengths: what today some might call a warrior ethic. The explicit objective of the Society, as expounded in its Constitutions and the *Ratio,* to make use of dramatic contexts to spread the word of God, further encouraged this type of public demonstration of fortitude or skill in an environment that was more than willing to accept it.

Commenting on the use of miraculous and dramatic cures as a means of furthering conversion efforts, Trevor Johnson has perceptively observed that in the later eighteenth century

> Jesuit sacramentals would come under the spotlight of enlightenment parody and the order itself would be lampooned for having apparently sunk from its position on the intellectual cutting edge in the sixteenth century to the level of peasant superstition in the eighteenth. The Jesuits were chided for sharing or colluding in the ignorance of the peasantry rather than attempting to reform it. Yet their very reluctance to attack popular culture may have been one of the key factors in the Jesuits' success in preserving the confessional

[45] David Sox, *Relics and Shrines* (London: Allen and Unwin, 1985), 124. A Baroque account is found in *Ioannis Ferrandi Anciensis e Societate Iesu theologi Disquisitio reliquaria* . . . (London, 1647).

identity not just of Catholic bastions but of the recently recatholicized areas of Germany.[46]

Moreover, the Jesuits have long been criticized for their willingness to adapt to local cultural conditions. Their adaptability has been interpreted as evidence that the Society lacked a moral compass, and their engagement with the surrounding culture has been denounced, by both Protestants and Catholics, as either a cynical manipulation of the less sophisticated or as a lack of their own inner convictions. In reality, some of these factors might seem to have made their way into the Society, but it would be wrong to ignore the relationship between this adaptability and the aesthetic of the Baroque itself. The Baroque, as manifested in the visual arts, featured common elements of sensuality, internal tension, grandiose presentation, and appeal to the emotions, each one of which was echoed in some of the mission and pastoral work of the Bohemian Jesuits. Yet the Baroque, without losing its transnational quality, was far more successful in achieving an integration with local folk elements than was either Renaissance classicism or Josephinian neoclassicism. The very difficulty confronting us in succinctly defining the boundaries of the Baroque derives from its ability to fuse and blend with existing local styles and to draw the viewer through an appeal to a subjective internal experience. If the Jesuits in their literary, theological, and artistic achievements on a high cultural plane are sometimes seen to epitomize the Baroque, then their missions among the peasantry deserve to be viewed in the same light.

Baroque Catholicism

The cluster of meanings attached to the word "Baroque" do not have an exclusively Catholic connotation: one need only recall the music of Bach or the architecture of Blenheim Palace to find outstanding examples of the Baroque that grew up in environments that were actively hostile to the Church of Rome. But the piety, public and private, that came to be associated with the Catholic Renewal of the mid-sixteenth century onward found its most powerful expression within the Baroque aesthetic.[47] So strongly has this Baroque aesthetic come to be associated with the era of Catholic Renewal that the term Baroque Catholicism has been put forward to convey the closeness of the relationship between the aesthetic and the religious experience.

---

[46] Johnson, "Blood, Tears and Xavier-Water," 201.

[47] Many writers almost unconsciously link the words "Baroque" and "Catholic" in the context of the seventeenth century. See William Monter, *Ritual, Myth and Magic in Early Modern Europe* (Athens, Ohio: Ohio University Press, 1983), 142 and passim.

Thomas F. O'Meara has identified three foci of Baroque Catholicism evident in the spiritual autobiographies, theologies, liturgies, and communities of the day. These foci are the self, method, and drama.[48] Each of these is an important element of the culture fostered by the Society in Bohemia through its teaching and preaching.[49] By the self is meant neither selfishness nor self-centered asceticism.[50] Rather, the awareness of the self is a heightened sense of one's own sensory, emotional, and cognitive experiences that enables the penitent to gain a greater awareness of the process of redemption and forgiveness, and helps the martyr to achieve a deeper understanding of his or her relationship to the specific sacrifice being made.[51]

The self under these conditions may have an increased awareness of objects around itself, and is especially conscious of its relationship to the divine. The self may be inspired to produce creative works or to embark on solitary undertakings such as pilgrimages, fasts, or vigils. The individual must rejoice, undergo moments of "desolation," to borrow a term from the *Spiritual Exercises,* experience reunion, and discover the need to communicate these experiences to others, who in turn can be guided towards their own encounters and transformations.[52] The language in which these experiences are described is often unabashedly sensuous or even erotic in its vocabulary and images as it struggles to convey this highly personal encounter. The degree to which the Baroque Catholic writer does not seek to exclude any aspect of human experience when recounting religious experience may surprise his reader. Yet this is not to say that the widest possible

---

[48] *The HarperCollins Encyclopedia of Catholicism,* s.v. "Baroque Catholicism," by Thomas F. O'Meara.

[49] It should be noted that unlike the devotional literature of the period, much of the homiletics of the seventeenth and early eighteenth centuries exhibited the ornate style of literary Baroque without always achieving this heightened sense of self. Abraham à Sancta Clara, the Jesuit-trained Austrian Augustinian who gained great renown with his attacks on the follies of rich and poor, used Baroque rhetorical devices in his vernacular preaching and writing, but did not focus on either himself or on his audience as self-conscious individuals (Kann, *Study in Austrian Intellectual History,* 56 f.).

[50] Baroque self-denial might take on forms that were not precisely ascetic, as when French Jesuits decreed that "religious modesty is enough to prohibit [bathing]" (quoted in Jean Delumeau, *Sin and Fear,* trans. Eric Nicholson [New York: St. Martin's Press, 1990], 437).

[51] Michel Foucault has called attention to the important distinction between confession and acts of public penance. Referring to the latter by a term used in late antiquity, *exomologesis,* Foucault describes the public identification and humbling of the self as obeying "a law of dramatic emphasis and maximum theatricality." The latter has obvious implications for the Baroque aesthetic of the Society (Michel Foucault, *Religion and Culture,* ed. Jeremy R. Carrette [Manchester: Manchester University Press, 1999], 712–72).

[52] *The Spiritual Exercises of St. Ignatius,* ed. and trans. George E. Ganss, S.J. (St. Louis: Institute of Jesuit Sources, 1992), no. 6 (p. 23), and passim. Hereafter this work will be abbreviated to *SpEx.*

range of sensuous experience is to be sought after as the ultimate goal; asceticism, paradoxically, was also a hallmark of Baroque Catholicism.[53]

The elevations of the individual experience in the Baroque may be high, but the low points of the experience are very low indeed; and the need for self-abasement, either as an act of contrition or as a warning to others, can be great. From a distance of more than two hundred years, it is not easy to determine the psychological origins of Antonín Koniáš's public acts of self-degradation, but what is clear is that some of his Jesuit contemporaries expressed admiration for behavior which to them exemplified a righteous life.[54] Recording Koniáš's life in print was itself as much a typically Baroque undertaking as his career had been, even though Leopold Scherschnik and František Pubitschka composed his biography at the very end of the Baroque period in Bohemia.[55] The hagiographic recording of the exploits of Antonín Koniáš and other less exhibitionistic Bohemian Jesuits had its roots in the Bollandist movement begun in the previous century, which has produced the multivolume *Acta sanctorum,* the most massive account of the lives and deaths of saints ever attempted.[56]

The coupling of this highly emotional, often seemingly spontaneous behavior with a carefully recorded method, the second of our foci, seems cumbersome today. The method, however, while generally demanding, was not intended to straitjacket the spiritual experience, but rather to provide a series of guideposts to assure the participant that he or she had not lost the path. In a world teeming with baneful heresies and dire punishments for those who strayed, the specificity of the method described in a work such as the *Spiritual Exercises* offered the opportunity for a personal encounter

---

[53] For example, the Marian sodalities of Munich produced plays focusing on the theme of asceticism even while the plays themselves were sensory experiences of some grandeur. These were published between 1737 and 1750 under the title *The Drama of Asceticism* (William Bangert, S.J., *A History of the Society of Jesus,* 2nd ed. [St. Louis: The Institute of Jesuit Sources, 1986], 315).

[54] His ragged clothing, unkempt appearance, and bloody penances were undertaken to win sinners back: "Veste attrita, capillo neglecto, calceis luto foedis in publicum prodibat. . . . In sceleratis vero ad frugem reducendis omne suppliciorum armamentarium in se expromebat, a vigiliis, jejuniis, flagellis sanguinariis non prius desistens" (Antonín Podlaha, "Dodatky a opravy k biografiím starších spisovatelů českých," *Časopis musea Království českého* 69 (1895): 324). A Freudian might find it of interest that the father of Koniáš the book burner was probably a book publisher.

[55] Internal evidence indicates that this biographical study of Koniáš, principally the work of Scherschnik, was composed after 1765, since the latter was born only in 1746 (Franz Martin Pelzel, *Böhmische, mährische und schlesische Gelehrte und Schriftsteller aus dem Orden der Jesuiten* [Prague, 1786], 289 f.).

[56] The *Acta* was one of the few High Baroque projects of the Society to be revived after its restoration: in 1836 Belgian Jesuits were once again publishing the series (C. J. Ligthart, S.J., *The Return of the Jesuits: The Life of Jan Philip Roothaan* [London: T. Shand, 1978], 200; Christopher Hollis, *A History of the Jesuits* [London: Weidenfeld and Nicolson, 1968], 127 f.).

without the danger of error-prone personal choice.[57] It was, of course, just this seeming lack of personal choice that made Baroque Catholicism so repugnant to such religious movements as the Anabaptists. Yet these guide-posts themselves were very attractive to many Catholics, conducting them through a comprehensible process towards spiritual growth. Devotional guides also provided opportunities to identify with others who had trod that path before and to express a devotion to saints that had long formed an important part of the lives of Catholics.[58]

Drama forms the third component of the tripartite aspect of Baroque Catholicism. Drama combined elements of both awareness of the self and of method in a way that brought them into direct interaction with one another. Dramatic performance requires, on its most basic level, awareness of one's own actions and appearance. It also, through the conventions of stage direction and characterization, requires awareness of and mastery of a method. The production of drama is a public undertaking, where the understanding of these elements provides the audience with a meaningful event. Jesuit drama thus shared much with the public processionals that wound their way through the streets of Bohemian towns. Robert Bireley has observed that Jesuit drama was a public affair, providing a stage on which the struggle between Christ and salvation on one hand and the forces of evil on the other was re-created and vivified.[59] Thus, these performances wit-nessed the fusion of the most ambitious aspirations of the Society as a teaching order and as an order committed to the "care of souls." The banning of Jesuit school drama in Bohemia, which preceded the suppression of the Society by a few years, was more than the symbolic elimination of a cornerstone of the Jesuits' Baroque project; it marked the end of a mode of expression that best captured the Jesuit approach to religious experience.

Empire and Dynasty

In the mid-eighteenth century, the Holy Roman Empire of the German Nation, shorn of almost all its temporal powers, gradually lost its claim to be the focus of Habsburg interest. Rich in symbolic significance, the empire had for centuries been a source of compelling imagery for the dynasty as it set about consolidating its territories, which lay both within and beyond the old empire.[60] The sacral nature of the empire, whatever its practical liabilities and limitations, had held the attention and commitment of the Habsburgs,

---

[57] For example, see the guidelines for penance in *SpEx* 82–89 (pp. 49–51), and passim.

[58] A. A. Mansi, "Le Icone di Maria: Un cammino teologico," in *Liturgia e spiritualità nell'Oriente cristiano,* ed. C. Giraudo (Milan: San Paolo, 1997), 237–48.

[59] Robert Bireley, *The Refashioning of Catholicism, 1450–1700* (Basingstoke: Macmillan, 1999), 128 f.

[60] Joachim Whaley, "Austria," 2–12.

who despite their great power, periodically still felt the insecurities of a younger dynasty.[61] But the events of the 1740s and later taught the dynasty to see itself once and for all as more than rulers of the empire.

The attempt and subsequent failure of the Wittelsbach emperor Karl VII to break the hegemony of the Habsburgs called forth a final flowering of the Austrian late-Baroque, as exemplified in the tombs of Maria Theresia and Francis in the Kapuzinergruft in Vienna.[62] In Prague the Theresian additions to the Prague Castle and the Jesuit Church of St. Nicholas are expressions of the reassertion and repetition of the message of Habsburg legitimacy and supremacy that directly influenced the relations of the Society with both the court and the people.

But this was to be the last appearance of the central-European Baroque in its older context of the Holy Roman Empire. As the eighteenth century wore on, the interests of the dynasty reached ever further beyond the boundaries of the old empire. On the eve of the suppression, the first partition of Poland brought the Habsburgs the vast tract of land known as Galicia, which had never been even indirectly connected with the politics of the old empire and which was inhabited by a large population of Jews, whose "oriental" appearance and customs were the target of much anti-Semitic attention.[63]

The transition from the Holy Roman Empire to the Austrian Empire that appeared after 1804 parallels the transition from the Baroque to other expressions of dynastic legitimacy and personal power adopted by the Habsburgs after 1780. We find a dramatic example of this shift in the sarcophagus of Joseph II, the last emperor to make concerted efforts to increase this power over other princes of the empire. Joseph's tomb lies literally in the shadow of his parents' tombs in the Kapuzinergruft. Joseph, who died in 1790, decreed that his tomb be as simple as a commoner's casket. Adorned with only a simple cross, the sarcophagus is both a refutation of the Baroque ostentation of his parents' monument and a rejection of

---

[61] Marc Bloc discusses the need for new dynasties to establish a form of sacral legitimazation (*Les Rois thaumaturgiques: Étude sur le caractère surnaturel attributé à la puissance royale particulièrement en France et en Angleterre* [Paris: Gallimard, 1983]).

[62] In addition to the work by Pawlik-van der Water, see the illustration of Maria Theresia praying at her husband's tomb in the Kapuzinergruft in *Dějiny českého národa od roku 1705 do roku 1780*, by Josef Svátek (Prague, 1898), 746. Even if this illustration dates from after her reign, it captures the public and theatrical (and thus perhaps Jesuit-influenced) elements of Baroque devotion expressed by the dynasty as they were remembered long afterwards in the Czech lands.

[63] Stanislaw Grodziski, "Les Réformes de Marie-Thérèse et de Joseph II en Galicie de 1772 à 1790," in *Unité et diversité de L'Empire des Habsbourg à la fin du xviiie siècle*, ed. R. Mortier and Hevré Hasquin, *Edition de l'Université de Bruxelles*, no. 15 (1988), 69.

the turbulent, emotional style of ecclesiastical art that had predominated a generation earlier.[64]

Joseph's dislike of Jesuits has often been exaggerated, but his determination to promote an aesthetic at odds with what the Society had so often chosen was very real. Practical, impatient, Joseph (who allegedly remarked to a subject kissing his hand, "It's not a holy relic!") was a more effective enemy of the Baroque aesthetic than any Enlightenment salon theorist; he felt no desire to retain any imagery of the Holy Roman Empire that could not support his reform plans in any meaningful way. Only a dozen years earlier, the words on the title page of the *Annales Provinciæ Bohemiæ S. J.* had been inscribed in an ornate blending of Baroque and traditional folk elements; Joseph's neoclassicism and austerity banished such effusions from the mainstream culture of Bohemia as completely as the Holy See had banished the Society itself.[65]

But even without the Emperor's determination to change everything within his own dominions, the Baroque aesthetic and much that went with it were doomed by midcentury. When the dynasty's focus on the old empire, an institution that was both universalist in its claims and highly regional in its actual functioning, shifted to the creation of a unified empire based on the territorial inheritance of the Habsburgs, there was no need to promote the Baroque as a medium for communicating the sacral functions of the dynasty. Francis I might strive to be as absolutist as any member of the eighteenth-century dynasty; but he did not need the intimate blending of ecclesiastical, classical, and dynastic imagery on which the House of Austria had so long relied to convey his intentions. The new Crown of the Habsburgs was in essence one of their own creation, descended from but no longer dependent upon the same endorsement of the Church that for so long had been the source of legitimacy for the dynasty. Nor, apparently, was there any further need to rely on the services of the Society of Jesus.

The Power of the Unseen

The reality of the unseen but potent world of the supernatural and emotional that the devotee encounters on a personal level is another hallmark of the Baroque that persists after the middle of the century in Bohemia, and was both sustained by and reflected in the Latinity of the Jesuits, as

[64] Joseph's choice of sarcophagus was both an explicit break with the ostentation of the immediate Baroque past of the dynasty, and a public demonstration of his commitment to practicality and economy, as he understood them. It may also be interpreted as a highly individualistic expression of his uniqueness and power as a despot (Derek Beales, "Was Joseph II an Enlightened Despot?" in *The Austrian Enlightenment and Its Aftermath,* ed. Ritchie Robertson and Edward Timms, Austrian studies, 2 [Edinburgh: Edinburgh University Press, 1991], 1).

[65] NK, 23/19, *Annales Provinciæ Bohemiæ S. J. ad annum 1768,* folio 78r.

it had been by their Czech writings a century earlier.[66] Writings of the members of the Society appearing in the eighteenth century retained for the most part the flavor of Baroque piety that was common during the previous century.[67] Leopold Fabritius, S.J., writing as late as 1760, exhibited in his Czech prose a conservative style containing elements of the Baroque and the less complex language of the people.[68] Even Leopold Scherschnik, whose intellectual interests overlapped Enlightenment philological and historical concerns, could introduce Baroque elements into his biographical sketch of the undeniably pre-Enlightenment Father Koniáš.[69]

Nor did the Baroque mentality express itself only in literary endeavors intended for public consumption. In the records of the Jesuit communities of Prague we find innumerable evidences of the survival of the Baroque world of miracles accomplished through the mixing of the physical and the spiritual. Those who suffered fevers reported glorious visions of St. Aloysius, "vultu resplendentem," who gave them comfort; others ate of the "farina Aloysiana" (flour of Aloysius) to cure diseases or sought solace in prayer to the Sacred Heart of Jesus, an example of the objectification of an emotional or spiritual concept in a human body part.[70] Pilgrimages, vigils, and public penance, practices that might have a "double" (that is, a literal and a symbolic) meaning were still part of the piety promoted by the Jesuits, a piety that stood in distinct contrast to Jansenist and Pietistic movements that disliked images or activities calling attention to the body or body parts.[71] The Shrine of Loreto, the goal of pious Catholics journeying to Italy, was exalted in an elaborate complex on the Hradčany a short distance from the Prague Castle, and relics from the shrine were the objects of devotion in the Jesuit church of St. Clement in the Staré Mesto.[72] The cult of St. Jan Nepo-

[66] Regarding the Catholic religious poetry of the high Baroque in Bohemia, Arne Novák writes that it "did not always limit itself to liturgical aims, and fostered the expression of feeling and sensuality; authors were encouraged to delve into their innermost being" (*Czech Literature,* trans. Peter Kussi [Ann Arbor: Michigan Slavic Publications, 1976], 81).

[67] See the bibliographies in Pelzel, *Böhmische Gelehrte,* passim, and in the *Dictionnaire de spiritualité,* s.v. "Tchèque (église): Époque baroque, des lumières a 1950," by Jaroslav Kradlec.

[68] For example, *Mrawna naučení na nedele celého roku* (Prague), Moravský zemský Archiv v Brně, Cerroniho sbírka II, 345, 78. Hereafter this source will be abbreviated to MZAB.

[69] A new look as Scherschnik's contribution is found in "Antonín Koniáš S. J. von seinen Ordensbrüdern dargestellt," by Martin Svatoš, *Humanistica Lovaniensia* 43 (1994): 411–24.

[70] NK, 23/17, *Annuæ Litteræ Collegii S. J. ad S. Clementem 1767,* folio 186r.

[71] NK, 23/17 *Annuæ Litteræ Collegii S. J. ad. S. Clementem 1766,* folio 168r; Marc Venard, "Popular Religion in the Eighteenth Century," in *Church and Society in Catholic Europe of the Eighteenth Century,* ed. William J. Callahan and David Higgs (Cambridge: Cambridge University Press, 1979), 153 f.

[72] NK 23/17 *Annuæ Litteræ Collegii S. J. ad S. Clementem 1766,* folio 168v.

mucký remained vital into the nineteenth century and likewise had as its focus the miraculous preservation of a body part.[73]

These expressions of devotion straddled two conceptions of a saint: the older concept, rooted in the earliest demonstrations of devotion to saints in the early Middle Ages and before, where the saint functioned as a wonderworker or even a quasi deity, and a later vision of the saint as moral exemplar, a concept that gained ground after Pope Urban VIII set down clear procedures for canonization.[74] By retaining elements of both conceptualizations of a saint, the Jesuits were able to make use of the saints as demonstrations of the immediacy of God's power in the corporeal world and to turn saints' lives into lessons for sermon or school. Nepomucký, whose own story both exemplified the miraculous and taught the lesson of fidelity to the secrecy of the confessional, illustrated how one saint could comfortably manage these two roles.[75] It was quite appropriate for Jesuits to emphasize Nepomucký, the "martyr of the confessional," considering that the confessional was one of their most characteristic ministries.

These expressions of the Baroque aesthetic, while sponsored by elites (frequently for their own benefit), always formed a connection with the common people, who after the long night of sterile rationalism of the Renaissance, welcomed the emotionalism, the color, the variety, and the immediacy of the Baroque.[76] The Society of Jesus, whose task was to bring the predominantly Protestant population of Bohemia back into the Catholic Church, found that it was of particular importance to exploit the media for its ability to speak to the masses. By decorating the Bethlehem Chapel in the Old Town with gold lamps, the very chapel where Jan Hus delivered sermons denouncing the venality of the Church, the Society sought to send

---

[73] Pierre Delooz, "Toward a Sociological Study of Canonized Sainthood in the Catholic Church," trans. Jane Hodgkin, in *Saints and Their Cults: Studies in Religious Sociology: Folklore and History,* ed. Stephen Wilson (Cambridge: Cambridge University Press, 1983), 210.

[74] David Morgan, *Visual Piety: A History and Theory of Popular Religious Images* (Berkeley: University of California Press, 1998), 71.

[75] Nepomucký may have fulfilled another, less obvious, function for the Jesuits. Not only is there circumstantial evidence that Nepomucký was put forward as a substitute role model for the heretic Jan Hus, but since the story of Nepomucký dwells on the evil behavior of his master, the Czech Premyslid/Luxemburg king Václav, it served to discredit this earlier dynasty, which included Charles IV, widely regarded as the greatest of Czech kings. The position of the more recently arrived Habsburgs in Bohemia would therefore be enhanced by the retelling of the martyrdom of Nepomucký. Catholic historians have long argued, not entirely convincingly, that Nepomucký was not promoted with the intent of obliterating the memory of Hus, and that the cult of Nepomucký was well established before the arrival of the Jesuits (*Dictionnarie d' histoire et de géographie,* s.v. "Bohême," by P. David).

[76] See Arne Novák, in his *Praha barokní* (1915), commenting on the common touch of the Baroque, quoted in *Società, chiesa, e vita religiosa nell' "ancien régime,"* by Carla Russo (Naples: Guida Editori, 1978), 372.

to those who might favor the religious reforms of the Hussites the typically Baroque message that the Roman Church was powerful, triumphant, and glorious.[77]

The Jesuits built lavish chapels in the Malá Strana (Small Side) of Prague in part to rival the city palaces of the highest nobility that were located in the vicinity. The splendor of these structures was intended not only to impress those who worshiped in them but also to captivate the passerby, much as Jesuit dramas performed in their collegia contained didactic messages for the youthful performers, but at the same time were intended for members of the wider community.[78] The rhetorical element of the Baroque aesthetic was also evident in the very lives of members of the Society. Antonius Khabes, a Viennese Jesuit whose sermons were a throwback to the rhetoric of the High Baroque, was active as late as 1771.[79] Yet it is important to remember that the architecture and the sermon were not necessarily aimed at uneducated persons; historically, the Jesuits had always sought to engage the most powerful and educated members of society.

In the second half of the eighteenth century, however, the support of some of the elites in the Habsburg domains was eroding. Pious cults, an important part of seventeenth-century Jesuit work in Bohemia, were under attack after 1750 by the descendants of the very families who had previously endowed and promoted them.[80] Thus, this expression of the Baroque sensibility began over time to be associated more with laypeople belonging to a particular social class and possessing a certain level of educational attainment. It seems strange that despite this development, highly educated Jesuits continued to produce devotional literature in the Baroque manner, in both Latin and Czech. Likewise, the personal letters and diaries of Bohemian Jesuits traveling to missions overseas frequently show a combination of shrewd observations and fragmented, unsystematic reports, so typical of the writings of their learned seventeenth-century predecessors.[81] As the next chapter will demonstrate, these contrasts and tensions remained a part of Jesuit culture until the suppression.

---

[77] NK, 23/17, *Annuæ Litteræ Collegii S. J. ad S. Clementem 1767*, folio 183v. The redecorating of Gothic churches in Baroque style was widespread throughout Europe and especially common in Prague, with political implications in many instances that did not involve the Jesuits.

[78] Kaufmann, *Court, Cloister, and City*, 350.

[79] Anna Coreth, "Priesterliches Wirken im baroken Wien: P. Antonius Khabes 1687–1771)," *Archivum historicum Societatis Iesu (AHSI)*, 61, no. 121 (1992): 71–89.

[80] Evans, *The Making of the Habsburg Monarchy*, 388.

[81] For example, the letter (in Czech) of P. Martin Schweyna sent back to Prague from the Quito missions, dated January 14, 1754 (Václav Schulz, ed. *Korrespondence Jesuitů Provincie České z let 1584–1770 z Archivu Musea Království Českého* [Prague: Nákl. České Akademie císáře Františka Josefa pro vědy, slovesnost a umění, 1900], 233–42).

Baroque visual art relied heavily on emblems, and likewise the Jesuits turned to emblems to communicate the most profound truths of their faith.[82] The enthusiasm for emblems and especially for emblem books reached its peak in the seventeenth century, but traces of this pedagogical technique lingered long into the Age of Enlightenment.[83] We have evidence of the tradition of emblematics and complex symbolism in the elaborately engraved theses produced for the Prague university well into the eighteenth century.[84] In Prague these theses were not unique to the university, but were also produced to commemorate graduations at the archiepiscopal seminary founded by Cardinal Harrach.[85] Emblematic theses complemented the symbolism found in Baroque churches and in the texts of Latin compositions created by students in Jesuit schools.

However, by the second half of the eighteenth century, the use of emblems was dwindling, supplanted by the growing interest in the exact sciences and hastened by the slow but steady decline of the decorative arts that supported emblematics and also gave it a context in which to flourish. While emblems were not limited to Catholic themes, the decline of emblems may also be regarded as paralleling the retreat of Baroque forms of Catholic piety among the more educated and culturally ambitious. Emblems survived longer in Hungary, where the Counter-Reformation had arrived later, and where Baroque visual arts remained vital into the nineteenth century.[86]

---

[82] The field of late Baroque emblematics still awaits an adequate study. The most complete documentation of emblems is *Emblemata zur Sinnbildkeit des XVI. und XVII. Jahrhunderts*, ed. Arthur Henkel and Albrecht Schöne, 2 vols. (Stuttgart: J. B. Metzler, 1967–76).

[83] The Jesuit emblem makers of the Baroque era strove to communicate two messages through their creations: one that was specific to Jesuit pedagogical and theological positions, and an implicit moral statement not uniquely linked to the Jesuits' agenda (Richard Dimler, "The Bee-Topos in the Jesuit Emblem Book," in *Selected Papers of the Glasgow International Emblem Conference, 13–17 August 1990*, ed. Alison Adams and Anthony Harper [Leiden/New York/London: E. J. Brill, 1992], 238 n. 21). Emblems executed in 1712 under the auspices of the Society are still displayed in the public spaces of the University of Graz (Grete Lorsky, *Barocke Embleme in Vorau und anderen Stiften Österreichs* [Graz: Auslieferungsstelle: Buchhandlung Styria, 1962], 140–144).

[84] An example from 1747 is found in "Teologická fakulta," by Karel Beránek, in *Dějiny Univerzity Karlovy*, ed. I. Čornejnová, 3 vols. (Prague: Univerzita Karlova, 1995–1998), 2:224. A very late thesis, produced in 1756, is reproduced in *Pražská sbírka universitních thesí*, by Oldrich J. Blažíček (Prague: Zvlastní otisk z Hollara sborníku grafického umění, 1940), 11 f. See also Louise Rice, "Jesuit Thesis Prints and the Festive Academic Defence at the Collegio Romano," in O'Malley, *The Jesuits*, 148–69.

[85] Hedvika Kucharová, "Slavností disputace a grafické listy tezí v arcibiskupském semináři v Praze," *Bibliotheca Strahoviensis* 2 (1996): 137–43. Hereafter this source will be abbreviated to *BS*.

[86] A very late example of emblematics is found in the engraving of the tomb or perhaps the *castrum doloris* of Joseph Bajzath, bishop of Veszprém, Hungary, who died on February 24, 1802 (Országos Széchény Könyvtár Budapest, 405–42).

Complementing the Jesuit preoccupation with the solitary objects that made up emblems was their interest in "curiosities" or objects from the natural world that could not easily be classified according to existing systems. Such a fascination for collecting curiosities occupied a special place in the world of the Baroque. As Krysztov Pomian has noted, the high Renaissance curiosity "enjoyed a temporary spell in power, an interim rule between those of theology and science."[87] Jesuit collections of curiosities reflected both the Society's search for the signs of God hidden in natural phenomena, and perhaps also the intellectual curiosity of some Jesuits who were moving towards a way of viewing and understanding nature closer to that of modern science.

The titles of two works by Ioannes Klausal, a Jesuit who died in Prague in 1768, illustrate how mixing an interest in natural history with theological conformity typified the Jesuit communities of Prague throughout the century.[88] Yet, by the middle of the eighteenth century, the tension with the empiricist, Enlightenment approach to preserving and identifying natural objects, as exemplified by the work of Lineaus, van Swieten, and the Scottish naturalist John Hope, had become almost insurmountable for Jesuit scientists working in the Habsburg realms.[89] Put another way, the Enlightenment approach to recording and organizing knowledge about the cosmos was unified and secular, but also systematic, increasingly specialized, and professionalized. By contrast, the Jesuit collections of curiosities, their pharmacopeias, and their hagiographies retained an earlier model from the Renaissance of the Tree of Knowledge or the House of Knowledge, whose collective whole was meaningful and whose constituent parts might contain emblematic insights into a greater truth that reached beyond the individual parts.

To this was added the Baroque passion to include everything imaginable in a complete, if often less-than-coherent whole. Jesuit polymaths of the High Baroque, of whom Athanasius Kircher was the outstanding example, sought to bring together elements of many disciplines in a way that seems to lack organization and a common theme. Yet such efforts were highly esteemed in an age when causal relationships, chronologies, and Linnean taxonomies were not yet indispensable elements of the intellectual

[87] Quoted in "Shrines, Curiosities and the Rhetoric of Display," by Stephen Bauer, in *Visual Display: Culture beyond Appearances*, ed. Lynne Cooke and Peter Woolen (Seattle: Bay Press, 1995), 24.

[88] Joannes Klausal, *Curiosa naturæ arcana inclyti Regni Bohemiæ et appertinentium Provinciarum Moraviæ et Silesiæ, quæstionibus philosophicis indagata* (Prague, 1724); id., *Controversiæ fidei particulares populari captui accommodatæ, cum Thesibus ex universa Theologia*, 2 vols. (Prague, 1733).

[89] See Brechka, *Gerhard van Swieten and His World*, 113; and A. G. Morton, *John Hope, 1725–1786: Scottish Botanist* (Edinburgh: Edinburgh Botanic Garden Trust, 1986).

landscape.[90] Such an unsystematic approach to knowledge was readily accepted by a populace, including that portion considered well educated, that could still believe in the possibility of alchemical transformations.[91] The cult of St. Jan Nepomucký, with its particular attention to a body part (the saint's tongue), continued to dominate the imaginations of many Prague ecclesiastics and lay people, a phenomenon Jesuits were happy to promote.[92] By reason of the attention he attracted from Jesuits and others, Nepomucký was the archetypal Baroque saint, and works devoted to him retained their Baroque flavor into the 1760s.

Elsewhere, mystery, metaphor, and lack of systematization, in the encyclopedic or taxonomic senses of the term, were hallmarks of much Jesuit writing, both on religious and more "scientific" subjects, and appear even in the works of Prague former Jesuits following the suppression.[93] It was against such an approach to acquiring knowledge that the *encyclopédistes* were striving, despite their own prejudices, to present information "objectively."[94]

The Baroque Mentality

To speak of the late Baroque is not necessarily to speak of decadent Baroque. (The classification "Baroque" itself originally applied to an expression in the plastic arts that was considered decadent in comparison to Renaissance norms that had preceded it, and only in the latter part of the nineteenth century did "Baroque" cease to have this negative connotation.) What is striking about Baroque visual art in Bohemia is that there is little evidence that it lost its vitality during the first eight decades of the eigh-

[90] Kircher, whom the Habsburg Ferdinand II showered with honors, produced a torrent of writing, some of it chaotic and pedantic; other pieces, however, conveyed a more impressive sense of the Baroque aesthetic that is only beginning to be appreciated today (Evans, *Making of the Habsburg Empire*, 433 ff.).

[91] In 1770 an English traveler reported that three thousand people in Vienna were still interested in the "Hermetic" sciences (cited in Fouchier-Magnan, *Small German Courts*, 62).

[92] Typical of the literary attention that Jesuits gave to Nepomucký is *Fortissimus Dei miles et martyr invictus sanctus Joannes Nepomucensis S. Metropolitanæ Ecclesiæ Pragensis Canonicus sub annuis solemniis in Templo honori ejusdem athletæ neo-Pragæ in Skalka erecto Panegyricus laudatus a Guilielmo Leopoldo Rogalsky* (Prague, Old City, 1763).

[93] For example, Antonius Strnad, *De divi Joannis Nepomuceni gloria, quam sibi loquendo . . .* (Prague, 1781).

[94] Yet the systematization of knowledge found in the *Encyclopédie* was not without its own hierarchies and tensions. Mental labor, for example, was viewed by the *encyclopédistes* as less potentially injurious to the individual than physical work (Harry Payne, *The* Philosophe *and the People* [New Haven/London: Yale University Press, 1976], 37 f.). Payne also points out that the hierarchies put forward by the *encyclopédistes* were on occasion ambiguous or contradictory, suggesting dynamics among the writers similar to those found among Jesuit writers in the final years before the suppression.

teenth century. This persistent vitality resulted from the pervasive influence of ideas, artists, and aesthetic values imported from Italy or Vienna, cradles of the Baroque, well into the middle of the century, as well as from the inherently cosmopolitan backgrounds of many of the aristocracy who sponsored the arts.[95]

To assess the vitality of late-Baroque forms of expression beyond the evidence of the visual arts is more problematic. First, we must say more about what here we define as the "Baroque" mentality. While this mentality includes, for example, belief in miracles, such belief is not an element unique to the Baroque, although aspects of the cult of miraculous relics in the seventeenth and eighteenth centuries are distinctive. Specifically, the Baroque preoccupation with miraculous relics differs from earlier expressions of this belief in the heightened theatricality of the presentation of the relic, and frequently by the degree of realism with which the body of the holy personage is portrayed from whom the relic was taken. For the Baroque exhibits a fascination with the body, its peculiarities and individual parts, a fascination that encouraged Baroque writers to name or describe body parts in new ways.[96]

Often this fascination manifests itself in ways that are bizarre, incomprehensible, or repulsive to modern sensibilities, yet are highly suggestive of how relics and representations of the body were perceived in a Baroque Catholic context. An example of this is found in the work of Frederik Ruysch (1638–1731), a Dutch anatomist who practiced the technique of injecting wax into anatomic specimens. The results are strange mélanges of body parts arranged more for aesthetic contemplation or moral reflection than for instructional use. One such presentation included in his *Thesaurus anatomicus* features three fetal skeletons (one of which is posed drying its nonexistent eyes with a cloth) grouped around an arrangement of preserved human organs and other tissues that vaguely resembles a rock garden.[97] Yet Ruysch was no mere sideshow exhibitionist of the macabre; he was a distinguished medical illustrator whose strictly anatomical engravings made an important contribution to the medical knowledge of the day. His wax

[95] Preiss, "Malby Františka Karla Palka," 144–67.

[96] In the eighteenth century many body parts, especially those concerned with sexual reproduction, had received names, analogous organs of the two sexes sharing common names; during this later period, the organs of both sexes were differentiated and received distinctive names (Thomas Laqueur, *Making Sex* [Cambridge, Mass./London: Harvard University Press, 1990], 149). Laqueur even goes so far as to claim that "sometime in the eighteenth century sex as we know it was invented."

[97] A *vanitas mundi* complete with fetal skeletons playing instruments made from preserved human tissue appears in *The Origins of Museums: The Cabinet of Curiosities in Sixteenth- and Seventeenth-Century Europe,* by Oliver Impey and Arthur Macgregor (Oxford: Clarendon Press, 1985), fig. 49. I am indebted to Lilla Vekerdy for bring Ruysch's work to my attention.

preparations illustrate several interacting themes within the Baroque as later expressed by the Jesuits of Bohemia. Another outstanding example of using skeletal body parts for decorative purposes can be found in the crypt of the Capuchin church in Rome, at the foot of the Via Veneto.

The first of these themes is the desire to arrest the process of decay, a theme repeated in the reports of the miraculous preservation of the body of Shimon Abeles and other saints and near saints.[98] Preservation was equated with virtue, and thus also with what is pleasing aesthetically, so that the usual associations of corruption, decay, and repulsion are replaced with a positive aesthetic experience. While the miraculous preservation of bodies or body parts is found in accounts of early Christian saints, the Baroque era carried the idea of preservation to new heights.

The second of these themes is the tendency to display elements of the human body in theatrical and visually arresting ways, unrecognizable at times and disconnected from their more familiar settings. This presentation was accomplished with great care and technical skill, but without any effort to achieve either a naturalistic or systematic presentation that would be the goal of Enlightenment scientists. The reliquary designed to display the supposed "tongue" of Jan Nepomucký is only one example of this form of presentation. Rather than realistically representing either Nepomucký or his tongue—the saint's tongue as part of a complete body—the reliquary emphasizes instead the splendor and miraculous nature of what has taken place, the relic's potential as a "living" object that can transmit its life force to those who come in contact with it.[99]

Next, the body or its parts fit within the context of the "curiosity" mentioned above. The body or body part became an object of edification, or possibly entertainment, somewhat as the anatomical lecture came to be regarded as a moralistic tour de force blended with voyeurism. Even if the relic is performing no miracle at the present, its existence demands attention from the viewer, much as the presentation of a Latin play or Greek oration, in a language and perhaps setting that were themselves "relics" for many of the audience, demanded respect and attention. The condition of the body or of a body part, as in the case of Shimon Abeles, is both morally edifying and evidence of God's power. The preservation of the body, or the special circumstances that surround its rediscovery or display, are recurring tropes

---

[98] Specific elements of the Abeles case as reported reflect preoccupations of the medical profession during the Baroque: the phenomenon of the bleeding corpse was the subject of a learned dissertation by M. F. Geuder entitled *De probatione per cruentationem cadaverum vulgo Baarecht, præside Eberh. Rud. Rothio* (Ulm, 1694), cited in *A History of Magic and Experimental Science*, by Lynn Thorndike, 8 vols. (New York: Columbia University Press, 1923–58), 7:370.

[99] *The Encyclopedia of Religion*, s.v. "Relics," by John S. Strong.

in Baroque Catholic hagiographies and were even applied specifically to one of the great early Jesuits, St. Francis Xavier.[100]

Finally, there is more than a trace of *memento mori* common to Baroque funerary art in the postures of the fetal skeletons. The display of these skeletons also raises the question of how viewers understood the humanity of their original possessors. A culture that did not always see the need for giving a newborn infant a funeral or a formal tomb regarded the humanity of the unborn and the newborn differently than we of the twentieth century might do.[101] These factors are of great relevance when considering the pastoral activities of the Jesuits and the care they bestowed on the living and dying of all ages; again, they suggest the distinctly pre-Enlightenment attitudes prevailing in the Bohemian Society, despite the scientific undertakings of some of its members, and despite the gradual emergence of the self in a devotional, Catholic context.[102]

It would be a mistake to consider Baroque taste the exclusive property of either the highest ruling elites or the most ignorant peasantry. The petite bourgeoisie of Vienna, despite their flirtations with Freemasonry, were profoundly influenced by the sensuous and theatrical elements of the Baroque aesthetic, and the same could be said of the burgher classes of Prague as well.[103] The processions, great choral Masses, and rituals associated with the dynasty were more than entertainment for the wealthy or distraction for the impoverished (although they undoubtedly served these functions as well). They also provided an element of cohesion for a society just beginning its passage to modern urban life, as the Jesuits instinctively understood. The emphasis of the Society on public ceremony and spectacle cannot be attributed exclusively to a classist or self-promotional base.

The emphasis on the importance of ceremony, when symbol and action were brought together, was likewise in accord with the tendency noted in Jesuit ethics to stress the specific act rather than the total personal-

---

[100] The appearance of his incorrupt body was noted, despite its having been buried in quicklime: "[E]jusdem [Francisci Xaverii] corporis integritas, color vividus, odor molissimus: e viva calce post aliquot menses educti miraculum" *(Ioannis Ferrandi Anciensis e Societate Iesu theologi Disquisitio Reliquaria . . .)*. This reference appears in the index of this book, but the indicated page does not contain a mention of Xavier.

[101] Even the deceased infants of royal houses are not always remembered by name, and crypts and cemeteries of the period, for instance, the crypt below St. Michael's Church in Vienna, are strikingly devoid of the tombs of infants. The Kapuzinergruft likewise contains tombs of imperial infants who go unnamed.

[102] Roy Porter, *A Social History of Madness: Stories of the Insane* (London: Weidenfeld and Nicolson, 1987), 26.

[103] Jean Bérenger, *A History of the Habsburg Empire, 1700–1918,* trans. C. A Simpson (New York: Longman, 1997), 120. Unlike Vienna, Prague was more dominated by its aristocracy and the servants of nobility than by an urban middle class, which remained small throughout the eighteenth century.

ity of the individual. Specific acts of piety, such as pilgrimages and participation in processions, were greater than moments of public commemoration; they were conscious endeavors through which the individual's life might be judged and seen publicly.[104]

The mere survival of literary works or the continued use of religious objects does not necessarily prove that a "Baroque" mentality persisted among those who wrote or worshiped. Compounding the historian's problem is the scarcity of evidence concerning what the majority of uneducated people really believed. The use of "St. Ignatius's water" (meaning water blessed on the saint's feast day or used to invoke his intercession), and the veneration of local saints and relics continued to be widespread throughout Catholic Europe in the eighteenth century.[105] The historian can generally only surmise to what degree these apparent acts of piety were motivated by habit, tradition, or social pressure.

Occasionally it is difficult to grasp the rationale by which eighteenth-century Jesuits distinguished between legitimate piety, expressed through one of the approved cults, and aberrant, dangerous practices. The position of Church authorities wishing to maintain control over doctrine and morals, and the reaction of local clergy to these forces are also important factors. Jan Royt describes an instance where an engraving of the pregnant Virgin showing rays of light proceeding from her (covered) womb and breasts was perhaps predictably denounced as a scandal.[106] The Society viewed the intent behind the "20 schedæ in honorem S. Coronæ ad obtinendam pecuniam" (twenty sheets(?) in honor of the holy Crown to obtain money) as dangerous. Although the nature of the danger is not spelled out in their *Litteræ,* the twenty *schedæ* were seized in 1759 by Jesuits in Prague.[107] Did all uses of the holy Crown of our Lord run the same risk?

In 1762, the Jesuits again seized other books dealing with the holy Crown that they maintained were being used for financial gain.[108] An instance reported in a rural setting, where a youth had apparently run amok while under the influence of the Crown, suggests how dangerous inappropriate devotion to it could be. The importance attached to the misuse of this particular holy object was not limited to the immoral purposes

---

[104] Palmer, *Catholics,* 37.

[105] Owen Chadwick, *The Popes and the European Revolution* (Oxford: Clarendon Press, 1981), 3–95; this discussion of popular Catholicism during the ancien régime deals mostly with conditions in France and Italy, but is still useful in suggesting the relation of the physical and spiritual in the daily life of the people in rural areas; it also sheds light on the material prosperity of the clergy.

[106] Jan Royt, *Obraz a Kult v Čechách 17. a 18. století* (Prague: Univerzita Karlova, 1999), 56 f.

[107] Strahov, D A III 33, *Epitome historiæ Dom. Prof. ad S. Nicolaum, anno* 1759, folio 4v.

[108] Ibid., anno 1762 folio 10r.

to which it might be put; merely coming under the influence of the holy Crown could be, in the narratives left by the Jesuit fathers, a great danger in itself. Danger through proclivity to evil, the complement to the curative properties of contact with the holy, made up much of the actual practice of Baroque Catholic piety. The *Litteræ* for the final years of the Society in Bohemia would in fact be very barren documents were they not enriched by the constant reporting of danger, whether this danger was from disease, foreign attack, or heresy.[109]

The investment in a worldview fraught with danger exposes another fault line within the Bohemian Society. There was much within the ideology of the Society from its inception onward that stressed the possibilities of this world; the aggressive intercontinental missionary efforts that the Society embarked on early in its history reflect this optimism, as do the founding of schools throughout Europe. Danger in such situations was not to be shunned; a martyr's death was always a highly desirable outcome of courting trouble for the faith. But the danger that lurks through the *Litteræ* is generally of another sort, a dread of possible contamination with heresy and Judaism and from the workings of the devil, who is behind each case of possession and responsible for each ill-considered pact made with him or his confederates. The Society needed this danger as a counterpoint to its own activities, and it needed to document the danger to justify these activities. Without the dark, the light of the Baroque was far too difficult to recognize.

Another feature of Baroque piety, although one not unique to this period, was the tendency towards the ascetical and a yearning for self-abasement. This asceticism existed alongside of and intertwined with the Baroque affinity for the sensual world, a connection evident in many of the reports of the miraculous that illustrated the bridge between the divine and the earthly. Jesuits combined an elevation of the material manifestation of the divine with an abasement of their own material selves.[110] In the obituary notice of Father Andreas Provin, we read about his humble devotion to the Blessed Virgin Mary and his practice of piously kissing her statue: "Numquam cubili egressus aut ingressus, quin humili osculo pedes B. V. in statua Mariæ Schenensi venerata fuerit"; it is also reported that he abstained from wine on the Sabbath.[111] Likewise, Father Carolus Cardell, who died

[109] The material deprivations brought on by the Seven Years' War are prominent themes in the *Litteræ;* for example, as in 1762, when Prussian soldiers made off with livestock and extorted money from the community in Kommotov (NK 1287, MS XXIII C105/15, "Status provinciæ," *An. Prov. Boh. 1762,* folio 254r). The same year in Děčín (Tetschin) occupying Prussian troops did thousands of florins' worth of damage (ibid., folio 312r).

[110] Karl Bosl ed., *Handbuch der Geschichte der böhmischen Länder,* 4 vols. (Stuttgart: A. Hiersemann, 1966–), 2:367.

[111] We find these data regarding him: Gettendorf, Austria, born 12.11.1695; entered the Soc. 14.10.1711; professed of the 4 vows, 2.2.1729; died 29.7.1761 (Strahov, D. A. III. 33,

while caring for Walloon troops in the service of the Habsburgs during the 1757 siege of Prague, practiced fasting and self-flagellation to honor the Virgin Mary.[112] During the seventeenth century several Bohemian Jesuits had become legendary for their asceticism, and other Jesuits reported with admiration that Fr. Koniáš slept next to the rotten carcass of a dog, and on other occasions rode in a peasant's wagon full of manure.

This practice of extreme self-mortification was an expression of more than simply devotion to religion; it was also a rejection of materialism, and thus represented a polar opposite of the rational empiricism that was gaining ground among Habsburg intellectuals, including some Jesuits. Simultaneously there was an undeniable element of Baroque theatricality in Koniáš's practices. Since among these intellectuals may be counted a number of Bohemian Jesuits, including Stepling, Tessanek, Dobrovský, Strnad, and Zeno, it is reasonable to conclude that serious tensions must at times have existed between these two worldviews, tensions that at times manifested themselves within the same individual Jesuit.[113]

Pious asceticism, enthusiastically practiced in the seventeenth century by Jesuits and laypersons alike, was on the wane in the eighteenth, but one could still find outstanding examples among the most devout. Franciscus Wissinger, who held high offices in Prague university and was later provincial, coped with the difficulty of attending banquets related to his elevated position by only pretending to partake of the food put before him, while maintaining his usual abstention.[114] This fact was reported admiringly in his obituary in 1773, on the very eve of the suppression, showing that whatever challenges were confronting the Society in its final months, at least its

---

Epitome annuariæ litterarum Prov. Boh. S. J., Hist. Dom. Prof. ad S. Nicolaum, anno 1761, folios 5v–6r).

[112] Pelzel, *Gelehrte,* 237.

[113] Strnad is a good example of this internal tension, composing devotional texts while he was conducting advanced astronomical observations. Franciscus Zeno, also famed as a scientist, was remembered many years after his death as a "great ascetic" (Strahov, D K II 16, Fischer, *Miszellen,* 2, 26). Jesuit administrators seem to have experienced this tension as well. Franciscus Retz, the Bohemian Jesuit who became the superior general of the Society in 1730, wrote privately to Koniáš endorsing his theatrical and assertive methods of mission work; but later, as general, when communicating with the provincial of the Bohemian Province, he took Koniáš to task, saying that he jeopardized the mission of the Society (I. Čornejová, *Tovaryšstvo Ježíšovo: Jezuité v Čechách* [Praha Mladá Fronta, 1995], 199).

[114] "Hunc [cibum inconsuetum] assidentibus ne gustatum quidem, non raro porrigebat; . . . a consueta refectionis norma nihil recedebat, quamvis edulia omnia delibare videretur" (MZAB, Cerroniho sbírka 345, 689). Yet the metaphor of eating and drinking could have positive connotations in Baroque Catholicism. Francis de Sales, for example, compared decorous eating with modest sexuality, and used the metaphor of eating and drinking to describe contemplation of the Divine (Milad Doueihi, *A Perverse History of the Human Heart* [Cambridge, Mass.: Harvard University Press, 1997], 108–10).

institutional commitment to such expressions of Baroque Catholicism remained intact.

The End of the Baroque

Several developments heralded the end of the Baroque in Bohemia. The aristocracy looked to the dynasty for models of artistic consumption, and the dynasty began to offer new models after 1765; thus it is better to regard this date as a watershed than 1780. F. A. J. Szabo discerns a connection between the increased interest of the widowed Empress in Jansenism and her retreat from the ornamentation of the late Baroque.[115]

Events in the wider world were also working against the Baroque. The loss of Silesia, an important part of the Holy Roman Empire, and the consequent reduction in the scope of the dynasty and the Holy Roman Empire also contributed to the breakdown in the Baroque expression of that relationship. When Joseph II decreed a reduction in the number of monasteries and convents, he unquestionably hastened a process that was already well advanced before he became sole ruler of the dynasty's lands. Equally indicative of the end of the Baroque attitude toward the body and death was Joseph's decree that attempted to have all new cemeteries in Vienna located outside the outer ring of defenses, thereby effectively separating the bodies of the dead not only from churches but from the living residents of the city.[116] Pragmatism and a desire for the efficient and hygienic were steadily winning out over the older notion that linked the living and the dead and kept the danger and mystery associated with the one constantly in the consciousness of the other. At the same time, the close relationship between Bohemian Baroque philosophy and the Middle Ages, a connection that perdured in the absence of a thriving middle class, could not be sustained in a new world that would soon bring forth nationalism, the beginnings of industrialization and a bourgeoisie, and even the threat of Jacobinism.[117]

In the visual arts, at least one commentator has detected a general stagnation in the Baroque after 1780.[118] The declining Baroque also had to deal with the increasing vitality of a totally different aesthetic, one that valued not only classical simplicity but linear efficiency as well. In contrast to

[115] Franz A. J. Szabo, *Kaunitz and Enlightened Absolutism* (Cambridge: The University Press, 1994), 221.

[116] Maria Theresia had proposed the separation of graveyards from churches as early as 1775 (Peter Hanák, "The Alienation of Death in Budapest and Vienna at the Turn of the Century," in *The Mirror of History: Essays in Honor of Fritz Fellner,* ed. S. Wank et al. [Santa Barbara/Oxford: ABC-Clio, 1988], 236).

[117] Stanislav Sousedík, "Böhmische Barockphilosophie," in Seibt, *Bohemia sacra,* 443.

[118] Oldrich J. Blažíček, *Rokoko a konec Baroku v Čechách* (Prague: Matice Česká-Orbis, 1948).

Joseph II's austere tomb, we may also consider his above-ground monument, Vienna's Allgemeines Krankenhaus (General Hospital), a monument to this new aesthetic that had no sympathy either with the sensuality and the ornamentation of the Baroque or with its otherworldly objectives.[119]

The suppression was both a result of and a contributing factor to the decline and extinction of the Bohemian Baroque. Although an eighteenth-century Jesuit might not have subscribed to the Baroque mentality, such a mentality could not have survived apart from an institution that had so long supported it. The Jesuits had elevated, legitimated, and perfected the Baroque in Bohemia, helping it to attain a level of development unsurpassed anywhere in the world. They had struggled to maintain its inherent contradictions and had created a more complex cultural entity out of these contradictions. Yet the tensions and contradictions within their order made it clear that even under optimal external conditions, the Society would have been hard pressed after midcentury to maintain the Baroque aesthetic and worldview with some of its most talented members striking out in new directions. The pressures of secularism and empiricism, however, along with the declining support for outward manifestations of piety, when combined with changing attitudes about death and the body, marked out the Baroque for extinction, and with it the unique culture of the pre-suppression Society.[120]

---

[119] Kaufmann, *Court, Cloister, and City*, 417.

[120] Space does not permit a full discussion of Baroque attitudes toward death, but it should be noted that believers often regarded death, not as a obstacle to be minimized and held at a distance, but as a liberator and a guide to reunion with God (F. W. Wentzlaff-Eggebert, *Deutsche Mystik zwischen Mitteralter und Neuzeit* [Berlin: Walter de Gruyter, 1969], 196). Expressions of this view of death are most prevalent among seventeenth-century mystics, such as Jakob Balde (1604–68), but are often detected as well in obituary notices of eighteenth-century Prague Jesuits.

chapter four

AMONG THE PEOPLE

A good symbol is the best argument, and is a missionary to persuade thousands.

—Ralph Waldo Emerson, *Letters and Social Aims*

This worldly, emotional, anti-intellectual kind of religion . . .

—Anthony Blunt, *Artistic Theory in Italy, 1450–1600*

Background

Until 1754 the Province of Bohemia included the historical territories of Bohemia, Moravia, and Silesia, all of which had been under the scepter of the Habsburgs since the first half of the sixteenth century. To appreciate the goals and the work of the Society in these territories, we must devote some study to these lands themselves, examining their relationship to the larger political unit of the Habsburg lands and to that shadowy entity, the Holy Roman Empire.

The lands of the Crown of St. Wenceslaus, as these territories were traditionally known, formed an important yet at times precariously held component of the lands of the House of Habsburg. These lands in general, and Bohemia in particular, constituted a kind of "internal colony" that the Habsburgs had ruled continually for centuries but nonetheless regarded in a very different light from the so-called Hereditary Lands *(Erblande)*, namely, the Austrias, Tyrol, Carniola, and Carinthia, which had been in its

Portions of this chapter appeared in a different form in "Antonín Koniáš, the Jesuits of Prague, and the Extirpation of Heresy in Bohemia," in *Proceedings of the Conference on Universities and Heresy*, held at Trinity College, Dublin, November 5–6, 1999, ed. Helga Robinson-Hammerstein. I also would like to thank members of the Faculty of Divinity, the University of Glasgow, for their comments and suggestions following a presentation of this material.

possession since the fourteenth century. The lands of the Crown of St. Wenceslaus were, in the first place, originally controlled by an early rival to the Habsburgs for the crown of the Holy Roman Empire, the Premyslids. Even long after the Premyslids had been eliminated as competitors for the imperial crown, the Bohemian lands had posed first a threat and then a challenge to the Habsburgs, in terms both of the dynasty's claims to the imperial crown and of the Habsburg mission to defend the Catholic Church.

After the death of Louis, king of both Hungary and Bohemia, in the disastrous battle of Mohács in 1526, control of the territories had passed to Ferdinand, brother of Charles V and later emperor in his own right. Yet the Bohemian Estates proved difficult to control, and the staunchly Catholic Habsburgs found themselves challenged at every turn by a populace with strong Protestant leanings as well as an immemorial conviction that theirs was a distinctive identity within a predominantly German empire.

The response of the Habsburgs to the rebellious Bohemian upper classes after 1618 was drastic: a transfer of ownership of land on a scale unparalleled in continental European history.[1] The consequences of this transfer of land ownership continued to dominate life in rural Bohemia throughout the eighteenth century and remained in the forefront of consciousness of Czech historians in the nineteenth, contributing to the legend of the *doba temna* (period of darkness).[2] The upheavals of the Thirty Years' War, the subjugation of the Czech-speaking population, the expulsion of Bohemian religious dissidents and intellectuals, and the encroaching night of the *doba temna* are points of cultural reference taught to every Czech schoolchild today, yet the role of the Jesuits in these events is not as clear-cut as it has often been portrayed.

As we have seen, the influence of the Jesuits in these events was great; the emergence of Czech-speaking Jesuits such as Balbín and Kadlinský shows that the involvement of the Society was more complex than merely that of a collaborator with an occupying power, for the identification of many seventeenth-century Jesuits with Czech culture is unmistakable. Nevertheless, there is ample evidence that in the seventeenth and early eighteenth centuries, many Bohemians felt themselves to be under the oppressive boot heel of an alien, occupying power, and regarded the Jesuits—as members of an institution, rather than as individual teachers,

---

[1] William Monter points out that after 1620 half of the one thousand landed estates of Bohemia changed hands, including 275 of the largest estates. This transfer of property was perhaps the greatest Europe had seen since the time of William the Conqueror (Monter, *Ritual, Myth, and Magic in Early Modern Europe*, 142).

[2] Tomáš Bílek, *Dějiny konfiscaci v Čechách po r. 1618* (Prague: V Kommissi u Františka Rivnace, 1883).

preachers, or writers—as collaborators with the oppressors. That many of these Jesuits were themselves ethnic Czechs only complicates this picture.[3]

Any assessment of the Jesuit relationship to the general population during the second half of the eighteenth century must therefore take into account the long-standing antagonisms and frustrations of the Bohemian people and the special economic and political difficulties that the Bohemian lands faced.[4] At the same time, the bonds of sympathy between Czech-speaking Jesuits and the oppressed Czech-speaking majority, which had been apparent in the seventeenth century, were much less evident in the eighteenth-century Society, although they would emerge again after the suppression in the works of Dobrovský and Cornova and more obliquely in the writings of many other former Jesuits.

The Society of Jesus, as it functioned in the Habsburg lands in the eighteenth century, must be understood, not as a monolithic organization, but as a worldwide religious order that within its hierarchical structure operated in three overlapping modes.[5] These modes, a natural consequence of the implementation of ideas set forth in the founding documents of the Society, can be described as the bureaucratic, the evangelistic, and the cultural. Each of these modes played a role in the development of Jesuit institutions as the Society strove to adapt itself to local conditions; but they might not have been identified as such by the Bohemian Jesuits themselves or their contemporaries, since both internally and externally the Society was widely perceived as having a single, unified mission that informed all of its activities.

The Society of Jesus originated in the passionately held religious convictions of its founder, St. Ignatius of Loyola, and his friends, who sought the blessing of the Pope to undertake the work of "caring for souls." Yet despite Ignatius's great energy and activity, he could not foresee every situation that would confront the Society as its mission expanded, nor did he ever believe that he could do so. Still, there remained the need to codify the rules and customs that developed in the Society with the passage of time.

---

[3] Data on the ethnicity of Jesuits are difficult to interpret, since neither geographical origin nor language mastery (the categories usually identified) is a sure indicator. After the debacle of White Mountain, however, it seems beyond doubt that there was a large minority, perhaps even a majority, of Bohemian Jesuits who were native speakers of Czech (S. Harrison Thomson, *Czechoslovakia in European History* [Princeton: Princeton University Press, 1943], 210).

[4] For the impact of famines, common in Bohemia throughout the eighteenth century, on peasant culture, see *Famine in Peasant Societies,* by Ronald E. Seavoy (New York: Greenwood Press, 1986), 7–30. The Bohemian famine of 1771–72 is discussed in John D. Post, "Nutritional Status and Mortality in Eighteenth Century Europe," in *Hunger in History,* ed. Lucile F. Newman (Oxford: Blackwell, 1990), 267.

[5] John Patrick Donnelly, S.J., "Religious Orders of Men, Especially the Society of Jesus," in *Catholicism in Early Modern History: A Guide to Research,* ed. John W. O'Malley, S.J. (St. Louis: Center for Reformation Research, 1988), 147–62.

This codification took its ultimate form in two documents, the *Constitutions,* and the *Ratio studiorum.*

Examining these documents today, the reader is struck by the flexibility built into their language, and the degree to which individual Jesuits carrying out the assignments described in them were (at least implicitly) allowed some freedom in their interactions with lay persons.[6] The instructor especially had found much to commend in the *Ratio.* Its goals were both easily discerned and relevant to the culture from which his students typically emerged.[7] The detail and structure of each of the documents, however, also lent themselves to a more rigid, bureaucratic interpretation, and thus to a more systematic and centralized understanding of the mission of the Society; thereby they fostered a tension between adaptability and conformity that dominates much of the Society's undertakings during the period under consideration here. The distinctly bureaucratic mode of operation is constantly in evidence in the records of the eighteenth-century Bohemian Province. The practice of moving Jesuit instructors from site to site could potentially damage the long-term effectiveness of its teachers; coupled with the rigidity of the curriculum of the *Ratio* relative to the changing conception of natural science, this loss of stability placed the Society increasingly at a disadvantage as the eighteenth century wore on.

Other elements of the bureaucratic mode of operation did not work in the Society's favor. Superficially, the uniformity of the Society's standard reporting procedure, namely, the *Litteræ annuæ,* promoted efficiency and aided the Jesuit central administration in Rome to compile data. But if we carefully examine the *Litteræ* composed over a period of many years, we see that the very uniformity adopted by the writers of the *Litteræ* posed difficulties, and not simply for historians trying to reconstruct events centuries later. The steadfastly triumphalist flavor of the accounts, the stereotypical characterization of the people with whom the Jesuits interacted, and especially the conversion and repentance experiences—as all of these are recounted, they mask the diversity of local conditions and the individuality of

---

[6] Suggestive of this level of interaction is the admonition in the *Ratio* that instructors should seek the reactions of their students to their teaching or, as it might be put today, "feedback" (*Ratio,* no. 25). M.-E. Ducreux has noted that Koniáš could adapt his message for crypto-Protestants, who preferred to read the written Scripture as their ancestors had done (M.-E. Ducreux, "Reading unto Death: Books and Readers in Eighteenth-Century Bohemia," in *The Culture of Print: Power and the Uses of Print in Early Modern Europe,* ed. Roger Chartier, trans. Lydia G. Cochrane [Princeton: Princeton University Press, 1989], 201).

[7] As Daniel Schlafly Jr. has noted, "The primary emphasis, especially on the lower levels, was acquisition of what was called *eloquentia,* or facility in reading, writing and speaking Latin." For more than a century after the publication of the *Ratio,* a high degree of fluency in Latin was in fact a most useful skill in most professions, and even of value in trade and commerce (Daniel Schlafly, Jr., "The *Ratio Studiorum* on Alien Shores: Jesuit Colleges in St. Petersburg and Georgetown," *Revista Portuguesa de filosofia* 55, no. 3 [1999]: 254).

specific cases. The talents and skills of individual Jesuits were submerged in the reports of their activities, to surface only occasionally, often in a stereotypical form, in their obituary notices.

Nor was this the only problem. The penchant for statistical reporting that the Jesuits in Bohemia and in other provinces demonstrated actually yielded less information than might seem to be the case. For instance, although in 1766 the Church of St. Ignatius in Prague reported 28,900 "communicantes" during the year, it is impossible to determine how this figure should be interpreted.[8] The relation of this number to the total population of the city or even of the neighborhood of the church is unclear, since each communicant might be represented many times in the total. This reliance on "body counts" and on the documentation of important personages present at Jesuit-sponsored events points to a deeper weakness in the institutional culture of the Society as it carried out its missions in Bohemia. In the overwhelming majority of cases, individual Jesuits in missions and schools probably established genuine, warm relations with the communities in which they worked. Yet the educational program and mission of the Society, as well as the thrust of the reporting system, followed a routinized approach that ran the risk of becoming impersonal, rigid, and off-putting, something quite the opposite of the encounters envisioned by Ignatius. Book burners such as Fr. Koniáš may have damaged the reputation of the Bohemian Society in contemporary Rome and among later historians, but a statistical approach to evangelizing damaged the mission of the Society from within.

For the Jesuit bureaucracy that received and filed these reports, the picture of steady success (occasionally punctuated by descriptions of natural calamities or the hardships brought on by war) belied the fluid and often unstable situation in Bohemia, where the archbishop of Prague might seem to favor the notoriously atheist Prussian king and his allies, and a bishop's throne might go unoccupied for long periods of time.[9] It is equally evident that the means employed to report conversions made no allowances for backsliders, although the more readily detectable return of converted Jews to their original religion was reported.[10] And, of course, statistics on conversions conveyed little or nothing about the religious understanding or commitment of those converted, which, in view of the shortage of priests

[8] NK, 2L/23/25F, *Litt. An. Prov. Boh. 1766*, folio 422v.

[9] Such was the case in Hradec Králové, which experienced rapid turnovers of authority and was without a bishop from 1760 to 1775; this was also one of the flash points of the peasant rebellion of 1775 (Svátek, *Dějiny*, vol. 6, fasc. 2, p. 148).

[10] Note, however, the case of the "perfidious wife of Kozak the Gypsy," described in "Missions and Schools of the Jesuits in Transylvania and Eastern Hungary, 1700-1773," in *Lesestoffe und kulturelles Niveau des niedrigen Klerus: Jesuiten und die nationalen Kulturverhältnisse*, ed. I. Monok and P. Ötvös (Szeged: ScriptumRT, 2001), 106.

and schools in rural Bohemia, must have varied a great deal. The leaders of the Jesuit missions, motivated as they no doubt were by the need to demonstrate the value of the Society at a time when it was increasingly coming under attack, continued to employ a mode of reporting established over a century earlier, expressed in a formulaic Baroque Latinity and vocabulary not always well suited to the task at hand. In so doing, they may have failed to alert their superiors to possible threats to the Jesuit mission in the field.

In the parish missions of the Society, when several priests spent short periods of time preaching and hearing confessions in various small towns, we find the essence of the second mode of Jesuit activities, the evangelistic, since much of the Society's mission work was undertaken at a time when the missionary was far more effective than the often nonexistent rural parish priest.[11] Even in locations where a parish priest could be found, the confraternities created and maintained by the Society promoted social cohesion and doctrinal fidelity as they complemented and prolonged the mission work of the Jesuits.[12] The mission to bring men to a knowledge and love of God was even more fundamental to the Society than its proclivity towards bureaucratization and formalization. All the activities of the Jesuits were supposed to have as their end bringing men closer to God, but some undertakings advanced this objective more directly than others.

The career of Josef Stepling, which was almost entirely devoted to scientific studies, could be justified by arguing that greater understanding of natural phenomena and mathematical expressions of reality lead inevitably to a greater love and understanding of God. Whether this was actually the motivation of Jesuits engaged in these activities is now extremely difficult to determine, just as it was in the eighteenth century. The means by which Jesuits sought to bring about this love and understanding might vary greatly as well, with a figure such as Fr. Koniáš relying more upon fear and theatricality, while another Jesuit preacher might focus more on the forgiving love of God.[13] Even the Spiritual Exercises themselves, the basis of all Jesuit

---

[11] See Louis Châtellier, *The Religion of the Poor: Rural Missions in Europe and the Foundation of Modern Catholicism,* trans. Brian Pearce (Cambridge: Cambridge University Press, 1997), 205. The lack of parish priests was widely noted by contemporaries, and may be put in the context of the "profound catastrophe" of the period following White Mountain (Jerzy Kloczowski, "Les slaves dans la chretienté aux XIVe et XVIIe siècles," in *The Common Christian Roots of the European Nations: General Sessions* [Florence: Le Monnier, 1982], 124).

[12] Prague could count twenty confraternities in 1769, of which the most eminent, the "Italian," was lead by an Italian Jesuit who may have fled to Bohemia after the expulsion of the Society from Naples (Antonius Podlaha, ed., *Relationes super statu ecclesiæ et archdiocesis Pragensis ad S. Congregationem Concilii ab Archiepiscopis Pragensibus factæ a. 1759–1781* [Prague: Cyrillo-Methodìjská knihtiskárna V. Kotruba. Nákladem vlastním, 1908], 36).

[13] See MZAB, Cerroniho sbírka, II, 345, 8; Podlaha, "Dodatky," 324. We should note that Koniáš's vision of the horrors of hell had a long pedigree within Jesuit homiletics. A century earlier Paolo Segneri (1624–94), a famed Italian Jesuit, had published sermons that described in

spirituality, might be presented to the lay public in a variety of ways: during the eighteenth century the fathers frequently compressed the thirty-day course of the Exercises into an accelerated three-day experience, which surely differed substantially from the longer version.[14]

The linking of these apparently disparate undertakings and modes of presentation of the religious encounter may seem forced and artificial to us today; but to many if not all Jesuits and to devout Catholics of the age, the contradictions and tensions would not necessarily have been obvious. What unites these varying expressions within the apostolates of the Society is the firm conviction that the claims of the Church are true despite its many opponents. This unwavering belief in the truth of revealed religion was in accord with attitudes that predated the Josephinian reforms, though they were already starting to face opposition during the Theresian era.[15] The positions of individual Jesuits, in Bohemia and elsewhere, vis-à-vis the commitment to revealed religion, like their individual understanding of the role of scientific inquiry, are veiled by the official language used by the Society and, as in the case of Stepling, by the caution individual Jesuits needed to employ when making public their ideas on any topic touching on religion.

The Nature of the Missions

The activities of the Jesuits of Bohemia, and of their colleagues in many other venues, were not limited to strictly educational undertakings conducted within the confines of a school, or to preaching in a church. The mobility of the Society and its commitment to "the care of souls" gave impetus to the Bohemian Province and to the Jesuits of Prague to reach out to surrounding communities.[16] Thus, in this section the term "Jesuit community of Prague" will be extended somewhat to include those Jesuits who had connections to Prague, but who during at least half of their careers worked in various mission settings; for if we do not take these activities into

terrifying detail the torments of those sent to hell. The appeal to fear of punishment in the afterlife was not the sole property of Jesuits, of course; indeed, it was typical of much Catholic devotional literature of the Baroque era (Delumeau, *Sin and Fear,* 379).

[14] *The New Catholic Encyclopedia,* 1967, s.v. "Spiritual Exercises," by J. Lewis.

[15] A historian sympathetic to Catholicism has characterized Josephinism as "a latent decline from a revealed religion to a natural religion" (H. Reiser, *Der Geist des Josephinismus und sein Fortleben,* cited in *The Church in the Age of Absolutism and Enlightenment,* vol. 6 of *History of the Church,* ed. Hubert Jedin, trans. Gunther J. Holst [London: Burns and Oates, 1981], 473).

[16] For example, the missions in Stará Boleslav (Alt Bunzlau) and Nová Boleslav (Neu Bunzlau), which were listed in the *Litteræ annuæ* of the Old City of Prague; and even Jesuits whose principal assignment was within the city of Prague might work for a time in missions in smaller communities.

account, we will fail to sketch an accurate picture of the life of the Prague Jesuit community. The city of Prague will still draw our attention, however, for it is there that the Jesuits not only worked within their schools and the university but also interacted with the public in the nine churches entrusted to them.[17]

The overall Jesuit mission in Bohemia was multifaceted. Although the majority of the population was nominally Catholic, their ecclesiastical and political loyalties were often in flux. The Jesuits reported these projects in detail in the annual reports they compiled and sent to Rome; in fact, these form the largest component of these reports. Originating from a region of low literacy where Catholicism had long been the only officially tolerated form of Christianity, the *Litteræ* not infrequently contain tantalizing hints about the religious beliefs of the people with whom the Society came in contact. For example, a list of "conversos" (converts) from 1767 included the entry "ab Husso 1," while elsewhere in the report for the same year is recorded "conversi . . . a secta Anabaptistarum 1 . . . a schismate Græcorum 2."[18] Three years later another category of heretic is recorded: among the "conversi" is listed "a secta libertina 1."[19] A stray Arian or syncretist might also turn up in Prague or in the countryside.[20]

How the Jesuits defined or identified quiescent Hussite beliefs more than three hundred years after the death of Jan Hus, or how they determined that a convert had been part of a band of libertines is not clear, but the fathers certainly suspected the presence of such beliefs. We may suppose that when the fathers encountered a nonbeliever whom they rescued "ab Alcorano Persarum" in the Silesian city of Kladsko (Glatz), they were able to identify the offending belief accurately, although how a Muslim came to reside in this provincial city is unknown.[21] The frequent references to the presence of "atheists" in the hinterlands of Bohemia, moreover, raises questions about the type of interactions that took place between the Jesuits and the convert.[22] Anyone admitting to atheism incurred real danger, and before the Patent of Toleration was issued, only the most convinced (or

---

[17] These were the Churches of St. Salvator and of St. Clement, both located at the Clementinum, the Churches of St. Aloyisius, St. Eligius, and Bethlehem in the Staré Mesto, the Churches of St. Ignatius, St. Xavier, and Corpus Christi in the Nové Mesto, and the Church of St. Nicolaus in Malá Strana. The endowment of each of these is reported in *Summarische Abstract aus denen pro Ano. 1778 eingelegten Rechnungen deren Exjesuiten Kirchen im Königreich Boheim* SÚA Exjesuitica, F3/1/701a.

[18] (Enumerating converts from Hus, the Anabaptists, and the schismatic Greeks), NK, 2L 23/19, *Litt. An. Prov. Boh. 1767*, folios 9v, 10v.

[19] NK, 23/19, *Litt. An.. Prov. Boh. 1770*, folio 213r.

[20] NK, 1287 MS XXIII C105/15, *An. Prov. Boh. 1762*, folios 256v, 258v.

[21] Ibid., folio 257v.

[22] NK, 1288 MS XXIII C105/15, *An. Prov. Boh. 1761*, folio 202v.

foolhardy) would have done so. Jesuit missionaries, however, may have concluded on their own that the object of their attention held atheistic beliefs.

Other designations recorded in the *Litteræ* are equally hard to assess. The listing under the "Conversi a Calvino" of one individual described as from the "liberorum Muratorum[?]" (from the free Masons), remains obscure.[23] Jesuits assigned to the missions were constantly on the lookout for heresy, and even more so for heretical books; for these might fall into the hands of the innocent faithful or those recently converted who did not understand the dangers lurking in writings that defended their preconversion beliefs.[24] The number of books confiscated in a single haul might run into the many hundreds.[25] Books thus seized might be pitched into a bonfire in the middle of the largest courtyard of the Clementinum (where, ironically enough, after the suppression, Jesuit records would also be consigned to the flames), or they might be burned where they had been impounded.[26] The Society was also prepared to seize printing presses, should they be the source of books featuring content that was either dubiously moral or heretical.[27]

In so doing, the Jesuits were supporting the measure of the Prague Consistory, which as late as 1760 was still expressing concern about the

---

[23] NK, 1287 MS XXIII C105/15, *Litt. An Prov. Boh. 1765,* folio 423v. Possibly this is a reference to the Freemasons.

[24] For example, NK, 2L 23/19, *Litt. An. Prov. Boh. 1767,* folio 10v. See also Vavák, *Paměti,* 1,2, 56–58.

[25] ". . . scatenentia [hæreses] sordibusque aliis infecta volumina conquisita 1479 et ultra" (The books spewing forth heresies and other filth numbered more than 1,479) (NK, 23/19, *Lit An. Prov. Boh. 1769* folio 171r.).

[26] "Bibliotheca integra hæresim olens combusta" (The entire library, reeking of heresy, was burned) (NK, 1287 MS XXIII C105/15, *Litt. An. Prov. Boh. 1762,* folio 257v). Civil authorities had recommended that book burning be discontinued, but the practice persisted until shortly before the suppression. For the background on book burnings earlier in the century, see Tomáš Bílek, *Reformace katolická neboli obnovení náboženství katolického v království českém po bitvě bělohorské,* 276 ff.

[27] In 1767 a "typographia" (print shop) producing "minus honestos amores" (less-than-proper love stories) was confiscated (NK, 2L 23/19, *Litt. An. Prov. Boh. 1767,* folio 41v). This account appears under the category of the "Archiepiscopal Missions," and as such may have involved non-Jesuit clergy (see n. 39 below). The *Amatoria* seized and burned in 1765 might refer to the poem by Ovid; if so, it would be the single documented instance of a classical work being seized by the Bohemian Society during this period (NK, 1287, *An. Prov. Boh. 1765,* folio 372v). Locally produced pornographic or salacious literature was extremely rare in the Habsburg lands before Joseph II lifted censorship, so we can only wonder whether the publications seized in many other instances were actually the more scabrous works of Ovid or some other classical Latin author.

importation of heretical works into the kingdom.[28] Books of "magic, incantations, and the illusions of superstition" were also targets.[29] Symptomatic of the widespread fusion of Catholic Baroque piety and other less orthodox practices was a "Zodiac" used by pilgrims on their way to Sacro-Montana, the Holy Mountain near Příbam. Along with a work known as *Patient Job* in Czech, written by Hieronymus Drenellus, the *Zodiac* was seized by the Jesuits in 1761 in the Nové Město of Prague.[30] Amulets, popular among Christians and Jews alike, were seized on occasion.[31] The Jesuits even seized and destroyed loose pages of presumably hand-written prayers and incantations.[32] Any object that seemed to encourage occult activities or promoted miraculous events not sanctioned by the Church was likely to be confiscated, even (or perhaps especially) if the owner was a person of consequence.[33] An "archiatrus superstitiosus" (superstitious physician) was relieved of a divining rod used to find hidden treasures and other things, and he was forbidden to use a small bone to work his spells.[34] Yet, even though the civil authorities supported the Jesuits throughout the Habsburg lands, it seems unlikely that the Jesuits' attempts to control the flow of heretical materials did much to curb the enthusiasm of many Czechs for this sort of material.[35] Persecution and oppression bred martyrs and further resistance, something that the

---

[28] "[Rumor fert] . . . libros hæreticos in utraque vernacula tum Bohemica tum Germanica recentibus typis editos in Regnum inferri" (it was rumored that recently edited Czech- and German-language heretical books were being brought into the kingdom; quoted in Kerner, *Bohemia,* 312). For the seizing of heretical literature throughout the eighteenth century, see M.-E. Ducreux, "Kniha a kacírství, způsob četby a knižní politka v Čechách doby baroka," *Literarní archiv PNP,* 27 [1994]: 61–89).

[29] NK, 23/19, *Litt. An. Prov. Boh. 1770,* folio 271v.

[30] NK, 1288 MS XXIII C105/15, *Litt. An. Prov. Boh. 1761,* folio 211v.

[31] NK, 1287 MS XXIII C105/15, *Litt. An Prov. Boh. 1762,* passim.

[32] "Five hundred pages of suspect prayers" *(500 paginas precibus suspectis conscriptas)* were burned in Kladsko (Glatz) (NK, 1288 MS XXIII C105/15, *An. Prov. Boh. 1761,* folio 203v). Manuscripts were often mentioned in the accounts of interrogation of suspected heretics from rural areas.

[33] The exact nature of occult materials circulating in Bohemia during this period is difficult to determine; far less work has been done on this topic than on the occult in Hungary. The primary sources that have been identified are mostly from a much later date. A manuscript recounting a special prayer for "good luck," identified in the Czechoslovakian State General Archives, dates from only 1895, although its oral antecedents are far older (Antonín Robek, *Lidové zdroje národního obrození* [Prague: Universita Karlova, 1974], 30, 153).

[34] NK, MS XXIII 105/15, *An. Prov. Boh. 1765,* folio 372v.

[35] One historian has even claimed, without proof, that in the previous century "Jesuit missions had probably made more Protestants than they had converted in Bohemia" (W. R. Ward, *Christianity under the Ancien Régime, 1648–1789* [Cambridge: Cambridge University Press, 1999], 185). Whether or not such a claim could be substantiated, the perception that the Society's efforts were counterproductive can be traced back into the nineteenth century and suggest that the missions and related activities were long ago viewed as failures.

Jesuits should have anticipated, for they had been beset by persecution and oppression elsewhere throughout their own history. Successfully or not, as long as they could, Jesuits spared no effort in attempting to regulate many aspects of daily life for the people of Bohemia, something for which the writers of the *Litteræ annuæ* saw no reason to apologize.[36]

While these reports meticulously discussed personnel and budget matters, often their allusions are more revealing than their outright statements. A typical example is a note included in the annual *Epitome historiæ* (summary of events) of the province for the years 1755: "In missione Archi-Episcopali a Judaismo 1, ab Apostasia 20."[37] Here we have evidence that on this occasion continual efforts on the part of the Society and its allies to convert Jews made some converts but could not prevent far more of them from reverting to their original faith. Backsliders were liable to appear in other quarters, too.[38] A "Missio de poenitenia" (perhaps what is now known as a parish mission) preached in the countryside in 1765 succeeded in bringing 104 "apostates from orthodox religion" back to the fold; how many apostates did not return is, as usual, not reported, but the number may well have been large.[39]

The reconversion of apostates and backsliders is a recurring feature of most missionary undertakings. Granted that we need not be surprised that the Society's work in Bohemia experienced these setbacks, still, these meager results must have had serious consequences for the Jesuits themselves. When we ponder the extant records recounting the labors of the Jesuit fathers, we can well imagine the frustration that was theirs as they dealt with a people so prone to recidivism.

Conversions from other faiths were also important, and the Society carefully distinguished converts from Lutheranism, who were considered to have received baptism, from "Baptizati" converted from Calvinism, who in

[36] Confessional catalogs compiled by Fr. Joannes Wydra, S.J., in the parish of Uhošt, near Tuchomerice, in 1717 show that the moral conduct of parishioners was noted and found its way into permanent records; for example, one Anna Kukowkin is described as living a "scandalous life" *(vitam scandalosam)* (*Zpovední Seznamy Arcidiecese Pražské z r. 1671–1725*, ed. J. V. Šimák, 3 vols. Díl 3, sv. 1: Plzensko a Loketsko [Prague: Nákladem hist. Spolku za pomoci minister. školství a národní osvěty, 1935], 423).

[37] *Epitome historiæ Provinciæ Bohemiæ Soc. Jesu ad annum 1758, 1759, 1760,* Strahov D D III 33; loose leaf in volume. In Olomouc in 1761, the ratio was one Jewish convert to twenty redeemed apostates.

[38] Ducreux reports that one Václav Polák relapsed and was reconverted no fewer than seven times ("Reading unto Death," 223).

[39] NK, 1287 MS XXIII C105/15, *An. Prov. Boh. 1765*, folio 387r. The "Missio de pœnitentia" differed from the "Missio archiepiscopalis," which also appears in the *Litteræ,* in that the former was an entirely Jesuit enterprise, while the archiepiscopal mission involved other clergy. I am indebted to Dr. Ducreux for pointing out this distinction.

the eyes of the Society had not been validly baptized.[40] Reports of other pastoral activities are harder to assess. In 1760 we read of an attempted suicide that was averted, an adulterer who reformed his ways, and a woman living with an "Illustrissimo" who had been persuaded to return home and behave herself ("in gremium suum et mores").[41] The general outlines of these reports are so formulaic and resemble so closely the accounts of Jesuit missions elsewhere that the reader may be tempted to put less than total credence in them, a credence further tested when one reads of the "invisible hand" *(invisibili manu)* that saved a would-be suicide's life.[42]

Moreover, these accounts, detailed in some aspects though they were, provide few clues as to their sources. Given the sanctity of the confessional and the Jesuits' enthusiasm for St. Jan Nepomucký, who supposedly underwent torture and martyrdom rather than violate the seal of confession, the sources of these stories must have been well-publicized testimony from those who experienced the miraculous events, or else hearsay. Each possible source poses problems; public declarations might be influenced by social pressures, and hearsay is, of course, extremely unreliable. The lack of independent corroboration compels us to concede that these second-hand accounts may in some instances reflect the values and experiences of the Jesuits who recorded them rather than of the individuals described therein.

Occasionally, however, the account of Jesuit intervention in the personal lives of sinners is so detailed and idiosyncratic as to persuade the reader that the report conveys at least what the reporter believed to correspond to the facts. A shocking case of incest in Hradec Králové was presumably resolved when the abuser and the victim, his daughter, both went to a Jesuit missionary.[43] Likewise, the 1760 case of a pregnant woman who, abandoned by her lover, contemplated drowning herself. How she was eventually saved is presented in portentous Baroque language that might

---

[40] A typical entry is found in the *Litteræ annuæ* of the collegium at the Clementinum for 1767: "Maria Josepha Barabara Straubin, Helveta Ottwillana Sectæ Calvinianæ prius addicta, nec legitime baptizata" (formerly a Calvinist and not legitimately baptized) (NK, 23/17, folio 181r); see also folio 181v for separate listings of "conversi a Luthero" from "baptizati." The reasons for the distinction made between Lutheran and Calvinist converts with regard to their status as baptized is problematic. It may be that Jesuit writers lumped Anabaptists together with Calvinists, although the rigor with which the Society trained its priests to function as controversialists makes this unlikely. The more probable explanation is that the structure of Lutheranism, while still abhorrent to Jesuits because it had abandoned confession and most other sacraments, adhered more closely to the Society's understanding of the sacraments.

[41] Strahov, D A III, 32, *Epitome historiæ Provincicæ Bohemiæ 1760*, folios 7r–7v.

[42] Strahov, D A III, 32, *Epitome historiæ Collegii S. J. ad S. Ignatii Pragæ ad annum 1761*, folio 80v.

[43] "Quidam, per longum tempus abutebatur incestuose filiam, permotus in confessione ipse pœnitens filiam quoque poenitentiam adduxit ad Missionarium" (Strahov, D A III 33, *Epitome historiæ Collegii Soc. Iesu Reginæ Hradeii Annus 1758*).

suggest personal contact with agents of the underworld.[44] The instance of a woman of Prague engaged in a "nefandum commercium . . . cum cælibe" (shameful intercourse with a celibate) who was assisted by a Jesuit to repent seems plausible enough; in fact, the reader might even wonder whether the "cælebs" so discreetly referred to might actually have been a member of the Society—though there is no evidence that he was.[45]

Another tale fraught with sexual implications recounts the conversion to a good life of a woman and the young ladies whom she had induced to sin with her.[46] As is often the case, the subsequent history of the characters in this drama is not reported. A more explicit instance of repentance and reform from sexual misconduct involves many "slaves of Venus" who after many years of depraved behavior, ceased to ply their libidinous trade.[47] Commerce with the devil himself and the danger of suicide are reported in the same context as more routine carnal lapses, and indeed it may be that these phenomena frequently occurred in tandem.[48] These reports are not presented in a salacious fashion, nor is the role of the Jesuits in bringing about a positive outcome given undue attention. Nevertheless, the sexual content of these accounts calls attention to how eroticism played an important role in the Baroque religious culture of eighteenth-century central Europe.[49] Bear in mind that this was not an exclusively Catholic phenome-

[44] "Optatus Alastor Stygius comparere abnuerat, mortem undis sibi consciscere parabat." The circumstances producing this pregnancy are described cryptically as "nefario concubitu" (NK, 1416 MSXXIII 105/18, *Annales Prov. Boh. 1760*, folio 11r).

[45] Strahov, D. A. III 33, *Epitome historiæ Collegii S. J. ad S. Ignatii Pragæ,* folio 7r.

[46] "Præterea mulier, quæ suis incontenta sceleribus, innocentes virgines iisdem contaminare invitatu suo ausa est, aspirante Divinā gratiā, cum seductis a peccandi licentia ad honestatem Christiano homine dignam revocata" (Strahov, D A III 33, *Epitome historiæ Domus Professæ ad S. Nicolaum, Anno 1759*, folio 4v).

[47] [Comperit] "pænitentiam quoque egere quamplurima Veneris mancipia post exactos nefandum in modum complures annos, quo in genere notasse duntaxat sufficiat quindecim, diocesis in locis domos, in quibus personæ libidini propositæ alebantur" (NK, 2L 23/19, *Litt. An. Prov. Boh. 1767,* folio 37r).

[48] Described is a sacrilegiously pregnant woman who had twice sold her soul to the devil, but when he did not appear at her call, she determined to fling herself into the Vltava: "Alia, quæ in sacrilego utero gerebat, eo delapsa est, ut bis animum suum Diabolo sanguine proprio subscripserit, quia tamen advocatus comparere renuebat, vitam sibi alio modo eripere firmum, fixumque habuit, quo fine etiam præter fluentem Moldavam accessit, animo se in fluvium præcipitandi" (Strahov, D A III 33, *Epitome historiæ Domus Profess. ad S. Nicolaum Anno 1760*, folio 7r).

[49] Promoters of the cult of relics understood how the charged emotional atmosphere in which the relic was displayed exposed the faithful to the risk of sexual responses to this religious event. The recommended solution to this problem was to segregate men and women, particularly when the relic was displayed at night. Jesuit records from Bohemia do not indicate whether this recommendation was followed (Petrus Moretto, *De ritu ostensionis sacrarum reliquiarum* [Rome, 1721], 124).

non: erotic overtones interlace even the Protestant documents generated by the Count Nikolaus Ludwig von Zinzendorf (1700–1760).[50]

On other occasions there was less need for secrecy, and the names of the individuals converted or rescued were reported with pride, especially if they were prominent people. When in 1768 Samuel Machel, the son of a Lutheran minister who had pursued medical studies in Dresden and Halle (the latter being the earliest and most outstanding alternative to Latin-based Jesuit higher education in the empire) became a convert, the *Annales* of that year triumphantly recorded the details of how the youth spurned his family and friends to embrace the truth.[51] A decade earlier, the unnamed daughter of one "Prænobilis D. Henricus Wolff" appears to have been in danger of damaging her reputation ("in manifesto amittendi visa periculo constituta"), but a Jesuit father encouraged prayer and penance before a silver crucifix, and thus saved the day.[52] An aspect of these reports that we find striking is the frequency with which Christian women—and Jewish women as well—were called back to pious living. Once again, women are vulnerable and victimized, either by human or superhuman agencies; once again, Jesuits help mediate the divine intervention and bring the story to a happy ending.[53]

Sometimes the recorded account has the flavor of a ghost story, or at least that of a highly moralistic sermon seasoned with elements of local folklore. One night in 1756 Joannes Wolfgang Fritz, a citizen of the New Town of Prague, was awakened, along with three of his children, by a loud voice that called out in the middle of the night. He soon discovered that his home was haunted by a twofold ghost *(duplex spectrum)* that could be banished only with specially blessed water, images of the saints, and prayers.[54] Dangers of the natural world also figured in Jesuit reports. As late as 1767 we find accounts of pictures of St. Ignatius being invoked along with relics of other saints in hope of preventing lightning from striking a building, a dramatic contrast to the experiments being simultaneously conducted by

---

[50] Many twentieth-century commentators have characterized Zinzendorf's ecstatic meditations on Christ as being suffused with a subconscious eroticism (William A. Clebach, *Christianity in European History* [New York: Oxford University Press, 1979], 216–22).

[51] NK, 23/19, *Litt. An Prov. Boh. 1768*, folio 113r. The theme of a young man who decides not to follow the wishes of his family but instead turns towards a life of greater piety is older in Catholic hagiography than St. Francis; but this scenario had a special resonance within the Society, as two of its great saints, Francis Borgia and Aloysius Gonzaga, had chosen service in the Society over worldly recognition.

[52] Strahov, D A III 33, *Epitome historiæ Domus Profess. ad S. Nicolaum, Anno 1758*, folio 2r.

[53] Yet this contact with women also fueled anti-Jesuit propaganda, especially when women allegedly performed physical acts of penance in the presence of Jesuits (Čornejová, *Tovaryšstvo*, 220).

[54] Strahov, D A III 33, *Epitome historiæ Domus Profess. ad S. Nicolaum Anno 1759*, folio 4r.

Stepling on the nature of electricity.[55] These two very different responses to a natural phenomenon illustrate a genuine tension within the Society, but they should be placed in a broader cultural context. Mid eighteenth-century central Europe was in much the same position that England and France had been some decades before, where scholars who associated natural phenomena with the supernatural simultaneously conducted scientific inquiry.[56]

"Si Sciant Legere . . ."

Though not a major aspect of the Jesuit mission, the publication of religious works in the vernacular had become part of the program of the Society by the middle of the century.[57] The Society printed five hundred copies of a "libellus precationis" (small prayerbook) in Brno, and in the same year, 1768, the Jesuits of Hradec Kralové purchased another thousand "Germanico et Bohemico idiomate vulgatos libellos" (books in German and Czech) for free distribution.[58] Such efforts to reach readers of the vernacular, and in particular to address the needs of those who read only Czech, must be placed alongside the evidence of the thousands of Czech-language books burned by Koniáš and other Bohemian Jesuits.[59] On balance, how-

[55] NK, 2L 23/19, *Litt. An. Prov. Boh. 1767,* folio 10v. An even more striking example of the combination of Baroque piety and allegiance to the political status quo is found in a description of an ordinary examination ("tentamenta consueta") that took place the following year in Prague. In this public defense, the recently published *Chronologium rerum Boemicarum* of František Pubitschka, a work that bore traces of the lingering Baroque notion of *Pietas Austriaca,* also featured an essay on magnetism and electricity (NK, 23/19, *Litt. An. Prov. Boh. 1768,* folio 116v).

[56] The first section of Newton's *Principia* to appear was printed in the *Transactions* of the Royal Society next to a report on picking herbs by the light of the moon in order to assure the potency of their medicinal properties! The author thanks Steven Harris for providing this information.

[57] Between 1622 and 1773 the Society's press in the Clementinum published fifteen hundred titles, the majority of which were in Latin, and illustrate the capacity of the Bohemian Society to generate the texts used in the training of its own members. An example of these is the text for all the Jesuit feasts celebrated during the year, for use in the Province of Bohemia: *Proprium Societatis Jesu: Pro Provincia Bohemiæ officia Sanctorum* (Prague, 1679). Religious texts aimed at Czech speakers were published in Prague and Olomouc (Josef Hemmerle, "Die Prager Universität in der neueren Zeit," in Seibt, *Bohemia sacra,* 417).

[58] NK, 23/19, *Litt. An. Prov. Boh. 1768* folio 115v. This printing had been undertaken by the *Hereditas S. Wenceslai,* which by distributing the "Catholic Bible of St. Wenceslaus," had displaced the older "biblie kralická" associated with Utraquism (F. Malínský, *Otázka svatováclavská v české historii* [V Brno: Nákladem svazu osvětových ústředí moravsko-slezkých v Brně, 1929], 39 f.).

[59] Heinrich Benedikt asserted, however, that Koniáš returned to their original owners many of the books that he confiscated, after striking out the offending passages with his pen. His source for this observation is not provided (Heinirch Benedikt, *Franz Anton Graf von Sporck (1662–1738)* [Vienna: Manz Verlag, 1924], 218).

ever, efforts to publish Czech-language books were largely offset by the campaign to confiscate heretical material.[60]

In fact, the format and content of these newly printed books sometimes resembled that of the forbidden books burned by the Jesuits, and the actual impact of either the destruction or production of books in the vernacular may have been exaggerated by some writers; after all, the level of literacy in the countryside, both among the German and the Czech speakers, was very low, even among local magistrates or *rychtáři*.[61] Teaching Czech in the schools of Bohemia had been banned in 1744, crowning a process of decline that had set in a century earlier.[62] That the Jesuit book burners impeded the development of literary Czech is beyond doubt, but it is also equally clear that their motives had much more to do with enforcing religious conformity than with the overt promotion of one language over another. These undertakings were expressions of the bureaucratic mode of operations as much as of the evangelistic, for the Society excelled in the rationalist process of producing, confiscating, and destroying books. Yet the consequences of the Society's production and destruction of books were also cultural, implanting a memory of the Jesuits as meddlesome and hostile to many aspects of the native culture. Koniáš himself conceded in the second edition of his index of proscribed books that the campaign to eliminate anti-Catholic texts only drove their owners to greater secrecy.[63]

The confiscation of books served another purpose as well. As personified by the bizarre figure of Fr. Koniáš, the Jesuit book burners also provided a useful villain for Czech nationalist writers in the nineteenth century determined to create a narrative rationalizing and explaining the *doba temna*

---

[60] Yet Jesuit printing houses were the training grounds of lay printers, such as František Augustin Hochenberger (1715–?), who learned his craft at the Prague printing establishment of the Society (Magdelena Sobatová, "Příbamští tiskaři v 18. století," *Středočeský sborník historický* 10 [1975]: 228). See also Josef Wolf, "Z dějin tiskárny v Hradci Králové v 18 století," *Časopis Českého Národního Musea* 104 (1930): 74–79.

[61] The documents generated in the wake of the peasant uprising of 1775 in northeastern Bohemia give us an idea of the level of active literacy (that is, the ability to write) among prosperous villagers. A group of *rychtáři*, who would have been among the most educated and prosperous in their respective villages, signed a document related to the prosecution of the fomenters of the uprising, but could do so only with Xs. Yet since the ability to sign one's name is no longer regarded as a strictly reliable measure of active or passive literacy, it is possible that some of these men may have been able to read Czech (Josef Hanzal, "Nižší školství," in Petráň, *Počátky*, 135).

[62] Joseph Frisz and Louis Leger, *La Bohême historique pittoresque et litéraire* (Paris: Libraire Internationale, 1867), 249 f.

[63] Quoted in *Vznik národné osvicenské ideologie v českých zemích 18. století*, by Alexandr Sergejevic Myl'nikov (Prague: Universita Karlova, 1974), 63.

in terms that did not reflect badly upon the Czech people themselves, but instead shifted the blame upon the Society.[64]

Celebration of Masses for the dead was another important responsibility of Jesuit priests of Prague, who were in charge of many of the most splendid churches of the city, where the wealthy generally worshiped. Much more documentation exists of Masses for the dead being offered for the wealthy or noble, although the Society no doubt provided this service for more humble persons as well. The Society made particular note of prominent individuals for whom Masses were offered when they had left money for the support of missionary and educational undertakings. Such was the case in December 1771, when services were held for Anna Barbara Widdinana, who had left a generous bequest to the Society.[65]

If the deceased was an especially august personage, special services might be held far from where he or she had died and was interred;[66] for example, special services were held in 1761 after the death of Isabella, the wife of Archduke Joseph, Maria Theresia's son. More generally, though, funeral rites were performed within the context of the local community, which both put Jesuits on display before the public and created (as they hoped) the impression that they were an invaluable element of that community. The same was true of sermons and other public addresses made by Jesuits. In a province where, in the previous century, the arrival of Jesuits had occasionally invited stones and jeers, it was of considerable importance that they cultivate such favorable relationships. Jesuits took full advantage of the opportunities to address the local populace in ways that the listeners would find agreeable and comprehensible, using both German and Czech in the city, in order to reach the maximum number of the faithful.[67]

These listeners frequently included women; the Ursuline Sisters housed in the convent of New Town of Prague, attended a service in the church of St. Salvator in the Clementinum complex, where they heard sermons on the Lord's passion.[68] There are also records of Jesuits leading

[64] J. Jungmann, *Historie literatury české* (Prague, 1849), 583 ff.

[65] NK, 23/19, *Litt. An. Prov. Boh. 1771*, folio 310v.

[66] For example, *Epitome historiæ Residentiæ Kossumbergensis Societatis Jesu ad annum 1761, 62 et 63,* folio 85v (Strahov, D. A. III 32).

[67] NK, 23/17, *Litteræ annuæ Collegii S. J. Pragæ ad S. Clementem 1767*, folio 185v. The same year in the "Missio de pœntitentia in Regno Bohemiæ," four priests were reported to be working in the German language and four in Czech ("Bohemico") (23/19 *Litt. An. Prov. Boh. 1767*, folio 9v). In Moravia, Jesuits even took on the local dialect ("moravici idiomatis") in their sermons (NK, 23/19, *An. Prov. Boh. 1771*, folio 337).

[68] ". . . similiter in templo Salvatoris, item apud SS. Virgines Ursulinas Neo-Pragensis et Hradschinenses sermo dictus de Passione Domini" (NK, 23/17, *Litt. An. Prov. Boh. 1766*, folio 171r). The Ursulines were regarded as an order that attracted women from the highest strata of society. Twelve years later Khevenhüller-Metsch repeated the gossip that the "Oberin" of the

the "virgines Elisabethinas" of the New Town of Prague, probably the Sisters of Elisabeth of Hungary, in contemplative exercises.[69] Even though Jesuits did not instruct women in academic subjects, they often served as spiritual advisors to female religious, thereby maintaining contacts with the aristocratic families, who frequently had relatives in convents. The Society also cared for women from the other end of the social scale; in the Old Town of Prague they induced a former prostitute to repent, and provided her with the means to subsist and not be compelled to return to her old life.[70]

The Glory of the Saints

Devotion to Mary

The *Litteræ annuæ* expatiate upon the activities of sodalities, organizations of lay persons under Jesuit auspices who were devoted to a particular saint and often to good works as well. Sodalities were an important setting for Jesuit interaction with the general populace from the sixteenth century onward, flourishing in settings such as Italy where fraternal organizations had played a crucial social function since the early Renaissance. Most popular were the Marian sodalities, which had existed from the earliest days of the Society and had first appeared in Prague the very year the Jesuits arrived there.[71] After 1751 some sodalities were organized especially for women and girls.[72]

The Virgin Mary as an object of devotion had undergone a slow but steady evolution in Catholic central Europe, starting in the early Medieval period. Mary had always occupied a special place among the saints, but in the post-Tridentine Church the unique position of the Virgin continued to grow in prominence. In neighboring Poland during the course of the seventeenth century, devotion to Mary had resulted in her being portrayed in art as a sort of co-redeemer, but in a more regional style and, in the words of one scholar, more "Polonized." There is evidence of a similar if less

Prague Ursulines was the natural daughter of Joseph I (Rudolph Khevenhüller-Metsch and Hanns Schlitter, eds., *Aus der Zeit Maria Theresias: Das Tagebuch des Fürsten Johann Joseph Khevenhüller-Metsch,* 8 vols. [Vienna: A. Holzhausens, 1907–], 3:195).

[69] NK, 23/15, *Litt. An. Prov. Boh. 1766,* folio 439r.

[70] "Neo-Pragensium quidam mox laudavit Vetero-Pragensis operarii studium æmulati, [qui] mulierculam atq. prostitutam ad pœnitentiam, sanioraque consilia vitam sustinendi effectu optimo perduxit" (NK, 23/19, *Litt. An. Prov. Boh. 1771,* folio 239v).

[71] Heinrich Donat, "Die Marianischen Congregationen," in *Die deutschen Katholiken in der Tschechoslowakischen Republik,* ed. H. Donat (Warnsdorf: Opitz, 1934), 209.

[72] Jedin, *Church,* 549. There is some evidence that women may have been involved in Marian-sodality activity in a less official capacity long before this date.

thoroughly documented process taking place in Bohemia.[73] There the cult of Mary had flourished long before the arrival of the Society, and the Virgin had always been called upon to cure the sick and to offer reassurance to the distressed.[74]

By the mid-seventeenth century, the prestige of Mary as a powerful intercessor with her Son had reached the point that prayers modeled on the Lord's prayer were being offered to her.[75] Promoting popular devotion to the Virgin had been an important element of the Jesuit mission from its earliest days; indeed, in 1577 no less a figure than Peter Canisius had written a lengthy work on the unique place of Mary in Catholic devotions. In Prague, sodalities were expressions of Baroque piety and of outward allegiance to the Catholic Church in a community whose commitment to the Church was often fluid.[76] One of the sodalities that continued to flourish in the eighteenth century is in fact documented in 1629, only a few years after the Society had regained control of many of the city's churches and was struggling to consolidate its position at the Prague university.[77] The Society also placed great emphasis on the oath attesting belief in the Immaculate Conception of the Virgin, a requirement of all candidates for university degrees.[78]

The sodalities of Prague thus had their roots in turbulent times, when Catholicism was not yet the religion held by the majority of the city's citizens, and when images of the Virgin dating from pre-Reformation times were miraculously rediscovered, thereby reigniting cultic activities.[79] But by

---

[73] Alexandra Witkowska, "The Cult of the Virgin Mary in Polish Religiousness from the 15th to the 17th Century," in *Common Christian Roots: Contributions to the Twelve Carrefours* (Florence: Le Monnier, 1982), 472–74.

[74] Among other ailments, Mary was invoked "against attacks from worms" (*Marienlexikon* (1988), s.v. "Böhmen," by C. Valasek.

[75] A "Mutter Unser" prayer was published in 1655 (Eduard Winter, *Tausend Jahre Geistestkampf im Sudentenraum* [Leipig: Verlegt bei Otto Müller, 1938], 230).

[76] NK, 23/17, *Litteræ annuæ Collegii S. J. ad S. Clementem 1767,* folios 183r, 184v, et passim.

[77] Hammerschmied, *Prodromus,* 432.

[78] Despite opposition from the Dominicans, whose theological position on this controversial point was somewhat different, the Jesuits insisted on the oath as long as they were able to retain any control of the university, and used the occasion of its administration to stage elaborate public events attended by the highest-ranking nobles: "Unde religio Iurisiurandi de Immaculato Conceptu Bmæ Virginis MARIAE acta est illinc in Præsentia Celsissimi Principis Archi-Episcopi, ac Excellentissi Regni Procerum, hinc coram Senatu, populoque academico, utrimq. Pro Immaculata e rostris Sancta nostris," noting in particular the exalted personages who attended this ceremony (NK, 23/19, *Litt. An. Prov. Boh. 1769,* folio 187v, 188r).

[79] The phenomenon of the "rediscovered" image of the Virgin, a pattern often repeated in the early Baroque era, is discussed in *Wondrous in His Saints: Counter-Reformation Propaganda in Bavaria,* by Philip M. Soergel (Berkeley: University of California Press, 1993), 224 f.

the eighteenth century the activities of these organizations did not suggest so much a drive to reintroduce Catholicism as simply an established component of the social environment.[80] A collection of dramatic works produced by a Munich sodality in 1766 and 1767 contains lists of prominent community figures performing and writing these musical productions. These are lyrical rather than controversial in nature and, performed in Latin as they were, it is unlikely that they had proselytizing as a major goal.[81] The financial support Emperor Charles VI offered to the Marian sodality of Prague early in the eighteenth century was not motivated by a concern that Catholicism had failed to establish roots in the community, but by a desire to strengthen an already existing institution valued by the population of the city.[82]

Baroque Prague was a community of outdoor processions, public demonstrations, and public devotions, activities that never completely lacked important social elements.[83] Events sponsored by the sodalities of Prague, as described in the *Litteræ,* are part of this culture: they do not give the impression of either coercion or overt political maneuvering. And although it is difficult to assess the specific role of the Society in the direction of these organizations, there seems ample reason to believe that sodalities enjoyed genuine support from their members, who according to the *Litteræ,* included some of the most prominent people in Bohemia and reflected the cosmopolitan makeup of these organizations.

Devotion to the Virgin was not limited to urban sodalities. It was a unifying theme in the Jesuit missions and other undertakings throughout the Habsburg lands.[84] This practice made easier headway in Bohemia, as in other areas of central Europe, because devotion to the Virgin in her various manifestations had similarities to pre-Christian beliefs, particularly in connection with the goddesses Lada and Devana.[85] The special Bohemian shrine of the Virgin, Maria-Schein, was the scene of many miraculous cures re-

[80] In Prague alone in 1760, there were five sodalities and ninety other smaller "conventus" under the direction of the Society (NK, 1416 MSXXIII 105/18, *An. Prov. Boh. 1760,* folio 7v).

[81] *Fundamenta virtutum: Thema quatuor meditationum Congregationis Latinæ Majoris monacensis B. Mariæ V.* ([Munich], 1768).

[82] *Annales Prov. Boh. 1760,* NK, MS XXIII C 105/18, folio 44r.

[83] See Marie Pavlíková, "Josefinská Praha," in *Pražský sborník historický* (Prague: Orbis, 1968), 85–112. The *Litteræ annuæ* of 1768 record a procession through the streets of the Malá Strana, complete with soldiers and music: "Dominica infra festi octavam post Vesperas decantatus instructus" (NK 23/19, folio 99r).

[84] Examples of this devotion abound: in the Austrian Province the visitation records of a Carinthian archbishop in Gorizia in 1762 furnish repeated examples of chapels maintained by the Jesuits and dedicated to the Virgin (*Die Berichte der Pastoralvisitationen des Görzer Erzbishofs Karl Micahel von Attem in Kärten von 1751 bis 1762,* in *Fontes rerum Austriacarum diplomatica et acta,* 87 [1993]: 513).

[85] Josef Virgil Grohmann, *Sagen aus Böhmen* (Prague, 1863), 33 ff.

corded in Jesuit reports.[86] This cult of the virgin, while it had direct ties to folk culture and resembled cults elsewhere, was not unrelated to dynastic concerns. As the Habsburg lands expanded eastward, so did the ambitions and hopes of the Church; and sodalities dedicated to the Virgin were an especially crucial component of the network of organizations planted by the Church in the eighteenth century to assure that its doctrines would take root.[87] Likewise sodalities provided a context for social interaction and fraternal association that was also more public and more approved of by the authorities than other associations, such as the Freemasons. Jesuit priests were often active participants in the public demonstrations of piety associated with sodalities.[88]

These organizations provided more than an outlet for religious sentiments, however; sodalities also performed good works, although reports of these activities convey the impression that they were of more symbolic than practical significance. On a Sunday in 1768, members of a sodality in the Old Town of Prague fed twelve "pauperes" (poor folk) in conjunction with the celebration of the Lord's Supper; that this event was noteworthy enough to be included in the annual report of the province might suggest, however, how rarely such an event occurred.[89]

A twentieth-century Jesuit historian has called the Baroque Marian sodalities "an instrument of the spiritual elites in all classes of society."[90] From this claim it is a short step to view sodalities as the source of lay allies of the Society who could provide important assistance in secular contexts. In Naples, Ferdinand IV apparently shared this suspicion, for when he expelled the Society, he took pains to specify that the lay persons linked to the Jesuits were also to be expelled.[91] In France an exasperated official dubbed

---

[86] Typical is the case of a woman suffering from partial paralysis who was cured miraculously, and left a "tabella" at the shrine as an expression of thanks (NK, 23/19, *Litt. An. Prov. Boh. 1771*, folio 320r).

[87] This expansion is dramatically illustrated in the map "Die Zuruckdrängung des Osmanischen Reiches und die Hierarchie in Südeuropa," in *Atlas zur Kirchengeschichte: Die christlichen Kirchen in Geschichte und Gegenwart*, ed. H. Jedin, K. S. Latourette, and J. Martin (Freiburg/Basel/Rome/Vienna: Herder, 1987), 96.

[88] After Fr. Joannes Flaschner died in 1761, his eulogist recalled, "Post DEUM DEI Matrem Virginem adamavit. Hanc singulis Sabbatis perpetua ad humilem mensam accubatione honoravit; amorem Huius in Sodalibus, quam poterat luculentissme, accendit; quod ad cultus hyperdulici augmentum conduceret, nihil omisit," describing the honor he paid to the Virgin on Saturdays and his infectious zeal in directing the Sodality, omitting nothing that would contribute to her honor (MZAB, Cerroniho sbírka, II 345, folio 483).

[89] NK, 23/19, *Litt. An. Prov. Boh. 1768*, folio 91r.

[90] Bangert, *History*, 106.

[91] Louis Châtellier, *The Europe of the Devout: The Catholic Reformation and the Formation of a New Society*, trans. Brian Pierce (Cambridge: Cambridge University Press, 1987), 193. The fate of sodality members following the suppression is a field so far ignored by scholars.

the congregations founded by the Society, including the Marian sodalities, "the light infantry" of the unstoppable Jesuit "phalanx."[92] Aristocrats were part of these auxiliary troops. Curiously, even Count Sporck, who had struggled with Antonin Koniáš regarding the "heretical" books of Jansenist leanings, towards the end of his life seems to have lent his support to Marian sodalities.[93] A letter written by Koniáš himself (and therefore perhaps suspect in its details) asserts that the count, who had joined a sodality and donated three hundred florins to the Jesuit missions, also gave money for the publication of "good Catholic books."[94] Despite the suspicions of more skeptical contemporaries, Benedict XIV supported the devotion embodied in the Marian sodalities, and he decreed that the cult of Mary should be spread throughout the world.[95]

The public and cultic nature of activities sponsored by sodalities reflects both the desire, widespread in eighteenth-century Catholicism, to experience religion in a group setting and the program of the Society, which was to call attention to the message of salvation in a public setting adapted to the norms of the local culture.[96] Sodalities could bring together large numbers of people in a socially approved setting; they could incidentally even function as gatherings where unmarried men and women could meet, much as did pilgrimages, though these attracted a much more general group of participants.[97]

By definition sodalities were not tied to exclusively Baroque forms of religious expression; still, in practice they flourished best in the atmosphere of Baroque Catholicism, which might on occasion include musical celebra-

---

[92] Ibid., 192.

[93] Sporck also appears to have published "scurrilous doggerel" about the Society while still in possession of his printing presses, making his change of heart, if sincere, all the more remarkable (Paul Bernard, *Jesuits and Jacobins* [Urbana/London/Chicago: University of Illinois Press, 1971], 13).

[94] Reported (without attribution) in *Z duchovních dějin českých*, by Josef Pekař (Prague: Melantrich, 1941), 202. Since Pekař, a distinguished Czech historian, was anything but an apologist for Koniáš, we can accord some credibility to this improbable tale.

[95] *Marienlexikon*, s.v "Jesuitenorden," by J. Stierli.

[96] Whether the changes instituted by Reform Catholicism decreased the influence of sodalities is a point debated by historians, who have only inconclusive evidence from which to draw a general conclusion (Monter, *Ritual, Myth, and Magic*, 94).

[97] In the small town of Mindelheim, Bavaria, an eighteenth-century Jesuit Marian sodality brought together 2,904 men and women (Châtellier, *Europe*, 196). For the relationship between religious and festive elements of the pilgrimage experience, see Mary Nolan and Sydney Nolan, *Christian Pilgrimage in Modern Western Europe* (Chapel Hill: University of North Carolina Press, 1989), 47 f.); for the pre-Christian roots of the pilgrimage, as understood by early etymologists of the word "Wallfahrt," see Wolfgang Brückner, "Zur Phänomenologie und Nomenklatur des Wallfahtswesen und seiner Erforscher," in *Volkskultur und Geschichte: Festgabe für Josef Dünninger*, ed. Dieter Harmening (Berlin: E. Schmidt, 1970), 384–424.

tions.[98] After the suppression, in the towns of central Europe sodalities and less formal cultic gatherings to honor a saint lost much of their significance as expressions of solidarity and piety, and never regained their prominence in nineteenth-century Bohemian Catholic culture.[99]

Nevertheless, there is evidence that in the countryside sodalities had performed an important function in providing the context in which the dead could be commemorated; like Jesuit secondary schools, they were sorely missed by the population after 1773.[100] The sodalities of the Bohemian Society thus transcended categories of "popular" and "elite" culture, appealing to both rich and poor, and to people in smaller communities as well as those in the metropolis.[101]

The Society also fostered a more private devotion to Mary, whether practiced by a wealthy aristocrat or an impoverished peasant. The "Sacro-Montana" founded near Příbam at the end of the seventeenth century was a focus of devotion to the Virgin and served as the source of souvenirs that the faithful could then venerate in private.[102] Meanwhile, Jesuits preached the cult of Mary in schools and from pulpits on Sundays.[103] As the *Litteræ* illustrate repeatedly, Mary was looked to for deliverance from an endless list of personal and private misfortunes and difficulties, some life threatening, others less serious.[104] The Virgin was more than a source of relief from

---

[98] References to events accompanied by a "choro musico" are rare, however (*Litt. An. Prov. Boh. 1771* NK 23/19, folio 316v). In Košumberk, three hundred florins were spent to pay for musicians and a singer: "pro iuvenibus musicis et cantore" (*Catalogus III Prov. Boh. 1764—Catalogus 3tiæ Residentiæ Kossumbergensis Soc. Iesu,* ARSI, Boh. 82 folio 32).

[99] See also the exhibition catalog *Die Jesuiten in Bayern 1549–1773: Ausstellung des bayrischen Haupstadtsarchivs und der Oberdeutschen Provinz der Gesellschaft Jesu* (Weissenhorn: Anton H. Konrad Verlag, 1991), 146.

[100] A memorandum sent to the Bohemian Landes-Gubernium in 1776 by the city fathers of Dečin(?) speaks longingly of the "sontägige Zusammenkünfte, bey welchen die Sodalitaeten vor die abgestorbenene die Tagzeiten zum betten pfleget, nicht mehr veranlasset" (SÚA, ÈG 16 [Exjesuitica] 396, F 2/40, 494, 2., Praes. 26. Jan. 1776).

[101] The Prague sodalities were gatherings of the elite. A Latin eulogy *(oratio funebris)* published in 1779 and written by the Jesuit Godefridus Graetzel was no doubt intended for the "higher" cultural groups who might appreciate the form, if not entirely understand the content, of such an address (Pelzel, *Gelehrte,* 272).

[102] Johanna von Herzogenberg, "Heiligtümer, Heiltümer, und Schätze," in Seibt, *Bohemia sacra,* 468.

[103] The holy crown of Mary was the subject of an address given at the *Convictus S. Wenceslai* in Prague in 1762 (NK, 1287 MS XXIII C105/15, *An. Prov. Boh. 1762,* folio 309r). While the crown figures in numerous Jesuit accounts as an object misused by the superstitious, it was nevertheless an important element in Marian devotion. The crown might be symbolic of a bridle wreath, or could suggest the crown of victory when applied to the Habsburg victories over infidels or heretics (*Marienlexikon,* s.v. "Krone," by F. Tchochner).

[104] Ailments cured through prayers to the Virgin included deliverance from bad habits, swallowing a bone, paralysis of the limbs(?), skin disease, and the bite of a poisonous serpent: "a

medical problems; she also furnished a calming and hope-inspiring female presence in a troubled landscape where women faced not only the medical risks of childbirth but also the profound psychological stresses ensuing from the illnesses and isolation that could follow in the course of raising a child.[105]

Setting aside the unanswerable questions surrounding the miraculous cures credited to the Virgin, we must also consider the effort and expense lavished upon her shrines, and the enthusiasm that pilgrimages in her honor generated. Jesuit records, potentially slanted in their presentation of data, perhaps, demonstrate the vitality of her cult among the people; in 1771, for example, a remarkable 6,067 Masses were celebrated at her shrine at Sacro-Montana, an average of over sixteen a day.[106] This genuine and enthusiastic devotion to the Virgin, something scorned by virtually all Protestant movements, is striking in a land where crypto-Protestantism remained strong.

The Society can be credited with promoting the cult of the Virgin and introducing institutions, such as the Marian sodalities, that provided a framework for the organized expressions of devotion to her. But considering the Jesuits' failure to accomplish many of their other objectives, most notably the extirpation of heretical texts, we probably should not attribute the people's Marian devotion solely to the efforts of the Society. To a great extent we may attribute this to her image as an accessible and merciful woman, a figure with which many other women could identify. The Jesuits undoubtedly understood this appeal; and, in contrast to (or as a complement to) the hellfire approach used by Fr. Koniáš and many other Jesuits in missions throughout central Europe, cultivated this expression of the Divine that was mild and approachable. Some peasants regarded Mary as an efficacious source of succor flowing from a sort of magical realm apart from the doctrines and restrictions imposed by the Church. In encouraging devotion to her, the Society strove to maintain in balance several somewhat incompatible positions.

---

pravis habitibus . . . a deglutito ossuculo . . . a membrorum, ut ajunt, contractura . . . a scabie . . . a morsu venenato" (NK, 1287 MS C105/15, *An. Prov. Boh. 1765*, folio 444).

[105] For the trials and tragedies of new peasant mothers, see Rebekka Habermas, *Wallfahrt und Aufruhr: Zur Geschichte des Wunderglaubens in der frühen Neuzeit* (Frankfurt/New York: Campus, 1991), 54–57.

[106] František Xav. Holas, *Dějiny poutního místa marianského Svaté Hory u Příbamě* (U Příbamě, Nákladem Matice Svatohorské, 1929), 450. We may judge the scale of this shrine when we consider that in addition to cultivated lands attached to the shrine, the Society also operated a brewery on the premises (ibid., 455). Sacro-Montana was also the scene of a gathering of perhaps 100,000 people in 1732, when the statue of the Virgin was crowned amid great pomp and a mission procession was conducted "in the Italian fashion," namely, in a dramatic and sensational style often banned from rural areas by authorities out of fear of public disorder (Jaroslav Vlček, *Dějiny české literatury*, 3 vols., 3rd ed. [Prague: Nakladatel L. Mazáč, 1931], 3, 2).

This cultivation of a mild female manifestation of the Divine, practiced by so many Bohemian Jesuits, contrasted not only with the baleful tones of a sermon by Koniáš but also with the rationality of a Stepling or the national consciousness of a Balbín or Cornova. The Virgin as wonder worker appealed to the people in their physical and personal difficulties, frequently in an immediate and often local manifestation that nevertheless transcended the immediate and local, the ethnic and national—Mary, unlike Nepomucký and other saints promoted by the Society, had absolutely no national identity; here and wherever else she is venerated, her Jewish nationality was completely expunged.[107] Mary epitomizes the nonintellectual aspects of the Divine, and also manifests a different sort of virtue than did a martyred Abeles or Wenceslaus, to say nothing of the soldier Ignatius or the apostle Xavier. Yet it was the former soldier and gallant lover Ignatius who hung his sword up on an altar dedicated to the Virgin; the connection between the more activist and stereotypically "masculine" side of the all-male Society and the holy Mother suggests the complexities attendant on the mission of the Bohemian Society.[108]

A Host of Saints

Devotion to a saint need not be as formalized as participation in a sodality. The cults of local saints, such as "Sanctus Patriæ Defensor et Bohemiæ Rex Wenceslaus," were promoted by the Society.[109] Other saints with origins much further from Bohemia, such as St. Barbara, for whom a "cœtus" or congregation was established in the Malá Strana, are mentioned frequently.[110] The most prominent Jesuit saints, Ignatius, Xavier, and Aloysius Gonzaga, were the objects of widespread and, it would seem,

[107] Along with the Trinity, one of the greatest stumbling blocks to Jewish conversion to Catholicism was the cult of Mary, which for many Jews seemed to smack of idolatry (*The Jewish Encyclopedia* (1907), s.v. "Trinity," by Samuel Krauss.

[108] *A Pilgrim's Testament: The Memoirs of Saint Ignatius of Loyola,* Parmanandra R. Divarkar, S.J., trans. (St. Louis: Institute of Jesuit Sources, 1995), nos. 17 f. (pp. 23–26).

[109] St. Wenceslaus (Svatý Václav), the patron saint of Bohemia and therefore a potential rallying point for nationalist sentiment, has become the object of scholarly speculation regarding his place in the Jesuit collection of approved saints. F. Malínský claimed that "some historians" have found evidence that Wenceslaus was not useful to the Society, because he had gained popularity on his own, without much Jesuit promotion. Even stranger, he asserts that the martyred duke received veneration from Bohemian "heretics" precisely because of the Society's lack of enthusiasm for him (František Malínský, *Otázka svatováclavská v české historii* [Brno: Nákladem svazu osvětových ústředí moravsko-slezských v Brně, 1929], 39 f.).

[110] NK, 23/19, *Litt. An. Prov. Boh. 1769* folio 150r. A (presumably Catholic) legend claimed that St. Wenceslaus was buried at the site of White Mountain, the scene of a great Catholic victory, and that when Bohemia was in such desperate straits that all its able-bodied men might be gathered under one tent, the king would return to fight for the land (Grohmann, *Sagen,* 24).

genuinely enthusiastic devotion shared by Jesuits and lay persons alike. Aloysius was, like Jan Nepomucký, one of the "Baroque saints" whose cults reached their apogee in the eighteenth century. A noble sixteenth-century youth who had entered the Society and died at age twenty-three after nursing plague victims, Aloysius was the special protector of young students and, like St. Stanislaus Kostka, another youthful hero of Jesuit sermons and writings, a frequent subject of sentimentalized biographies.[111]

The cult of St. Aloysius Gonzaga was promoted throughout the world, and his image served as a visual icon of the Society's commitment to young men. The saint became the subject of one of the last major works of art dealing with Jesuit education produced before the suppression, an allegorical painting in the Baroque style attributed to Francesco de Mura, now in the Art Museum at Princeton University.[112] Both St. Aloysius and St. Stanislaus Kostka died virgins, so they could be held up as models of purity on the physical level as well as examples of sacrifice and spiritual achievement.[113] The resemblance of these examples of chastity to the virginal innocence of Shimon Abeles is not without significance, as is the relationship of these saints to disease and corruption.[114] Moreover, on occasion this purity had the power to cure real physical infirmities.

According to reports, the miracles attributed to water or oil brought in contact with the relics of these young saints could be spectacular: during the year 1766 the "benisons of Aloysius" *(Aloysii beneficia)* included three persons cured of poisonous pustules, 190 victims of fever, 3 persons suffering from burning fever, 2 persons suffering from "inveteratis febribus" (persistent fevers), 18 from "madness" *(phrænisi),* and 118 people afflicted

---

[111] Aloysius was canonized in 1726 and throughout the century served as a model for young Jesuits (many of whom entered the Society at fifteen or occasionally younger). Kostka, canonized the same year, had been a protégé of Canisius; before he died at the age of eighteen in 1568, he had already begun to acquire a reputation for "angelic innocence" (*The Book of Saints,* complied by the Benedictine monks of Ramsgate [London: Adam and Charles Black, 1966], 38, 654). The iconography of Kostka is highly developed; for a number of representative images from the seventeenth and eighteenth centuries, see *Sw. Stanislaw Kostka* (Warsaw: Nakladem XX. Jezuitow w Warszawie, 1928).

[112] The uplifted gazes and the zigzag compositional structure of this dramatic painting place it in the high-Baroque tradition, even though it may have been painted in the second half of the eighteenth century. Such a form of presentation supported the idea of "heroic virtue" of candidates for canonization articulated in the treatise *De servorum Dei* of Benedict XIV, and effectively conveys the ideal held by Bohemian Jesuits (Marcus B. Burke, *Jesuit Art and Iconography, 1550–1800: Introductory Essay and Exhibition Catalogue* [Jersey City: St. Peter's College, 1993], 4 ff.).

[113] Châtellier, *Religion of the Poor,* 173.

[114] This interest in the magical ability of some dead bodies to resist corruption also manifested itself in the growing interest in vampirism noted in the eighteenth century in several parts of the Habsburg domains (Gábor Klaniczay, *The Uses of Supernatural Power: The Transformation of Popular Religion in Medieval and Early Modern Europe,* ed. Karen Margolis, trans. Susan Singerman [Oxford: Polity/Blackwell, 1990], 176 ff.).

with various other maladies.[115] The reports do not say how long these individuals remained cured, or what was known about their conditions previous to their healing; but the sheer number of persons involved speaks for itself. The needs of the Bohemian peasantry were great, and the claims of the Jesuits proffering the hope of a cure were readily accepted. There remains the important question of the degree to which the participation of the populace in these "thaumaturgia" may be read as evidence of Catholic piety, of traditional folk belief in the miraculous, of mass hysteria, or of a mixture of these elements.

In a few instances, the behavior described bears a resemblance to paranoia, although intentional deception also cannot be ruled out.[116] The case of a seventeen-year-old girl whose "phrænisis" defeated the efforts of the physicians, but who received relief from the wonder-working powers of the "farina Aloysisii" (flour[?] of Aloysius) raises other questions about the stresses placed on young adults, and especially on young women, in a culture filled with so many dangers from childbirth, disease, and nutritional deficiencies.[117] Naturally, the Jesuits recording these events seemingly were scrupulous in noting the exact numbers of those affected and cured, yet they did not differentiate among the motivations or states of mind of the participants.[118] In virtually every case, moreover, corroborating evidence of these miracles is lacking; the afflicted did not leave diaries, nor did civil authorities keep systematic reports on these events. And, in any case, neither of these secular sources would have been automatically more trustworthy.[119]

---

[115] NK, 2L 23/15F, *Lit An. Prov. Boh. 1766*, folio 456v.

[116] For instance, the case of a boy of noble birth who was convinced that he had made a pact with a demon in his own blood ("schedam, qua suomet sanguine Dæmoni sese denotaverat"), and who fled in vain hopes of hiding from his tormentor (NK, 1288 MS XXIII 105/15, *An. Prov. Boh. 1761*, folio 203r).

[117] NK, 23/19, *Litt. An. Prov. Boh.* 1769, folio 164v. The Bohemians' lack of proper nutrition was reflected in the poor physiques of conscripts called up for service in Maria Theresia's armies (Betty Behrens, "Government and Society," in *The Economy and Organization of Early Modern Europe,* ed. E. E. Rich and C. H. Wilson, vol. 5 of *The Cambridge Economic History of Europe,* ed. M. Postan, C. Coleman, and Peter Mathias, 8 vols. [Cambridge: Cambridge University Press, 1977], 614).

[118] The reader is left to ponder the significance of such entries as the following, in which witchcraft, superstitions, instruments of divination and healing, books of incantations, and all else harmful to man and beast were stamped out or consigned to the flames: "Maleficia ad nocendum hominibus, et pecoribus inventa plane fuere destructa. Superstitiones, divinandi, medendique[?] artes magicæ pluribus in locis abolitæ sunt. Libelli, et incantationum instrumenta ad Nostrorum exhortationes ultro porrecta pro merito jussa sunt igne cremari (ARSI, *Relatio missionum Boh. Prov.* 194, 67, [1770]).

[119] In a few cases the reports written by the Jesuits suggest indirectly how peasants themselves regarded supernatural phenomena. In 1760 a Jesuit recorded one man's efforts through black magic to cause his enemy to go blind: "hunc arte magica visu privare constituit." Here it is not clear whether the Jesuit missionary is repeating a story narrated to him by a local

The categories identified in Jesuit reports, however, provide some clues to the range and nature of the preternatural experiences and of those suffering from them.

Along with physical ailments, psychological disturbances figure prominently in Jesuit reports; and despite the undifferentiated and nonclinical modes of reportage, the distress of the afflicted is beyond doubt, as are the surprisingly large numbers of people involved in these faith healings.[120] Suicide is a common theme, as is demon possession. Other cases involve adolescents seized with mania or delusional and obsessive behaviors.[121] Exposed to periodic famine, war, poor diet, and lack of medical treatment, the peasant and town-dwelling communities of Bohemia as a whole were vulnerable to whatever might produce symptoms of madness, alienation, or melancholia, conditions that Jesuits might interpret as examples of demonic possession.[122] The continuing Baroque leitmotiv of the terrors of hell, declaimed not merely by the fanatical Koniáš but by many other Jesuits, heightened the emotional tension felt by believers and kept the image of the devil and his minions in the mind's eye of the faithful.[123]

When one considers that in 1769 alone, 2,211 sermons were preached to the populace through the efforts of the *missio de pœnitentia,* it becomes clear how great an impact the Jesuit understanding of demonology could have on the entire region.[124] The tendency of the Society to view exceptional behaviors as evidence of demonic or diabolical meddling is echoed throughout central Europe, and reflects a difference in the ways Catholics and

---

resident, who affirmed the supernatural character of the event, or whether he expects his readers to accept the account as factual. Though it is likely that the Jesuit believed that the story told him corresponded to reality, the point of the story as recorded here was the intervention by the Jesuits to put an end to a disreputable practice (NK, 1416 MS XXIII C105/18, *Litt. An. Prov. Boh. 1760* folio 62v).

[120] The reputed power of the relics of Jesuit saints was exceptional: relics of Xavier were believed to have cured hundreds and even brought people back from the dead (*Die Jesuiten in Bayern,* 164).

[121] For example, a report dating from 1764 in which a woman allegedly sold the consecrated Host to the Jews (presumably so that they could desecrate it during one of their "diabolical" ceremonies) and then began to write in her own blood (ARSI, 194 *Relatio missionum Prov. Boh.*, 56).

[122] The Society's records are noticeably silent on the ongoing problem of hunger in the region. An exception is a passing comment that the people of the kingdom are "oppressed by hunger, diseases, and violent deaths" (NK, 23/19, *Litt. An. Prov. Boh. 1771* folio 319r).

[123] Rudolf Zuber, *Osudy moravské církve v 18. století 1695–1777. VI. Díl. Dějiny olomoucké arcidiecéze* (Prague: Česká katolická Charita v Ústředním církevním nakladadelství, 1987), 233.

[124] While the content of these "dictiones" must be inferred, the steady stream of supernatural cases reported in connection with the mission provides some sense of how often these themes would have been addressed (*Relationes super statu ecclesiæ et Archidiœcesis Pragensis ad S. Congregationem concilii ab archiepiscopis pragensibus factæ a. 1759–1781,* A. Podlaha ed. [Prague: Cyrillo-Methodějská knihtiskárna V Kotrba, 1908], 40).

Protestants dealt with the common phenomenon of deviant behavior. R. Po-Chia Hsia has pointed out that as the seventeenth century progressed, Protestant Germany increasingly tended to incarcerate its "mad," while Catholics and particularly the Jesuits preferred to resort to "Church magic."[125] This approach placed exceptional behavior within a theological framework that, once accepted, would increase the credibility of the theology itself and, it might be argued, strengthen the position of its proponents.

Yet the claim that the Society significantly perpetuated belief in atavistic rituals and a nonexistent supernatural world must be balanced with the realization that long after the suppression and the disappearance of the Jesuit missions, such beliefs persisted among the rural communities of Bohemia. The Society may have worked to reinforce superstitious practices that predated its arrival—or may have attempted in vain to extirpate them—and to institutionalize and elevate the cult of saints, but these already deeply rooted beliefs possessed enough innate power to survive on their own.

Serving the Emperor

Jesuits also served as chaplains in the armies of the Habsburgs, a mission that combined the care of souls with service to the temporal ambitions of the House of Austria. In the earlier part of the century, the Bohemian father Georgius Hess had served with the imperial army in the Austrian Netherlands, although it was unusual for a chaplain to travel so far from home.[126] Fr. Joannes Forst, born in Vienna, was a chaplain in the regiment of Heinrich Daun who died at his post in 1759.[127] Fr. Josephus Tusinsky died in Hungary on August 30, 1762, while serving his third year as a chaplain in the Bukovian Legion.[128] Joachim Pleiner, born in Suckograd in Bohemia in 1706, spent many years as a chaplain in both the imperial and Saxon armies, and wrote two devotional works intended specifically for soldiers.[129]

---

[125] R. Po-Chia Hsia, *Social Discipline,* 168.

[126] MZAB, Cerroniho sbírka II, 345, folio 43. One of the first projects undertaken by the Society in its early days in Italy was a home where former prostitutes were rehabilitated.

[127] Born in Vienna, 1700; entered the Society, 1718; professed of the four vows, 1736; died February 5, 1759 (*Epitome historiæ Coll. S.J. ad S. Nicolaum Pragæ, Anno 1759* (Strahov D A III 33 folio 3r).

[128] Born in Znoymo, March 7, 1726; entered the Society, October 14, 1743; professed of the four vows, 1762 (ibid., *Anno 1762,* folio 11v).

[129] Joachim Pleiner, *Die Glaubens- und Sittenlehre nach den Evangelien gerichtet, zum Gebrauch der Polisch-Sächsischen Truppen,* 1746; id., *Der in Lebensgefahr begriffene Soldat, durch trostreiche Ermahungen und anmutige Gebeter zu einem Ermangung eines priesterlichen Beystandes, zum Trost dem in sächsichsen Diensten befindlichen Soldaten vorberieitet* (Dresden, 1748). The latter work was intended specifically for the wounded or ill soldier who did not have the opportunity to confess to a priest, a situation that must have been very common in all armies of the day.

Even in comparison with other Jesuit activities, a chaplaincy with the imperial army was a hard assignment, generally not sought out by Jesuits with aspirations to literary or scientific accomplishments. The Habsburg army, prior to the reforms of Joseph II, was indeed capable of winning battles, but it was certainly no better than most other European armies of the time, filled with the castoffs of society and often commanded by incompetent officers who owed their commissions to birth and connections.[130] In addition to the rigors of camp life (with its attendant diseases) and the dangers of war, Jesuit military chaplains were isolated from their colleagues and not infrequently surrounded by soldiers hostile to Catholicism. No reports survive of any fathers who actually died on the battlefield, but the lives of many were doubtless shortened by military service. Yet Jesuit chaplains were also in a position to influence larger numbers of men through preaching and example, and the *Litteræ annuæ* record many conversions made among the soldiery. Unlike missions in the countryside, Jesuits working among soldiers netted no forbidden books. Imperial soldiers apparently were not readers.[131]

Far from the battlefields, Jesuits encouraged the penitential activities of imperial troops; for example, in 1760 in Kutná Hora a large number of soldiers devoted a week to "sacramento pœnitientiæ."[132] Whenever the opportunity presented itself, the fathers also reminded soldiers of their duty to the Habsburgs, calling attention to the importance of the dynasty.[133] Difficult though it might be, work among the soldiers of the empire and its allies held real appeal for some members of the Society, and the tradition of this service continued long after the suppression. In 1800, when Napoleon's armies had inflicted serious losses on the Habsburg forces and the dynasty turned to detachments of soldiers made up of citizens and students, former Jesuit F. X. von Schönfeld served as a chaplain in the *Studentenlegion* raised from Bohemian university students.[134]

Field chaplains were not the only Jesuits seen on the battlefield. During the Seven Years' War, missionaries visited two hundred Prussian prisoners of war and preached to them in German.[135] In 1758, after an

---

Pleiner died in Prague in 1769.

[130] Andrej Romaňák, "Reformy armády," in Petráň, *Počátky,* 118.

[131] NK, 1288 MS XXIII c105/15, *An. Prov. Boh. 1761*, folio 143v.

[132] NK, 1416 MS XXIII 105/18, *An. Prov. Boh. 1760,* folio 10r.

[133] When Emperor Francis I died in Innsbruck in 1765, Austria was at peace, but still maintained a large standing army. Jesuit chaplains delivered a funeral sermon on the Emperor to the troops that year; they also commemorated the marriage of Joseph II to the daughter of the Elector of Bavaria (NK, 1287 *An. Prov. Boh. 1765*, folios 375r, 347r).

[134] Goedeke, *Grundriss,* 6:718.

[135] NK, 1416 MS XXIII 105/18, *An. Prov. Boh. 1760,* folio 48r.

unnamed military engagement, they administered the last rites to 297 dying Prussian soldiers (who had presumably become converts or had been Catholics previously), among whom were three officers. During the same campaign, a Jesuit priest presided over the burial of a high-ranking French officer.[136] In carrying out these duties, the Society was following a general policy observed in the Habsburg lands during the war, one that viewed prisoners of war as entitled to spiritual care.[137] The impressive dedication of the Jesuits who undertook these difficult tasks is in part to be weighed against their bureaucratic obsession carefully to keep track of numbers. Success on the battlefield was measured in the same way as elsewhere: the transcendent experience of personal encounters with the Divine was somehow validated by keeping records of how many individuals were initiated into the experience.

In addition to performing special services for deceased members of the House of Austria and serving alongside soldiers fighting for the Habsburgs, Jesuits engaged in other activities that tied them to the dynasty. They solemnly commemorated the name day of their monarch, Maria Theresia, in a public ceremony attended by the royal prefect of Prague and two regiments of soldiers.[138] In 1767 the Queen's recovery from a serious illness was celebrated with even greater ceremony. In the New Town of Prague as well as in Olomouc, Klatovy, Kutná Hora, and other towns throughout the province, the fathers organized processions in the streets, sometimes including the students of the local collegium.[139] A rare and important event for the Society was the visit of Emperor Joseph himself to the Jesuit community in Hradec Králové in 1766. From the account given in the *Litteræ annuæ,* the reader would never suspect what antipathy Joseph would later show towards some religious orders. Joseph, after arriving in a Jesuit mission on one of his lightening trips through the kingdom, leaped down from his horse and paused for half an hour as he prepared to continue his journey. While there, he chatted with the Jesuits and an assemblage of locals and accepted their good wishes.[140] The young emperor's visit recalled a similar visit from

[136] NK, 1416 MS XXIII 105/18, *An. Prov. Boh. 1760,* folio 57r.

[137] Lutz Voigtländer, *Die preussische Kriegsgefangenen der Reichsarmee 1760/1763* (Duisburg: Gilles & Franke Verlag, 1995), 196–200.

[138] "In qua hoc anno [1761] Supremi militiæ Caesero-Regiæ Præfecti Pragæ presentes cum duabus legionibus festum Sanctæ Matris Theresiæ Augustissimæ Dominæ nostræ Nominis diem more suo solemniter celebrarunt" (Strahov, D A III 32, *Epitome annuarium litterarum Provincicæ Bohemiæ ab anno 1761 usque ad annum 1763: Compendium annalium Collegii Societatis JESU Neo-Pragæ ad S. Ignatium ad annum Domini 1761,* folio 82r).

[139] *An. Prov. Boh.1767* (NK, 23/19, folios 13v–14r).

[140] "[A]dvenientes ex equo desiliens benevolentissime allocutus, singula missionis munia diligenter exquissivit, atq. cognita collaudavit, dimidiæque horæ spatio sermocinatus[?] dum iter parasset prosequi fortunam suam, regnorumque felicitatem precibus missionariorum, collectique populi impense [commendavit]" (NK. 2L 23/15F, *An. Prov. Boh. 1766,* folio 461v). The trip in

his father in Jindřichův Hradec (Neuhaus) in Moravia fifteen years earlier, in which Francis had greeted members of the Society and received their blessings.[141]

In descriptions of public disputations conducted in Jesuit schools, the famous and the nobles in attendance were always recorded, and we find the same attention to the aristocracy in accounts of Jesuit missions. In 1769 the Jesuits could report with pride that Count Metternich and Count Kollowrath were among those attending sermons preached in connection with the Society's mission activities.[142] Not only did members of the aristocracy serve as sponsors for converts baptized by the Jesuits, but many nobles continued to make financial contributions toward the maintenance of churches and schools, as well as to provide (or so the Society hoped) a sympathetic ear to the concerns of the Jesuits. In the 1760s it was still possible to view the local aristocracy, the Society, and the dynasty as natural allies in holding together the existing institutions. Even though by the end of the century the nobility would play a key role in promoting Czech national consciousness (which contained much that was hostile to the overt institutional goals of the Jesuits), at the time of the suppression these developments still lay in the future.

The efforts of Vienna to centralize the administration of Bohemia were already well underway by the third decade of Maria Theresia's reign; but they were not explicitly tied to Germanization and did not yet inspire the resistance that would transform some Bohemian nobles into Czechs who haltingly spoke their "native tongue" in the presence of their sovereign to illustrate their newly rediscovered identity.[143] The decline in enthusiasm among the nobility for the Baroque piety promoted by the Society is harder to assess. It is not at all surprising that no trace of this decline makes its way into the reports written during the years immediately before the suppression; whether this omission was deliberate or simply the result of blindness on the part of the Bohemian Society is hard to say. The religious attitudes of this group probably ranged over a considerable spectrum of beliefs. Those aristocrats no longer motivated by personal religious convictions or *pietas Austriaca* would have stayed away from the events described in the *Litteræ*,

---

question is probably the one charted in *Österreich zur Zeit Kaiser Josefs II,* ed. Karl Gutkas (Vienna: Niederösterreichische Landesausstellung, 1980), 715.

[141] NK, 1288 MS XXIII C105/15m, *An. Prov. Boh. 1750,* folio 15v.

[142] NK, 23/19m, *Litt. An. Boh. Prov. 1769,* folio 174r. Franz Georg Count Metternich-Winneberg (1746–1818), was the father of the famous Austrian chancellor, and by all accounts much more sincerely devout than his son (Karl Otmar Freiherr von Aretin, "F. G. von Metternich," in *Neue deutsche Biographie,* 19 vols. [Berlin: Duncker und Humblot, 1953–], 14:235 f.).

[143] This was happening by the time Leopold II journeyed to Prague in 1791 (Emil Franzel, *Der Donauraum im Zeitlater des Nationalitätenprinzips* [Bern: Dalp-Taschenbücher, 1958], 46).

while those still motivated by piety would be the most active in their support of the Jesuits' missionary work, which continued unabated until the suppression.

Beyond the tokens of aristocratic patronage, the Jesuits had reasons to tell themselves that their missions were on the right course. In hunting out heretics, Jesuits were complying with the spirit of the archbishop of Prague's directive of 1762, which commanded every parish priest to determine the "Stand der Häresie" in his community.[144] As late as 1765 the Holy See still found reason to praise the missionary efforts of the Society in the archdiocese of Prague.[145] Yet many nobles were probably ambivalent or uncommitted; few were sympathetic enough with the position of the Jesuits in Bohemia to transform their religious convictions into concerted efforts on behalf of the Society.[146]

The missions of the Jesuits of Prague based in smaller communities functioned in a different world from the one inhabited by the aristocracy. In the country the Society focused much less on formal education than on missionary efforts among backsliders and heretics, administering the sacraments and maintaining enterprises that would support their pastoral work. The statistics reported from the Jesuit residence in Tuchoměřice give a very rough idea of the scale of the activities carried on in these Jesuit outposts (while making allowances for the limitations associated with Jesuit-generated statistics, discussed earlier). In 1769 three priests and one lay brother worked in this community, where in the course of a year they baptized twenty people and distributed Holy Communion to 13,640 recipients. Moreover, they acquired more property, on which were 226 trees.[147] To their satisfaction, they had also successfully constructed a new fishpond.[148] Maintaining focal points of devotion in rural settings was a major concern of the Society as it sought to combat crypto-Protestantism in one of its strongholds.[149] A statue of St. Jan Nepomuký located in a remote part of the countryside near a small chapel dedicated to St. Francis Xavier was, it was reported with pride, the object of many devotees.[150] The enter

[144] Winter, *Tausend Jahre Geisteskampf,* 230.

[145] Clement XIII to Archbishop Przichowsky, June 5, 1765 (*Synopsis actorum S. Sedis in causa Societatis Jesu 1605–1773* [Louvain: Ex Typographia J.-B. Istas, 1895], 493).

[146] Tomáš Bílek, "Reformace katolická v Čechách 1650–1781."

[147] NK, 23/17, *Litt. An Prov. Boh.1769,* folio 232v.

[148] NK, 23/19, *Litt. An. Prov. Boh. 1769,* folio 228r.

[149] In the Bohemian Province in 1767, three individuals are reported "Conversi . . . a naturalismo." Since Lutherans and Hussites are (generally) listed separately, this category suggests Jesuit encounters with more localized Protestant sects or with individuals whose beliefs were not easily understood or classified by the missionaries (NK, 23/19, *Litt. An Prov. Boh.1767,* folio 10v).

[150] Ibid., folio 233v: "Fructus administrationis Chwalensis in Spiritualibus." Thomas Da Costa Kaufmann has pointed out that in the accounts of Nepomucký's life written and preached

prises of the Society were, of course, not immune to the vagaries of rural life. In 1769 an epidemic in the countryside killed seven hundred sheep belonging to the Prague Jesuit community, but spared the community's cattle. For all these favors, according to reports, the Jesuits gave thanks to God.

Sudden misfortune hit the urban properties of the Society as well. Fires were common and disastrous occurrences. On September 23, 1767, a fire within the precincts of the Clementinum destroyed a building containing all the gardening tools *(omnem apparatum)*, as well as equipment used in the wine cellars.[151] Five years earlier, detachments of soldiers and teams of scholastics had battled through the night to keep the Clementinum itself from burning down.[152] Urban life brought other challenges. During the year 1760 thieves broke in and stole lamps from the Churches of St. Ignatius and St. Salvator in Prague; the lamp in St. Salvator weighed seven pounds and was encrusted with semiprecious stones.[153]

In addition to serving as military chaplains, Jesuits made prison ministry a mainstay of their mission. The work here must have been at times especially grim, for example, when five French-speaking prisoners (possibly prisoners of war or, more likely, accused spies) were enjoined to prepare for their approaching death.[154] The Jesuits of the collegium of St. Ignatius in the New Town likewise ministered to a man condemned to death who, even after being tortured a second time, still proclaimed his innocence.[155] The inclusion of such detailed accounts in the *Litterae annuæ* may be taken as evidence of their relative rarity, but it is equally evident that the Society saw such ministrations as an essential aspect of its mission. An even clearer instance of Jesuit work in prisons was reported from Olomouc in 1760,

---

by the Jesuits, the saint was martyred for his "devotion to the sacrament of confession," which had been later abolished by the Protestants. Thus, the promotion of the cult of Nepomucký had as a subtext the reaffirmation of the sacraments against those who had repudiated them, the followers of John Hus (Kaufmann, *Court, Cloister, and City*, 345).

[151] NK, 23/19, *Lit An. Prov. Boh. 1767*, folios 57v–58r.

[152] NK, 1287 MS XXIII C105/15, *Litt. An. Prov. Boh. 1762*, folio 289r.

[153] NK, 23/19, *Litt. An. Prov. Boh. 1768*, folio 78r.

[154] In carceribus . . . quinque Gallico [indiomate] ad iter æternitatis rite comparati sunt (Strahov, D A III, 32, *Epitome historiæ Collegii S. J. Vetero Pragae ad annum 1761*, folio 81r).

[155] In carcere inclusus . . . unus capite damnatus, cum ante supplicium innocentem se esse proclamaret, ad tormenta nova sustinenda se resolvit, quæ et heroice sustinuit, probe nunc instructus in pietatis studio vitam transivit (Strahov, D A III, 32, *Epitome annuarum litterarum Provinciæ Bohemiæ ab anno 1761 ad annum 1763: Compendium annalium Collegii Societatis JESU neo-Pragæ ad S. Ignatium anno Domini 1761*, folio 7v). The tone of this entry suggests that the writer had some admiration for the accused, or perhaps even considered him innocent.

when another condemned man specifically asked for a Jesuit to help guide him through the harrowing experience that lay ahead.[156]

It is perhaps in such cases that the explicitly stated mission of the Society seems to the modern reader most at odds with the scientific and rationalistic undertakings of some of its other members. Yet Jesuits viewed these acts as deeds of mercy in an age when many in prison could be offered little other comfort. The Baroque understanding of a "good" or "pious" death, which expressed itself in the founding of Societies of the Happy Death, guided the actions of many Bohemian Jesuits.[157] Among those Jesuits concerned with guiding souls to a good death even if they were not affiliated with an organization having this as its specific goal, was Joseph Piczardi, who made use of Italian, French, Hungarian, and English both to guide converts to the true Church and to prepare believers for departure from this life.[158] On the other hand, the motivations of the Jesuits who worked to free six people from prison where they were held for an unspecified reason are easier for the modern mentality to grasp.[159] But the Jesuit vision of charity, it should be recalled, did not make a distinction between those acts that benefited the body and those that assisted the soul; instead, they interpreted both forms of activity as advancing the salvation of the soul.

The Problem of Possession

The "diagnosis" of demonic possession, a recurring theme in Jesuit documentation of mission work, lies at the center of the problem of understanding how the Jesuit missionaries related to the populace. Baroque Catholicism acknowledged the existence of demons, and religious literature described in detail the nature of the interaction between demons and those who could call on relics and other holy objects in struggling with them.[160] Clergy of all

[156] ". . . nostrum elegit, per quem ad mortem fortiter subeundam disponeretur . . . inter summarum virtutum actus capite pleno occubuit" (*Annales Prov. Boh. 1760,* NK, 1416 MS XXIII C 105/18, folios 68r–68v). See also the discussion of Jesuit interactions with Jews accused of various crimes in chapter 5 below.

[157] On June 3, 1730, Franciscus Retz, superior general of the Society, had issued a letter regulating the involvement of Jesuits with lay persons active in the Society of the Happy Death (Arhivele Statului Cluj-Napoca, Fondul Liceal Romano-Catolic, unnumbered dossier).

[158] Strahov, D D III, 32, *Epitome annuarum litterarum Provinciæ Bohemiæ ab anno 1761 usque ad annum 1763: Compendium annualium Collegii Societatis JESU, Neo-Pragæ ad S. Ignatium ad annum Domini 1761,* folio 82r.

[159] Ibid. , folio 81v.

[160] An eighteenth-century manual on the proper use of reliquaries advised that "apud reliquarias dæmones rugiunt, et inhabitores . . . illorum se sentire præsentiam confitentur," affirming that in the presence of reliquaries the demons howl and the bystanders can sense that they are nearby (Moretto, *De ritu*, 124).

sorts fostered the belief in demonic possession; the decrees issued from Vienna by the express order of Maria Theresia in the 1750s demonstrate this. These laws prohibited the Moravian clergy from exhuming bodies in order to perform *magia posthuma* (posthumous magical rites) on them, and insisted that persons suspected of being possessed by the devil be examined by a competent physician.[161] The willingness of Jesuits in particular to identify mental illnesses as possession and to seek to cure them through supernatural means can illustrate how the Society could adapt to local cultural circumstances that were already well entrenched and endorsed by local priests. The missionaries understood, moreover, that this accommodation would provide opportunities for them to display the power of the faith.[162] Folk culture, furthermore, was carefully studied within the Society, and Jesuits in Europe and elsewhere collected and recorded information about local customs whether they conformed to Catholic doctrine or not.[163]

There were risks inherent in approaching the question of demonic possession: the involvement of Jesuit priests in the exorcism of demons from women in particular has often given rise to stories of improprieties and scandal.[164] The age, gender, educational attainment of the people afflicted and, especially, their religious knowledge (or lack thereof) also influenced the atmosphere in which demonic possession was recognized, diagnosed, and cured.[165] Thus, a fair degree of skepticism regarding the actual beliefs

---

[161] *Theresianisches Gesetzbuch,* Bd. 3, p. 172f. (Nr. 383), Wien 1. März 1755, in *Der Josephinismsus: Ausgewählte Quellen zur Geschichte der theresianisch-josephinischen Reformen,* ed. Harm Klueting (Darmstadt: Wissenschaftliche Buchgesellschaft, 1995), 42. By 1758 Vienna's stance was even more uncompromising in its desire to bring the process under civil jurisdiction: "Der Geistlichkeit ist das Exoriziren, wenn sie sich nich vorher mit dem Politikum einverstanden, nicht erlaubet" (ibid., 47, Bd. 3 p. 416 f. [Nr. 499)], Wien, 27. Juni 1758).

[162] Some areas of the Habsburg realms were even more in thrall to the most severe forms of superstition than was Bohemia. While accusations of witchcraft (as opposed to demonic possession, an important distinction in the minds of many in the eighteenth century) were rare in the regions near Prague, Transylvania, long the scene of witch crazes, had a witch burning as late as 1752 (Henry Charles Lea, *Materials towards a History of Witchcraft,* ed. Arthur C. Howland, 3 vols. [Philadelphia: University of Pennsylvania Press, 1939], 3:1209).

[163] In the neighboring Austrian Province, István Csiba, in his treatise on the mountains of Hungary, included seemingly pagan customs of miners (*Dissertatio historico-physica de montibus Hungariæ* [Nagyszombat (Trnava), 1714], reported in Tekla Dömötör, *Hungarian Folk Beliefs* [Bloomington: Indiana University Press, 1982], 111, 286). At the end of the eighteenth century, Josef Dobrovský pioneered the systematic study of folk culture in the Czech lands (Karel Fojtík and Oldřich Sirovátka, "Czech Ethnology and Folklore: A Short Outline of Their Development," *Man and Culture II: Contributions of the Czechoslovak Ethnologists for the VIII International Congress of Ethnologists in Tokyo 1968* [Prague, 1968], 1).

[164] In France in the eighteenth century, a Fr. M. J. B. Girard had been the focal point of tales of immoral contact with a woman, "La Cadière," said to be possessed (M. A. Arnould, *Les Jésuites depuis leur origine jusqu'à nos jours,* 2 vols. [Paris: Duterte, 1846], 1:165–225).

[165] Ducreux documents the lack of knowledge among suspected heretics interrogated by missionaries ("Reading unto Death," 214–17). Vavák supports this evidence with a somewhat

of the Jesuits who became involved in cases of possession may not be out of order. Yet the obituary notices and other records of the personal beliefs of Bohemian Jesuits discount the idea that the Society shrewdly accepted these supernatural phenomena in order to maintain its control over the populace or to keep pace with the activities of local parish priests. It seems far more likely that many Jesuits believed that they were dealing with supernatural possession and that the remedies they offered for them would be helpful.[166]

As Trevor Johnson has suggested, the Jesuit missionaries and the people they encountered shared a religious culture whose lines of influence worked both ways. University-trained Jesuits brought a sophisticated dramatic performance and a carefully tuned level of rhetoric to their mission efforts, as well as an awareness of the history and traditions of their Society that might be used to recruit future Jesuits from the populace. For their part, the peasants and townspeople who received the Jesuit message brought their rich folk traditions to the encounter. Many of these practices were deemed heretical by the Jesuits; but the prevailing climate of belief in preternatural intervention in the lives of ordinary people helped keep alive this dimension of spirituality among the Jesuits, and the apparent cures of the "possessed" encouraged missionaries to continue to believe in the powers of their exorcisms.

Social historians have sometimes regarded as a standard scenario demonic possession or mad behavior associated with relations with the devil; medical problems, psychological disturbances, or other influences drove people so afflicted to claim that they had relations with these supernatural beings or even that they were such beings themselves.[167] There is also

---

contemptuous account of a peasant unable to describe the heretical faith to which he belonged (*Paměti,* vol. 1, fasc. 2, pp. 56–58). Although in both instances feigned ignorance to escape punishment may have motivated the performance of the person being interrogated, for the interrogators to accept such a stance as plausible illustrates how low the level of religious knowledge was held to be among Bohemian peasants.

[166] The situation is somewhat more ambiguous when Jesuits recorded the activities of the devout in which the Society was not necessarily the sole motivator. A characteristic instance is a procession held in Prague during Passion Week of 1767 to prevent the "scourge of earthquakes" ("supplicatio instituta ad advertendos terræ motus"). The reporting of such an occurrence implies that it met with the approval of the Society, although individual Jesuits may have had scientific explanations for the origins of such natural phenomena, relative to accepted Church teachings (NK, 23/19, *Litt. An. Prov. Boh. 1767* folio 86v). In 1761 a Jesuit named Malagrida was burned by the Inquisition in Portugal for claiming that the Lisbon earthquake has been a punishment from God (Monter, *Ritual, Myth, and Magic*, 126). This atrocity was also a demonstration of Pombal's political power.

[167] Roy Porter relates the story of Christoph Haitzmann (?–1700), a Bavarian Catholic who believed that he had twice signed a pact with the devil. He found peace of mind only when he became "Brother Chrysostom" and entered a monastery. Porter rejects Freud's theories regarding this case, which postulated that the devil was a father substitute (Porter, *A Social History of Madness,* 89).

irrefutable evidence that those interrogating suspected witches or sorcerers prompted them to "confess" their dealings with the forces of evil, and that they perhaps actually internalized the demonology forced upon them by their judicial tormentors. The tendency for people to explain their interior experiences in such terms can be traced to influences other than local folk culture; post-Tridentine Catholic dogma supported these beliefs in no uncertain terms.[168] Yet these considerations leave us very far from resolving the question of what actually transpired when Jesuit missionaries exorcised demons. We can no longer determine with any certainty the causes of the mental sufferings described in Jesuit letters to Rome, but the relationship between these ailments and the general climate of social instability and material deprivation found in the communities where the Society labored cannot be overestimated. The question remains to which existing documents provide us with no confident answers: Did the sufferers described by the Jesuits come to the fathers already believing that they were tormented by supernatural forces, or did the Jesuits suggest this idea to them?

There seem to be cases occurring elsewhere in which the Jesuits did suggest such a diagnosis. Hanns Bächtold-Stäubli cites an instance from 1767 in Landsberg an der Lech where Jesuit efforts to combat an outbreak of witch hysteria actually promoted belief in this phenomenon.[169] But considering the general level of superstition in Bohemia, we may suppose that often the sufferers arrived at a "diagnosis" of possession on their own or with the help of their neighbors and relatives.[170] In such a context bodily pain or mental discomfort manifesting itself in physical symptoms could easily be attributed to the supernatural, because in folk culture the body itself was a portal through which evil might enter. In both a classic Baroque and in a traditional folkloristic milieu, the body was seen as the potential home of malignant forces, whose power might even continue after the death of the "host" individual.[171]

---

[168] Even after Vatican II Catholic dogma could still assert "all that is affirmed of the natural essence of the angels must be ascribed to [demons] too" (Adolf Darlap, "Demons," in the article "Devil," *Sacramentum Mundi: An Encyclopedia of Theology*, ed. Karl Rahner, 6 vols. [New York: Herder and Herder, 1968–1970], 2:72).

[169] Hanns Bächtold-Stäubli, ed., *Handwörterbuch des deutschen Aberglaubens*, 10 vols. (Berlin/New York: Walter de Gruyter, 1987), 4:663.

[170] For example, see František Vavák's uncritical relation of how a villager's evil ways resulted in his being turned into a toad (Vavák, *Paměti*, vol. 1, fasc. 1, p. 15).

[171] Thus in 1755 peasants in Hermersdorf, on the border with Silesia, exhumed the body of an alleged female vampire, beheaded it, and burned the remains. Maria Theresia's revulsion at these and similar occurrences, motivated, not by Enlightenment skepticism, but by her own understanding of Catholic orthodoxy, contributed to the eventual "Article," issued in 1766, which placed severe restrictions on the circumstances that would allow the prosecution of individuals accused of witchcraft or vampirism (Edmund M. Kern, "An End to Witch Trials in Austria: Reconsidering the Enlightened State," *Austrian History Yearbook* 30 [1999]: 169).

Such beliefs increased the number of reported instances of the supernatural and widened the range of circumstances that might be attributed to the supernatural. Yet at the same time, acts to cure physical ailments that to the Jesuits smacked of heresy or commerce with the forces of evil were not always perceived as such by peasants, who instead regarded them as "good" magic.[172] In an environment that blended folk remedies, superstitions, and both orthodox and heretical religious practices, many peasants regarded the use of magic more tolerantly than did the Society when they employed cures viewed as "superstitions" by the fathers. The philosophy of such individuals was simple and pragmatic: often they did not consider that methods which seemed to alleviate suffering could be wrong.[173] Thus, the Jesuit chroniclers might record many more instances of individuals straying from orthodox Catholicism than those straying might consider justified. All these factors contributed to the narratives ultimately produced by the Jesuits, which leave the impression of a countryside seething with immoral acts and demonic relations.

The complex relationship between Jesuits and the people they assisted was not limited to these perceptual issues. The constant presence of death, particularly infant death or the death of women in childbirth, contributed to the somber, if not morbid, atmosphere in which Jesuit missions were undertaken.[174] Fear and material need were constant companions of the Jesuit missions, and the need they perceived precipitated the curative activities associated with them and conditioned people to hope for a possible cure.[175]

Another element present in the hectic climate of popular piety that brought forth such miraculous "cures" was the competition among various

[172] In 1767 occurred a curious variation on the use of a holy relic to prevent harm from coming to the possessor. Josef Brabeneč returned to Bohemia from Lusatia, where he had absorbed heretical ideas. Earlier he had purchased the thumb of a hanged man from an executioner, believing that it would protect him from prosecution by the authorities. The grisly relic was proved ineffective, however, and Brabeneč was convicted of scandalous speech and suspected heresy (Ducreux, "Reading unto Death," 212).

[173] See the discussion of the "bona intentio" of German Catholic peasants practising popular magic in "Witchcraft and Popular Religion in Early Modern Rothenburg ob der Tauber," by Alison Rowlands, in Scribner and Johnson, *Popular Religion,* 116.

[174] Mortality in rural Bohemia in the 1760s was high by modern standards, if slightly lower than in previous years; but infant mortality, a problem directly related to nutrition, was noticeably higher during this decade (Victor-Lucien Tapié, *L'Europe de Marie-Thérèse* [Paris: Fayard, 1973], 281).

[175] See James George Frazer, *The Golden Bough: A Study in Magic and Religion,* 1-vol. abridged edition (New York: Macmillan, 1922), 138 f. Frazer discusses the impulse toward chaste behavior, seeing it as motivated by a desire for food or victory. Chastity was an important element of the message of the Jesuit missions and was no doubt related in the minds of peasants to reduction of danger or the granting of better harvests through divine favor.

objects of devotion.[176] The devotees of a particular portrait of the Virgin or relic of a saint might attach so much significance to the object of their devotion that they would dismiss or disparage other such objects. St. Ignatius himself was held to be a healer of the possessed, and thus was in potential competition with other healers promoted by other orders.[177] Locally accepted "cures" might be ranged against those sanctioned and promoted by the Society, which could present testimonials of "cures" wrought through their efforts. The wars and military occupations that temporarily closed shrines such as Maria-Schein heightened the tension of believers seeking cures and frustrated the Jesuits who sought to satisfy their needs.[178] The *Litteræ annuæ,* of course, have little explicit to say of such complications, and the reader must content himself with a brief mention of the wonder-working image or object.[179] In some instances the behaviors of the afflicted as the *Litteræ* described them suggest serious mental illnesses that would have required therapy that lay outside the capabilities not only of the Jesuits, but of the most enlightened physicians of the day.[180]

Far from Home

The Jesuits of Bohemia had a long history of missionary work far from their homeland. In addition to service in a number of provinces in "the Indies," which might include both the New and Old Worlds, Bohemian Jesuits had traveled to Russia, from which they were twice expelled, the

[176] Even a highly sympathetic Jesuit writer on devotions has conceded, "There is a certain competitive element in devotions" (John J. MacKenzie, S.J., *The Roman Catholic Church* [London: Weidenfeld and Nicolson, 1969], 182).

[177] Bächtold-Stäubli, *Handbuch,* 2:671.

[178] Maria-Schein was closed for an extended period after the Prussian army occupied it (NK, 1288 MS XXIII C105/15, *An. Prov. Boh. 1761,* folio 162r).

[179] For example, the *Litteræ annuæ* of 1771 record that a distraught father's invocation of the "Diva Ruthenica"(Ruthenian goddess) enabled a passing stranger to help rescue his son who had fallen into a river (NK, 23/19 folio 323v).

[180] The *Litteræ annuæ* record many such instances. The following is the case of a desperate, obviously very distraught man. Burdened with an enormous debt, he fled deep into the forest and offered to pledge his soul to the hellish throng if it would provide him with money. When no help was forthcoming, he ceased from his fearful blasphemies and turned toward God and against his demon; then free of all this, he wandered about in the forest: "Unus erat qui paupertate gravissima pressus, cum nomina contracta ereditione vehementius urgente delere non potest, domo in sylvarum abditum profugit, ubi gentis infernalis opem identidem inclamans, animam si desiderato aere sibi subveniri cognosceret pignori relinquere paraverat, quo dantem hunc in modum levamen nullum inopiæ impetraret, ad deum versus demonem convertit a vocibus summæ blasphemiæ, a quibus identidem solutus silvas oberrebat" (NK, 2L 23.19 *Litt. An. Prov. Boh.1767,* folio 46r).

second time in 1719.[181] Even as the signs became clearer that the Society was facing a grave crisis, the Bohemian Province persevered in its commitment to missions beyond its borders. The range of its activities in the years preceding the suppression is testimony to the degree to which it regarded itself as part of a worldwide mission.

A responsibility peculiar to the Jesuit community of Bohemia was the so-called Saxon Mission. Although ruling over a predominantly Protestant region (and the historic home of some of the original defenders of Lutheranism), the court in Dresden had been Catholic since the end of the seventeenth century, when Elector Frederick August converted to Catholicism in order to become king of Poland. While the courts of Catholic Europe moved to exclude the Society from their innermost workings, the Saxon Electors continued to receive Jesuits throughout the 1760s. Fr. Constantius Caldonazzi, who died in the Clementinum on November 5, 1771, had spent six years "in missione Saxonica."[182] As late as 1773 fourteen Bohemian Jesuit priests were listed as assigned to Dresden, four to Leipzig, and one to Hubertusburg.[183] Among those assigned to Dresden were the confessors of the Elector, his mother, and his wife; the court chaplain; and tutors to two of the princesses.[184] Other Jesuits of the Bohemian Province, such as Joachim Pleiner, mentioned above, who later served in Vienna as the province's representative at the imperial court, worked in prisons and schools in the Saxon capital.[185] The Society was thus arguably in an extremely influential position at the Saxon court, although the exact nature of the relationship between individual Jesuits and members of the electoral family has yet to be fully investigated.[186] The Elector also was known to have attended dramatic performances at Jesuit schools when visiting Prague.[187]

---

[181] Antonín Vasilejevic Florovský, *Čestí Jesuité na Rusí* (Prague: Nakladatelství Vyšehrad, 1944), 380 ff.).

[182] MZAB, Cerroniho sbírka II, 345, folio 465.

[183] *Catalogus personarum & officiorum Provinciæ Bohemiæ Societatis Jesu an. MDCCIII,* 30 f.

[184] Franciscus Schirmer (born May 10, 1732, Cestice; died March 15, 1795, Prague) served as confessor to the Princesses Kunhut and Elisabeth (Čornejová and Fechtnerová, *Slovník,* 371).

[185] Born Sukorady, Jan. 19, 1706; professed of the four vows, Feb. 2, 1741; died at Prague, Nov. 16, 1769 (MZAB, Ceronniho sbírka II, 345, 601 f.).

[186] The Saxon mission had its moments of uncertainty. At one point in 1769, rumors circulated that the common people were secretly ridiculing the Catholic practices of the court, and that because the new eighteen-year-old elector, Frederick Augustus III, was no longer able to claim the Polish crown, he would be tempted to turn to the "opinionibus Lutheri." At the end of the year, however, the Society could still claim the elector and his wife as devoted to the Church and not converted to Lutheranism (NK, 23/19 *Litt. An. Prov. Boh 1769,* folio 176r).

[187] NK, MS XXIII C105/15, *An. Prov. Boh. 1761,* folio 234v.

It is clear, however, that in the post-suppression period, former Jesuits did not enjoy any special privileges or considerations in Saxony, and may in fact have fared worse than the Jesuits of Silesia, to whom Frederick the Great extended many courtesies. As for any influence that the Jesuits might have had in rallying support in Dresden for their traditional patrons, the Habsburgs, it is worth noting that in the War of Bavarian Succession in 1778, Saxony sided against Joseph II in his bid to acquire Bavaria. It might be argued that the Jesuit presence continued in Dresden after the suppression, in that former Jesuit Alois Schneider (1752–1818) served as confessor to the Elector and King of Saxony, although ties to the communities of Bohemian Jesuits were lost for good.[188]

Throughout the eighteenth century the Bohemian Province also maintained what might be called a mission to the imperial court in Vienna. In the 1760s Ernestus Puschmann and Johannes Bleiweis were among the priests whose full-time assignment was to represent the province in the *Residenzstadt*.[189] Considering the increasingly vulnerable position of the Society and the traditionally strong ties between the court and the Jesuits, the Vienna mission, we might assume, enjoyed the services of men of outstanding ability, who would have left records of their efforts to shore up the deteriorating position of the Jesuits and seek out allies for their cause. In fact, the opposite is true. Neither Bleiweis, Puschmann, or any other Bohemian Jesuits sent to Vienna were outstanding figures, and no letters or reports survive that recount the accomplishments of these men at court during this crucial period. Prince Khevenhüller-Metsch's exhaustive and gossipy diary passes over these Bohemians in silence, and the controversial literature of the day likewise ignores the Bohemian mission to Vienna. The lacuna raises one of the most significant questions in the pre-suppression history of the Bohemian Society, but it can be explained as symptomatic of the degree to which anti-Jesuit forces in Vienna were carrying the day. The leadership of the Bohemian Province may have seen the assignment of talented Jesuits to the court as merely a waste, although it is more likely that superiors in Prague comprehended neither how perilous the situation facing the Society had become nor how the Habsburgs had adopted new tactics in order to hold on to power. While Jesuits remained loyal to the older principle of the legitimacy of the dynasty and had not been swept along by the "dynastic patriotism" that was becoming the new cornerstone of Habsburg internal policy, not only were the opponents of the Society able to thwart its

[188] Schneider was apostolic vicar of Saxony and, after 1801, protonotary. Shortly before his death he became titular bishop of Argos (Wilhelm Katz, S.J., "Exjesuiten als Bischöfe," *ARSI* 6 (1937): 200).

[189] Bleiweis died in Vienna on February 2, 1760; Puschmann's assignment apparently kept him in Vienna until the suppression, and he may have died there sometime later (Čornejová and Fechtnerová, *Slovník*, 31, 356 f.; Pelzel, *Gelehrte*, 204).

relationship with the court, but the Society itself was unaware of how the times were changing.[190]

Given the growing pressures on the Bohemian Province in the late 1760s, it is surprising to discover that in 1768, the Province embarked on a missionary project in far-off Transylvania.[191] The connection between this principality, one of the most remote and unstable in the Habsburg realm, and Bohemian Jesuits is shrouded in mystery. After some notable successes, the Society had been expelled from the principality in the early-seventeenth century by the Calvinist prince Gábor Bethlen.[192] Much of the Society's missionary effort had been directed at German-speaking "Saxons," who were both farmers and burghers in several fortified towns.[193] Ultimately, the Bohemian-directed mission, like other efforts of the Society in Transylvania, did not produce many lasting results. Frs. Joannes Koffler and Matthias Schmidt were in Transylvania in 1770, an assignment that placed them at the easternmost limit of popular Catholicism in central Europe.[194] In 1771 Fr. Ignatius Adam, who hailed from Bohemia, died in Hermannstadt (now Cibiu, Romania); no successor was reported in the *Litteræ annuæ* for that year.[195]

Although the Transylvanian project was small and not as successful as many other undertakings of the Bohemian Society, its significance is considerable. The willingness of the Jesuits to embark on this mission when they did demonstrates how confident the Society still was in the dynasty and its

[190] For the principle of dynastic legitimacy, see Peter F. Sugar, "The Rise of Nationalism in the Habsburg Empire," *Austrian History Yearbook*, 3 (1967): 95. The notion of dynastic patriotism *(Kaisertreue)*, which had existed even before the accession of Maria Theresia, but which increasingly supplanted the older sacral and legalist arguments, is addressed in "The Nature of Non-Germanic Societies under Habsburg Rule," by Peter F. Sugar, *Slavic Review* 22 (163): 2ff.

[191] NK, 23/19, *Litt. An. Prov. Boh. 1770*, folio 26r.

[192] Dominic Kosáry, "Gabriel Bethlen: Transylvania in the XVII Century," *Slavonic and East European Review* 17 (1938–39): 162–72.

[193] By one estimate, a high proportion, perhaps two-thirds, of all the Jesuits involved in missions outside of the Bohemian Province were native speakers of German (Anton Stahl, S.J., "Der deutsche Priester- und Ordensnachwuchs in der Tschechoslowakei," in *Die deutschen Katholiken in der Tschechoslovakischen Republik*, ed. Heinrich Donat [Warnsdorf: Verlag A. Opitz, 1934], 140).

[194] *Catalogus Personarum et Officiorum Provinciæ Bohemiæ Societatis Jesu 1770*, 32. Koffler, born in the New Town of Prague in 1711, spent many years in the Far East and remained in Transylvania after the suppression, dying there in December 1780. His history of that region, written in Latin, was lost (Johann Nepomuk Stöger, *Scriptores Provinciæ Austriacæ Societatis Jesu* [Ratisbon: Manz, 1855], 190; Constant von Würzbach, *Biographisches Lexikon des Kaisterthums Österreich*, 60 vols. [Vienna: Wilhem Braumüller, 1854–1860], 12:271–272; Johann Georg Meusel, *Lexikon der vom Jahre 1750 bis 1800 verstorbenen teutschen Schriftsteller*, 15 vols. [Leipzig, 1802–16], 7:260).

[195] NK, 23/19, *Litt. An. Prov. Boh. 1771* folio 386r.

ability to safeguard the future of its Counter-Reformation agenda, and how misguided they were in being so. Transylvania itself, while not contiguous with Bohemia or inhabited by many settlers from that region, was of notable strategic importance to the Habsburgs. Not only did the principality have a history of Hungarian-led resistance to Habsburg rule, but it was inhabited by "Wallachs" (Romanians) who constantly proclaimed their desire to be included among the four "received nations" of the land.[196]

Romanian culture and language, neither Slavic nor Magyar in origin, were rallying points for the peasant leaders who would stage a full-scale rebellion in 1784.[197] By laboring in this less-than-fruitful vineyard, Bohemian Jesuits were doing more than trying to strengthen the commitment of the Uniate Church to Rome; they were also establishing a Catholic Baroque presence, overlaid with rituals that commemorated the dynasty, in a potentially hostile territory.[198] Moreover, they were working in an environment where the practical necessity of numbers dictated tolerance of the Orthodox majority. The Habsburgs were neither willing nor able to eliminate the influence of the Orthodox Church in this region, and so Bohemian Jesuits found themselves officially supported by a far-off bureaucracy, but unable to bring the same pressure to bear against local religious practices that had been possible in Bohemia.[199]

The presence of a Protestant church, in this case Calvinist, in Transylvania meant that Bohemian Jesuits would encounter implacable resistance from yet another quarter. But even though Calvinism is linked by some writers with the beginnings of the Enlightenment in the Netherlands and Scotland, this was not the case in the easternmost realms of the Habsburgs. Here Calvinism expressed a resistance to the Catholic dynasty that was free of any tendencies towards rationalist philosophies or notions of tolerance. In Transylvania possessors of two visions of a well-articulated absolute truth

---

[196] Never unwilling to meet a new linguistic challenge, Jesuit missionaries soon were preaching in Wallachian (NK, 23/19, *Litt. An. Boh. Prov. 1771,* folio 350r).

[197] David Prodan, *Supplex libellus Vallachorum; or, The Political Struggle of the Romanians in Transylvania during the 18th Century,* trans. Mary Lazarescu (Bucharest: Publishing House of the Socialist Republic of Romania, 1971), 165 f.

[198] In Transylvania, Uniate intellectuals, many of them priests, resisted Jesuit efforts to draw Transylvania closer to Roman dogma and ritual. In this environment Jesuit missionaries faced a much more difficult task than in Bohemia, where there was no clergy opposing them who were capable of offering organized resistance (Keith Hitchins, "Religion and Rumanian National Consciousness in Eighteenth Century Transylvania," *The Slavonic and East European Review* 57 [1979]: 214–39).

[199] Ludwig Binder, "Die evangelische Kirche in Siebenbürgen zur Zeit der Reformen Joseph II: Mit besonderer Berücksichtigung des Toleranzpatents," in *Im Lichte der Toleranz: Aufsätze zur Toleranzgesetzgebung des 18. Jahrhunderts in den Reichen Joseph II., ihren Voraussetzungen und ihren Folgen,* ed. Peter F. Barton (Vienna: Institut für Protestantische Kirchengeschichte, 1981), 172.

collided, and the Society made little headway among the adherents of the Reformed Church.[200]

Other Bohemian Jesuits were employed on an individual basis at various foreign courts, for the structure of the Society allowed priests to pass many years outside the boundaries of their own province. Although Joannes Hillebrandt spent the majority of his career as a Jesuit in Spain and Sicily, he was still listed in the roster of the Bohemian Province.[201] Franciscus de Paul Cardell, a native of Prague, spent thirteen years in the service of the King of the Two Sicilies in Naples, dying at the age of fifty on January 8, 1768, in Trent.[202] Joannes Diesbach, who after the suppression would become the mathematics tutor of Francis, the future emperor, served in Linz as the "Hofmeister" of the teenaged Count von Browne.[203] Similarly, Franciscus Schirmer, who had taught Latin and Greek in the Philosophical Faculty of Prague university, served as a tutor in the household of Graf von Sternberg after the suppression.[204] Joannes Wendlingen spent many years in Madrid, where he published a text in Spanish on mathematics, and was an instructor to the King's children.[205] When the Society was expelled from Spain, he returned to Prague, where he directed the Museum mathematicum, one of the most important collections of scientific instruments in Europe east of the Danube.

Finally, a handful of Jesuits of the Bohemian Province worked in much more remote European settings, the most remote of them being the mission of the Bohemian Province to Wallachia, which lay beyond the boundaries of the Habsburg domains.[206] Other Jesuits were assigned to Loreto, a major goal of pilgrimages in the Baroque era, as well as to Rome,

---

[200] Hugh Trevor Roper makes this important distinction between various national varieties of Calvinism in his *European Witch-Craze of the Sixteenth and Seventeeth Centuries and Other Essays* (New York: Harper Torchbooks, 1967), 139.

[201] Hillebrandt, who had been confessor to the Queens of Spain and the Two Sicilies, died in Madrid on January 11, 1764 (MZAB, Cerroniho sbírka, II, 345, folio 521).

[202] Ibid., folios 467–68. The court of Naples was one of the linchpins of the diplomatic network maintained by Maria Theresia and Joseph, and the position of ambassador frequently went to one of the greatest princes of their realms (Gates-Coon, *Landed Estates*, 42–44). Cardell was probably the one Jesuit reported in the *Litteræ* of 1767 who was still active in Naples (NK, 23/19, folio 5v).

[203] Pezlel, *Gelehrte*, 262. Joseph II, supposedly vehement in his anti-Jesuit sentiments, appointed Diesbach to the imperial post in 1784 when he no longer had a Jansenist spiritual director (Jean Bérenger, *A History of the Habsburg Empire*, 72, 174). Bérenger, who identifies Diesbach as the young archduke's confessor (a position he might have held concurrently with that of tutor) credits the former Jesuit with helping foster Francis's conservative Catholicism. It seems likely, however, that Francis needed little encouragement in this direction.

[204] Born in 1723; died in 1795 (Čornejová and Fechtnerová, *Slovník*, 398 f.).

[205] *Catalogus personarum Prov. Boh. 1767*, 68; Pelzel, *Gelehrte*, 226.

[206] ARSI, Boh. Prov. 194, *Relatio missionum*, 70 f.

Vienna, and Lvov.[207] Many Bohemian Jesuits were still working in the "Indies" during the last years before the suppression: in 1750, forty-nine were "transmarini" (stationed overseas).[208] Despite the distances and the slowness of travel and communications, the centralized organization of the Society enabled Bohemian Jesuits, wherever they were assigned, to remain in contact with their superiors in Prague and Rome.

We should also mention Jesuits who traced their origins to the Bohemian Province and who sometimes ventured even farther from home. Ignacio Tirsch, a native of Komotov, sailed to Mexico after completing his studies in Brno. In Baja California, thousands of miles from Bohemia, Tirsch helped found a mission and left behind a collection of vivid watercolors of local flora, fauna, and products of the native culture.[209] Tadeus Javier Henis or Enis, also a native of Bohemia, achieved somewhat greater notoriety.[210] The superior in the Paraguayan reduction of San Ignacio-Guazu, Henis was said to have written a diary describing the abuses practiced by the Jesuits in their Paraguayan missions. Opponents of the Jesuits used the diary, which may never have actually existed and has in any case disappeared from sight today, to bolster their arguments for the destruction of the Paraguayan "republic" established by the Society.[211] Enis did not return to Bohemia after the expulsion of the Society from Spanish territory, and we do not know where or when he expired, although he may have survived in the trackless Paraguayan forests until 1769.[212] Men such as Tirsch and Enis were exceptions, but they did reflect a tradition, stretching back to the beginning of the previous century, of Jesuits from the Austrian and Bohemian Provinces traveling to remote missions.[213]

---

[207] Ibid. There was also an important, if unofficial, link between the Austrian and Bohemian Provinces. At the time of the suppression, there were forty-five Jesuits born in Bohemia or Moravia in the Austrian Province, of whom ten resided in Hungary (Ladislaus Szilás, S.I., "Die österreichische Jesuitenprovinz im Jahre 1773: Eine historische-statistische Untersuchung," *AHSI* 47 (1978): 128 f.).

[208] NK, 1288 MS XXIII C105/15, *An. Prov. Boh. 1750*, folio 5r.

[209] *The Drawings of Ignacio Tirsch, a Jesuit Missionary in Baja California*, narrative by Doyce B. Nunis, Jr., trans. Elsbeth Schulz-Bischoff (Los Angeles: Dawson's Bookshop, 1972).

[210] "Né en Bohême le 29. juillet 1711" (Sommervogel, *Bibliothèque*, 4:270). Many other details of Enis's life are lacking.

[211] Vicente D. Sierra, *Los Jesuitas Germanos en la conquista espiritual de Hispano-America: Siglos XVII-XVIII* (Buenos Aires, Faculdades de Filosofia y Teologia, 1944), 391.

[212] V. Rynes, "Los Jesuitas Bohemicos trabajando en las missiones de America Latina despues de 1620," *Ibero-Americana Pragensia* (1971), 201.

[213] Rudolph Grulich has cited a typescript list of Jesuits from the Bohemian Province during the seventeenth and eighteenth centuries ("Der Beitrag der böhmischen Länder zur Weltmission des 17. und 18. Jahrhunderts," *Archiv für Kirchengeschichte von Böhmen- Mähren-Schelsien (A.f.KB-M-S)* 5 [1978]: 376 f. 7). The writer has not been able to examine this list, identified as P. Pitrau, "Seznam jesuitských misionářů české provincie ze 17.a 18. stol. o. O. o. J."

Since their emergence as a religious order two hundred years earlier, the Jesuits had sought out connections with royal and noble houses, and had often served as confessors to emperors and kings, a vocation that earned them much jealousy and criticism on the part of their rival religious. The charge that Jesuits exercised undue influence over rulers was complemented by the accusation that, in turn, the rulers often manipulated Jesuit policies. Modern historians have acknowledged that this was often true. Dauril Alden, writing about the Jesuits of the Portuguese Assistancy, notes the complex factors that compelled Jesuits to submit to temporal authority:

> [T]he Society of Jesus, far from being disdainful of Portuguese royal authority, were markedly submissive to it and undertook many assignments that had no direct bearing on the Order's perceived spiritual mission. Jesuits were compliant with the king's wishes partly because they found it difficult to refuse appeals from the high and mighty, but also because they recognized, as did perceptive royal officials, that in some of the king's domains there were few people who could be trusted to do a job competently and honorably.[214]

Much the same could be said about many Jesuit undertakings for the Habsburgs. Before the innovations and reforms of the latter part of Maria Theresia's reign, the dynasty lacked the bureaucracy to carry out its wishes effectively. Later Joseph II, struggling to bring about radical changes in the 1780s, found himself without the human resources to execute the stream of edicts he produced. Jesuits were obvious candidates for many assignments in the service of the Habsburgs, and some of them equaled or surpassed the enthusiasm Alden detected in the Jesuits of the Portuguese Assistancy.

Several factors account for this. First, many important Jesuits of the Bohemian Province had ties to Habsburg Austria, having been born or undergone formation there. Next, the relationship between the ruling family and Bohemia was much closer geographically than the connection between the far-flung Portuguese overseas dominions and Lisbon. Roads through Bohemia were at least as bad as elsewhere in central Europe, but in good weather a messenger on horseback could reach Prague from Vienna in less than two days. Prague itself, the "Matka měst" or mother of Bohemian cities, was located in the center of Bohemia, with roads and waterways radiating out in all directions to other cities. Most important of all, the alliance between the Society and the Habsburgs was no contested arrangement where control over schools, estates, or other enterprises was occasionally disputed or where the apparent goals of the Society and the civil authorities were in constant conflict. No autonomous reductions such as those developed in Paraguay were ever envisioned for Bohemia, nor were the Jesuits

---

[214] Dauril Alden, "Tribulations of a Special Relationship; The Society of Jesus vs. the Crown of Portugal, Sixteenth to Eighteenth Centuries," in *Render unto Caesar: The Religious Sphere in World Politics,* ed. Sabrina Petra Ramet and Donald Treadgold [Washington, D.C.: The American University Press, 1995], 166).

ever embroiled, even in the days of their most tumultuous confrontations with Archbishop Harrach, in any conflicts of the magnitude that troubled the Spanish and Portuguese Assistancies.

In short, the Society had worked closely with the Habsburgs, in Bohemia and elsewhere, for more than a century and a half before the suppression. More often than not, the connection between the Bohemian Jesuits and the dynasty, fostered initially at the bureaucratic level, had grown intimate and mutually advantageous; yet a distinctive feature of the period under consideration here is that the assumed closeness of this relationship was under unmistakable strain, and that this strain was influencing the way Bohemian Jesuits recorded their activities.[215] We have touched upon the overall decline in support for the Society earlier in chapter 2 and elsewhere; to the problems of an antiquated curriculum and enemies both within and outside the Catholic Church must be added the general sentiment growing in Vienna that every aspect of life in the realm must be approached from a rational perspective. Reports of Jesuits continuing to encourage and participate in pre-rational folkways that were not in keeping with the new agenda of the monarchy were reaching Vienna by midcentury, providing ammunition for reformers who sought to remove Jesuits from all positions of power.[216]

The inability of so many of the Jesuits of the Habsburg realms to respond adequately to this challenge in part resulted from the persistence of a vital Counter-Reformation worldview among Jesuits in many corners of the dynasty's empire, including Hungary, where the belated encounter with the forces of the Counter-Reformation continued into the 1760s.[217] The image of the Habsburg monarch as a protector of the Church and therefore of those religious orders who defended and expanded the Church's influence was a powerful one, not easily abandoned after several centuries of proving its validity.[218] Even a few short years before the suppression, some Jesuits were choosing, unwisely, to ignore developments outside the Habs-

---

[215] David Sorkin develops the thesis of a widespread anti-Jesuit movement within the ranks of Reform Catholicism, as distinct from those forces, epitomized by Pombal of Portugal and the Bourbon monarchs, who opposed the Society largely because of their desire to seize its reputed power and wealth, and because of their indifference or hostility to orthodox Catholicism (David Sorkin, "Reform Catholicism and Religious Enlightenment," *Austrian History Yearbook* 30 [1999]: 187–219).

[216] The removal of Jesuits from chairs of canon law as a result of pressure from the reformist Studienhofkommission is detailed in *State Absolutism and the Rule of Law: The Struggle for Codification of Civil Law in Austria, 1753–1811,* by Henry E. Strakosch (Sydney: Sydney University Press, 1967), 162. Strakosch paints a vivid picture of the severely, even brutally, "rational" program introduced by Joseph after 1780; elements of this style of governance were becoming evident during Maria Theresia's lifetime.

[217] R. J. W. Evans, "Comment," *Austrian History Yearbook,* 30 (1999): 231.

[218] Kurt Agustin Huber, "Der Sudetendeutsche Katholizismus," *AfKB-M-S,* 1 (1967): 45.

burg world and, blissfully confident that all would turn out well, carry on as before.[219]

Conclusion

Viewed in the light of these larger political and strategic considerations, the mission activities of the Bohemian Society do not appear to have contributed to its survival; indeed, they may even have hastened its demise. But the story is not a simple tale of a backward-looking religious organization that was finally done in by the forces of progress, a scenario offered by many historians, who assume that fears of witchcraft and other preoccupations with the supernatural emerge from a popular culture that is irrational and autonomous. In this scenario, the forces of enlightenment, usually led by secular authority, must rescue the people from their own delusions.[220] Yet the series of events described in this chapter do not demonstrate that the Society of Jesus falls within the category of either the enlightened force determined to bring material improvement or the obscurantist organization seeking to keep the people in darkness.

This statement is true even if we leave out of consideration the purely scientific undertakings of a Stepling or Tessanek, for the Society easily mixed its supernatural and more concrete approaches to human problems. To the degree that the Society encouraged belief in ghoulish or bizarre practices that the devout Maria Theresia abhorred, it jeopardized its future, and jeopardized the legitimacy of its other (for example, educational) programs. But when the same desire to help the unfortunate motivated Jesuits to offer support and care to a woman struggling through a difficult childbirth, the Society was contributing to an outcome of which the Empress wholeheartedly approved, and which even Joseph II might have looked upon with approval.[221] Where it could recognize practical benefits, the

---

[219] In addition to the papal encyclicals and other documents originating from Rome that have already been alluded to, there were also periodic signals that the wealth of the Society, however it was being put to use, was also a liability. The papal encyclical *Cum primum,* issued on September 17, 1759, reiterated the point that the clergy should not seek temporal wealth (Claudia Carlen, ed., *Papal Encyclicals, 1740–1878* [Raleigh: Consortium, 1973], 121).

[220] H. C. H. Erik Midelfort, "Witch Hunting and the Domino Theory," in *Religion and the People, 800–1700,* ed. James Obelkevich (Chapel Hill, University of North Carolina Press, 1979), 279.

[221] Joseph's view of the miraculous is harder to assess than might appear at first glance. Like most of his siblings, Joseph was probably tutored at some point by Jansenist teachers (Derek Beales, "Joseph II and the Monasteries of Austria and Hungary," in *Religious Change in Europe, 1650–1914: Essays for John McManners,* ed. Nigel Aston [Oxford: Clarendon Press, 1997], 169). Yet many of the anti-ecclesiastical statements attributed to Joseph have been shown to be fabricated or greatly exaggerated (Derek Beales, "The False Joseph II," *The Historical Journal* 3 [1975]: 494).

dynasty was in no rush to destroy existing institutions. The degree to which the political leadership regarded the mission activities of the Society in Bohemia, as opposed to their schools, as beneficial is unclear, and the documentation left by Jesuit writers sheds no light on this question. The Bohemian Society itself strove to develop mission strategies that were more systematic and less potentially disruptive.[222] What the *Litteræ,* obituary notices, and other records generated by the Society do reveal is a stubborn resistance to change, and a refusal to acknowledge forces at work beyond the Bohemian countryside that were threatening the entire missionary undertaking. These records also, so repetitive and wedded to traditional procedures, suggest that the mission program lacked the potential to sustain momentum and commitment among the populace after the missionaries had moved on. As rumors of the stubbornness and ineffectiveness of the Society circulated in Vienna, they only bolstered the arguments of those at court and elsewhere who asserted that the Society must go.

The Society in Bohemia worked in a complicated ethnic environment, and one must proceed with caution when applying conventional ethnographic models to the encounter between the Jesuits and the communities of Bohemia. Advances in interethnic research suggest that earlier models which grouped individuals in eastern-European communities into convenient "language islands" for study were inadequate, for they presupposed an isolation and level of self-containment that did not exist even in the early-modern period. Although some groups of German and Czech speakers existed in Bohemia, sometimes in mutual isolation, more often the two groups intermingled, and even uneducated individuals were often bilingual and familiar with more than one set of cultural norms. Overlapping cultural boundaries, survivals of earlier communities, and innovations are now recognized as part of the pattern of life in such ethnic communities.[223] In smaller towns and villages, contacts between Jews and Christians were the norm as well. Therefore, to approach Jesuit mission activities from the standpoint of a monolithic religious organization interacting with one isolated cultural group after another is misleading.

We must also stress that many of the Bohemian Jesuit missionaries were themselves members of the culture to which they ministered, or had at

[222] While the "Italian" style of missions continued throughout much of the century, a newer style developed by the Bohemian Jesuit Ignaz Parhamer gained ground after midcentury. This approach was far more systematic than its predecessor, and aimed at greater understanding for participants. Groups of peasants receiving instruction were watched over by examiners, who in turn were supervised by prefects. Austrian Jesuits were so impressed that they sent their colleagues to Bohemia for retraining (Ward, *Christianity under the Ancien Régime,* 63).

[223] Ingeborg Weber-Kellermann, "Problems of Interethnic Research in Southeast Europe: A Consideration of Method," in *German* Volkskunde: *A Decade of Theoretical Confrontation, Debate, and Reorientation,* ed. and trans. J. R. Dow and H. Lixfeld (Bloomington: Indiana University Press, 1986), 171–83.

least emerged from these cultures before beginning their formation in the Society. The precise nature of the relationship between missionary and peasant can never be completely known, but it is safe to say that the individual characteristics of all the participants complicated such relationships; and the specifics of each encounter, be it dominated by the dangers of illness, the stresses of marginal existence, or previously held religious beliefs, added to the mélange of complications.

The traveling fathers must often have inspired fear, not merely of divine justice or even ecclesiastical censure, but of civil justice in this life as well.[224] Paying a "confessional Kreutzer" to all confessing priests, a practice that was not discontinued until 1767, further complicated this relationship, introducing elements of a financial arrangement into a relationship already saturated with overtones of religious fervor and pressure to conform.[225] At the same time, the institutional approach of the Society to missions was, as we have seen, relatively consistent between groups, and this itself further complicated the specific interactions between Jesuit and peasant, town dweller, or city resident.

Discussing Jesuit missions requires us to emphasize what for lack of a better term is generally called popular religion, although the connotations of the term can be misleading. The culture of popular religion itself, in which the interactions between missionary and men, women, or children took place, should not be dichotomized as either identical to or the reverse of formal ecclesiastical or state institutions.[226] The term "popular culture" with all its implied contrast with higher culture, is misleading in the mission context as well. In the countryside aristocrat and peasant frequently worshiped at the same church and sought out the same miraculous relics and images. Of course, the actual experiences of these two individuals, their expectations, fears, and responses to the Baroque aesthetic of contrast and danger may have been quite different; but the evidence left behind by the

[224] Close to nine hundred heretics were put to death in Bohemia and ten thousand interrogations took place between 1701 and 1780 (Marie-Elisabeth Ducreux, "La 'question tchèque' exorcisée?" in *Les Religions de l'est,* ed. Patrick Michel [Paris: Les éditions du Cerf, 1992], 46). Persons who possessed heretical books were fined, and the money was sometimes donated to the Hereditas S. Wenceslai.

[225] Josef Svátek, *Dějiny národa českého,* 173. This was a small sum of money intended to supplement a priest's income. Jesuits were forbidden to accept money under such circumstances.

[226] Richard C. Trexler, "Reverence and Profanity in the Study of Early Modern Religion," in von Greyerz, *Religion and Society,* 246. Trexler points out that the German academic tradition has also taken a "discrete confessional approach" to the study of religious and theological matters, which adds another unhelpful dichotomy to much of the existing literature. See also Stanley Brandes, "Conclusion: Reflections on the Study of Religious Orthodoxy and Popular Faith in Europe," *Religious Orthodoxy and Popular Faith in European Society,* ed. Ellen Badine (Princeton: Princeton University Press, 1990), 185–99.

Society stresses the similarities with which pastoral or missionary work was carried out, not the differences.[227] The Jesuit preoccupation with titled aristocracy is impossible to overlook, but the fathers remained constant in their presentation of the verities of their faith, regardless of the status of the communicant. An investigation of the encounter between the Jesuits, with their own ethnic identities, and the communities where missions were conducted must acknowledge the complexities of the encounters as well as their commonalities, even if they cannot be fully explored from the side of the lay participants.

Moreover, two centuries later it is not easy to determine all the elements of the experiences described in the *Annales* composed by Jesuit priests. How can we measure the actual effect of the "opem Virgineam" (assistance from the Virgin) that a blind child is reported to have received?[228] What are we to make of the testimony of a non-Catholic surgeon who pronounced the healing of a woman's tumor "beyond the powers of nature"?[229] Should this experience be called delusion or faith? Is the reporter misunderstanding the experiences he describes or providing a valuable insight into the mindset of the Baroque? The answers depend in part on whether the worldview held by the Jesuit writer and presumably by the afflicted women as well is accepted as valid. As the individual case studies are reviewed, the immeasurable gulf that separates the Jesuit chronicler of these events from the modern researcher becomes increasingly evident. Despite the contributions of Jesuits to Enlightenment scholarship and even science, the reader of these accounts is continually under the impression that he has entered a pre-Enlightenment world whose principles of causality are at variance with modern thinking and, indeed, with the thinking of Jesuit empirical scientists of the day.

---

[227] Sometimes only the passing mention of a legacy inherited or a connection to high-ranking court officials provides a clue as to the social standing of the individuals described in Jesuit mission narratives. The tale of a young heiress who was rescued from the "perversion" of her Protestant mother's beliefs by Maria Theresia herself is characteristic (NK, 1288 MS XXIII c105/15, *An. Prov. Boh. 1761*, folio 207v).

[228] NK, 23/19, *Litt. An Boh. Prov. 1768* folio 95v. On this occasion both mother and child survived the "periculoso partu"; often the outcome, of course, was not as happy, although the Jesuit writer tried to put the best face on the situtation: "Versabatur quæpiam Dresdensis mense septimo prægnans ac phrenesi laborans in extremo vitæ discrimine. . . . Sectione mortuam prolem frustratim eximendam censerit, auxilium mulier a Thaumaturga flagitavit, atq. etiam obtinuit, si quidem 7. diebus lapsis absq. dolore omni humanaeq. manus adjutorio mortuam prolem edidit" (A woman in her seventh month of pregnancy was out of her mind and in danger of death. When all means to deliver her dead infant failed, she asked help of a wonderworker; seven days later she delivered a dead infant painlessly and without human assistance) (NK, 23/19, *Litt. An. Prov. Boh. 1767* folio 95v).

[229] When this cranial tumor was reduced with the help of "oleo Aloysiano," "[c]hirurgus utut a fide nostra alienus ultra naturæ vires esse asseruit" (NK, MS XXIII c105/15, *An. Prov. Boh. 1765*, folio 456v).

Nor is this the only difficulty to confront anyone investigating the Society's missionary undertakings. Among the many differences between the viewpoints held by the eighteenth-century Jesuit and the modern historian, one of the most important is the gap between the clergy historians who were involved in the events they recounted and the lay historian.[230] Until less than a century ago, it was Jesuits who were involved in the events who wrote Jesuit history, and Jesuit historians have continued to make important contributions in recent years.[231] The responsibility of these men was to safeguard revealed religion, often in an apologetic approach to the topic. By contrast, the task of the secularly trained historian is to derive meaning from the record of the past, a responsibility that includes acknowledging cultural norms very different from those of the investigator.

This profound shift in the writing of ecclesiastical history in the past century and a half places new burdens on anyone who writes about the experiences of the participants in the Jesuit missions.[232] The collection of quantitative data regarding religious participation makes an important contribution to our understanding of late-Baroque Catholic culture; but by itself it cannot provide a picture of the experience of individuals.[233] Ultimately, we cannot know the internally perceived and understood characteristics of the experiences that dominate the accounts of the missions; yet, since such experiences lie at the heart of much of the entire Jesuit enterprise, the historian must address the phenomenological issues they raise.

Lacking the personal testimonies of the afflicted, the repentant, and the converted, as well as evidence from other witnesses, we must turn to such indirect and analogous evidence as ex voto art from the region to gain a sense of the experiences of those whom the Society believed it was aiding with the miraculous cures it attempted to offer.[234] Popular songs, the alma-

---

[230] In other words, a fundamentally intellectual culture aspiring to rationality has become the heir of one whose basis was revealed truth, causing a profound shift in methodology and in the motivations of the writer (Edward Norman, "Epilogue: The Ecclesiastical Historian," in Aston, *Religious Change,* 405).

[231] Not all Jesuit historians, however, can be classified as part of this participant category. One of the outstanding characteristics of Jesuit historiography in the past century has been its conscious move (with some exceptions) towards objectivity and self-criticism of earlier Jesuit history.

[232] A lucid discussion of the shifts in methodology and focus that have occurred in both Jesuit and Catholic historiography in general is found in "The Historiography of the Society of Jesus: Where Does It Stand Today?" by John W. O'Malley, in O'Malley, *The First Jesuits,* 24–29.

[233] An exhaustive case study focusing on quantitative data is Michael Pammer, *Glaubensabfall und wahre Andacht: Barockreligiösität, Reformkatholicizmus und Laiscizmus in Oberösterreich 1700–1820* (Vienna: Verlag für Geschichte und Politk, 1994).

[234] The literature in this field is as yet underdeveloped. The most complete work on the subject is Lenz Kriss-Rettenbeck, *Das Votivbild* (Munich: Verlag Hermann Rinn, 1958), which contains many examples from the eighteenth century but only one from Bohemia from this

nacs and popular writings of the day, and naïve religious art—all provide clues to the range of internal experiences that emerge from the missionary encounter.[235] Yet the internal, subjective elements of the engagement with the supernatural that constitute the core of the Jesuit mission encounter can only be discussed and analyzed from a distance. This distance involves not only time, but also the profound differences in worldview between the twilight of the Baroque and our own time.[236]

The mission programs of the Society were the heart of its work in Bohemia; even its schools must be viewed in the light of their perceived missionary and evangelical purpose. The detailed presentation of mission work in the *Litteræ*, when contrasted with their silence concerning the renowned accomplishments of the Steplings, Cornovas, Vydras, and other intellectuals and teachers of the Society, says a great deal about how the Bohemian Province wished to portray itself to Rome, and how many of its own members understood their mission.[237] While charitable works were both an important element of the Jesuits' undertaking and a part of the activities of the sodalities that the Society supported, they too were subordinated to the religious mission that was the fundamental purpose of the Society. All the missionary endeavors of the Society in Bohemia must therefore be understood from the perspective of the ultimate goal of the Jesuits, which was to bring men and women to the truth of revealed religion, and to safeguard both the members of the Church and the Church itself from the enemies of the true faith.

---

period. However, the pathos and danger of pregnancy and childbirth is powerfully conveyed in many of the images, including one that portrays a group of children in a German family who did not survive; accompanying it is the inscription "Lieber Gott acht Kinder sind bei Dir, so schenk das neunte mir" (91).

[235] Popular literature in Czech included saints' lives, books of herbal remedies, adventure tales, and moralizing stories, many of which were illustrated with woodcuts. Hundreds of different books were produced in the eighteenth century, not counting shorter tracts whose number is unknown (Jiří Pokorný, "České literární kultura," in Petráň, *Počátky*, 246 f.).

[236] Temporally, this gap is not as great as might be supposed. As noted elsewhere, the Baroque as a cultural (and therefore psychological) moment lasted longer in Bohemia than in many other parts of western Europe; the evidence for this is found in the popular art of the nineteenth century (Oldřich J. Blažíček, *Iskusstvo cheskogo barokko* (Leningrad: Ministersvo Kulturi SSSR, 1974). The illustrations in the popular literature alluded to in the previous footnote likewise exhibit Baroque elements. Then, too, elements of the Baroque might appear in the training of a Jesuit whose career would stretch far beyond the period of the last Bohemian missions. Josef Dobrovský, whose fame lies in a direction far removed from most of the topics dealt with in this chapter, is described as having received a "Baroque" training (that is, one stressing the Baroque expressions of piety) in his early schooling in Klatovy (Jan Milíč Lochman, *Duchovní odkaz obrození* [Prague: Kalich, 1964], 28).

[237] The *Litteræ* were apparently read and reviewed carefully by officials at each site, so that the reports reflect not merely the viewpoint of individual writers and communities, but the Province of Bohemia as a whole (NK, 1287 MS XXIII C105/15, *An. Prov. Boh. 1762*, folio 252r).

Because the Society's intellectual traditions included the utilization of science and learning in the service of this faith, there was some room in the Bohemian Jesuit mission for the science of Stepling, even if there was no room for him in the reports that formed the official record of the province. The Province of Bohemia, like its counterparts throughout the Jesuit world, was rife with such tensions until the suppression put an end to it all. Only when we recognize this fact can we reconcile the seemingly incompatible activities of rationalist scientific inquiry and reliance on the miracle-working properties of relics and their corollaries (objects that had been brought into contact with relics, such as the *farina* of St. Aloysius).

While evaluating the work of the Society, the historian must choose whether it is possible to assess, from the distance of more than two centuries, the achievement of its all-encompassing and sometimes broadly defined goal. The long lists of persons converted and the anecdotes about repentant prostitutes and pious believers show beyond a doubt what the Jesuits believed and hoped they were accomplishing. Yet, given the impending collapse of the entire enterprise and the warnings of this collapse, we must indeed ask whether the goal as stated continued to be the real objective of the majority of Jesuits in Bohemia during their last years. There might also have been a self-conscious attempt to make the work of the Society seem especially important as its enemies circled ever closer. But, of course, the Jesuits' trusting faith that God would somehow come to their assistance might have been an important factor in their reactions to the events swirling around them. The answer to this final puzzle is complicated by the overlapping of the bureaucratic and missionary elements in the records that the Jesuits left behind, and by the multiple roles that Jesuits played as teachers, scientists, exhorters, guardians of the Church, and providers of access to the miraculous. In this complex and opaque mix is located the elusive essence of the Bohemian Jesuit mission enterprise.

chapter five

JEWS AND JESUITS

Jews are not hated because they have evil qualities; evil qualities are sought in them because they are hated.

—Max Nordau

Jesuitry and Jewry have many things in common.

—Étienne Pasquier

As the 1694 case of Shimon Abeles makes clear, relations between Jews and Jesuits in Bohemia were complicated and, generally, far from cordial. The Society inherited and did nothing to alter a centuries-old hostility toward Jews that was already embedded in Bohemian literary and ecclesiastical history and sustained in popular culture.[1] It also inherited the relationship between Bohemian Jews and the hierarchy of the Catholic Church, which had been characterized by the Church's support of the restrictive measures and outright persecution implemented by the civil authorities.[2] Most Jesuits saw it as their duty to strive to convert Jews to Catholicism, and the conversion process was frequently accompanied by attacks on Judaism itself and on the character of the Jews as a people. It is perhaps no surprise that few Jews were converted, and that a significant number of those who did accept baptism became "apostates" soon after; that is, they returned to the religion of their fathers.

Under these circumstances, the Society directed much of its proselytizing efforts toward children, who, like young Shimon, could sometimes be persuaded to convert after being separated from their parents. Jesuit tactics were persistent and, according to their own records, often successful, to some extent because Jewish parents had no legal right to defend their claims

[1] Jakob Apella, a wicked apostate who desecrated altars, is described in the *Czech Chronicle of Cosmas*, one of the oldest medieval histories of Bohemia (*Kosmova Kronika Česká*, Přeložili Karel Hrdina a Maria Blahová [Prague: Svoboda, 1972], 200).

[2] Pěkný, *Historie*, 179f.

to the children once the child had been baptized. Jesuit records abound with accounts of such cases. In 1766 a Jewish woman in Rakonice who had converted to Christianity left her child with her unconverted Jewish husband. Two talkative Jewish children told a Jesuit priest about the child, and he endeavored to have it taken away from its father by order of the captain of the district. He received permission to take the child, and the Society was able to report with pride that the child was baptized and sent to the "Italian Hospital" to be educated. The reaction of either parent (or, of course, of the child) to this development is not recorded.[3]

Both the involvement of secular authorities and the role of the Jewish woman in seeking a Christian upbringing for her child are commonplaces in Jesuit accounts of contacts with Jews. Likewise the stock character of the Jewish youth seeking to join the Church appears repeatedly in Jesuit reports.[4] (In the same year as the above-mentioned case, 1767, a deaf Jewish boy, "contra parentium minas, et blandimenta constans," was persuaded to be baptized.)[5] This pattern is repeated endlessly in Jesuit reports: in 1760, nineteen Jews from the countryside *(pagos),* led by an older man, sought the refuge provided by the Society, and among them was one young man who wished to undergo conversion.[6] The emphasis placed on the potential redemption of Jewish youths can be interpreted as evidence that Jesuits believed the "perfidious" qualities of Judaism were not innate, but acquired through exposure to the corrupting influence of Jewish ritual law. This point should be borne in mind when we consider the relationship between Jesuits and Jewish women.

Women were special targets of Jesuit conversion efforts and figure prominently in the *Litteræ*. A woman, described as "nearly the richest [Jewish?] woman in Bohemia," despite the efforts of her parents to arrange a marriage with a Jewish man, persisted in her efforts to be baptized. After her wedding, she fled from her new husband, and after pleading before the Royal *Gubernium,* was allowed to receive baptism.[7] Finally, another Jewish woman who had been converted was then "dolo malorum Christianorum" returned to her husband. (The motives of these Christians are not explained, but their appearance in the account suggests that at least some

[3] NK, Praha 23/17, *Litteræ Annuæ Collegii S. J. Vetero-Pragæ ad S. Clementem 1767,* folio 188v.

[4] The Jewish youth is often portrayed as having grown disgusted with the rituals of his religion: "fastidivit is a septimo ætatis anno Judaicos ritus" (NK, 1288 MS XXIII C105/15, *An. Prov. Boh. 1761,* folio 147r).

[5] That is, the boy seeking baptism braved the threats and resisted the appeals of his parents (NK, 27/17, *Litteræ Annuæ Collegii S. J. Vetero-Pragæ ad S. Clementem 1766,* folio 173r).

[6] ". . . confugere 19, inter hos adolescens duce seniore" (NK, MS XXIII 105/18, *An. Prov. Boh. 1760,* folio 79v).

[7] NK, 23/19, *An. Prov. Boh., 1769,* folio 173r.

Bohemian Christians may not have approved of the Jesuits' tactics.) After she became seriously ill, she feared for her soul and received the sacrament of baptism from a priest.[8]

Intermarriage between Jews and Christians was extremely rare. An occurrence in 1767 illustrates the complications attending such unions.[9] A Catholic man was married to a Jewish woman who had apparently not yet been converted; after she became pregnant, the couple disagreed as to the faith in which the child should be raised. When the child was born, the Christian midwife, fearing that it might die, baptized it, following a widespread practice of dubious legality. In the legal struggle that followed, the mother gave up the child, and a more official baptism was performed, again at the "Italian Hospital." The case as reported is of added interest because the linguistic abilities of one of the Jesuits ("noster linguagnarus") enabled the Society to learn of the struggle from two Jews, perhaps by eavesdropping, or perhaps from the Catholic party or from second-hand accounts.[10]

The Jesuit reports leave the impression of constant efforts on the part of the Society to convert Jews. Even when Jews did not actually convert, Jesuit chroniclers took pains to dwell upon the efforts made to persuade them, for example, by using "modulis musicis" at vespers and distributing a small book written in three languages. Reportedly, the populace eagerly requested copies of this book and always seemed to draw profit from it.[11] The report that Jews in Polna ended their Sabbath prayer early in order to listen to the preaching of the Fathers seems unduly sanguine. Some readers might see in this either a complete fabrication on the part of the Jesuits or perhaps a Jewish community so frightened at the possibility of a pogrom that it was willing to abridge its rituals in the hope of escaping violence.[12]

These accounts, included in the official annual reports to Rome, undoubtedly leave unstated familial and personal crises, social and economic pressures, and spiritual doubts no longer accessible to the historian. What is apparent is the willingness of Jesuits to break up Jewish families, isolate children, and press potential converts when their immortal souls were at

---

[8] NK, 2L 23/17, *Litteræ Annuæ Collegii S. J. Pragæ ad S. Clementem 1767*, folios 188v–189r.

[9] NK, 2L 23/19, *Annales Prov. Boh. 1767*, folio 49v.

[10] The language in question would have been either Yiddish or Judeo-German. Both tongues are very close to German; but the acknowledgement of the special skills of this particular Jesuit implies that not all members of the Society were able to understand the native tongues of Bohemian Jews.

[11] [L]ibellique idem argumentum triplici idiomate pertractantes quemadmodum avidissime expetibantur ita quoque liberalissime distribuebantur (NK, 1416 MS XXIII 105/18, *An. Prov. Boh. 1760*, folio 12r).

[12] "[S]ibi consuetas preces ante statutam alias horam ea de caussa persolvere, ut dictiones Patrum exciperent" (They cut short their usual prayers so that they could attend the fathers' sermons) (NK, 1416 MS XXIII 105/18, *An. Prov. Boh. 1760*, folio 48r).

stake.[13] Nothing else equaled the importance of embracing the faith, and virtually all accounts of contacts with Jews turn on this point, even when conversion did not actually take place. In the case of young Abeles, only a few decades after his death officially sanctioned accounts transformed his contemplated conversion into an actual conversion.[14]

It is also clear that Jewish converts were of special importance to the Society, and that their admission to the Church was accompanied with at least as much fanfare as that of converts from Lutheranism or other heresies.[15] These conversions are described more often and in greater detail than conversion from other faiths, and their narratives contain the recurring theme of the potential convert, often a vulnerable woman or child, who fled from ("profugit") fellow Jews in search of the safety that the Church and the civil authorities alone could provide.[16] Private citizens sometimes came to the aid of Jewish women and children. A case reported in 1765 has a ten-year-old Jewish girl and her mother escaping from an oppressive household and seeking baptism, only to be recaptured by the girl's father, who with the connivance of other Jews, held them captive. In the end they were rescued by a "cive Catholico" who conveyed them to the Clementinum, where both

[13] Nor was this tendency unique to Jesuit missionary efforts. In a celebrated case in Berlin in 1699, three young Jewish children fled from their parents to become Christians, a decision supported, not surprisingly, by the civil authorities. Cotton Mather, among other Protestant divines, took a keen interest in the case (Mel Scult, *Millennial Expectations and Jewish Liberties: A Study of the Efforts to Convert the Jews in Britain up to the Mid-Nineteenth Century* [Leiden: E. J. Brill, 1978], 54 f.).

[14] By 1723, in a major survey of Prague and its history, it was reported that Abeles had became a convert (Hammerschmied, *Prodromus*, 30).

[15] The Jesuits attached great importance to these public acknowledgements of conversion from apostasy: "[Q]uni *(sic)* catechumeni ad superstitionem redissent curatum ut hi secundum Perfidiæ pœnam mulctarentur exilio[;] immunitate vero quæ catechumenis ab Aula Clementissi. concessa fuerat inviolati servarentur[;] curatum item ut iidem a vexationibus, quibus impeti consueverunt liberi viverent librosque sibi noxios aut eripi aut corrigi paterentur" (NK, 2L/23/15/F, *Litt. An. Prov. Boh. 1766*, folio 490v). According to this passage, when(?) some Jewish catechumens relapsed into their previous superstitions, they were to be exiled as a punishment for their infidelity; but they were mercifully pardoned and allowed to live free of the usual harrassments, but they had to allow their harmful books to be either confiscated or emended.

[16] The spiritual refugee might, however, be a man. The annual report of 1766 recorded with approval the strenuous efforts of a Jewish man who, wishing to free himself from all encumbrances, abandoned all his possessions in Bohemia, sold his properties, and fled to Telcz; there he eagerly requested to be instructed from the documents that bring salvation; finally, he was admitted to the bosom of Holy Church through baptism: "Notandus item ex Hebræis ille, qui ut omnibus impedimentis sese expedisset, relictis in Bohemia sibi aliis necessariis emendoque complurium milliarum spatio ad Telczenses profugit, ac documentis salutaribus institui ardenter exoptavit . . . ad sacrum lavacrum Ecclesiæ Sanctæ gremium est admissus (NK, 2L/23/15/F, *Litt. An. Prov. Boh 1766*, folio 491r).

were baptized. Miraculously, the father too was persuaded to become a Christian.[17]

In a few cases the flight of the persecuted Jewish convert is described in even more dramatic terms. In 1768 a "most excellent wife [made] a heroic flight to the Catholic community, where she received instruction in our rite."[18] The author of these passages, steeped in Scripture, seems to be echoing biblical accounts of the flight of the Holy Family into Egypt, seeking safety from the persecution of the Jewish king Herod. The tendency to make the protagonists in these accounts seem "heroic" may have been unconscious, but its result was to increase the drama of the narrative, and thereby also to call attention to the role of the Society in helping bring about these wondrous events.

The most detailed and provocative account of events related to conversion is found in the *Litteræ* of 1760.[19] The story opens with a young Jewish man in captivity for some unstated reason. His people exerted every effort to persuade him not to become a Christian. In order to escape the danger that he might succumb to their blandishments, by an unheard-of provision of the Praetor, using faculties conferred on him by the Most Reverend Office [the Roman Holy Office(?)], he arranged to live at the guest house of the [bishop's(?)] curia, so that he might be baptized. Once he had received this sacrament, he was freed of all legal penalties levied against him.[20]

While this narrative as recorded contains several obscure passages, and while the reader must make allowances for the tendency of such accounts to follow stereotyped formats, it is still of great value for the light it

[17] NK, 1287 MS XXIII C105/15, *Litt. An. Prov. Boh. 1765*, folio 387r.

[18] "Lectissima conjuga . . . heroica fuga ad Catholicos, inter quos per nostrum rite instituta est." In doing so, this woman also fled from her young Jewish husband (NK, 23/19, *Litt. An. Prov. Boh. 1768*, folio 113r).

[19] NK, 1416 MS XXIIIC 105/18, *An. Prov. Boh. 1760*, folios 68v–69r: "Adolescens autem ex Hebræis inter captivos erat, multa pecunia, aliisque artibus, ad abiiciendum religionis Christianæ suscipiendæ propositum a suis tentatus, utque ab omni deinceps periculo esset remotior, effectum, ut a Judæis non . . . in carceribus [molestaretur], . . . maioris securitatis ergo, apud curiæ hospitium ademptis compedibus habitaret, idque etiam lata relegationis sententia, privilegioque nemini ante concesso, . . . ut is cursu tecto ad Theynensem basilicam ab urbis Prætore babtismatis caussa promoveretur, cuius conferendi potestatem a Reverendissimo Officio sibi concessam . . . qui subinde plenam a constituta pœna immunitatem babtizato impetravit."

[20] Note that prostitutes also were obliged to wear a yellow band on their clothing that identified their occupation (Merry E. Wieser, "Paternalism in Practice," in *The Process of Change in Early Modern Europe: Essays in Honor of Miriam Usher Chrisman*, ed. Phillip N. Bebb and Sherrin Marshall [Athens, Oh.: Ohio University Press, 1988], 186). See also the requirement from 1750 that Jewish *women* in Prague wear "einen gelben Fleck an der Stirn," in "Handschrifliches zur Geschichte der Juden in Prag in den Jahren 1744–1754," by Salomon Hugo Lieben, *Jahrbuch der Jüdisch-Literarchischen Gesellschaft*, 3 [1905–6]: 272).

sheds on official Jesuit perceptions of Jews and Judaism, individually and collectively. The virtuous motivations of a lone Jew, young and presumably innocent and vulnerable, are contrasted with the depravity, anger, and unreasonableness of the Jews *as a group,* led presumably by the educated adult males, who would have known enough about their own religion and Christianity to present an attack on the latter. The risks of contact between Jewish males and Christian women are reiterated, and the necessity of cooperation between the civil authorities and the Society is stressed. Themes of danger and sanctuary, threats and deliverance, predominate.

The local Jewish rabble function like the crowds in key scenes of a Baroque passion play: they heighten the emotional tension without becoming individually differentiated. The climax of the story, the conversion, is brought about through the faculty granted by a "Reverendissimo Officio," which because of its high rank and power was able to override local laws and customs. A story of this kind confirms the solemnity of the event and suggests the close relationship of the Society to such authorities, who in turn conferred legitimacy on the Society's actions. As is so often the case, the curtain drops before we can learn anything about the life of the young convert. Like Abeles, he remains forever youthful in the story, a model for other youths seeking baptism.

The distinction made here and elsewhere between the capacities of individual Jews to seek salvation and the collective guilt of Jews as a group, that is, being "Christ killers," among other such insulting designations applied to them by some Christians, is most noteworthy. Not only are the institutions of Judaism unworthy, but the group behavior and the inherited culpability of the Jews as a religion (but not as a "race" in the post-nineteenth-century sense of the term) render them despicable. The first step toward the saving power of God's love, in the view of the writers who composed the *Litteræ*, is physical separation from the Jewish community, an act involving risk and the danger of recapture at the hands of other Jews. Yet in eighteenth-century Bohemia, the motives for this separation are not always clear, nor are the results of the separation always what the Jesuits might desire.

Conversions Sincere and Insincere

During the time when the *Litteræ* were written, insincere Jewish conversions were very much on the minds of Bohemian Jews and Christians alike. One of the best-known Jews in the region, Jacob Frank (1726–91), had undergone a highly publicized conversion to Catholicism in 1759, after having previously embraced and then abandoned Islam. But even his most recent conversion was suspect, since he had long claimed to be the reincarnation of Sabbatai Tsevi, the charismatic mystic whose Messianic claims in the previous century had attracted a large following throughout the worldwide Jewish community. [21] The seemingly immoral behavior of some of Frank's followers cast even more doubt on the value of his conversion. Sabbatai himself had also ultimately converted to Islam when threatened with execution by the Ottoman sultan, a move that baffled many of his disciples and led others to believe that he would someday reveal his true power and rise above the debasement he had allowed himself to undergo.[22] But such an event never came to pass.

The Jewish conversions chronicled by the Society in the middle of the eighteenth century were thus taking place not only because of intense pressure from Christians but also of bitter disappointment that their hopes for a Messiah to deliver Jews from centuries-old oppression failed to be realized. The Jews of Bohemia had had more than their share of mystics who made appealing claims to the community, claims that fell short of the expectations they aroused. This climate of disappointment, suspicion, and anger hindered intellectual advances among the Jewish communities of Bohemia and fragmented a community already coping with poverty, banishment, and the constant threat of violence.

As a result, Jewish intellectual leaders lost status as they fended off attacks, not from Christians, but from coreligionists. Jonathan Eybeschütz (1690–1764), a gifted rabbi who achieved great success in Prague, was also suspected of dabbling in the mystic doctrines of Sabbataism; eventually he emigrated first to French Metz and then to Danish-controlled Altona.[23] The failure of such a Messiah to appear tempted some Bohemian Jews to accept other faiths, at least superficially; and in any case, the insularity and self-sufficiency of the Bohemian Jewish community that had sustained it though so many trials was starting to reveal fissures, despite its accepted religious leaders' struggles to maintain continuity.

From 1755 until 1793, the leading spiritual figure among the Jews of Bohemia was Rabbi Ezekiel Landau (1713–93), who had come to Prague

[21] Frank's followers were highly visible figures in the cultural life of Jews in Bohemia and Moravia throughout the century (Mordechai Breuer and Michael Granz, ed., *Tradition and Enlightenment, 1600–1780,* trans. William Templer, vol. 1 of *German-Jewish History in Modern Times,* ed. Michael A. Meyer, 4 vols. [New York: Columbia University Press, 1996], 233).

[22] Although there is no definitive evidence of contacts between Jesuits and members of the Sabbataian movement, the categories recorded in the *Litteræ* make clear that Jesuits perceived distinctions between various Jewish groups. An entry under "Conversi" for 1765 lists one convert from the errors of the Sadducees (NK, 1287 MS XXIII C105/15, *Litt. An. Prov. Boh. 1765,* folio 423v). The sect of the Sadducees had disappeared during the late Classical period, and thus the writer was apparently groping for some term somehow related to Baroque Latinity that would convey the different beliefs held by the convert. Could this person have been a follower of Sabbatai or even of Frank?

[23] H. I. Bach, *The German Jew: A Synthesis of Judaism and Western Civilization, 1700–1930* (Oxford: Oxford University Press, 1984), 42 f.

from Podolia.[24] Landau, receptive as he was to some of the reforms proposed by Joseph II, was nevertheless fundamentally a conservative who resisted innovation. He once wrote, "The essence of things is faith, not reason and investigation." Landau's insistence on a pre-Enlightenment view of learning and of relations between Jews and Christians would cause some Bohemian Jews to withdraw into the Medieval world of their forefathers, but it also drove others to look beyond the confines of the ghetto and to participate more willingly in the larger, Christian-dominated world.

But did these developments encourage Jews to be more receptive to Jesuit efforts to convert them? Probably not. Some historians have speculated that the majority of Jewish converts in Bohemia and Moravia were motivated either by their desperate poverty or by the oppressive laws that restricted marriages among Jews.[25] These possible motivations, of course, played no part in the narratives written for the records of the Society. Moreover, the Jesuit reports make no explicit references to the dawning of the *Haskala* (Enlightenment) that was beginning to make inroads among Bohemian Jewry, or the new choices becoming available to this generation of Jews that were denied to their ancestors. Although these tensions within the Jewish community cast a different light on the act of conversion than would have been the case a century earlier, the accounts written by Jesuits in the 1750s and '60s were couched in the same phraseology as they were long before Shimon Abeles had accidentally become an almost-Christian martyr. Again, the innate conservatism of the Society's methods of collecting, assessing, and reporting information blunted Roman superiors' ability to take these new developments into account. These methods also make it harder for us to assess the extent to which individual Jesuits grasped the changes affecting the Prague Jewish community. Instead, Jesuits on the official and institutional level continued to operate in a high-Baroque mode, oblivious to trends that in a few decades would bring Jewish students into the Philosophical Faculty of the Prague university, formerly one of the pedagogical high points of the Jesuit educational undertaking.

Jewish Women: Strayed, Rescued, Converted

The Jewish women who earned a place in the *Litteræ* of the Society display a variety of motivations and personalities and thus achieve a more vivid

---

[24] Hillel J. Kieval, "Autonomy and Independence: The Historical Legacy of Czech Jewry," in *The Precious Legacy: Treasures from the Czechoslovak State Collections*, ed. David Altshuler (New York: Summit Books, 1983), 88.

[25] The *Familienantengesetz* instituted by Charles VI in 1726 restricted the number of Jewish families that could live in the lands of the Bohemian Crown, and forbade all but the eldest son to marry, a ban that could be relaxed upon payment of a large sum of money (Meyer, *German-Jewish History*, 1:250; Pěkný, *Historie*, 77).

characterization than did their male counterparts. This characterization tended to focus on the women's emotional nature and to devote less effort to the supposedly intellectual qualities of the Jewish man, who might rely on the Torah or other literature to justify his obstinacy.[26] Some Jewish women, like their Christian counterparts, came to an understanding of the "true faith" only after encounters with evil derived from their own so-called false faith. The *Litteræ* of 1768 report the almost incredible tale of a "person," possibly Jewish and probably a woman, who by showing devotion to an idol attempted to force a demon to do her bidding. After listening to the sermons of the missionaries and seeing the error of her ways, she did penance and entered upon a better life.[27] The story then describes a man who from his youth was devoted to a demon; but going into a heretical land and marrying a non-Catholic wife, he came to understand the evil of his ways. So wishing to do penance, he went where he knew some missionaries could be found. But he could not persuade his wife to embrace the true faith, so he seized her corrupt Bible, which had confirmed her in her error, and brought it to the missionary. It is not stated explicitly whether either of the protagonists in these accounts was Jewish.

The first tale is especially hard to deconstruct. The Jesuits undoubtedly knew enough about Orthodox Judaism to realize that it viewed idols and commerce with spirits of any kind as abominations. Thus, if it indeed deals with a Jew, this story must either reflect the Jesuits' profound misunderstanding of what this convert had actually believed, or else it is a distortion of Kabbalist or Sabbataist practices widespread among eighteenth-century Jews.[28] Or perhaps the story as written down reflected the unreliable alley gossip based on third-hand reports brought to the fathers. From the Jesuit point of view, the difference may have mattered little; the story as told was further evidence of the murky and loathsome nature of Jewish culture in general and Jewish religious practices in particular.

Jesuit records also provide a glimpse of the relations between Jewish converts and Christian men and women of high birth, although the exact

---

[26] There are many instances when the heart of a Jewish woman was "moved"; for instance, see NK, 1281 MS XXIII C105/16, *Litt. An. Prov. Boh. 1757*, folio 188.

[27] "Inter plures in semitam salutis reductos Missionarii de poenientia Boemi memorant personam in omne prius facinus projectam, atq. DEI veri odio ita æstuantem, ut dæmonem, quem ad vota sua promptum cupiebat in idolo coleret; hæc enim exceptis in Missione dictionibus immanitatem admissorum criminum agnoscens, ac propterea pænitentiam agens vitæ melioris rationem iniit, atq. non nemo a prima ætate dæmoni devotus demumque in terras heterodoxas decedens alienam a fide uxorem duxit, qui tamen ad crimina sua respiciens ac pænitentiam acturus, locum in quo missionarios versari intellexerat, adiit; quodq. uxorem ad sacra nostra amplectenda nullo molimente adducere posset, erepta biblia corrupta, qui conjugem in erroribus firmabant, interim ad Missionarium detulit" (NK 23/19, *Litt. An. Prov. Boh. 1768*, folio 114r).

[28] Pěkný, *Historie*, 159–61.

connection between the parties must be placed in the context of the Bohemian Society's own needs and agenda. In 1769 several Jewish youths whom the Society had converted were about to receive baptism in a public ceremony, sponsored by an impressive gathering of some of the highest aristocracy of Bohemia. Among the sponsors was the Countess Josepha of Solhicz.[29] Sponsorship in this context probably did not necessarily entail close or continued contact, and the association of the distinguished names of the sponsors reflected as much glory on the Society (through whose efforts presumably the conversions had taken place) as it did on those converting. Like the reports of the noble students who attended Jesuit schools or the noble members of the audience during a Jesuit dramatic production, the identification of aristocratic patrons of Jesuit-assisted converts was a way for the Bohemian Society to demonstrate to Rome how politically secure it was, though time was to reveal how feeble this security could become.[30]

These vulnerable Jewish converts, the fleeing woman or the pious child, were surely objects of real concern and interest to Jesuit missionaries, but they were also minor characters in a larger drama in which the embattled Society struggled on many fronts to justify its existence, demonstrate its value to those in power, and solidify its position in the eyes of its superiors. The presence of wealthy and aristocratic allies of the Society at christenings, displaying all the ostentation associated with their rank, contributed to the image that the Jesuits wanted to convey: an organization that itself possessed considerable rank and status, one actively engaged in an important religious and civic responsibility, namely, the conversion of the Jews.[31]

The Jew as Other

The Jesuit chroniclers who recorded the struggles and conversions of Jewish women and children may not have intended thereby, even subconsciously, to suggest a rationale for the Society's continued efforts; but they portray an encounter where the Jew, converted or not, was almost always

[29] "In Sancti Ignatii publica ceremonia Judæorum cui adstitere sponsores, testesq, Illustriss. Dni. Dni. Comites Procopius a Kollowrath, Michael a Kaunitz, Nobilis Dnus. De Ruber, Excellentissima Dna. Josepha Comes de Sohlicz" (NK, 23/19, *Litt. An. Prov. Boh. 1769*, folio 138v).

[30] Evans, *Making*, 388, cited above in chap. 1. While the enthusiasm of some of the most independent-minded nobility for Jesuit-sponsored Baroque piety waned, the longstanding connections between noble families and the Society did not dissolve completely, as the presence of members of these families at such events as baptisms demonstrates. See also Szabo, *Kaunitz*, 241 ff.

[31] The importance of ostentatious public display in events initiated by the Society cannot be overestimated. Such display, as Max Weber pointed out, is an indispensable function of rank. This is especially true during the Baroque era (quoted in Norbert Elias, *The Court Society*, trans. Edmund Jephcott [New York: Pantheon, 1983], 64 f.).

viewed as an "other," whose personal characteristics and circumstances are ignored or subordinated to the demands of an emerging crisis, and who was to be looked upon as a stranger. Jews were constantly viewed as different, subject to different moral standards, and guilty until proven innocent. Jewish historians have dwelt upon the tendency of Christians during the early-modern period to apply completely different standards to Jews when a question of morality or public dignity was at stake, or when the welfare of Christians was in jeopardy. While such claims should be examined carefully, there is much in the history of Christian-Jewish relations in the eighteenth century to suggest that this was often the case.[32]

The story of Jud Süss Oppenheimer is illustrative of the perils awaiting the eighteenth-century Jew, even if he successfully served a Christian master. Süss worked as a *Hofjude* in the court of Württemberg; he demonstrated great loyalty to his prince, Duke Charles Augustus, performed difficult tasks, and not coincidentally, lived according to Christian rather than Jewish customs. Jud Süss also entertained extravagantly, and was no more scrupulous in his amassing of wealth than were Christian court functionaries. When the prince died, the enemies of Süss seized him and had him publicly executed in a spectacle reminiscent of the torture of Loebl Kurtzhandl, thus making him a kind of scapegoat.[33]

Kurzhandl and Süss were men. In the world of the Bohemian Jesuits, the heroism and virtue of Jewish women wishing to convert contrasted with the venality and even obscenity of the Jewish male, often nameless and without distinguishing characteristics beyond the nature of his depravity.[34] Whenever possible, Jesuit chroniclers took note of the crimes and base behavior of Jewish men with whom they came in contact, even if the ostensible point of the story was to recount a conversion or change of heart. Strange is the case of several old Jewish men who, when brought before the magistrate and accused of rape, declared themselves dedicated to Christ.[35]

---

[32] A telling instance of the application of the separation of the Jews occurred during the great famine of 1771, when rations were issued to Jews and Christians at separate locations, supposedly at the request of the Jewish supplier (Erika Weinzierl-Fischer, "Die Bekämpfung der Hungersnot in Böhmen 1770–1772 durch Maria Theresia und Joseph II," *Mitteilungen des Österreichischen Staatsarchivs,* 7 [1954]: 496).

[33] Meyer, *German-Jewish History,* 1:115–17.

[34] Bohemian Jesuits were not the only ones to characterize Jews this impersonally in their narratives about the communities in which missions operated (Paul Shore, "Missions and Schools of the Jesuits in Transylvania and Eastern Hungary, 1700–1773," in *Lesestoffe und Kulturelles Niveau des niedrigen Klerus: Jesuiten und die nationalen Kulturverhältnisse,* ed. I. Monok and P. Ötvös (Szeged: ScriptureRT, 2001), 101–18.

[35] "Ex senis *[sic]* præterea Judæis crimen violentæ rapinæ Pragæ ad Judicium raptis bini Xto dedere" (NK, 23/19, *Lit An. Prov. Boh. 1768* folio 113v). We may also suppose that the victim of this attack was probably not Christian, since such a detail would have been added to the account. This brief entry calls to mind the story of Susanna and the elders, found in the

We are not told the outcome of the case, or what the circumstances were that led to this case being brought. From the Jesuit perspective, the acknowledgement by Jews of the Christian Messiah warrants mention in the annual report, for it represented evidence, however slight, of the impression Jesuit proselytizing was presumably making on the Jewish community.[36]

Immediately following this account, the Jesuit chronicler recorded a story that bears a striking parallel to the case of Shimon Abeles some three-quarters of a century earlier. A Jewish criminal who had been imprisoned for twenty-one years was baptized in jail the day before he was sentenced. When confronted with the horrors awaiting him, a public execution by being tied to a wheel (the same punishment given to Loebl Kurzhandl), the criminal showed a visible change in his demeanor, and faced his death with great resignation to the will of God.[37]

Several messages may be inferred from this story: First, that the power of Christian faith is very great, bringing solace and salvation even to someone facing death because of a capital crime. This theme is not restricted to accounts dealing with Jews, for as we have seen, the *Litteræ annuæ* stress the role of the Jesuit in offering solace and guidance to those facing execution.

The contrast between the breaking of the body and the strengthening of the soul, a Baroque commonplace, is also underscored in this as well as in other narratives that have come down to us. Here the converted convict shares an experience with the Jesuit ascetic tradition that can be traced back to Ignatius and is not associated exclusively with the depraved or unbelieving. Yet lurking behind these themes is the ever present reminder of the criminal depravity of the Jew, whose more recent crimes echo his first and greatest crime, the killing of Christ, and his later crimes against Christian children and against the consecrated Host.[38] Presented collectively, these elements titillate as they instruct, calling attention to the important work of the Society while drawing upon the unfavorable attitude that most Chris-

---

Apocrypha and in Dan. 13. A popular theme of Baroque artists, this narrative significantly combines Jewish feminine virtue (and beauty) with revolting Jewish male sexuality.

[36] Unlike many Protestant missionaries of the day, the Society did not view the conversion of the Jews as a necessary precursor to the Second Coming; instead, the emphasis was on the elimination of a religion that had rejected Christ and had therefore excluded its adherents from salvation (Scult, *Millennial Expectations*, passim).

[37] "Alter annum agens supra vigesimum in carceribus fonte ablutus cum die sequente sententiam audierat, quo capite decusso rotæ implectendum cognoscebat, turbari visus est in voluntatem DEI resignatissismus" (NK, 23/19, *Litt. An. Prov. Boh. 1768* folio 113v). There remains the possibility that the "alter" mentioned in the text does not refer to another Jew, but simply to another depraved individual. Yet the context of the presentation of other explicitly Jewish converts, and the lack of any indication that the criminal was converting from a known heresy makes his Jewish identity almost certain.

[38] Desecration of the Host was one of the most common charges leveled at central-European Jews (Meyer, *German-Jewish History*, 1:26 ff.).

tians harbored toward Jews. The shocking and depraved nature of some of the crimes attributed to Jews holds the attention of the reader, while the moral lesson is driven home in various ways.

True, the documents from which these accounts are derived were undoubtedly intended to be read in Rome, not Prague; still, it seems likely that Jesuit preachers made use of such incidents, many of which would have been well known in the community. The writings of Fr. Eder on the Abeles case illustrate how effectively stories about Jews could be turned to serve the missionary work of the Society.

The consequences of the pressure tactics employed by the Jesuits to convert Jews can be only partially assessed, given the lack of complementary documentation from Jewish sources, and given the tendency of Jesuits to report these events in both a formulaic and self-promoting fashion. Superficial changes in the identity of the convert are evident: one Isaac Kauders emerged from baptism with the remarkable new name of Maria Carolus Fridericus Reiner. Kauder's new surname and the elaborate Christian names assumed by himself and his family may be an acknowledgement of his sponsor; his Christian names reflect his espousal of Catholic culture as well as religion.[39] While some conversions may have been pro forma, many resulted in profound changes in the daily life of the converted; but Jesuit records are silent on the subsequent lives of Jews who embraced the Faith.

Even allowing for the climate of hostility and the designation of the Jews as "others," the outward differences among Jews, Christians, and converts to Christianity in the western Habsburg lands were nevertheless slowly shrinking throughout the second half of the century. As the Baroque era approached its end, the differences based on dress and appearance between converted Jews and Christians became less noticeable: some of the former began to appear more frequently in public dressed and behaving exactly like their Gentile counterparts. Even more shocking, non-converted Jews began appearing on the streets dressed exactly like Christians.[40]

This breakdown in visible difference was perceived in some quarters as a threat to public morality. When in the 1770s some Jews, probably those having greater contact with Gentiles, ceased to wear beards, the Bohemian-Austrian chancellery felt compelled to step in and regulate the contacts that Jews might have with Christians in public places, now that their appearance

---

[39] *Litteræ annuæ Collegii S. J. ad S. Clementem 1766,* folio 181r. For the popularity of various saints' names during the late Baroque, see *Pieté baroque et dechristianisation en Provence au XVIIIe siècle,* by Michel Vovelle (Paris: Plon, 1973), 179ff.

[40] This development produced consternation and outrage among conservative aristocrats, one of whom remarked, in a council of state, "It is evident . . . that young Jewish men, contrary to all custom, now go about in public dressed indistinguishably from Christians . . . some even with swords at their sides" (quoted in Wangermann, *Achievement,* 112; also see n. 80 below).

might no longer mark them as Jews.[41] Nor did this trend toward conformity with Christian styles slow after patents were issued admitting Jews to the university of Prague. A generation later, one professor at the Prague university might identify Jewish students as such, but other professors might not, suggesting that the visible differences between Christians and Jews were in some cases disappearing altogether.[42]

The gradual reduction in visible differences between the two groups was an element in the relations between Jews and Christians that increased anxiety on the Christian side, but it was difficult to assess the Jewish motivations and attitudes. One way of reading this development is to see the act of conversion to Christianity as a less drastic step from a Jewish standpoint than it had been before. However, from the perspective of Rabbi Landau and other conservative Jewish leaders, any move toward conformity with Christian norms would have been an abandonment of fundamental elements of Jewish identity and therefore never acceptable. The Jesuit viewpoint regarding this vanishing difference in outward appearance is unclear, although in practice it was most probably negative. The theology put forward by the Society rejected any inherent virtue in Judaism or in Jewish customs, although in principle it asserted that a baptized Jew's soul had as much worth as that of a born Christian's. Thus, as it became increasingly possible for an unconverted Jew not to be recognized in Christian society, the prejudice against the Jewish "deception" and "perfidiousness" that could place Christians at risk was confirmed, therefore reinforcing the most negative stereotypes of Jewish character.

Despite the significant number of Bohemian Jews who ultimately proved to be apostates, some Jews did genuinely convert. The willingness of some Jews to submit to Jesuit pressure and convert, or at least seem to do so, must be viewed against the context of the life a Jew had to lead before Joseph II's *Toleranzpatent* of 1781. In those harsh times, Jews could not even practice most manual trades or found an industrial enterprise.[43] Enlightenment ideas of Judaism and Jewish humanity, as typified by Lessing's *Nathan der Weisse*, had made little headway in Theresian Prague, as the often hostile popular reactions to the patent show.[44] Jews understandably mistrusted

---

[41] The chancellery sought through a decree of January 17, 1778, to restrict Jews from theaters and other public places (Coelestin Wolfsgruber, *Christoph Anton Kardinal Migazzi Fürstenbischof von Wien* [Saulgau: Hermann Kitz, 1890], 430).

[42] Paul Shore, "Jewish Students at the University of Prague, 1782–1822," *AUCP-HUC* (awaiting publication).

[43] Wolfgang Häusler, "Das österreichische Judentum im Zeitalter der josefinischen Toleranz," in *Österreich zur Zeit Kaiser Josefs II*, ed. Karl Gutkas (Vienna: Amt der Niederösterreichischen Landesregierung, 1980), 166–69.

[44] For example, the anonymous tract published in Prague in 1782, *Über der Unnütz und Schädlichkeit der Juden im Königreich Böheim, und Mähren.*

Jesuits, and references to the "perfidy" of Jews abound in the *Litteræ annuæ* of the Bohemian and Austrian Provinces. These slurs are matched by the attacks on Jews that we read about in the records of communities throughout the Habsburg lands.[45] Yet there was an occasional Jewish presence in the halls of the Faculty of Medicine in the university. As candidates for degrees, Jews were completely excluded from the Prague university until the promulgation of the *Toleranzpatent*. Yet even while they were thus marginalized, as early as 1687 the university Faculty of Medicine, which had little direct contact with or oversight from the Society, examined Jews for such positions as midwife or barber-surgeon.[46]

Jews and Christians had limited contacts with one another; still, the economy of Prague was hurt rather than helped when the Jews were expelled from the city during the War of Austrian Succession, after Maria Theresia accused the community of traitorous dealings with the Prussians.[47] Yet the unfeigned hatred shared by the educated and the rabble as well is evident at every turn in the records of eighteenth-century Prague. The hostility and arrogant indignation of Prague university students who were sanctioned in connection with an anti-Semitic brawl makes it clear that few if any members of Prague's Christian community were yet prepared to grant Jews even minimal toleration.[48] For these Christians, as well as for the Jesuits, Judaism was more than simply a misguided religion; it was a "superstitio," a malformed and incomplete set of beliefs unworthy of serious consideration or respect.[49]

---

[45] For example, townspeople in Hungary, in a petition to the National Diet, referred to Jewish and Greek traders as "godless vermin" ("heyloser Ungeziefer") (Gates-Coon, *Estates*, 125). Gates-Coon's chapter on the Jewish communities of the Esterházy estates, pp. 115–33, though it deals with Hungary, contains many characteristic examples of anti-Semitism similar to those the Prague Jews had to contend with, including the assumption that by nature Jews were dishonest in business dealings and that their religion was "perfidious."

[46] Although Jewish barber-surgeons sometimes practised their trades without a certificate of examination, records show that between 1727 and 1753 at least twenty-three were examined (*Matricula Facultatis Medicinæ Pragensis MDCLII*, folios 515r–519r). Jewish women were also licensed as midwives in the eighteenth century (ibid., folios 523r–526r).

[47] *Beschreibung des Auszugs der sämtlichen Prager-Judenschaft aus Prag . . .* (Nürnburg, 1745). This contemporary account is cataloged in *Bibliografický přehled židovské Prahy*, by Otto Muneles (Prague: Státní židovské muzeum, 1952), 254.

[48] When three university students were taunting a Jewish man held in the stocks, others (Jewish, perhaps) defended the helpless Jew against their abuse. When a brawl ensued, police took the rioters into custody. Some university students protested the punishment inflicted upon their fellow students, and were themselves sanctioned. They retaliated by publishing a broadside against their treament at the hands of the authorities (V. J. Novák, "Studenské nepokoje v Praze roku 1767," *ČČH* 15 (1909): 463 f.).

[49] NK, 23/19, *Litt. An. Prov. Boh. 1768* et passim. In the late seventeenth century, Abraham à Sancta Clara, a Viennese preacher noted for his attacks on Jews and his generally theatrical style, in his sermons made arbitrary distinctions between superstition and legitimate

Yet at the same time some Jesuits may have paid more attention to aspects of this *superstitio* than their in-house records suggest. The Jesuit predilection for emblems and numerological riddles has tempted scholars to speculate about an unacknowledged relationship between cabalistic practices, which by the seventeenth century had become a central feature of Jewish mysticism, and baroque Jesuit mysticism.[50] We may never know with any certainty to what extent Jesuits understood Jewish ritual and mysticism.

One searches in vain for a clear sense of how eighteenth-century Jesuits actually viewed their Jewish neighbors, as opposed to how both institutional pressures and local cultural norms compelled them to respond publicly and on paper.[51] The *Litteræ annuæ,* intended as official reports to distant Rome, are filled with predictably negative references to Judaism. Yet in their reports Prague Jesuits sometimes demonstrated, if not acceptance, at least an awareness of Jewish culture. In 1772 the new baptismal names of female Jewish converts (and there were generally more female than male converts reported) are followed in that year's *Annales* by the converts' Jewish names, and, more surprisingly, by the designation "bas" ("daughter of" in Aramaic).[52] The willingness to acknowledge the Jewish identity of the converts in their own linguistic tradition is striking.

In fact, Jesuit knowledge of Jewish languages was by no means limited to the grammar and restricted vocabulary of Old Testament Hebrew. Bohemian Jesuits applied their typical energy and awareness of contemporaneous conditions to the linguistic problems of Jewish culture. Leopold Tirsch in 1773 published a Jewish-German/German dictionary, probably the first of its kind to appear in Bohemia.[53] Tirsch, who served as the censor of Hebrew books from 1764 onward, was preceded in this post by František Zeleny, a Prague Jesuit who had himself published learned treatises on

---

beliefs. Though he was not a Jesuit, Sancta Clara had received his training in a Jesuit school (Kann, *A Study in Austrian Intellectual History,* 56 f., 62 f.).

[50] This connection is not entirely a figment of twentieth-century speculation; in the eighteenth century Friedrich Nicolai reported that he had encountered a "Buchstabenzettel" from the Domus Professa in Vienna which contained a formula that Gerhardt Kapner associates with the Kabbala (*Barocker Heiligenkult in Wien und seine Träger* [Munich: R. Oldenbourg, 1978], 126).

[51] In 1744, after the Christians of Prague had looted the Jewish ghetto and caused soldiers to be sent in to restore order, the city's clergy called upon citizens to return stolen property to its rightful owners, or if this was not possible, to return it to the "Jüdisches Rathaus" (S. H. Lieben, "Handschriftliches zur Geschichte der Juden," 248). Whether Jesuit preachers figured among those who made this plea is unknown.

[52] For example, "Maria Anna Friedin, in Judaismo Chava bas Node" (NK, 23/19, *An. Prov. Boh. 1772,* folio 411v).

[53] *Handlexicon der jüdisch-deutschen Sprache, in welchem all den Juden entweder eigene, oder aus dem hebräisch- oder Rabinischen entlehnte Redensarten, etc., enthalten sind* (Prague, 1773; cited in Sommervogel, *Bibliothèque*, 8:52).

Hebrew grammar and the Pentateuch.[54] What is most significant, Prague Jesuits frequently revealed familiarity with more specific aspects of Jewish life in Prague. In 1766 a rumor ("fabula") found its way into the annual Jesuit report: some Jew averred that Elijah had appeared to him and that he had received a revelation that Moses was coming next year.[55] That the recorders of the official account of the Jesuit community would see the need to note such developments suggests how closely the Society observed its Jewish neighbors; no comparable level of attention to any other communities in Prague, Catholic or heretical, can be deduced from surviving Jesuit records.

The repeated use of the term "superstitio" in Jesuit records dealing with Judaism reflects, in an indirect way, how much attention they paid to Jewish religious practices; they were not merely uttering uninformed slurs. Some of these practices were the subject of fierce debates both within and outside the Jewish community in the eighteenth century. The "early burial" controversy illustrates the concern expressed over some traditional practices.[56] Critics claimed that the custom of burying the dead in less than three days' time ran the risk that a person might inadvertently be buried while still living. Although there were no documented cases of such an occurrence, even Jewish reformers such as Marcus Herz took up the theme, and one book on the topic even featured an illustration of a Jewish cemetery with what was thought to be a corpse rising out of a shallow grave.[57]

Even though the issue was not of momentous importance, such debates revealed the degree to which almost all Jewish practices, real or mythical, were objects of suspicion. Kosher butchering practices, circumcision, and rumors that the false Messiah Sabbatai had "married" the Torah in a bizarre ceremony were all lumped together as evidence that Judaism was an incoherent and indefensible collection of ancient superstitions. Unintentionally, Jesuits who decried Jewish *superstitio* were aligning themselves with reformers and Enlightenment figures of both Jewish and Christian backgrounds who challenged traditional customs that did not seem to have a

---

[54] Born in Nové Město (Neustadt) in Moravia in 1721, Zeleny also taught poetry and grammar in Prague. He died in Klatovy (Klattau) on February 1, 1765 (Pelzel, *Gelehrte,* 243).

[55] "[D]etecta est, cura nostri fabula qua Hebræorum non nemo sibi Eliam comparuisse deq. Mossiæ adventu anno sequente futuro revelationem sibi accidisse" (NK, 2L/ 23/15/F., *Litt. An. Prov. Boh. 1766,* folio 490v). The rumored return of the Messiah or some other personage to the Jewish communities of central Europe was a constant source of agitation in these communities throughout the eighteenth century. See Pěkný, *Historie,* 159 ff.

[56] Meyer, *German-Jewish History,* 1:280–281, 347.

[57] It should be recalled that Shimon Abeles had been buried in a shallow grave and without sufficient ceremony, conduct that added to the indictment against his father and to the general horror associated with the case.

have a practical value.[58] Ironically, the nonrational encounters that were so central to the Society's mission work were the targets of many of these same reformers, as was the Society itself.

Like almost all other Christians in Baroque central Europe, the Society of Jesus was able to make an unconscious distinction between the Jews whom they encountered in the Bible and those with whom they shared the cities and towns of the region. The former were for the most part essential elements in the story of God's plan of salvation (with the notable exception of the Jewish foils presented in the Gospel of John). Some, such as the patriarchs and prophets, were even exemplary figures of righteousness who were favored by God. Perhaps the Jesuit writers who, following a tradition in religious orders, repeatedly referred to St. Ignatius as a "patriarch" were even trying to draw a subtle comparison between the founder and the first leaders of the Children of Israel.[59] Jesuit playwrights had no difficulty drawing upon tales of Jewish military heroes from the Old Testament and the Apocrypha as allegories for the victory of Habsburg arms.[60] Even the Jewish queen Esther, whose story has no relationship to prophecies of the coming of the Messiah, was enlisted by Jesuit playwrights as a virtuous heroine.[61]

But the Jews who lived in the same time and place as the Jesuits illogically but inevitably fell into a separate category.[62] The Jews' initial

---

[58] Diderot and Voltaire, while denouncing persecution of Jews as human beings, held Judaism in contempt and regarded it as filled with archaic and superstitious practices (Arthur Hertzberg, *The French Enlightenment and the Jews* [New York/London: Columbia University Press, 1968], 312 ff.).

[59] NK, 2L /23/15, *Litt. An. Prov. Boh. 1766*, folio 448 et passim. Whether the reference to the Old Testament patriarchs was deliberate or not, the recording of details of a *cultus* of St. Ignatius in terms suggesting his parental role in the Society is another example of the solidification of the corporate identity of the Society.

[60] The work of Johann Baptist Adolph, a Jesuit working in Klagenfurt in the early eighteenth century, provides many examples of this use of Jewish heroic figures. Adolph's *Judas Machabeus* was produced in Vienna before a distinguished audience (Kurt Adel, *Das Wiener Jesuitentheater und die europäische Barock-dramatik* [Vienna: Österreichischer Bundesverlag, 1960], 164). The Jesuit university in Trnava (Tyrnau, Nagyszambat) presented a drama with protagonists such as Moses, Simon Macchabeus, and Samuel (Milena Cenaková Michalová, "Divadlo na trnavskej universite," in *Trnavská universita v dejinach školstva a vzdelnosti: Zborník referatov vedeckej konferencie konanej v Bratislave dňu 26. Novembra 1985 pri príležitosti 350 výrocia založenia trnavskej university* [Bratislava, 1986], 114).

[61] *Regina Esther de Amano triumphans*, produced at the Erfurt *Jesuitengymnasium* in 1734 (*Bibliographia dramatica et dramaticorum*, ed. Reinhart Meyer, 12 vols. [Tübingen: Max Niemeyer Verlag, ca. 1986], vol. 2, fasc. 9, p. 175).

[62] This distinction between the Jews of the Old Testament and contemporary Jews was rationalized in two ways. First, the Jews of Germany were "talmudic" rather than followers of God's word. Second, they belonged to a different "race" than Jews of ancient times, and thus were not the true heirs of Moses (R. Po-Chia Hsia, "Printing, Censorship, and Antisemitism in

rejection of Catholic Christianity was the most obvious reason for this division, but it was not the only source for the hatred that Jesuits could heap upon them. From the Jesuit point of view, the propensity of converted Jews to return to their ancient faith was an especially galling proof of the "perfidiousness" of this people, a matter that called for firm, even extreme measures. When an anonymous Jesuit wrote, "For not a few [Jews] who after conversion later fall away from the saving Faith are brought back to the Church through acts of penance," he was expressing both a deep anxiety and a profound conviction.[63] The Jesuits felt anxiety because their efforts to convert Jews seemed to have failed; at the same time, they held to the conviction that the particularly Baroque path to salvation through severe acts of penance was an especially efficacious one.[64] The only remedy that the Society was able to devise for the situation was to redouble its efforts to convert Jews, an activity it pursued energetically until the suppression.

These anxieties and convictions were expressed in the context of a culture that seems brutal to modern sensibilities. The severe treatment of Jews, and especially of Jewish converts who reverted to Judaism, was more than an expression of anti-Semitism; it was also part of a severe and unsparing approach to the physical human being, be he a Christian or an unbeliever, so typical of the Baroque. Distinguishing the harsh physical treatment of Jews prevalent in the Baroque period from that meted out to their contemporaries is extremely difficult. The brutal treatment of the suspects in the Shimon Abeles case should be compared with the equally inhumane treatment of Bohemian peasants in the uprising of 1775 or with the torture of political prisoners.[65] The world of the *Nemesis Theresiana* and the Habsburg state still recognized torture as a legitimate tool; and it was during this

---

Reformation Germany," in *The Process of Change in Early Modern Europe: Essays in Honor of Miriam Usher Chrisman,* ed. Phillip N. Bebb and Sherrin Marshall, 137).

[63] "[E]tiam non pauci qui postquam a fide salvifica defecissent, tamen facti pœnitentes ad Ecclesiam rediere (NK, 2L/23/15F, *Litt. An. Prov. Boh. 1766,* folio 491).

[64] The culture of flagellants and others in Bohemia involved in the more severe forms of Baroque piety has been inadequately explored, but there is scattered evidence of a widespread enthusiasm for the most extreme expressions of this piety, including frenzied flagellation that left the walls of pilgrimage sites spattered with blood (Peter F. Barton, " Der östereichische Barockkatholizismus: eine unerreichte Blütezeit kirchlicher Leben?" in *Horizonte und Perspektiven: Festschrift für Erik Turnwald,* ed. Gerhard Messler [Heidelberg/Vienna: Johannes-Mathesius Verlag, 1979], 102).

[65] Many examples from this uprising might illustrate this point; the beatings and executions of the leaders of the peasant uprising reveal that cruelty was not reserved exclusively for any group considered to be "perfidious" (M. Toegel et al., ed., *Prameny k nevolnickému povstání v Čechách a na Moravě v roce 1775* [Prague: Academia nakladetelsví československé akademie věd, 1975], 496 et passim).

era that methods of physical abuse were illustrated graphically in the Penal Book of 1769 for the edification and intimidation of the populace.[66]

These considerations help to explain (but not excuse) the recommendations of inhumane treatment for the Jews that permeate the official annals of the Bohemian Society in the 1750s and '60s. But they shed little light on how individual Jesuits viewed Jews, or indeed what any Jesuit's understanding of Jewish religious beliefs and ethical principles might have been. It is safe to say that, like any group of individuals, the Jesuits of the Bohemian Province varied considerably in their attitudes toward reality. The presence of a Stepling, a Cornova, and a Koniáš simultaneously in the same organization illustrates how diverse the Bohemian Society was. The Spiritual Exercises performed by all Jesuits in the course of their training could conceivably have been a force for either tolerance or bigotry, depending on the guidance the initiate received and the values he brought to the process.

The Exercises, drawing upon a tradition of medieval devotional literature, but surpassing much in that tradition by insisting on immediacy, vividness, and visualization, can draw the initiate toward a greater empathy for other human beings while he reflects on the Passion.[67] Yet, as is the case with the Passion plays and much of the high-Baroque art work centered around the Passion, the experience of the Exercises might fan hatred of the Jews, who could easily be portrayed as "responsible" for the sufferings of the Savior. The Exercises may also have increased, in those who made them, the sense of their own spiritual superiority. While such an outcome would not have been Ignatius's intention, it is easy to imagine, in the overheated religious climate of the late Counter-Reformation, that Jesuits emerged from the experience of the Exercises with a decreased rather than an enhanced appreciation of the spiritual content of the religions that seemed to threaten the Catholic position. Fired with the conviction that they alone possessed the truth, Jesuits, like many others in the late-Baroque period, were prone to go to excesses in their zeal to convert.

Other aspects of Jesuit formation could contribute to the attitudes held toward Jews. Despite the attempts of some twentieth-century Jesuit historians to describe the historical mission of the Society as all-encompassing and inspired by Ignatian ideals as opposed to confrontational, and imbued with the ideology of the Counter-Reformation, the records left by the Bohemian Society leave no doubt that the official mission of the Jesuits, right up until the suppression, included an aggressive posture toward all religious beliefs other than Catholicism. The training of the Jesuits of the

---

[66] Wangermann, *Austrian Achievement,* 133 ff.; the illustrations refer specifically to the execution of the murderer Franz Zahlheim in 1786. See also Bodi, *Tauwetter,* 289.

[67] Paul Shore, "The *Vita Christi* of Ludolph of Saxony and Its Influence on the *Spiritual Exercises* of Ignatius of Loyola," *Studies in the Spirituality of Jesuits* 30 (1998): 1–32.

Bohemian Province during the 1750s and '60s was imbued with both a Baroque mysticism that resisted rational argumentation and a defensive view of the position of the Church. It is also likely that directly or indirectly, young Jesuits were indoctrinated with anti-Semitic ideas in their collegium schooling, whether it was gained through studying the Church Fathers or through a didactic play that cast Jews in a negative light.[68]

From a Catholic standpoint, Bohemia was a dangerous place, where the Church and its faithful needed to be especially vigilant and assertive in protecting the true faith. Not only was Bohemia the home of the Hussite heresy, but it also gave shelter (however grudgingly) to an alien community in its midst. The conversion of the Jews was therefore a necessity not only because of the need to save the souls of the Jews themselves but also because of the threat to the integrity of Christianity posed by this alien community. Unlike Jesuits in China, who could find ways to tolerate local practices, such as the burning of incense before the tombs of one's ancestors, and who noted with approval the moral teachings of Confucius, for several reasons the Jesuits of Bohemia were not moved to discover parallels between Catholicism and Judaism, nor to defend the beliefs and practices of the latter. First, the Jesuit community in Bohemia had to operate within a larger culture saturated with hostility toward Jews and resistant to accepting any element of Judaism. Although Jesuits were not infrequently prepared to defend the underdog (as in the case of the Paraguayan reductions), the unanimity of opinion among Bohemian Christians as to the inferiority and contemptible nature of the Jews provided the Society with no allies for such a countercultural defense.

More important, we may assume that the majority of the members of the Society were themselves products of the Bohemian society nurturing them and lacked the ability to recognize and rise above their own cultural prejudices. These attempts were for a long time reinforced by the pro-

---

[68] There was no need to add an anti-Semitic Baroque flourish to many of the authors covered in patristic studies, a central part of Jesuit theological training. Explicit attacks on Jews abound, for instance, in the works of St. John Chrysostom; for example, his eight *Discourses against Judaizing Christians,* trans. Paul Harkins (Washington, D.C.: Catholic University of America Press, 1977). A dramatic production produced at the Jesuit collegium in the Rhineland town of Jülich in 1724 had the title *Acolastus, sive Servus nequam iusta talionis pœna castigatus;* it contained the following lines, spoken by a Jewish character:

> Mein Kunst ist, bey Christen liegen
> Sie mit falsher Muntz betriegen
> Was nicht taucht, ich kauser mach
> Alsdann in mein Faustlein lach.

(cited in *Die Jesuitenorden,* by Paul von Hoensbach, 2 vols. [Bern/Leipzig: Paul Haupt, 1926], 2:812 f.). Von Hoensbach, a former Jesuit who left the Society before taking final vows and who wrote polemics against the Society, was nevertheless careful when citing documents, and the verses quoted above fit the portrayal of Jews found in the Eder's writings on the Abeles case.

foundly intolerant religious climate of the region and of the Society. The Jesuit who wrote in 1760 about the "perfidy" of the Jews was only one generation removed from the notorious expulsion in 1731 of the Protestants of Salzburg by the city's prince archbishop.[69] Inflexibility and intolerance were still considered virtues by the rank and file of the Society, whatever the intellectual curiosity of individual thinkers such as Boscovich or Stepling might have been. Such attitudes of intolerance were also common among the elites whom the Society regarded as its allies.

In addition to these factors, there remains the problem of the common elements of Judaism and Christianity. If the inhabitants of Prague hated Jews because their peculiarities of dress, diet, and religious ceremony set them apart from Christians, the Jesuits also found them potential threats when they had to confront the similarities and commonalities between the two religions on scriptural matters. Jesuits confronting Confucian ancestor worship or the rites of the Malabar coast would have found it easier to recognize commonalities between these practices and Christian ones because of the distance of these traditions from European culture and because the religious practices of these regions did not offer such a specific rebuke or challenge to believing Christians.[70] Central-European Judaism fell into another category; its mere presence in the midst of a Christian world promoted, in the view of Benedict XIV, "faithlessness" among Christians.[71] Even the contact between Jews and Christians necessitated by the Jewish prohibition against working on the Sabbath was deemed dangerous to Christians.[72] Judaism could never be viewed as the faith of a distant civiliza-

---

[69] Prince Archbishop Leopold Anton von Firmian expelled twenty thousand Protestants from his territories, an act that generated controversy at the time but which was viewed with approval by the leadership of the Society (Reinhold J. Wolny, *Josephinische Toleranz unter besonderer Berücksichtigung ihres geistlichen Wegbereiters Johann Leopold Hay* [Munich: Verlag Robert Lerche, 1973], 39; Frank Eyck, *Religion and Politics in German History* [New York: St. Martin's Press, 1998], 343).

[70] The Chinese-rites controversy was resolved to the disadvantage of the Society early in the eighteenth century, and may have left some members of the European provinces less willing to make accommodations with local non-Catholics out of fear of disapprobation from Rome (F. A. Rouleau, "Maillard de Tournon, Papal Legate at the Court of Peking," *AHSI* 31 [1962]: 204–323). However, the Society did exhibit some flexibility in dealing with the Uniate Church of Transylvania, which retained some elements of the Eastern Rite (*Historia critica Regni Hungariæ stirpis Austriacæ* . . . a Stephano Katona [Buda, 1809], 512 f.; Petru Tocanel, "Attestamento delle missioni in Bulgaria, Valachia, Transilvania, e Moldavia," in *Sacræ Congregationis de Propaganda Fide memoria rerum,* ed. J. Metzler, vol. 2, 1700–1815 [Rome/Freiburg/Vienna: Herder, 1973], 722–42).

[71] *A quo primum,* June 14, 1751, section 2 (in Carlen, *Papal Encyclicals,* 42).

[72] Christians were forbidden to work for Jews on the Sabbath (as *Shabbas Goyim*) to perform tasks that devout Jews could not perform on that day: "Effecit etiam, ne Christiani Sabbato Hebræis famularentur" (Strahov, D A III 33, *Epitome historiæ Collegii Soc. Jesu, Reginæ Hradeii annus 1760,* unnumbered folio).

tion whose qualities a Jesuit missionary could learn to respect even as he sought to convert its members.

The inescapable fact that much of Jewish scholarship drew upon the same sacred texts as the Society utilized did not make the Jesuit feel a fraternal connection with the Jews, but more likely the "incorrect" interpretation of these texts by a people who had rejected the prophecies regarding the Messiah fostered further resentment, scorn, and hatred in him. The traditional Christian view of the Old Testament as a precursor to the New and its fulfillment, placed a barrier between the Jesuits and Jews that was not crossed by the sorts of debates and disputations still taking place in Protestant Germany.[73] The use of the Old Testament by the Jews seemed yet another behavior calculated to affront the defenders of the faith. The scholarly quality of the Jewish approach to these writings was a danger, not something to be admired; for the very skill with which Jewish scholars approached the texts made their interpretations dangerously seductive to Christians.[74] The appearance in rural Bohemia of "Abrahamites," who were circumcised and followed some of the dietary practices of the Pentateuch, would have confirmed such fears.[75]

The special attention that the Jesuits of the Bohemian Province devoted to Jewish women is not easily explained. As a group skilled in disputation and comfortable in their interactions with women (although their mission never explicitly included teaching women), the Jesuits were well equipped to proselytize Jewish women. Yet the amount of space in the *Litteræ* given to the trials and triumphs of these women suggests a special interest on the part of the Jesuits. Perhaps Jewish women, lacking the formal training in theological disputation that at least some Jewish men would have acquired, were more easily persuaded by the Jesuits' arguments. And possibly the desire of some mothers to ensure a better life for their children led these women to contemplate baptism for themselves and their offspring. Or perhaps the tactics of the Jesuits when interacting with Jewish women took on a softer tone; perhaps they regarded these women as victims, however they defined this victimhood. The evidence left behind by

---

[73] In 1704 the Lutheran Elector George Louis of Hanover (later George I of England) presided over a debate between a converted Jew and the chief rabbi of Schaumburg-Lippe, during which the rabbi was apparently treated with respect (Meyer, *German-Jewish History,* 1:162).

[74] Even in the first half of the twentieth century, Pius XI warned in an unpublished encyclical of the "perils that this unbelief and hostility might make for the faith and mores of the flock" (quoted in Georges Passelecq and Bernard Suchecky, *The Hidden Encyclical of Pius XI* [New York: Harcourt, Brace, 1997], 252).

[75] Pěkný, *Historie,* 195. According to this account, Koniáš himself was instrumental in causing the leader of the Abrahamites, a tailor named Jan Pita, to be executed.

the Jesuits themselves is inconclusive, but some observations may nevertheless be made.

The Jewish family, the cornerstone of Jewish society, was in many ways a threat to the missionary program of the Jesuits. Conversion of individual Jews seemed possible only by severing the bonds that held parent to child, thus preventing cultural and religious traditions from being passed on. And although the Jewish family was patriarchal in significant ways, the Jewish woman played a key role in the management of the family. Her role was not limited to raising children. In a traditional Eastern European Jewish community, when the father was a scholar his wife supervised the day-to-day family affairs and the family business, so that her husband could busy himself with the more prestigious activity of study.[76] In effect, this meant that it was the women who often materially supported the scholarship that helped sustain the Jewish connection with its religious roots. For all their contempt of Jewish culture, circumstantial evidence suggests that some Bohemian Jesuits had some understanding of this pattern and the vital role Jewish women played in it. By bringing these women to Christianity, Jesuits may have thought they could undermine the support system of Judaic scholarship and thereby smooth the path for more conversions.

The problem of male Jewish sexuality, as reported in the documents sent to Rome, occupies a murkier region where explicit and implicit values influence perceptions of gender and ethnicity. Elsewhere this author has argued that because Jewish students admitted to Habsburg universities for the first time in the late eighteenth century sometimes retained their secondary sexual characteristics (especially beards), they were regarded as a threat to Christians, and especially to Christian women.[77] The frequency with which very young Jewish men, especially if they were seen as too young to be sexually active, were reported as converted also points to the ambivalence that Jesuits seem to have felt toward the adult Jewish male.[78] The cartoons and caricatures circulating in the 1780s following the issuance of the Patent of Toleration make clear that whether the adult male Jew was viewed as comically apelike or merely degenerate, his physical appearance was the object of the horror and scorn of Christians, who accused Jews of attempting

---

[76] Mark Zborowski and Elizabeth Herzog, *Life Is with People: The Jewish Little Town of Eastern Europe* (New York: International Universities Press, 1952), 83, 240.

[77] Paul Shore, "Sex, Lies, and Jewbaiting," paper presented at the annual conference of the Popular Culture Society, Louisville, Ky., October 1992.

[78] For example, Samuel Fischel, a seventeen-years-old unmarried Jewish tailor, was baptized, taking the name "Francis Xavier Joseph ("Samuel Fischel Hebræus e Bohemia officio sartoris an. 17 cælebs in Baptismo Franciscus Xaverius Josephus [nuncupatus])" (*Epitome historiæ Collegii S. J. Pragæ ad Sanctum Ignatium anno 1759: Nomina conversorum* (Strahov, D A III 33, unnumbered folio).

to hide their true nature.[79] Seldom were Jewish women the target of eighteenth-century attacks in the press, even though their appearance might seem as exotic or alien to the outsider as that of Jewish men. The Jewish female was apparently less threatening than the adult male and therefore more approachable by Jesuit missionaries.[80]

Jesuit documents dealing with Jews during the period are highly suggestive in what they do not address. They are noticeably free from any references to Jewish usury *(Wucherei)* or to the longstanding role prominent Jews, known as *Hofjuden,* played as financial backers of the Habsburgs. Nor is much attention given to other common Jewish occupations that would have typically attracted scorn from some Christians, such as tavern owner or seller of used merchandise. The scope of the focus devoted to Jews in the *Litteræ* is far narrower, concentrating on the written "blasphemies" of the Jews and on the necessity of conversion.[81] From this we might conclude that the prejudice against the Jews that the Bohemian Jesuits exhibited on the institutional level was strictly religious rather than racial or cultural in origin. In view of the subsequent history of relations between Jews and Christians in Bohemia and in central Europe in general, this is an important distinction.[82]

The Society, its mission defined as the spreading of the Gospel throughout the world, was prepared to accept converted Jews, as exemplified by Shimon Abeles, regardless of their "blood." Surviving records of the Society reveal no traces of an underlying prejudice toward converted Jews, although, as has been noted, apostates came in for especial criticism. Anti-Semitism, or more precisely, anti-Judaism, was part of the spectrum of officially endorsed attitudes held by Jesuits against anyone who did not hew to the line of orthodox Catholicism.

Yet this is not the whole story. Anti-Judaism was compounded by the locally held prejudice against Jews that went beyond religious intolerance and spilled over into what might be categorized as racial prejudice. Individual Jesuits, both as products of Bohemian culture and as members of an

---

[79] An anonymous book of the period, *Der getaufte Jude: Weder Jude noch Christ* (Vienna, 1781), shows a Jew dressed as an upper-class Gentile, removing a mask to reveal another face beneath.

[80] By the late eighteenth century, the same physical features that contributed to the picture of the "repulsive" Jewish male were coming to be seen as "exotic" and appealing in a woman (Deborah Hertz, "Seductive Conversion in Berlin, 1770–1809," in *Jewish Apostasy,* ed. Todd Endelman [New York/London: Holmes and Meier, 1987], 50).

[81] The recurring theme is one of either "correction or destruction": "curatumque est ut Hebræorum libri blasphemia quæque continentes aut corrigerentur, si possent, sin minus ut flammis darentur (NK, 23/19, *Litt. An. Prov. Boh. 1770,* folios 270v–271r).

[82] A. Stein, *Die Geschichte der Juden in Böhmen* (Brünn: Jüdischer Buch-und Kunstverlag, 1904).

institution committed to accommodation with local cultural norms, may also have crossed the line between religious intolerance and racial prejudice. There is little evidence that Bohemian society became less prejudiced against Jews after they acquired some civil rights; in fact, hatred became even more intense in the years when Jews were starting to make real gains in their civil status within the Habsburg Empire. The combination of these factors created the hostile and unforgiving atmosphere in which the encounter between Jew and Jesuit took place.

Conclusion

While the same might be said of any of the facets of the Jesuit undertaking in Bohemia, it is especially true that further investigation into Jewish-Jesuit relations is needed to clarify both the interaction of the Society with the Jewish community and the dealings of the Jesuits with converted Jews. Surveying the available documents, I was struck not only by the estrangement between the two groups but also by the absence of any continued contact between converted Jews and Jesuits. It is not surprising that, unlike Jesuit missions elsewhere that ultimately produced Jesuits who were from the local culture, the Jesuit apostolate to the Jews of Bohemia resulted in no such Jesuits; for although such key figures in the early history of the Society as Polanco and Laínez were descended from converted Spanish Jews, such individuals were effectively barred from the Society by the early seventeenth century.[83]

Yet the complete absence of a record of even economic relations between the two groups is striking. Jesuits do not report visiting the Jewish ghetto, nor are Jewish converts visible in the picture of Catholic Prague painted by the *Litteræ annuæ*. By contrast, in Transylvania Jesuit priests noted when they purchased furniture from Jews, and described contacts with converted Jews who were serving in nearby military installations. Among the Jesuits of Bohemia, there is no further notice of the academic progress of Jewish children who converted or who were placed in Christian families, even though the success of such children would have reflected well on the missionary work of the Society. Texts of sermons in which Jesuits might have lashed out at Jews have not survived, leaving us to speculate whether the venom flowing through J. Eder's account of the Abeles case

[83] In 1593 at the Fifth General Congregation of the Society all descendants of Jews and "Saracens" were debarred from membership in the Society, a policy that was reiterated in a somewhat mitigated fashion by the Sixth General Congregation, which stated that applicants to the Society must prove that for five generations their ancestors were not members of these "infamous" races (John W. Padberg, Martin D. O'Keefe, and John L. McCarthy, eds., *For Matters of Greater Moment: The First Thirty General Congregations: A Brief History and a Translation of the Decrees* [St. Louis: The Institute of Jesuit Sources, 1994], 204, 232 f.).

conducted so many years before is representative of the attitudes of other members of the Society.[84]

The size of the Jewish community of Prague, its high local visibility before and after its expulsion in 1745, and its close proximity to the Clementinum make the lacunae in the records left by the Society in Prague all the more remarkable. While the Jewish community of Prague did not leave any systematic record of its dealings with its Jesuit neighbors, the annals of other central-European ghettos may furnish clues enabling us to develop a more complete understanding of relations between these two groups.[85] Although at least one history of the Prague Jewish community told from the Jewish perspective has survived, such sources have not been utilized in the study of the Prague Jesuits and their relations with Jews.[86] To an even greater degree than in the case of Christians who interacted with Jesuits in mission or educational contexts, the perceptions of Jews who encountered Jesuits must be taken into account in assessing the nature of these encounters.

The pervasive climate of suspicion and intolerance is an important element in the cultural mix surrounding the encounter between Jew and Jesuit. Jews who remained loyal to their ancestral faith and who refused to abandon the visible signs that set them apart from Christians were easily made into victims in a culture that shunned "otherness." Hugh Trevor-Roper has argued for the "interchangeability" of witches and Jews during the early phases of the Counter-Reformation in Germany and elsewhere in central Europe. He cites the telling example of how accused witches in medieval Hungary were forced to stand in the public pillory wearing a "Jews' hat."[87] When the interest that the Inquisition and other bodies dedicated to enforcing religious conformity began to shift toward witchcraft in the late-sixteenth century, the systematic persecution of Jews slackened somewhat. It is worth considering whether the end of the witch craze in central Europe, which occurred at the close of the seventeenth century, may

---

[84] Eder, *Mannhaftige Beständigkeit.*

[85] For an overview of possible directions for future inquiry based on materials from throughout the Czech lands, see Jan Heřman, "Jewish Community Archives from Bohemia and Moravia," *Judaica Bohemica* 7, no. 1 (1971): 4.

[86] In addition to the anonymous Hebrew manuscript mentioned above, other histories of Prague may have been composed by local Jews (Vladimir Sadek, "From the MSS Collections of the State Jewish Museum [MSS of Historical Content]," *Judaica Bohemica* 9, no. 1 (1973): 19 f.). Abraham Trebitsch of Miklov also composed a historical work entitled *Qorot ha-'ittim* (Events of time), covering the period 1741–1801, with special emphasis on events in the Habsburg realms (Jiřina Sedinová, "The Hebrew Historiography in Moravia at the 18th century—Abraham Trebitsch [around 1760–1840]," *Judaica Bohemica* 10, 1 [1974]: 51–61).

[87] Trevor-Roper, *The European Witch-Craze,* 112.

be traced to the intensified pressure placed on Jews in the eighteenth in places like Vienna and Prague.

Once again the otherness of the Jews earned them the attention of forces, including but not limited to the Jesuits, that needed an outsider to victimize. The apparent stalemate that the Jesuits had reached by the mid-eighteenth century in their efforts to bring crypto-Protestants back into the embrace of Mother Church was also a contributing factor in the renewed efforts undertaken to convert the Jews. The continuing existence of Jewish communities could provide both an explanation of why Catholicism had not completely succeeded in overcoming the Protestant leanings of some Bohemians, and a target for the frustrations of Catholic missionaries, who had achieved so little in this regard. Each component in this process denied Bohemian Jews an identity, instead reducing them to the objects of various agendas generated by other concerns. The only ray of hope in this discouraging history is found in the relatively sympathetic portrayals of those Jews who, according to accounts, voluntarily embraced Christianity. While denying their original faith any credibility or respect, Jesuit writers could not discuss Jews in their triumphalist narratives without according them some recognition as human beings possessing souls and the capacity to choose the virtuous path. In the context of the persecution Jews had experienced and continued to encounter in Bohemia, this is little reason for rejoicing; but the ability of Jesuits to see Jews as human beings does reveal a slightly more human side of the Jesuits themselves.

chapter six

SCHOOLS

Consule scholas Jesuitarum!

—Francis Bacon

Arguably, during the eighteenth century the Society of Jesus exercised its greatest influence on Bohemia through the schools it conducted. For several centuries the collegia of the Jesuits defined, both through their prescribed curriculum and their instructional methods, what it meant to be educated within Catholic Europe.[1] Although the schools of the Piarist fathers, which also operated in many part of Bohemia, rivaled those of the Jesuits, the Jesuit educational system had the advantage of the tested curriculum of the *Ratio,* as well as the prestige and material resources of the Society itself. Because the Jesuit collegia had existed for so long and had received such support from the elite of Bohemia, they functioned as an integral part of the cultural landscape and were recognized as such by outsiders.[2]

Even many of the Enlightenment opponents of the Jesuits had themselves been educated in the Society's schools; Count Sporck, who for many years had waged a running battle with the Society, was only one of the most conspicuous examples. Dominating as it did the universities in Prague and Olomouc, controlling extensive tracts of land, and affiliated internationally with such distinguished institutions as the Roman College, schools of the Society could shape the direction of education in Prague and the surrounding area to an almost unbounded degree, at least in theory. But the Society as a teaching order was moving toward a crisis even before the suppression put an end to its academic activities.

[1] By 1626 the Society already had 444 collegia worldwide, some of which were parts of existing universities (*Historical Dictionary of Catholicism,* s.v. "Universities and Colleges").

[2] For example, the reference to the school in Krumlov in *Historische und geographische Beschreibung des Königreiches Böheim, Erster Theil . . . ,* by Rochezang von Isecern (Frankfurt/Leipzig, 1746), 139.

The greatest potential strength of the school envisioned by the *Ratio* was the instructor. "Potential," because if the instructor lived up to the standards prescribed in this detailed document, the quality of instruction would be high; of course, it is hard to know how many attained this ideal. The ideal teacher was devout, tolerant, engaging, and able to exhibit a "prudent charity" when presenting interpretations of material that might offend the sensibilities of some Catholics. Books by heretics, of course were to be excluded.[3] Not only would the teacher serve as a moral arbiter regarding the classical literature that was the foundation of the curriculum, but he was also expected to set an aesthetic tone through his own formalized and extemporaneous use of Latin in class and by his correction of the Latin style of his pupils. Whatever the subject matter he was presenting, the instructor was always to model eloquence in both prepared and extemporaneous speech and superior auditory recall. And, of course, this speech was in Latin, never in the native tongues of teacher or student. The teacher would encourage competition among students, but temper these contests with "moderation and harmony."

Bohemian Jesuit records are conspicuously silent on the topic of unsuccessful teachers, who must have appeared at least occasionally; and the continued popularity of the Society's schools cannot be seen as proof that the majority of teachers attained the very high ideal described here. On the other hand, considering the unceasing attacks leveled at the curriculum and the methodology of Jesuit secondary schools in the mid-eighteenth century, it is significant that, even during the *Brochürenflut* of the 1780s, no documented reports of incompetent, vicious, or ignorant Jesuit teachers have come down to us. The high regard with which many Jesuit teachers, such as Ignac Cornova, were regarded by their students shows that the Society continued to attract talented school masters.[4]

From the hindsight of the twenty-first century, it is easy to spot the deficiencies in the Jesuit curriculum and in some of the instructional techniques employed. Physics, a field transformed by the work of Newton in the previous century and arguably the most dynamic of the sciences in the late Baroque period, was completely neglected in the official curriculum until 1832.[5] Modern languages, increasingly the medium through which not

---

[3] I. Cornova, *Die Jesuiten als Gymnasiallehrer* (Prague: Calve, 1804), 70.

[4] Cornova, who taught grammar and eloquence in Bohemian collegia before becoming a university professor, was so well liked by his students that when he announced his retirement in 1795, his students asked if he could stay on until his replacement was appointed (K. Kazbunda, "Dvě kapitoly z dějin 'stolice dějin' na Prazské universitě," in *Od pravěku k dnešku: Sborník prací z dějin československých* [Prague: Historický Klub, 1930], 2:295 f.).

[5] The revised *Ratio studiorum* of 1832 included ten additional rules for the professor of physics, the first systematic acknowledgement of the advances made in the field. The 1832 revision has never been officially replaced; in fact, it was not universally adopted either (John

merely the ideas of the Enlightenment but also the poetry and fiction of the new age were communicated, were likewise excluded; and the Society's opposition to any movement toward the vernacular became one of the flash points of debate in the eighteenth century. The Jesuit technique of employing students to act as *decuriones* or *censores,* who would monitor the conduct of other students and then report back to the teacher, appears archaic and counterproductive to modern educators, although there is no evidence that contemporaries were troubled by this tactic.[6] The reporting practices of the Jesuits reveal their bias toward aristocratic students—muted though it was in the original *Ratio;* we see them taking pride in recording the number of nobles of each rank attending the Prague *Convictus* connected with the Collegium Clementinum.[7] Yet this bias was not peculiar to the schools of the Jesuits, and in some other settings was even more blatant.[8] The practice of moving young instructors from place to place and from subject to subject has already been noted; while perhaps fostering loyalty to the Society, the custom of discouraging permanent connections for scholars and teachers probably made it harder for the Society to defend itself as an entity when the final crisis came.

Another drawback implicit in the school structure as outlined in the *Ratio* was perhaps inevitable, but potentially devastating: the top-down model of administration placed the young, inexperienced, and vulnerable instructors at the mercy of their rector. Because all teachers in the Jesuit secondary school were Jesuits themselves and therefore bound by vows of obedience, and because techniques for remedying problems were sometimes hard to build into a system based on obedience, a dictatorial or incompetent school rector could work havoc on a collegium. Of course, this drawback was not unique to the Jesuit model; to a greater or lesser degree, it was present in most schools then existing in Europe. The difference was that in the second half of the eighteenth century it was the Jesuit curriculum and

---

W. Donohue, S.J., *Jesuit Education: An Essay on the Foundations of an Idea* [New York: Fordham University Press, 1963], 53). However, by 1766 students in Prague were conducting disputations on the works of Newton, which had been translated by Joannes Tessanek (NK, 23/17, *Annuæ Litteræ Collegii S. J. Pragæ ad S. Clementem 1766,* folios 175r–175v).

[6] Alfred Herr, "Zur Geschichte des Egerer Gymnasiums," *Mittheilungen des Vereins für Geschichte der Deutschen in Böhmen MVGDB* 74 (1936): 136.

[7] The names of especially distinguished families, Kaunitz, for example, were also noted. The reputation of the two "Konvikten" directed by the Society in Prague was positive throughout the century (P. V. Bělohlávek, "Konvikt prazský," in *Dějiny ceských křížovníků s červenou hvězdou* [Prague: Nákladem Českých K Křížovníků v Praze, 1930], Díl 1, 200; NK, 23/17, *Litteræ annuæ Collegi S. J. Pragæ ad S. Clementem 1766,* folio 175r).

[8] In Ulm, for example, poorer students wore different-colored academic robes from those of the wealthier (W. H. Bruford, *Germany in the Eighteenth Century: The Social Background of the Literary Revival* [Cambridge: The University Press, 1959], 233).

the Society adhering to it that were subjected to continued criticism and calls for reform, not the schools of the Piarists or Benedictines.[9]

To counter the critics who found Jesuit education stultifying and out of touch with newer developments, the Society would have needed a way of reforming its program that took into account the ideas of talented younger teachers and recognized the possible benefits of incorporating acceptable elements of other educational programs.[10] This the leadership of the Society refused even to consider. Yet, these reforms alone would not have been enough to save the Society or its schools, for these schools existed in a world whose concept of secondary school as an institution was changing.

The increasing clarity with which educators viewed pre-university studies in the late eighteenth century posed a practical as well as a polemical challenge to the model of Jesuit secondary schools. This shift toward a clearer articulation of pre-university studies may be detected in the trend toward more systematic documentation. At the beginning of the century, there was little thought given to the sort of documentation, if any, that should be required in order to determine whether a student was prepared to begin university studies. Many students studied privately and then simply appeared for admission to a university, hoping to pass whatever formal or informal entrance requirements might be demanded of them. In the German-speaking world, Prussia took the lead in formalizing the process of preparing for the university when it adopted the *Abitur,* or standardized entrance examination, in 1788.[11]

But the desire to draw a clearer distinction between secondary school and university had long existed among German educators and intellectuals. The Jesuit commitment to a model that divided studies into "upper" and "lower," but which made no clear qualitative distinction in "philosophical" studies undertaken by secondary students as opposed to university scholars was out of step with this thinking.[12] Jesuit hostility to the determinist philos-

---

[9] In the relatively freewheeling exchange of pamphlets and other polemical writings that took place in the 1750s and '60s, the Jansenists relentlessly attacked the Society for its antiquated teaching methods and outdated curriculum (Hersche, *Der Spätjansenismus in Österreich, 346).*

[10] Following the suppression, the Josephinian educational reformer Josef von Sonnenfels published a devastating critique of Jesuit schooling, denouncing its philosophy as "about one hundred years behind the times," and lambasting its reliance on rote memorization and Renaissance notions of rhetoric. Had innovative younger Jesuit teachers such as Cornova been given a voice in restructuring curriculum, the most egregious aspects of this curriculum might have been revised (Gerson Wolf, *Das Unterrichtswesen in Österreich unter Kaiser Josef II.* [Vienna: A. Holder, 1880], 5 f.).

[11] Karl A. Schleuns, *Schooling and Society: The Politics of Education in Prussia and Bavaria, 1750–1900* (Oxford/New York/Munich: Berg, 1989), 11.

[12] Ignatius had originally envisioned a collegium of three faculties: languages, arts, and theology; this was revised in successive versions of the *Ratio* up until 1599, which saw the

ophy of Christian Wolff (1679–1754) was also costing the Society supporters among educators and the families of prospective students, especially in German-speaking regions where Wolff's influence was greatest.[13]

The low degree of urbanization in Bohemia meant that schools were far apart and resources were relatively scarce, and in the short term these factors worked in favor of the Society and its policy of changing only slowly. One of the obvious advantages that the Society enjoyed in Prague and the surrounding region was its dominance over other schools. The Society could afford to pay little attention to the teaching of more practical skills, and throughout the first half of the century these were neglected by most educators.[14] But when direct attacks on the Jesuits grew more intense in the 1760s, the human resources of the Society were so dispersed that it was less able to defend itself.[15]

Public Performances

A favorite element of the Jesuit secondary-school curriculum and arguably its most distinctive characteristic, a feature that distinguished it from many other curricula of the day, was the mounting of public *exercitationes,* often before an assembly of distinguished personages, each performed in Latin and invariably intent upon promoting a moral message. While this practice had its roots in the late Renaissance, *exercitationes* were still offered in the mid-eighteenth century. The synopsis of one such production dating from 1757 produced at the Malá Strana collegium offers a scene from Livy in

---

codification of the system that remained in place until the suppression (Karl Hengst, *Jesuiten an Universitäten und Jesuitenuniversitäten* [Paderborn: Ferdinand Schöningh, 1981], 64, 70).

[13] Wolff strove to prove the existence of God from natural rather than revealed or biblical evidence, an approach acceptable at many Protestant universities of the day but, of course, not at Jesuit schools (John V. Burns, *Dynamism in the Cosmology of Christian Wolff* [New York: Exposition Press, 1966]; also W. R. Ward, *Christianity under the Ancien Régime,* 173 f.). The determinism of Wolff, along with the Cartesian doctrine of the body, was particularly unacceptable to the Jesuits because of this theory's incompatibility with the Jesuit belief in the Real Presence of Christ's body in the consecrated Host (Marcus Hellyer, "Jesuit Physics in Eighteenth-Century Germany: Some Continuities," in O'Malley, *The Jesuits,* 546. Yet Josef Stepling was corresponding with Wolff as early as the 1740s (Eduard Winter, *Tausend Jahre Geisteskampf in Sudetenraum: Das Religiöse Ringen zwei Völker* [Salzburg: Otto Müller, 1938], 267 f.).

[14] An exception was Otthmar Zinke (1700–1738), who founded a short-lived "Winterschule" for the sons of farmers in Břevnov, a short distance from Prague (Franz Machilek, "Reformsorden und Ordensreformen in den böhmischen Ländern von 10. bis 18. Jahrhundert," in Seibt, *Bohemia sacra,* 78).

[15] For example, in 1763 it was decreed that the Society would have to pay back "Promotionstaxen" that had been collected at the graduation of students from its universities since 1622 (Nittner, "Erzbistum," 183).

which Hannibal confronts his Roman adversaries.[16] Another public performance, probably not staged or in costume and produced the same year in the Malá Strana, featured Pompey on the isle of Rhodes.[17] These performances date from long after the great era of Jesuit-produced plays in the seventeenth century.[18]

By midcentury such publicly performed plays were on their way to becoming a rarity in the Bohemian Province.[19] Plays performed in schools were outlawed completely in 1768.[20] Apparently, public performances served the same function for the collegia as the earlier plays, showcasing the Latinity of the students and generally promoting the image of the Jesuit

---

[16] "In exercitationes rursum cum publicas, tum privatas e Titi Livii Patavin . . ." (Strahov, F K IV 28 16).

[17] Ibid., 19.

[18] The outstanding Czech Jesuit playwright of this period was Carolus (Karel) Kolcava (Kolczawa; 1655–1717) (F. Kavka, J. Polišenský, and F. Kutnar, *Přehled dějin československa v epoše feudalismu III* [Prague: Státní pedagogické Nakladatelství, 1963], 215).

[19] Jesuit drama had its greatest worldwide impact in the seventeenth century, and some scholars date its decline from before the middle of this period. By 1620 the stage effects of plays produced by the schools of the Society were already tending toward the sensational and blood curdling (Curt von Faber du Faur, *German Baroque Literature* [New Haven: Yale University Press, 1958], 243). Jesuit plays also served as venues for glorifying the House of Habsburg and its military accomplishments, as did the production of *Mars Austriacus* by the students of the Klagenfurt collegium during Fasching in 1728 (Kurt Wolfgang Drozd, *Schul- und Ordenstheater am Collegium S. J. Klagenfurt (1604–1773)* [Klagenfurt: Landesmuseum für Kärnten, 1965], 227).

By the 1750s such plays were very seldom produced anywhere in the Bohemian Province. Possibly the latest documented reference to a Jesuit-produced play is found in the *Litteræ annuæ* of 1760, which report that a drama was staged on June 17 of that year before a distinguished audience (NK, 1416 MS XXIIIC 105/18, folio 76r). The popularity of these productions does not seem to have decreased in their final years. The obituary notice of Ferdinand Silbermann, who died in 1770 after many years of teaching in Prague, contains the following passage that suggests the amazement, pleasure, and betterment that the plays occasioned: "admirationem magis ac animorum modo hilaritatem modo salutarem oculorum oblectationem [dederunt] . . . adeo omnia semper plena erant maturæ eruditionis, jocunditatis, affectus ac efficacitatis (NK, 23/19, *Litt. An. Pro. Boh 1770*, folio 289r). Even if the plays alluded to date from a much earlier period in Silbermann's career, this passage shows how highly the business of producing plays was still regarded within the Prague Jesuit community shortly before the suppression. It is also evident that the "jocunditas" of comedy was as acceptable as the sometimes heavy-handed "eruditio" of more didactic Jesuit plays. A nineteenth-century historian asserted that the Habsburg government banned Jesuit plays in schools in 1765, ostensibly because of the comic content of works by Ignac Cornova (Oskar Teuber, *Geschichte der Prager Theater,* 2 vols. [Prague: A. Haase, 1883], 2:23). The author has been unable to find independent documentation of this claim.

[20] This was by imperial decree, October 19, 1768 (V. Maiwald, "Geschichte der öffentlichen Stiftsgymnasiums in Braunau," *Beiträge zur österreichischen Erziehungs-und Schulgeschichte* 13 [1912]: 276). December 19 of that year is given as the day that "Lateinische Schuldramen" were banned (Gerald Grimm, *Die Schulreform Maria Theresias, 1747–1775* [Frankfurt a/M: Peter Lang, 1987], 213).

collegia as bulwarks of morality and piety, although the writers of the *Litteræ* were not afraid to note the occasionally comic content of the plays.[21] Public performances restated the position of the Society on various ethical issues and kept the message of the post-Tridentine reformed Church before the public. Like the outdoor gardens that were the passion of Baroque princes, public performances offered stylized versions of natural life in a patterned ritualism that reinforced the notions of stability and permanence without sacrificing aesthetics. The *excertationes* also sustained the agonistic oral culture of the *Ratio*, which placed high value on rhetorical excellence and the ability to convey complex or elevated ideas in Latin. It is likely that this rhetorical tradition was no longer as vital in the 1750s and 1760s as it had been a century earlier, but Jesuit records from both the Bohemian and the Austrian Provinces show that the Society tried to continue the practice of public performances until the suppression put an end to its activities.

Apparently the choice of subject matter or literary work to serve as the focal point of the public performance was not always limited to the ancients. The *Historia Bohemica*, written in the fifteenth century by Aeneas Sylvius (later Pope Pius II) was featured in a public performance of 1766, "in disputationibus externorum vulgata historia."[22] In the same year a work of the Croatian Jesuit Ruder Boskovich, "De turbine," which had been translated by Jesuits from Italian into Latin, was also the subject of a public disputation.[23]

The importance of the public disputations and performances cannot be overestimated, and it is clear that contemporaries paid attention to the occasions when Jesuit schools displayed their students' learning and their teachers' literary skills. Listing in the *Litteræ annuæ* the names of the nobles in the audience is evidence that the Jesuits regarded public performances as

---

[21] Comic pieces may not have been performed for the general public: "tam in publicis tentamentibus litterariis, quam in comicis exercitationibus," suggesting, perhaps, the difference between a test or examination and an exercise or practice (NK, 1288 MS XXIII C105/15, *An. Prov. Boh. 1761*, folio 215r). See also n. 16 above.

[22] NK, 23/17, *Litt. An. Boh. Prov. 1766*, folio 175r. The choice of Aeneas Sylvius is especially significant, because the Italian humanist cast a predictably negative light on the contemporaneous Hussite uprisings and the sects that sprang up in their wake. Yet choosing a history of Bohemia instead of a classical or biblical theme by itself suggests that Prague Jesuit educators possessed an awareness of the historical antecedents of eighteenth-century Bohemia, and thus provide a context for the later researches of a proto-nationalist such as Josef Dobrovský. An even clearer evidence of this connection to Bohemian history is the subject of a 1770 performance: "In occasione prodiit Decas . . . ex Bohuslai Balbini manuscriptis descriptum" (*Litt. An. Prov. Boh. 1770*, folio 227v). Balbín, the seventeenth-century Jesuit defender of Bohemian cultural achievement, wrote an apologia for the Czech language that would not be published until 1777 (J. Hanuš, "Bohuslava Balbína, *Bohemia docta*," *ČČH* 12 [1906]: 137). Elsewhere, scripturally inspired "dissertationes" performed in public were published in Czech as well as German (NK, 23/19, *Litt. An. Prov. Boh.*, 1771, folio 309v).

[23] NK, 23/17, *An. Prov. Boh. 1770*, folio 227v.

demonstrating their institutional ties to the highest levels of Bohemian society, and as a means to reinforce their religious and educational values in a setting endorsed by the powerful. The tie between the aristocracy and Jesuit schools was not limited to performances of topics of more general interest, such as Bohemian history. At a 1772 performance of "Prælectiones dogmatico-speculativæ" put on by the second-year philosophy students, a dazzling array of aristocrats was present, whose ranks and, in one instance, whose actual name are dutifully reported.[24]

In addition to the collegia in Prague's Old Town and Malá Strana, the Society also operated two other schools in the city. One of these, the Seminary of St. Wenceslaus, had been founded in 1580 with support from Baron Lobkowitz, a prominent nobleman whose family remained loyal to the Habsburgs during the reign of the "Winter King." This seminary, which educated the sons of nobility as well as members of religious orders, had also been endowed by Albrecht von Wallenstein, the mercurial general whose double-dealing had led to his assassination in 1634 on the orders of the Emperor.[25]

Another school educated both the future priests and boys receiving a stipend from a fund established by that same emperor, Ferdinand II, in 1629. This institution, the Convictus ad S. Bartholomæum, had been created in 1560, in the first wave of efforts to regain Prague for Catholicism.[26] In 1771 the school enrolled "tam ecclesisatici quam liberi universim 93" (both future clerics and other boys as well).[27] There is only fragmentary documentation that either of these schools survived long into the post-suppression era, and the students whom they would have served were probably absorbed into the *Gymnasien* that flourished through the Josephinian period.[28] In any case, the need for a strictly religious education was waning among the aristocracy and wealthier urban bourgeoisie who formed an important part of the potential student body. With the suppression of the monasteries a few years later, the entire social context that had sustained these schools was irretrievably shattered.

---

[24] Moreover, barons and knights were in attendance as well: "Nostros inter auditores Ill'mus Josephus Comes Buquoi de Longuevall, Barones 9, Equites Nobiles Armigeri cum rubea Stella 16" (*Litt. An. Boh. Prov. 1772*, folios 174v–174r). The Buquoi family was one of the leading landowners of the kingdom; Count Johann Nepomuk Buquoi was known as one of the few landed aristocrats to promote peasant home industries (Paul P. Bernard, "Poverty and Poor Relief in the Eighteenth Century," in Ingrao, *State and Society*, 243 f.).

[25] Hammerschied, *Prodromus*, 102–6.

[26] Ibid., 361.

[27] NK, 23/19, *Litt. An. Prov. Boh. 1771*, folio 368v.

[28] Karel Beránek, "Teologická fakulta," in Čornejová, *Dějiny*, 2:87.

To gain a better-rounded picture of the students attending Jesuit schools, we must turn to the surprising evidence of members of other religious orders who were enrolled. In Cheb (Eger), a town located on the western frontier of Bohemia, the Jesuit collegium in 1769 counted ten Franciscans from the Province of St. John of Capistrano among its students.[29] This province was located in Hungary, making it highly probable that many of the students were ethnic Hungarians, hundreds of miles from home. The presence of such strangers must have had a significant impact on the small provincial school, and would have driven home the message of the worldwide mission of the Church.

Other orders also enrolled in Jesuit schools in Prague: a member of the Paulinists, often aggressive rivals to the Society, was studying poetics at the Prague university in 1768.[30] Considering the animosity between the Jesuits and other teaching orders that had been a part of the educational environment of central Europe for over a century, these contacts are significant. Perhaps no other schools were available where clergy could receive religious training. Yet it is equally possible that the polemics and jealousies in which the high-ranking officials of the competing orders indulged themselves were not of much significance to those occupying the lower ranks of the Jesuits and their rivals.

The enduring contribution of Jesuit schools goes beyond its curricular and instructional base; and despite all the criticisms noted here, Jesuit schooling never lost all its considerable prestige.[31] This was often attributable to the teachers themselves. Some Jesuits were beloved figures in the community, providing a noteworthy contrast to the terrifying performances of Fr. Koniáš and his fellow hellfire preachers. F. M. Pelzel remembered the long-dead Ferdinand Silbermann as a white-haired man of seventy surrounded by his students, who continued to walk to and from his classroom in the foulest weather.[32]

All the foregoing suggests an educational system well established in the seventeenth century and still flourishing in the eighteenth, but increas-

---

[29] NK, 23/19, *Litt. An. Prov. Boh. 1769*, folio 176r.

[30] NK, 23/19, *Litt. An Prov. Boh. 1768*, folio 116v.

[31] Compared to many nineteenth-century writers, twentieth-century critics of Jesuit schooling have been much more favorable in their assessment of its overall impact and surviving prestige. Even an author whose sympathies were with the *philosophes* rather than with the Society could write about the Jesuits' "unequaled methods of instruction" (Harold Nicolson, *The Age of Reason* [New York: Doubleday, 1961], 384.

[32] "Ich habe oft diesen siebzig jährigen mit einem Silberhaar gezierten Mann, von der Jugend umgeben auch im schlechtesten Wetter in und aus der Schule gehen sehen" (Pelzel, *Gelehrte,* 193).

ingly beset with difficulties that the Jesuits did not or could not remedy.[33] Why? First we may list the Jesuits' lack of understanding of the danger facing their Society. Earlier we noted the tendency of the Bohemian Society to carry on its business as usual during its final years. This ability to continue and even expand operations was the result of a naiveté and trust in royal protection that resulted, not unreasonably, from the high prestige that the Society enjoyed during the first half of the eighteenth century.[34] Expressions of confidence that the champions of the Society would come to its rescue were on the lips of Jesuits almost until the moment of the suppression. In Spain in 1766, even as the King planned the expulsion of the Society, a Jesuit could write, "Yo espero que el rey nos hará justicia."[35] In Bohemia the hope and belief in royal protection went so far as to include a conviction that the aristocracy who for so long had been educated in Jesuit schools would ultimately come to their defense.

It is true that in the official documents of the Society the degree to which powerful personages served as protectors was frequently exaggerated, if not fantasized.[36] Nevertheless, the confidence that the Society placed in the aristocrats whose names adorned the pages of its reports was not baseless. Indeed, these aristocrats continued to enroll their sons in Jesuit schools and take part in Jesuit-sponsored religious activities until the bitter end. Even as the days of the Society grew short, the Jesuit schools were seen as the fitting place in which clerical students of all kinds could receive training: in 1772 the Seminarium S. Wenceslai had a healthy enrolment of 199.[37] In the countryside, despite hard times, enrollments dipped but did not plummet: in Cheb, the collegium counted 230 in 1770 and 194 in 1773.[38] What did not occur, however, was a spontaneous and effective rallying of support among the leading families of Bohemia for the Society in its hour of need. Because the wealthy could avail themselves of a few other options for education and the other religious orders offering instruction were more

---

[33] The only published records of a Bohemian Jesuit collegium from the seventeenth and eighteenth centuries are the annual records of the school in Krumlov (P. Rudolph Schmidtmeyer, "Beiträge zur Geschichte des Jesuiten-Gymnaisiums [Gymnasium Rosense] in Krummau," *Beiträge zur österreichischen Erziehungs- und Schulgeschichte* 13 [1912] 289).

[34] J. C. H. Aveling, *The Jesuits* (New York: Stein and Day, 1981), 256; Geoffrey Cubitt, *The Jesuit Myth: Conspiracy Theory and Politics in Nineteenth Century France* (Oxford: Clarendon Press, 1993), 19.

[35] Ludwig Freiherr von Pastor, *History of the Popes* trans., C. E. Peeler, 40 vols. (St. Louis: Herder, 1899–1953), 37:100.

[36] As when Clement XIII was referred to as the Society's "faventissimo protectore" (NK, 23/19, *Litt. An. Prov. Boh. 1769* folio 132r). Clement suffered greatly for defending the Society against its enemies.

[37] NK, 23/19, *Annales Prov. Boh. 1772* folio 420r.

[38] Herr, "Zur Geschichte des Egerer Gymnasiums," 153.

flexible in their educational programs, there came to be less enthusiasm for Jesuit schools.[39] The rapid acceptance of the reforms proposed by the Piarist Gratian Marx in 1775 is evidence of how ready the upper-class clientele of the Jesuit schools was for substantive reform.[40]

During the War of Austrian Succession, Prague was under attack and the students of the Clementinum formed a *Studentenlegion* that fought to defend the city and to support Maria Theresia against the claims of the Bavarian Elector to the imperial throne.[41] Jesuit schools also suffered during the Seven Years' War and its aftermath, coping with the physical destruction of schools and communities, and with additional war taxes and the burden of quartering soldiers.[42] In Silesia the war brought wholesale destruction and atrocities, and signaled the continual decline of Jesuit schools in the region. The upheavals of war also called potential students away from the classrooms of the collegia and universities, and disrupted the agricultural enterprises that were a source of income for the schools.

Yet these difficulties do not seem to have had a long-term effect on the day-to-day functioning of the schools, which despite fluctuations in enrollment continued their work unremittingly through periods of war, famine, peasant uprisings, and rumors about the impending demise of the Society. Jesuit schools were well-established entities in Prague and in provincial cities and thus found it easier to survive. Moreover, the forces of inertia and resistance to innovation visible in many areas of Bohemian society would also have been assets to Jesuit schools. The majority of men who had attended school in Bohemia were themselves alumni of collegia and thus a natural pool of potential allies and a source of new students. Even when the Society had opponents nearby, there were many who did not seek the destruction of the school system it had created.

Had the Society not been suppressed, probably its schools as institutions would have survived the Josephianian reforms and perhaps even the

---

[39] Hugo Hantsch, "Die Aufklärung Böhmens," in *Tausend Jahre,* 163.

[40] Marx introduced the teaching of German (some years before Joseph II's Germanization program), and divided the *Gymnasium* into three grades of grammar and two of humanistic studies (Československá vlastivěda [Prague: Sfinx: Bohumil Janda, 1931], 10, 12). Nor did those who could pay enjoy the only option available. The *Ritterakademien* that catered to the aristocracy provided another alternative to the classical curriculum of the Jesuit collegia (Wangermann, *Achievement,* 55). Likewise, the *Stiftsgymnasium* established by Abbot Rautenstrauch in Břevnov offered an alternative to the traditional Latin school (Maiwald, "Geschichte der öffentlichen Stiftgymnasiums," 1–288.)

[41] The Prague *Studentenlegion* was active in 1744, two years after the occupation of the city by Prussia and its allies (F. A. Slavík, *Dějiny českého studenstva* [Prague: Nákladem vlastním, 1873], 29 f.).

[42] The collegium in Malá Strana struggled with an "annona militaris" (war-time provisions) during the war and, along with the *domus professa,* was obliged to billet soldiers (NK, 1416 MS XXIIIC 105/18, *Annales Prov. Boh. 1760* folio 84r).

stresses induced by the Napoleonic Wars. At the same time, the curriculum, already under pressure to change, could not resist the demands of the reformers forever.[43] Yet the enemies of Jesuit schooling within Bohemia, the rival religious orders, the readers of *philosophe* writings, and crypto-Protestant peasants and townspeople, were far from a unified force.[44] The potential supporters and clients of the Society's schools still existed; but certainly without the explicit support of the Habsburgs, mother and son, the Jesuit collegia could not have survived without modifications.

Even though Maria Theresia was in no position, even if she had wanted to do so, to prevent *Dominus ac Redemptor noster* from being issued, she could have taken steps to preserve the essential form of the Society's schools if she had so desired. Neither she nor her co-regent, however, had any strong inclination to salvage at least some vestiges of the Jesuit system, although their reasons for not taking any such steps were not identical.

The Jesuits' educational enterprise in Bohemia was doomed because its underlying reason for being, the promotion of the values of the Church, became less important to all the most powerful elements of society as the eighteenth century wore on. While sincere devotion to these values did not die out with the beginnings of Theresian reform, and in fact continued to play an important role in the history of the region for several centuries, the Baroque enthusiasm that had sustained the Jesuit collegia during their earliest years was fading among the crucial cluster of highly placed nobles of the kingdom. The purely practical value of Jesuit schooling as a preparation for a career, while still recognized in many quarters, was not held in high enough esteem to sustain its educational principles after the suppression and beyond.

The Diminishing Jesuit Role in the University

The university in Prague was not the only responsibility of the Jesuit community, but it was by far its most complex and most visible one. To understand the relationship of this community to the city and to the rest of

---

[43] Christoph Anton Migazzi, the Cardinal Archbishop of Vienna, later famous for his opposition to the reforms of Joseph II, had been appointed by Maria Theresia in 1760 to oversee the Studienreformcommission. With such powerful figures committed to moving reform forward, no amount of resistance, passive or otherwise, on the part of the Society could have permanently prevented further changes in the curriculum (Otto Vicenzi, *Das Gymnasium: Eine Chance für Europa* [Vienna: Hermann Böhlaus Nachfolger, 1983], 48).

[44] With the exception of a tiny circle in Prague, the actual impact of ideas coming from France was probably minimal until after the suppression. The papers of the Paars, a family of wealthy landowners, reveal that periodicals from France were received on the family estate in 1779. To what degree these publications reflected *lumière* ideas is not clear, nor is it certain that many other great families also had exposure to periodicals from France (Harvard Business School C-1 1766–1788, P111).

Bohemian society, one must first understand the currents within the university and the shifting position of the Jesuits during the 1760s and '70s.[45] As we have seen, the Society was directly connected to the university following the Decree of Unity in 1654; but throughout the eighteenth century, external and internal forces were steadily attenuating this relationship. The government of Maria Theresia strove to extend its direct control over the universities of the Habsburg domains; some of its measures, such as the rescript of 1744 regulating the visits that students of the Faculty of Medicine could pay to their patients had only slight impact on the teachers of the Society. But the Theresian reforms extended far beyond the "practical" disciplines of medicine and law, and had a major impact on the organization of the Faculties of Theology and Philosophy, long the preserve of the Jesuits. These reforms, embodied in the new plan of studies of 1752, were intended to place all branches of the university more directly under the supervision of Vienna, but were by no means in opposition to some of the educational objectives of the Jesuits. As long as the devout Empress lived, there was hope that she would support orthodox Catholicism, which, in the view of the Jesuit leadership, was synonymous with the theological position of the Society.[46] Events would prove that this assumption was not necessarily correct.

The University Crisis of the Eighteenth Century

The Prague university in the middle of the eighteenth century shared with many other European universities some significant difficulties, of which declining enrollments was the most easily identifiable.[47] While enrollment figures for the earlier part of the century are not available for all faculties of

---

[45] This brief discussion makes no claim to being a complete history of the university during the 1750s and 1760s. The most useful works on this topic are W. W. Tomek, *Geschichte der Prager Universität*, and I. Čornejová, *Dějiny Univerzity Karlova*. The history of the Faculty of Theology is detailed in an unpublished manuscript by Maximillian Millauer, *Geschichte der Theologischen Fakultät der K. K. Prager Universität* (Národné Muzeum [NM], VII A 5).

[46] Despite signs of danger to the Society from the mid-1760s onward, there were reasons to believe that Maria Theresia's commitment to orthodox Catholicism would continue to take the forms it always had. The unsophisticated could still read Pope Clement XIII's awarding of the title "Apostolic Majesty" to the Empress in 1768 as evidence of her support of the *status quo* (Mary Clare Goodwin, C.S.A., *The Papal Conflict with Josephinism* [New York: Fordham University Press, 1938], 43).

[47] Total enrollments at German universities averaged between 8,100 and just under 9,000 between 1700 and 1755; this number declined to below 7,000 from 1791 to 1795, and continued to decline until the end of the century, despite a gradual increase in the total population of the region (Charles E. McClelland, *State, Society, and University in Germany, 1700–1914* [Cambridge/New York: Cambridge University Press, 1980], 63). Some Habsburg institutions suffered far more than Prague: enrollment at the university of Graz slipped to a mere 22 in 1781 (Paul P. Bernard, *Jesuits and Jacobins* [Urbana/London/Chicago, University of Illinois Press, 1971], 15).

the Prague university, it is likely that enrollments declined in all divisions or at best remained constant in the seven decades of the eighteenth century. For the years 1705 to 1709, the total number of students enrolled in the Faculty of Law was 638, but this figure declined to 180 between 1745 and 1749. Between 1701 and 1750, 313 students were enrolled in the Faculty of Medicine; this compares with a total enrollment of 218 for the years 1751 to 1783.[48] The total number of students enrolled in the Faculty of Medicine slumped to 27 in 1793.[49] Given the upheavals confronting not only the Prague university but all educational institutions in Bohemia during this period and during the Seven Years' War, this decline is not surprising.[50]

But the decline in enrollments had causes that were more complex than simply the social instability of Bohemia. Although the motivations of prospective students are extremely difficult to establish, it is safe to say that the fading reputation of the institution contributed to its inability to attract as many students as it had enrolled at the beginning of the century. The appointment of Joseph Stepling as "director of studies" in the Faculty of Philosophy was not simply an expression of the desire of the court in Vienna to gain more control over its universities; it was also a tacit affirmation that the central government sought to improve academic standards in Prague.[51]

Indeed, the most basic internal challenge facing not only the Jesuit-dominated faculties of the university but the entire institution had to do with academic quality. Much of the ferment of the Enlightenment took place apart from, and even in opposition to, the culture found in both Catholic and Protestant universities. To many, universities now seemed holdovers from medieval times whose curriculum and means of instruction were outdated and unappealing and whose whole purpose for existing was merely to transmit existing knowledge and to perpetuate the traditional means of transmission. Even Oxford and Cambridge reached a low point in their fortunes during this century, with dilettantism and drunkenness dominating university life. Universities in the German-speaking world were seen as

---

[48] Čornejová, *Dějiny*, 2:243.

[49] Ibid., 2:247.

[50] Many examples can be given; the collegium in Kladsko (Glatz), in Silesia, was devastated by the Prussian army in 1759, whose commander not only seized its funds and buildings but even publicly hanged a priest (probably not a Jesuit) "in publico patibulo" (A. Podlaha, ed., *Relationes super statu ecclesiæ et Archidiocesis Pragensis ad S. Congregationem Concilii ab Archiepiscopis Pragensibus factæ an. 1759–1781* [Prague: Cyrillo-Methodějská Knihtiskarna V. Kotrba, 1908), 6).

[51] A modern Czech historian has called Stepling in the role of "director of studies" the "long arm" of the imperial court, as he answered only to the state, not to the university chancellor (Marie Štemberková, *Universitas Carolina Pragensis* [Prague: Charles University, 1995], 34 f.).

caught in a "trade guild" mentality that had little to offer society, but rather prevented these institutions from rising above the level of mediocrity.[52]

We have already seen the externally driven criticism leveled against the Prague university from the time of the Birelli report onward, yet we should note that it was not only secular-minded reformers who found fault with Catholic universities.[53] Cardinal Giuseppe Garampi, touring German Catholic universities in the 1760s, declared them to be "in a state of stagnation."[54] Two young Italian aristocrats who visited Prague in 1752 rendered a similar verdict when they found the books in the university library lacking in quality.[55] These negative assessments probably impress modern readers more than they did the members of the Society who directed the activities of the two nonprofessional faculties of the university. These men still felt they could view Prague university as a securely established institution that did not have to compete with salons and well-patronized and highly visible societies of learned persons, in contrast to universities in Britain or France. The university had the additional advantage of having completely dominated intellectual life in the lands of the Bohemian Crown during the previous century and a half. Its position, therefore, might have seemed less vulnerable than that of the Jesuits at the university of Vienna, which underwent a dramatic change in its intellectual orientation from 1735 to 1764.[56]

The very poverty of literary life in Bohemia worked to the advantage of the university as an institution, ensuring that it would, in effect, remain the only game in town.[57] There was no discernible pressure from religious

---

[52] Daniel Fallon, *The German University: A Heroic Ideal in Conflict with the Modern World* (Boulder: Colorado Associated University Press, 1980), 6. This problem had existed in the previous century as well. Of the handful of German universities considered in the seventeenth century to be of superior quality, none were Jesuit (Martha Ornstein, *The Role of Scientific Societies in the Seventeenth Century* [Chicago: University of Chicago Press, 1928], 227).

[53] Ivana Raková, "Les Essais de réforme à l'Université de Prague dans la première moitié du XVIIIe siècle," *Les Grandes Réformes des universités europeénes du XVI au XXe siècles: Zeszyty naukowe uniwersytetu Jagiellonskiego. Prace historyczne* 79 (1985): 75–82.

[54] Robert Haass, *Die geistige Haltung der katholischen Universitäten Deutschlands im 18. Jahrhundert* (Freiburg: Herder, 1952), 14.

[55] Josef Kollmann, "Praha v polovině 18. století očima italských cestovatelů," *Pražský sborník historický* 16 (1983): 119–30.

[56] During these years the Society was effectively forced out of its positions of power at the university (Helmut Engelbrecht, *Geschichte des österreichischen Bildungswesens; Erziehung und Unterricht auf dem Boden Österreichs*, 5 vols. [Vienna: Österreichischer Bundesverlag, ca. 1982–ca. 1988], 3:189–91).

[57] This absence of a vital literary culture (particularly in the vernaculars) resulted from socioeconomic conditions as much as from the persistence of the Latin schools. Bohemia simply lacked those classes that could be the bearers of a cultivated linguistic tradition (Robert Auty, "Language and Society in the Czech National Revival," *The Slavonic and East European Review* 35 [1956–1957], 243).

dissenters to be included in the university community; in fact, decades would pass before a Protestant would be appointed to the university faculty. Nevertheless, the university was in a less than entirely secure position in the second half of the century, in that its curriculum, particularly in the Faculty of Philosophy, was beginning to seem archaic and far removed from curricular developments embraced elsewhere.[58] The decision of the Society, after a rancorous internal battle, to remain committed to Aristotelian philosophy and physics only added to the conviction that the Society's philosophical program was out of date and even hostile to new developments.[59]

There was a perceptible drift on the part of students away from the themes stressed in the Jesuit curriculum of the Faculty of Philosophy and the works that were deemed worthy of publication by the university press.[60] Those students of the 1760s who did go on to make significant contributions to the sciences or liberal arts seem to have absorbed little if any of the doctrine put forth by the Jesuits, who in their Faculty of Philosophy program had long placed major emphasis on the training of clergy.[61] Typical of these was František Antonín Steinský (born Jan. 16, 1752), who studied, *inter alia,* Church history and theology in the Faculty of Philosophy after 1769, but whose interests lay much more with the practical sciences. Steinský, who corresponded with Benjamin Franklin, went on to become professor of Allied Historical Sciences at the Prague university, but demonstrated little respect for his Jesuit teachers and seems to have been little influenced by them.[62] Likewise J. K. Bohač, one of the greatest experimental scientists to come out of the Prague university, pursued a line of inquiry as a professor

---

[58] Not all of these developments foreshadowed the later evolution of modern university disciplines. The field of "Raritätkunde," the study of and care for curiosities stored in a university's or school's cabinet, was a curricular innovation in the eighteenth century (Friedrich Paulsen, *Geschichte des gelehrten Unterrichts auf den deutschen Schulen und Universitäten,* 2 vols. [Leipzig: Von Veit & Comp., 1896], 1:551).

[59] The defeat in 1751 of the reformers (known as the "weisse Raben" because of their opposition to the older curriculum of the "black fathers") had long-range effects on the curricula of many Jesuit schools, although in Prague, as in other settings, more innovative content was occasionally, if discreetly, taught (Gerhard Oberkofler and Peter Goffer, *Geschichte der Universität Innsbruck [1669–1945]* [Frankfurt a/M: Peter Lang, 1996], 48 f.).

[60] In 1771 the Jesuit press in Prague published "Commentarius Joan. Fran. Cigna e Miscellaneis philosophicis Taurinesibus" (NK, 23/19, *Litt. An. Collegii S. J. Pragæ ad S. Clementem 1771,* folio 405v). This now obscure work was not innovative, but merely a recapitulation of other scholastic philosophers, and was probably intended as a textbook.

[61] Ernst Nittner, "Erzbistum und Prager Universtät in der Zeit von der Neugründung bis zur Entkonfesionalisierung (1654–1873)," in *Tausend Jahre Bistum Prag,* 182 ff.

[62] Alena Petranová, "Z korespondence Františka Steinského, prvního profesora pomocných ved historických na Karlové Universite," *AUCP—HUC* 2 [1958]: 105 f.

and researcher largely unrelated to the prescribed content of courses at the university.[63]

It is especially noteworthy that after the Societas incognitorum was established in Olomouc, it did not turn its attention to the academic categories that were the focus of the university curriculum, but concerned itself instead with literary matters.[64] Still, although many Bohemians in the second half of the eighteenth century regarded the program offered by Jesuit universities as stale, the absence of significant institutional rivals or an awareness of the massive reforms that lay ahead prevented Jesuit administrators from feeling any great need to strive for reform.

Never at Rest

The Society, unlike the monastic orders of the Middle Ages, was committed to mobility and freely moved its teachers and professors from site to site.[65] While this mobility contributed to the vitality of the Society in its earliest days and kept teachers from becoming sedentary, it became a handicap in an era when the body of knowledge was expanding, and an instructor could not simply repeat the information he had originally acquired as he moved from place to place. Not all professors and teachers moved regularly (Stepling, for example, did not leave Prague for over twenty years); but the case of Jan Dreyhuasen is not untypical.[66] After completing his tertianship, or third stage of formation, at a *domus probationis* in Chomutov in 1727, Dreyhausen served as the historian of the collegium in Olomouc. In 1732 he was in Wrocław (Breslau), in 1733 in Lehnice, from 1734 to 1737 in Klatovy, from 1738 to 1739 in Hlohov, and by 1742 he was in Prague at the Clementinum. While serving as the confessor to the bishop of Litomerice from 1744 to 1749, Dreyhausen spent some years gathering data for a projected history of the Bohemian Province.[67] Then he performed other duties in various communities, including three years in Kutná Hora as

---

[63] Petr Svobodný and Ludmila Hlavačková, "Lékařská fakulta," in Čornejová, *Dějiny,* 2:190 ff.

[64] Knut Walf, "Kirchliche Aufklärung," in Seibt, *Bohemia sacra,* 155. This non-Jesuit slant was also influenced by the enduring Protestant climate of Olomouc and nearby Silesia.

[65] This mobility was enhanced by, but did not originate with, the emphasis placed on obedience in the Constitutions, whereby Jesuit teachers might be quickly sent wherever superiors deemed they were needed (*Cons.,* nos. 606, 609).

[66] Jan Moravek, "Schmidel Balbín a Ware: Příspevek k jesuitiské historiografii v Čechách," *ČČH,* 19 (1913): 69 f.

[67] A decade later this last assignment would have been impossible, for the new bishop, Emmanuel Waldstein, would be a known enemy of the Jesuits (Umberto dell'Orto, *La nunziatura a Vienna di Giuseppi Garampi, 1776–1785* [Città Del Vaticano: Archivio Vaticano 1995], 25 f.).

minister of its collegium. Finally he returned to Prague to become prefect of the library in the Clementinum, a post he held from 1758 until 1771.[68]

Such a career speaks well of the energy and versatility of men like Dreyhausen; and in the first several centuries of the Society's existence, this versatility was one of its greatest assets. But in Dreyhausen's case, this peripatetic life denied him the chance to become an effective historian (his planned history of the province was never completed).[69] Constant breaks in the administration of collegia also ultimately did more harm than good. Sometimes egregiously inappropriate mismatches must have been the result of such a policy. When we read that the terrifying Antonín Koniáš taught *poesis* in a collegium early in his career, we can be sure that many students (and teachers) must have suffered through periods of misdirected teaching efforts.[70] Conversely, when Jesuit professors were allowed to stay in one place for years or decades, their prestige grew, as well as the renown of the school in which they taught.[71] In his diary, side by side with accounts of battles and high-level diplomacy, Prince Khevenhüller-Metsch recorded Maria Theresia's decision to erect a monument to Joseph Stepling.[72]

The Faculties of Philosophy and Theology

The Faculty of Theology was not the largest of the branches of the university—this distinction usually belonged to the Faculty of Philosophy—but the program of studies provided for Jesuits studying in this faculty was the most rigorously structured, and thus sheds light on the Society's role in the university and in the outside world.[73] In chapter 2 we saw how the curriculum of the Faculty of Philosophy in particular was popular with both Catholics and Protestants alike, who appreciated its organization and content. However, the curriculum developed in these two faculties at the

[68] Anna Fechtnerová, "Klemintinští knihovnici od roku 1609 do roku 1773," *Miscellanea oddelení rukopisu a vznacných tisku* 2 (1985): 88.

[69] There are other instances of Jesuit historians who did not write much history. Antonín Sindt (Sündt; born 1704, died 1766) taught at the Clementinum, and from 1762 until 1766 was historian of the Bohemian Province, but left no surviving writings of any kind. Since other Jesuits holding this post had been productive writers, the exact nature of Sindt's assignment remains unclear (Čornejová and Fechtnerová, *Slovník*, 426 f.).

[70] MZAB, Cerroniho sbírka, 345, II, 565.

[71] For example, Karl John, whose productivity as a philosopher grew during his years of work in Prague, published his *Institutiones philosophicæ activæ* in 1772, and received praise for it in the *Prager gelehrte Nachrichten* (J. Hanuš, "Počátky král. České společnosti nauk," *ČČH* 14 [1908]: 152; Sommervogel, *Bibliothèque*, 4:10). Like other Jesuit professors in Prague who were scholars or scientists, John also produced panegyrics on New Testament themes.

[72] Khevenhüller-Metsch and Schlitter, *Aus der Zeit Maria Theresias*, 7:455.

[73] The following is taken largely from Čornejová and Fechtnerová, *Slovník*, XIII ff.

university level was strictly hierarchical and also had as one of its goals the advancement of outstanding Jesuit scholars to positions within the university or a similar institution. In order to rise to the position of a chair in either the Philosophical or Theological Faculties, a young Jesuit had to complete a complex and demanding program most often entailing the completion of studies in the philosophical faculties of one of the Society's universities or collegia.[74] To review this period of training briefly, after being admitted to the Society, the candidate entered upon a two-year "novitiate," which for the Province of Bohemia took place at the Brno Collegium. During this period the novice might return to secular life if he chose.[75] At the end of his novitiate, he took his first vows and returned to the classroom. A brief period at the collegium and three more years of study in the Faculty of Philosophy preceded another distinctive feature of the Jesuit system, the *repetitio humaniorum,* in which the young Jesuit was trained to teach the subjects he had recently pursued as a student.

Customarily Jesuits trained in this fashion then embarked on a period of teaching in the collegia of the province, a policy of the Society that provided an important link between its university and pre-university educational programs. In some cases talented scholars immediately after completing their studies in the Faculty of Philosophy would begin work in the Faculty of Theology, which was considered "higher" than the Faculty of Philosophy in the Jesuit study program. Whether the Jesuit spent time teaching at the pre-university level or advanced at once to further university studies, the expectation was that in the third year of work in the Faculty of Theology Jesuits would be ordained priests.[76]

---

[74] We have already noted that it is difficult to distinguish between a course of study within a collegium as opposed to one undertaken in a Faculty of Philosophy at a Jesuit university. The term "gymnasium" also poses problems. In Czech historiography after 1773, "*gymnasium*" is commonly used for all pre-university secondary schools, and is contrasted with the Jesuit collegia. In one instance, a Czech historian asserts that after the reforms of 1752 the collegia "system" of the Society was done away with and replaced with *Gymnasia* (Josef Petráň, *Nástin dejin filosofické fakulty,* 72 f.). However, the Jesuit *Litteræ* continue to use the term *collegium* until the suppression. Cornova's *Jesuiten als Gymnasiallehrer* deals with the pre-suppression period, while Čornejová and Fechternová refer to the "gymnázium" education of the young Jesuit. Here the term *collegium* will be used to denote the pre-suppression schools of the Society.

[75] Not surprisingly, the Society's records do not dwell upon those Jesuit students who elected to leave the program at an early stage. However, the absence of references to Jesuit training in the biographies of Bohemian laymen for most of the eighteenth century points to the ability of the Society to retain the most able of its prospects. Ignac von Born, who did leave while still a novice, and about whom we shall shortly hear more, is one of the first such cases recorded.

[76] Third-year theology students were also given positions in the community. Anton Pilat, a third-year student, served as a "bidellus" in the collegium in the Clementinum (Strahov, B C I 53, *Catalogus personarum,* 1761, xxii).

The highest degrees that a young Jesuit might earn after his philosophical studies were the master's degree or the doctorate; in this instance the titles were virtually interchangeable and were earned after three years of study.[77] The Jesuit university in Prague might also grant a doctorate of theology, but it conferred this degree less frequently than it did other degrees. As Čornejová and Fechtnerová point out, the doctorate in theology opened the path to the highest-ranking posts in the university, and we may conclude that the Society carefully controlled the number of individuals who gained this degree, in order to perpetuate the patterns of leadership that it had established in the seventeenth century.

Although Jesuits who had advanced through the program in the Faculty of Theology were, by the standards of the day, no longer young, their formal training was not yet at an end. The "tertianship," a stage in formation unique to the Society, was the next step and involved further studies in spirituality and the Constitutions of the Society. Bohemian Jesuits undertaking this "second novitiate" studied in Telč, Jičín, and Chomutov. It was after completing the tertianship that some Jesuits pronounced the fourth vow of obedience. These men were now the true "corpus Societatis"; and only those who professed the fourth vow could ever rise to the level of provincials and assistants (the advisors to the general for groupings of provinces), or be selected as general of the Society. These Jesuits carried on the tradition of the "athletæ" who in the first years of the Society were sent to the Collegium Germanicum in Rome to receive training for the aggressive propagation of the true faith.[78] The entire program of study, from early adolescence on, was in some sense a preparation for this highest level of leadership, although only a minority of Jesuits ever achieved it.

The preceding pattern of advancement has been described in some detail because its systematic and hierarchical sequence continued to shape the character of the Prague university even after the academic reforms of 1752.[79] There were, of course, no shortcuts to advancement within the Society. Originating in the spirit of mid-sixteenth-century Catholic reform,

---

[77] A bachelor's degree was granted after two years of study and an examination. The title of "Magister liberalium artium" was regarded as archaic in the seventeenth and eighteenth centuries, although it might still be legally granted by a Jesuit university. The Society preferred the title "Philosophiæ doctor."

[78] The *Collegium Germanicum* opened its doors in 1552, at the point when the Society's first serious campaign to regain central Europe was beginning (Paulsen, *Geschichte des gelehrten Unterrichts*, 1:288).

[79] After 1752 patristics, Church history, Semitic languages, and liturgy become standard features of the Faculty of Theology curriculum (Josef Hemmerle, "Die Prager Universität in der neueren Zeit," in Seibt, *Bohemia sacra,* 418). "Oriental languages," as they were called, meaning Hebrew and Aramaic, were repeated like other humanities. But the collegium at the Clementinum in Prague in 1761 enrolled only four students in this course (*Catalogus personarum Prov. Boh. S.J. 1761*, Strahov, B C I 53, xxiii).

the hierarchical system of the Society abhorred the Renaissance phenomenon of teenaged bishops and cardinals and ill-prepared parish priests and teachers. It was committed to a program of training in which each high-ranking member of the Society (and thus of the universities run by the Society as well) had been indoctrinated in its values, trained in the same linguistic skills, and drawn into a common cause through the fourth vow. Such a policy assured the survival of the Society's educational program through periods of social stress and material hardship, but it also made innovation and reform from within virtually impossible.

At the same time, the Society did make efforts to place its members in roles that were appropriate for them. If Jesuits showed a talent for library work, there were positions at the Clementinum and at other libraries in the collegia.[80] As we have seen, Jesuits were also chosen for work as chaplains and for service in missions in the countryside or to foreign courts.[81] There was the opportunity for those who excelled in legal studies to pursue canon law at the university, although these studies were completely divorced from the curriculum of the Faculty of Law.[82] Few other alternatives existed. The lack of flexibility in the training provided to young Jesuits placed a great deal of responsibility on the leadership of the Society in deciding where to place some of its members, while it also placed those who served in non-pedagogical capacities at a potential disadvantage from the standpoint of the larger culture, since their education did not include many branches of learning already accepted in the eighteenth century as standard.[83] Yet for

[80] A. Fechtnerová, "Klementinští knihovnici," 93–124, 140, 143. Many of the librarians of the Clementinum held important posts or had experience overseas: Nicolaus (Mikuláš) Krebs was president of the Museum mathematicum in Prague, and Franciscus (František) Wolff died in the prison of St. Julian in Lisbon after the suppression of the Society in Portugal.

[81] The accounts of Jesuits' careers as reported in obituary notices in *Litteræ* suggest that those chosen for pedagogical work often did little service in missions, and vice versa. This was undoubtedly a contributing factor in the tensions among the literary, scientific, and evangelizing roles of the Bohemian Society. However, a Jesuit might be transferred out of teaching assignment for very different work, as in the case of Franciscus de Paul Cardell, who after many years of teaching and work at the shrine of Loreto, was sent to the court of the King of the Two Sicilies (MZAB, Cerroniho sbírka, II, 345, 229).

[82] The careers of Jesuit priests who taught canon law were divorced from the activities of the Faculty of Law and remained completely integrated into the usual broad range of assignments teachers in the Society received. For example, Joannes Gremmer (Gremner) (born Oct. 27, 1695; died June 15, 1757) combined assignments teaching moral theology in Olomouc and canon law in Nisa with direction of the choir in the collegium in Breslau (Čornejová and Fechtnerová, *Slovník,* 124 f.; Pelzel, *Gelehrte,* 192; Strahov, FX IV 28 18–e). P. Joannes Flaschner (born May 25, 1761) also taught canon law at the Prague university (NK, 1288 MS XXIII, C105/15, *An. Prov. Boh. 1761* folio 234v).

[83] As the careers of many Jesuit scientists show, these limitations did not stop some of the most intellectually agile members of the Society. Occasionally university-trained Jesuits would even show a flair for applied sciences. Franciscus Gerck designed fortifications for the city of Olomouc that were of service in the Seven Years' War (Wydra *[sic], Historia matheoses,* 70).

those who remained within the ambit of the Society, such considerations were not serious problems.

The rigidity of the program of studies required for Jesuits had an impact on non-Jesuits as well. Students aspiring to a career outside the Society were taught in the Faculty of Philosophy by instructors, most of whom would eventually be ordained, and were presented a curriculum that, even though it was not designed exclusively for the Society's program of advancement, certainly addressed the Society's expectations for its future leaders and reflected the Society's official rigid view of theological and philosophical orthodoxy. This limited academic program was not necessarily detrimental to the education of all lay students. For the sons of the nobility, the training imparted at the Jesuit university surpassed what private tutoring could offer in rigor and in the depth to which Latin would be mastered. In addition, the Prague university featured a variety of instructors, and offered the possibility that a student would come into contact with a master teacher such as Ignac Cornova or a figure of international stature such as Josef Stepling. For the future village priest, the university offered an education superior in breadth and organization to what many European seminaries could provide.

Yet the orientation of so much of the curriculum of the Faculty of Philosophy toward the process of advancement within the Society was a liability in an environment where this curriculum was under attack from without. But neither the institutional configuration of the Society nor the organization of the schools themselves as outlined in the *Ratio* readily lent themselves to a reform of the system. Like the curriculum itself, the organizational model of the Jesuit-designed faculties of the university served as an anchor for conservatives fearing or despising change. But rather than saving those who clung to it, the weight of this anchor doomed the supporters of the traditional organizational model.

Despite these difficulties within this structure, individual Jesuits found ways to pursue their own interests. Johannes Nepomucenus Polanský conducted experiments in physics while teaching at the university, but he also published works on theology along with his treatises on optics.[84] Joannes Zobel, laboring in the Museum mathematicum of the Clementinum until his death in 1770, collected specimens of wood from the length and breadth of Bohemia.[85] Thus, in the university we find individual Jesuits functioning

Stanislav Vydra himself performed a similar service for Hradec Královéin the 1780s (Ivo Korán, "Přelom ve vývoji výtvarné kultury," in Petráň, *Počátky,* 272).

[84] Born Feb. 7, 1723; died Oct. 13, 1776, at Olomouc (Čornejová and Fechtenrová, *Slovník,* 349; Pelzel, *Gelehrte,* 249; Sommervogel, *Bibliothèque,* 6:948). One of Polanský's treatises, published in Olomouc in 1756, bears the title *De animabus brutorum dissertatio,* indicating his interest in the "souls" of brute animals.

[85] Wydra, *Historia matheseos,* 96.

in two settings, the confessional and the scientific, pursuing goals that would be regarded today as distant or even antithetical. When men such as Polanský ventured into the realm of confessional literature, were they practicing as individuals the same accommodation to culture that Jesuit missionaries adopted when they ventured into the world of folk religion? While such a hypothesis is plausible, we must admit the real possibility that Polanský and others like him saw no conflict between theological investigations and empirical science. In this, his actions would have reflected the continuing acceptance and promotion of the miraculous found among the missionaries who traveled the backroads of Bohemia.

Thus far the picture of the Prague university in the second half of the eighteenth century to a large degree conforms to the accepted view of the period as a time of "stagnation" for universities. But each case presents its own unique characteristics, and Prague was no exception. The most salient of these characteristics was the relationship of the university to the city of Prague itself. In fact, it is not possible to consider the role of the university and its influence on the intellectual currents of the day without taking into account the city in which it was located.

In the City

Prague, the historic capital of the lands of the Crown of St. Wenceslaus and a city of perhaps seventy thousand in the mid-eighteenth century was far smaller than the largest European metropolises, a community where those dwelling in its medieval center continued to live a life of face-to-face relationships.[86] It had been the residential city of Rudolf II in the late sixteenth and early seventeenth centuries and one of the great cultural centers of Europe; but during the Thirty Years' War Rudolph's collections had been looted by the Swedes, and after the Peace of Westphalia the city had never regained its prominence. Instead, Prague had evolved into the largest provincial city in the Habsburg realms, but one that no longer played a major role in international politics. Repeatedly under attack during the seventeenth and eighteenth centuries, the city had sustained tens of thousands of cannon volleys during the siege and subsequent occupation of 1757, when scores of houses had been destroyed and many public buildings damaged.[87]

---

[86] The exact population of Prague at midcentury cannot be determined with complete accuracy. Census data from 1768 suggest a population of 54,294, although data from only three years later show a total population of "77,577 legal and 78,874 actual" (P. G. M. Dickson, *Finance and Government under Maria Theresia, 1740–1780,* 2 vols. [Oxford: Clarendon Press, 1987], 1:51).

[87] For example, the Carolinum library, which was still in need of repair four years later (M. Pavlíková, "K osudu pražské universitní knihovny v 18 století," *Knihovna* 4 [1950]: 130, no. 42).

Eighteenth-century Prague was in some ways less conspicuously "medieval" in appearance than it would become in the next century; the romantic "restoration" of many landmarks and the completion of the towers of the cathedral of St. Vitus would be an expression of a Czech national sentiment only beginning to coalesce during the 1760s and '70s. Although a distant second in size behind Vienna among the cities of the Habsburg realms, Prague possessed an imposing urban landscape that took advantage of the natural assets of the Vlatava River and the surrounding hills. The development of Prague as a Baroque city came about in part because these realms were by no means as politically centralized as the kingdoms of France or England, allowing regional centers to take on special importance. Moreover, since their return to Vienna in the early seventeenth century, the Habsburgs had not transformed their city residence, the Hofburg, into a center of the arts, which in turn discouraged much aristocratic architectural activity in the *Residenzstadt* and made it possible for regional centers such as Prague to be the focus of more ambitious building projects.[88] By the time the high-water mark of construction had passed in the 1760s, Prague was a baroque treasure, crowded with private and public buildings unsurpassed by any city in the Habsburg realms, or arguably by any city in Europe.[89]

In this small city the Society was highly visible. Jesuits and former Jesuits living in Prague were well known not merely to their neighbors but to visitors from the countryside. František Vavák recorded in his memoirs that a Fr. Jan Groh, who was born in Nová Pecka in 1730, entered the Society in 1747, and was ordained at St. Ignatius in Prague in 1759. Groh continued to work as a secular priest after the suppression, and after his death in 1781 was buried in the Church of St. Maria before Tyn.[90] Prague residents who did not know Jesuits personally were still likely to encounter them. Jesuit teachers were seen on the streets of the city, and sodality celebrations, religious holidays, and events commemorating the Habsburgs thrust Jesuits into the public eye.

Prague, which a century and a half earlier had been the residence of the Habsburg emperors, remained a community with a distinct and well-developed, if provincial, culture. Like Vienna, Prague had "green spaces" within its confines: the Jesuits themselves could count thirty-five hundred vines in its city garden of St. Apollinaris.[91] In the 1780s, the earliest point

[88] Hellmut Lorenz, "The Imperial Hofburg: The Theory and Practice of Architectural Representation in Baroque Vienna," in Ingrao, *State and Society*, 103 f.

[89] *Prazské Baroko: K vystaní umění v Čechách sedmnácteho až osmnácteho století* (Prague: Umělecká Beseda, 1938).

[90] Vavák, *Paměti*, vol. 1, fasc. 1, p. 134.

[91] NK, 1287 MS XXIII C105/15, *Litt. An. Prov. Boh. 1762*, folio 311r. It is not clear whether the wine produced from these vines was consumed entirely by the Society or was sold.

for which we have data, university students would make up 2 to 3 percent of the male population, and close to 18 percent of the adult male population had some post-elementary education.[92] Probably about 1 percent of the population could claim noble birth, while at least 10 percent were Jews.[93] The latter had considerable contact with the Gentile population, although in certain trades, such as barber-surgeons, this contact was restricted. Jewish merchants probably had encounters with Jesuits and former Jesuits, although there is little clear documentation confirming this. Former Jesuit Antonín Strnad purchased books from Jewish merchants: books in his library bore such inscriptions as "Strnad emptus a Moyse," and "Gratias tibi, Hebræe!" thus demonstrating the Jewish provenance of these books.[94]

In Vienna and Berlin, 15 percent of the population consisted of servants, who in many cases would have come from the countryside seeking work.[95] Prague had a servant population of comparable proportions. A few who worked for foreigners might have been of foreign origin themselves, adding to the cosmopolitan character of the city. Some servants would have been employed in the great city palaces of the high aristocracy, but a good many would have worked in households that engaged only a few servants, for the most part country people. The peasant character of Prague remained one of its distinguishing characteristics well into the next century.

Poverty was an inevitable element of eighteenth-century urban life, and Prague had its share of beggars and social castoffs, increasingly so after the periodic famines that decimated Bohemia. The residents of Prague accepted their poor neighbors as inevitable; in the attitudes of Jesuits and others may be seen traces of the earlier view that regarded the poverty of Christ as holy and thus, by analogy, the poverty of ordinary humans as imbued with some of this holiness.[96] As elsewhere in Catholic Europe, the Church considered relief of the poor as one of its major responsibilities.[97] The mendicant, whether in the robes of a religious order or in the discarded garments of his betters, was viewed as earning an eternal reward for

[92] Josef Petráň, "Pražská metropole," in Petráň, *Počátky,* 86.

[93] In 1784, 1,401 clergymen, 618 nobles, and 7,901 Jews lived in Prague (Dickson, *Finance,* 1:5, no. 1).

[94] Otto Seydl, *Knihovna astronoma Antonína Strnada ředitele pražské hvězdárny (1746–1799)* (Prague: Tiskárna "Prometheus," 1939), 12.

[95] Counting liveried lackeys, 40,000 servants resided in Vienna in 1795, which then had a total population of 240,000 (George Rude, *Europe in the Eighteenth Century: Aristocracy and the Bourgeois Challenge* [London: Weidenfeld and Nicolson, 1972], 63).

[96] Robert Jutte, *Poverty and Deviance in Early Modern Europe* (Cambridge: Cambridge University Press, 1994), 194.

[97] William Doyle, *The Old European Order, 1660–1800,* 2nd ed. (Oxford: Oxford University Press, 1992), 157.

his humility and resignation.[98] By the 1780s a few intellectuals and bureaucrats were beginning to see poverty as harmful to society; but most citizens of Prague regarded the poor, not as a problem to be solved, but an unpleasantness to be avoided, or perhaps an opportunity to perform good works. The swarms of beggars who congregated on the Charles Bridge and elsewhere in the city were as normal and acceptable a feature of urban life as the ostentation flaunted by the city's resident aristocracy.

Up until the relaxation of censorship under Joseph II in the 1780s, Prague retained, at least publicly, a closed intellectual climate. Czech-language drama was unknown, and plays in German were few and far between. As late as 1779, copies of Bayle's *Dictionnaire politique et critique*, placed on the list of banned books by van Swieten in 1765, were being seized from bookstores.[99] Privately, small groups of Enlightenment-influenced intellectuals, many of them with ties to Freemasonry, were active. The most noteworthy of these men was Ignac Ritter von Born.[100] Born in 1742 in Alba Iulia, the son of a noble Transylvanian family of German origin, Born was educated by the Jesuits in Vienna, and even studied briefly to become a Jesuit. He arrived in Bohemia in 1762 and worked almost without interruption in and around Prague until 1776. Born's interests, however, were practical rather than theological, running to mineralogy and penal reform; and during the "thaw" in censorship under Joseph II, Born published a scathing attack on religious orders, which he likened to various subhuman species.[101] The work, *Joannis Paysiophili specimen monachologiæ methodo Linnæa* (Vienna, 1784), used the Enlightenment taxonomy of Carl von Linné as a starting point for lampooning the appearance and activities of the religious orders, whose numbers had been so severely reduced by Joseph II in 1781.[102]

An active Mason, Born was an acquaintance of Mozart and is said to have been the model for Sarastro in the *Zauberflöte;* in any case, Born and the composer were both members of the Vienna lodge Zur wahren Eintracht, and were certainly aware of each other's work.[103] The young nobleman had entered the intellectual life in Prague in 1769, engaging in a

---

[98] A thoughtful discussion of this attitude and its decline and ultimate repression during the period of Josephinian reforms is found in Gates-Coon, *Estates*, 140 ff.

[99] Jiří Klabouch, "K počátkum protischolastických proudů pražské university v 18. století," *AUCP—HUC* 2 (1958): 96.

[100] Josef Haubelt, "Profil," in Petráň, *Počátky*, 290–292.

[101] Leslie Bodi, *Tauwetter in Wien*, rev. ed. (Vienna/Cologne/Weimar: Böhlau Verlag, 1995), 289.

[102] The choice of a rationalist taxonomy in Born's lampoon was itself evidence of how far some Vienna and Prague intellectuals had come from the Baroque approach to theories of knowledge.

[103] Nicholas Till, *Mozart and the Enlightenment* (London: Faber and Faber, 1992), 121–23.

polemic with the historian Galasius Dobner. During the last years of the Society's activities in Prague, Born was busy publishing *Prager Gelehrte Nachrichten*, the first scientific journal of its kind in the kingdom. After the suppression, Born was one of the founders and editors of the *Abhandlungen einer Privatgesellschaft in Böhmen*, another journal that published scholarly and scientific treatises by many former Jesuits, including Stepling and Leopold Scherschnik.[104] Born's wide-ranging interests and activities and his willingness to quarrel with clerical scholars, such as M. A. Voigt, are characteristic not merely of an Enlightenment intellectual but also of a writer educated by the Society who utilized the rhetorical and scholarly skills acquired in Jesuit schools to take on the religious conventions of the day. In this Born shared company with Voltaire and other Jesuit-trained polemicists of the period.

The highly visible presence of a personality such as Born in the Bohemian capital was more than a fluke; it was a symptom of both the breakdown in the control that had traditionally been wielded by religious educators and writers, and of the presence of the skeptical and practical-minded spirit of the French Enlightenment, which was gradually but steadily making headway in the imperial capital, frequently with aristocratic support. In Born's case, his most important noble fellow traveler was František Josef Kinský, soldier, sometimes defender of the Czech language, and bibliophile.[105]

The impact of such Enlightenment figures on life in Prague in the 1760s and '70s cannot easily be quantified, and certainly many residents were only dimly aware of the controversial and innovative ideas that Born and others were promoting in Prague's Enlightenment circles. On the other hand, the systematic investigation of such topics as extinct volcanoes, Czech-grammatical issues, and numismatics had long been the preserve of the Jesuits. The tone of these new debates, far more varied in their points of view and no longer wedded to a natural science completely governed by theology, permanently changed intellectual life in Prague and set the stage for the flowering of the National Awakening in the next decades.

Prague was one of the largest cities in the Holy Roman Empire, which in the mid-eighteenth century, was predominantly made up of German-speaking subjects. Victor-Lucien Tapié, echoing travelers' reports, has asserted that by 1780 "Prague . . . was in the process of becoming a great German provincial town."[106] There is some truth in this claim, for Prague

---

[104] Scherschnik's essay on the transfer of control of the Clementinum library to secular authorities appears in the 1776 volume of the *Abhandlungen* (Strahov, A A XIV 22).

[105] V.-L. Tapié, *Rise and Fall of the Habsburg Monarchy*, 199; Marie Pavlíková, "Vznik a vývoj univerzitní knihovny" in Čornejová, *Dějiny*, 2:212–15; Jaroslav Vrchotka, "Vědecké knihovny a muzejní sbírky," in Petráň, *Počátky*, 302.

[106] Tapié, *The Rise and Fall of the Habsburg Monarchy*, 200.

had for two and a half centuries been dominated by a dynasty whose power base was in a German-speaking area, and by its supporters, many of whom spoke German as their first language. But in striving to call attention to the very real differences between Prague and the surrounding countryside, Tapié both oversimplified the complexity of the cultural elements introduced into Prague and neglected to point out the enduring influence of the indigenous and ever-growing Czech population.

Nor were Czechs and Germans the only ethnic elements present in the city. In particular, the architecture of midcentury Prague bore the stamp of Italian taste. This was in part because of the influence of Charles VI, who was the last Habsburg to habitually use the Italian language and who had received an Italian education as a young archduke.[107] Gothic churches, such as St. Mary before Tyn and St. James, had their interiors redone in a warmer Baroque style, a transformation that affected their worshipers and altered the tone of public life in the city.

This combination of cosmopolitan and rural elements making up the culture of eighteenth-century Prague affected the climate in which Jesuit preachers, educators, scientists, and confessors worked. Prague's position as a crossroads of central Europe and its heritage as a former imperial capital were counterbalanced by the flow of newcomers from the nearby countryside and the cultural isolation experienced by Bohemia as a whole throughout the eighteenth century. Jesuits writing and ministering in the city did not need to modify their techniques in any significant way; those used in rural communities continued to serve. Fireworks and large religious processions might be more common in Prague, but the reactions of the people in both places to Baroque displays were notably similar.[108]

Prague, as a city and a seat of a university, therefore, represented an intersection of the more cosmopolitan tendencies of the Habsburg realms and of the folk and traditional elements that had long dominated the culture of Bohemia. Looking back, in the years immediately preceding the suppression, we can easily discern the rising level of interest in matters rationalist and secular that would form an important component of the National Awakening to come. Even though the gatherings of intellectuals and writers were numerically small, they laid the groundwork for the more ambitious projects that would be undertaken when censorship was lifted and a broader public sought to participate in the debates and investigations of the 1790s and the early 1800s.

---

[107] Josef Polišenský, "Società e cultura nella Boemia del Barocco," in *L'arte del Barocco in Boemia* (Milan: Bramante, 1966), 10.

[108] The recovery of Maria Theresia from illness, celebrated throughout the kingdom, was an occasion for fireworks in the Old Town (NK, 23/19, *Litt. An. Prov. Boh. 1768*, folios 87r–87v).

Even the most sympathetic defender of the Jesuits and their educational program cannot deny that while the Prague university would serve as one of the cradles of the National Awakening in the late eighteenth and nineteenth centuries, its role in the mid-eighteenth century was peripheral at best. Significantly, those Jesuits and former Jesuits affiliated with the university who would play important roles in the intellectual and cultural revival did not show many ties to these developments while working in the pre-1773 university itself. It was as if the traditional curriculum and instructional program of the university and the related collegia masked an intellectual curiosity and restlessness that could only come into the light when its possessors were free to work outside the models of the *Ratio*. It is to these men and their contributions, both within and beyond the framework of the Jesuit mission, that we now turn.

chapter seven

THE MEN OF PRAGUE

Individuality . . . lies at the root of all progress.

—Gandhi

Among the Jesuits of the Prague community were a number of men whose significance as intellectuals and teachers belongs in a broader context than merely their province or the Society. Some of these who were active in the 1760s and 1770s made their greatest contributions following the suppression; others were well-established figures by 1773. Most, but not all, were directly connected with the Prague university, and many managed to maintain this connection after the suppression, contrary to the expectations of the secular powers who had wrenched the suppression of the Society from the Pope. A few, in fact, made their greatest contributions after 1773. Let us now consider the careers of several of the most notable of these.

The most prominent scientist in Bohemia during the middle of the eighteenth century was Josef Stepling, a Jesuit priest famed for his contributions to mathematics and astronomy.[1] Stepling's biography, perhaps to a greater extent than that of any other Bohemian Jesuit of the period, illustrates the tensions and possibilities inherent in the varying roles Jesuits found themselves playing during the last years before the suppression, as well as the difficulties we experience as we attempt to determine the motivations of such men. Stepling was born to a Czech mother and German father, the latter of whom was a secretary for the imperial embassy in Regensburg

[1] The literature on Stepling is voluminous, starting with a lengthy funeral oration delivered by his colleague: Stanislav Wydra, *Laudatio funebris J. Stepling* (Prague, 1778); S. Wydra, *Vita admodum reverendi ac magnifici viri J. Stepling* (Prague, 1779); F. Comes de Wiezenek, *Adhortatio ad Senatum Populumque Academicum dum Augusta Josephi et Mariæ Theresiæ munificentia Iosepho Steplingo monumentum erigitur* (Prague, 1780[?]); S. Wydra, *Oratio ad Monumentum a Maria Theresia Augusta Iosepho Steplingo in Bibliotheca Clementina erectum* (Prague, 1780[?]); Pelzel, *Gelehrte*, 227–30. A list of Stepling's publications appears in Čornejová and Fechtnerová, *Slovník*, 444 f.; Raimundo Diosdado Caballero, *Bibliotheca scriptorum Societatis Jesu, supplementum primum* (Rome, 1814), 263; Sommervogel, *Bibliothèque*, 8:1564–68.

in 1716.[2] Following the death of his father, Stepling, a child of delicate health, moved to Prague. By the time he entered the Society, he had attained the age of seventeen, a typical age for entrance.

Stepling spent his novitiate in Brno, and then was sent to Olomouc, where he studied for two years at the philosophical faculty of the university. Teaching assignments in the collegia of Kladsko and Svdinice followed; and then at the age of twenty-six Stepling returned to Prague, where, aside from a one-year tertianship at Jicín, he passed the remainder of his life. From 1748 until 1776 Stepling was successively professor of mathematics and experimental physics, director of philosophical studies, and director of mathematical and physical studies at the Clementinum. But his academic titles only hint at the range of activities that Stepling undertook.

Stepling shared the Enlightenment's fascination with electricity. As early as 1745 he conducted an experiment demonstrating the conduction of electricity along an iron chain, said to be eight hundred meters long, running along the flagstoned corridors of the Clementinum.[3] Starting in 1748, he began to publish monographs on meteorological, astronomical, and mathematical topics; his report on meteorites that fell in the Srtkov district of Bohemia, published posthumously, was one of the most complete accounts of its kind.[4] Stepling also wrote one of the first German-language descriptions of a lightning rod, and corresponded with other scientists investigating phenomena connected with electricity.[5]

But it was in the field of astronomy that Stepling made the most important original contributions.[6] Between the years 1749 and 1777, Stepling built the astronomical observatory and the meteorological observatory in the Clementinum, the latter being the third oldest of its kind in Europe.[7] In the meantime, he continued to fulfill his obligations as a Jesuit university professor. Beginning in 1754, Stepling delivered lectures on analytical

---

[2] Koch, *Jesuitenlexikon,* 1691.

[3] Voigt, *Klementinum,* 68.

[4] *De pluvia lapidea anni 1753 ad Strkow et ejus causis meditatio per Josephum Stepling Soc. Jesu Sacerdotem* ([Prague], 1754).

[5] "Anmerkungen über die elektrischen Ableiter," *Abhandlungen einer Privatgesellschaft in Böhmen,* dritter Band (Prague, 1777), 284 f.

[6] Stepling was not alone among clergymen belonging to religious orders in the eighteenth-century Habsburg realms who contributed to astronomy. In addition to the Hungarian Jesuit Maximillian (Miksa) Hell, who became court astronomer in Vienna, the Benedictine Dom Placidus Fixlmillner was appointed the first resident astronomer at the Kremsmünster abbey in 1759 (Emil Kisbán, *Hell Miksa: A magyar czillagász* [Budapest: Publicationes ad Historiam S. J. in Hungariam Illustrandam, 1942], 1–20); Dom Aiden Bellenger, "'Superstitious Enemies of the Flesh'? The Variety of Benedictine Responses to the Enlightenment," in Aston, *Religious Change,* 152).

[7] Petráň, *Nástin Filozofické Fakulty,* 64.

geometry and differential and integral calculus, subjects that had not traditionally found their way into the Jesuit university curriculum.[8] Stepling helped assemble a collection of books on mathematical topics that later become part of the Clementinum collection and subsequently part of the National Library; moreover, he is credited with founding a "Concentus litterati," or scientific society, which met until the upheavals of the Seven Years' War disrupted life in Prague.[9] Stepling's other interests lay in areas of applied science: he was named the "assessor" of the newly created Agriculture Society of Prague, and in 1764 was enlisted by the imperial court to bring the weights and measures of the Kingdom of Bohemia into conformity with those of Austria.[10] Most important of all, Stepling, along with Prague Jesuits Jan Tessanek and Antonín Strnad, both of whom had been his students, was one of the founders of the Soukromá *spolecnost* or private society, that grew into the Royal Bohemian Academy of Sciences.[11]

Stepling did not fit the picture of an eighteenth-century Jesuit committed to either pastoral, polemical, or academic theological concerns. The pedagogical techniques of the *Ratio* do not appear to have inspired him in his student years.[12] A story that circulated in the nineteenth century has Stepling as a young professor resigning his assignment to lecture on Aristotle, "for as a sensitive person, he could not subject others to something he himself despised."[13] Nor did he resemble the active Jesuit man of affairs, the diplomat, or naturalist; for while he was remembered as the mentor of several Jesuit intellectuals, he shunned public life.[14] Stepling was not one to thrust himself into the forefront of reform movements. When in 1755 reforms initiated by Piarists were proposed for the curriculum of the Prague university, he voted with his fellow Jesuits against them.[15] Unlike his Croatian contemporary, Boskovich, Stepling did not travel or accept commissions from foreign governments, nor did he become embroiled in political

---

[8] Luboš Nový, "Mathematika na pražské universitě v druhé polovině 18. století," *AUCP-HUC* 1 (1961): 35–57.

[9] Unfortunately little is known about these gatherings, for their minutes have not survived.

[10] S. Wydra *[sic], Historia matheseos in Bohemia et Moravia cultæ* (Prague, 1778), 73; see also Josef Hanzel, "Studium zemedelství na pražské university (1775–1844)" *AUCP-HUC* 4 (1963): 144.

[11] Josef Hanuš, "Počátky Král. české společnosti nauk," *Český časopis historický* 14 (1908): 317 ff.

[12] "Im Jahre 1743 endlich begann er die eigentliche theologischen Studien, in denen er weniger auf die Voträge der Lehrer Acht hatte, als sich in die Quellen selbst vertiefte" (von Würzbach, *Biographisches Lexikon,* 37:228).

[13] *Ottův slovník naučný,* 28 vols. (Prague: Otto, 1906), 24:107.

[14] Stepling took an interest in the young Josef Dobrovský while the latter was only a student (Franz Palacky, *Joseph Dobrowsky's Leben und gelehrtes Wirken* [Prague, 1835], 9.)

[15] Josef Haubelt, "Seminarum publicum a Gelasius Dobner," *ČČH* 27 (1979): 108.

controversy.[16] Pelzel, who no doubt knew Stepling personally, recorded that "he lived a retired existence, never called on people, and whoever wanted to see him would have to pay a visit to him."[17] Even after Stepling had reached adulthood, his health, which had never been robust, did not improve; doubtless this reinforced his reclusive tendencies.[18]

It is interesting that university and provincial records reveal little evidence of Stepling's activities as a priest. We do not read of him officiating at Mass, leading colleagues or lay people in the Spiritual Exercises, or conferring the other sacraments, although like other Jesuit scientists he was obliged to teach catechism. His interests seemed to have lain entirely within the realm of the exact sciences, in a world that stretched from his Clementinum observatory to the Museum mathematicum described by his colleague Stantislav Vydra. One may, perhaps, speculate that Stepling, as a youth with a mathematical bent, chose the Society as a career path because virtually no other options were at hand, and stayed with it because no others appeared later. When pressed, Stepling occasionally found it necessary to defend the orthodoxy, or at least the inoffensiveness, of his researches. Corresponding with P. Ioannes Timoni, the vicar-general of the Society, Stepling asserted that in his astronomical studies "there was nothing that should alarm Orthodox Religion."[19]

Once Stepling had begun his academic career, he appears to have enjoyed considerable freedom to pursue his interests and to carry on an extensive correspondence, despite the frequently conservative official position of the Society on many topics that might be taught in its schools.[20] This privileged position was undoubtedly enhanced by the esteem in which Maria Theresia herself held him. Striking evidence of the respect she accorded the scientist is the monument erected to him after his death, which is located

[16] Ruder Josip Boskovich, S.J. (1711–87), was one of the greatest mathematicians of his day. He conducted research on astronomy, hydraulics, optics, archaeology, geo-sciences, and pure mathematics, and was called upon by the Holy See to assist in repairing cracks in the dome of St. Peter's. After the suppression, Boskovich was appointed director of naval optics of the French navy, and eventually became a French citizen. His relations with the Society were at times strained; and he seems to have traveled throughout Europe, not at the direction of his Jesuit superior, but at his own volition. I am indebted to Dr. Stipe Kutlesa for providing this information.

[17] "Er lebt eingezogen, machte keine Besuche, und wer ihn bey sich sehen wollte musste ihn zu sich laden" (F. M. Pelzel, *Abbildungen böhmischer und mährischer Gelehrten und Künstler* [Prague, 1782], 4:170).

[18] Archivum Romanum Societatis Iesu, *Catalogus trien.* ad annum 1770, vol. 1, 234.

[19] *Litterarum commercium* (Wrocław [Breslau], 1782), lxxv 462–69, (April 17, 1759).

[20] This correspondence has been characterized as of great importance for the history of science and for the Catholic Enlightenment, although most writers on Stepling do not demonstrate much familiarity with it (Eduard Winter, *Barock, Absolutismus und Aufklärung in der Donaumonarchie* [Vienna: Europe Verlag, 1971], 217).

today in one of the courtyards of the Clementinum.[21] By the time the Society was suppressed, Stepling's productive years were for the most part over, and he does not seem to have played a significant role in the preliminary phase of the "National Awakening" that was underway by the mid-1770s, although he did lend his name to the *Privatgesellschaft* or "Soukromá společnost" mentioned above, and his publications continued to appear in the *Prager Gelehrte Nachrichten.*[22] With the passage of time, his Jesuit identity increasingly faded from view; and in his own lifetime, his name even appeared in print without the designation of "Father."[23] Stepling died in 1778, respected by his contemporaries, but increasingly forgotten by the next generation of Romantic Czech nationalists, who could find in his biography evidence neither of patriotic sentiment nor of the passionate, tortured genius that was so admired in the Romantic era. A century later he received only a modest entry in a standard German history of mathematics, and today his mathematical contributions are scarcely known or understood.[24]

One would like to place Joseph Stepling, who was born early in the reign of Charles VI, in the category of the divided late-Baroque Jesuit, committed to the principles and mission of his Society while struggling to internalize and integrate knowledge incompatible with those principles. The case of Stepling resists so simple an analysis, however. The retiring scientist left behind no evidence of conflicts between the traditional role of the Society in Counter-Reformation Bohemia and the point of view of the rigorous empiricist or theoretic scientist. His responsibilities to the Society after the first years of obligatory teaching in collegia were apparently slight, and whatever resentments that his privileged position might have engendered among his confreres have left no traces in the official documents of the Society. Stepling, the outstanding example of the Bohemian Jesuit intellectual, remains, on a personal level, a mystery.

In the second rank of scientists behind Stepling, Tessanek, or Strnad was Franciscus Zeno, who is sometimes called the father of Czech geology. A Moravian, Zeno was born in 1734 and entered the Society at the age of fifteen.[25] His career was spent teaching mathematics in Olomouc in his

---

[21] Voigt, *Klementinum,* 80.

[22] It is a reflection of the diverse interests of the Prague literati and of the former Jesuits involved in the *Nachrichten* that bardic poetry was well regarded in this publication. The Viennese Jesuit Johann Michael Cosmas Denis, who had translated *Ossian,* played a role in promoting such an agenda (Hanuš, "Počátky Král česk. společnost," 147; Wangermann, *Achievement,* 118 f.).

[23] In the third volume of Pelzel's *Abhandlungen,* published in 1777, Voigt and Dobner are identifed with a "P" (= Pater), but Stepling, Strnad, and Tessanek are not.

[24] *Vorlesungen über die Geschichte der Mathematik,* ed. M. Cantor, 4 vols. (Leipzig: Teubner, 1900–1907), 4:197.

[25] Pelzel, *Gelehrte,* 268 f.; Cerroniho Sbírka, II, 345, 42.

native Moravia and Prague, where he was employed at the Convictus nobilium; and later, when Joseph Stepling retired as astronomer in the Clementinum, Zeno succeeded him in that post.[26] The details of his family background are obscure; still, he was able to donate thousands of florins of his own money to purchase scientific instruments for the observatory in Prague. Zeno, remembered as an ascetic in the Baroque tradition, lived eight years after the suppression, publishing an essay on fossils and a work on morals during this period. Raised to the knighthood with the title "Ritter von Tausanen," he divided his time between his scientific pursuits and his duties as a confessor to the Celestines in the Nové Město.[27] Zeno's premature death on June 14, 1781, at the age of forty-seven, left a gap in the scientific fields in which he had specialized that was not filled for many years.

Ignac Cornova was a generation younger that Stepling, born in 1740 in Prague, the son of an Italian merchant from Como.[28] He entered the Society in 1756 (not in 1754, as is sometimes reported) and was a student of František Pubitschka, who no doubt encouraged his interest in history. Cornova worked inconspicuously as a teacher in the collegia in Chomutov and Klatovy until 1773, publishing nothing and showing few signs of his future prominence. Thus, he was not a member of the Prague Jesuit community during its last years, although he was a native of that city and returned to it as soon as the Society was suppressed. Cornova produced no surviving literary works during these years; his first known publication was a collection of poems in German that appeared in 1775.[29] It is as a former Jesuit, moving in the circles of restless Czech nationalists, Freemasons, and freethinkers, that Cornova made his mark, although his interests also included poetry and the university curriculum.[30] Cornova himself was a member of the Prague lodge, "The Three Crowned Pillars of the Orient," as early as 1778.[31] During this same period he made his debut as a historian, publishing three articles on Czech leaders of the Middle Ages in the *Abhandlungen einer Privaten Gesellschaft in Böhmen*. In these and later works, Cornova anticipated the nationalist historians of the next century, who would help return Jan Hus and his followers to their pre–Counter-Reformation status of publicly acknowledged national heroes. That a former Jesuit would work to rehabilitate one of the most renowned critics of the authority of Rome is noteworthy, and here we may discern a tension between the Czech and

[26] Otto Seydl, "Z nejstarších dějin pražské hvězdárny," *ČČH* 44 (1938): 499.

[27] Strahov, D K II 16, Fischer, *Miszellen*, 2:25.

[28] Pelzel, *Gelehrte*, 280 f.

[29] *Gedichte von Ignaz Cornova* (Prague, 1775).

[30] František Kutnár, "Život a dílo Ignace Cornovy," *ČČH* 36 (1930): 327–50, 491–519.

[31] Cyril Stranka, "Reforma pražských zednarských lozí r. 1778," *ČČH* 31 (1925): 129 ff.; Kutnár, "Život a dílo," 340.

Catholic elements of Cornova's intellectual heritage. Almost impossible to determine, however, is whether this tension was present in the years before the suppression.

The creation of a Chair of Universal History at the Prague university in 1783 provided Cornova with a position of high prestige and visibility from which to promote his views on Czech history before a receptive public.[32] Equally important, the establishment of such a chair, the first of its kind, freed the discipline of history from the connections with heraldry, geography, and literature that Jesuit administrators had imposed upon it.[33] Yet Cornova was also promoting the cause of Czech identity at a moment when Joseph II's Germanization program was taking form; the messages from Vienna were in fact mixed, for the Emperor was not hostile to other expressions of Czech identity as long as they did not thwart his reform program.[34]

In 1784 Cornova's comedy *Der Undankbare* appeared, and the following year he published a history of an orphanage founded in Prague by the Freemasons. In an age of prolific authors, Cornova distinguished himself by the range and volume of his output. He translated and edited Pavel Stranský's *Staat von Böhmen* during a ten-year period, while carrying out his teaching responsibilities. Cornova's 1804 work, *Die Jesuiten als Gymnasienleher,* probably published in Prague, is both a well-argued defense of the work carried on by the Society during its final decades and a valuable source of information about the workings of Jesuit secondary schools. So, despite Cornova's willingness to praise opponents of the Church hierarchy, he evidently still felt considerable loyalty toward the suppressed Society. Throughout the first decades of the nineteenth century, Cornova remained active in his efforts to popularize his version of Czech history.[35] Cornova lived until 1822 and saw the Society restored, even though it was not welcomed back into Bohemia; but like his fellow former Jesuit Josef Dobrovský, Cornova never made an effort to become affiliated once again with the resurrected order.

Ignaz Cornova's later career raises the question of what nationalist sentiment existed among his fellow Jesuits before the suppression. While serving in an international, or transnational, order, Bohemian Jesuits were both a part of and formed by the culture around them. Not only could they

---

[32] Sommervogel, *Bibliothèque,* 2:1476. Cornova also wrote patriotic literature for young readers, for example, *Unterhaltungen mit jungen Freunden der Vaterlandsgeschichte Böhmens,* 4 vols. (Prague: Calve, 1799–1803).

[33] J. F. Zacek, *Palacky: The Historian as Scholar and Nationalist* (The Hague: Mouton, 1970), 9.

[34] Bérenger, *History,* 108.

[35] Among these works was *Der Grosze Böhme Bohuslav von Lobkowitz* (Prague [?], 1808).

not escape from the controversies that arose concerning national identity, but sometimes they even initiated these debates. At the time when the oldest generation of Jesuits still active in the 1760s (those born before 1700, that is) were receiving their formation in the Society, notions of nationality based upon one's native tongue were not developed in central Europe. Cornova's keen sense of Czech identity as related to language is all the more remarkable considering his Italian heritage and the type of formation he would have gone through before his ordination. Unlike Dobrovský, Cornova never indulged in criticism of the Society of which he had once been a member, and his *Jesuiten als Gymnasienlehrer* is neither a critique of nor an apology for the teaching techniques of the Jesuits. Without openly breaking with the Jesuit intellectual traditions in which he had been trained, Cornova grew beyond them and was himself the teacher of an entire generation of teachers and writers who acknowledged little of their intellectual inheritance as originating from the Baroque Society.

Stanislav Vydra was of the same generation as Cornova, being born in 1741 in Hradec Králové.[36] After receiving an education at a Jesuit gymnasium, he entered the Society in 1757, as had his older brother and several other family members. Vydra's early career as a Jesuit followed predictable lines: he spent his novitiate in Brno, and at the age of eighteen was sent to Klatovy to begin teaching classical languages, geography, and history. Returning to Prague to complete his philosophical studies at the university, Vydra came in contact with Stepling, who acted as the young scholar's mentor. Vydra was appointed adjunct in astronomy at the Clementinum, but in keeping with the spirit of the pre-suppression Society, he maintained an interest in theology and other nonscientific subjects that would surface again after 1773. Vydra was also among the younger Prague Jesuits who focused their attention on Czech history. In 1769 Vydra, now an ordained priest, was sent to Jičín; some sources describe this move as the result of conflicts with the more conservative elements of the Society, but such transfers, as we have seen, were common for Jesuit academics. Shortly before the issuance of *Dominus ac redemptor noster,* Vydra was back in Prague to occupy the chair of mathematics at the university, a post vacated by the death of Franciscus Zeno; probably Stepling played a major role in winning this promotion for him. The events of 1773 seem to have had little impact on Vydra's teaching career, although it is noteworthy that his first publications appeared only at this time. By the mid-1780s, Vydra was an instructor "of great renown," whose position at the university seemed secure.[37]

Vydra remained a highly visible and active member of the university community for the next three decades. He lectured in the new quarters of

---

[36] Unless otherwise indicated, the biographical data in this section are taken from "Vydra, Stanislav," *Ottův Slovník naučný,* 27:21 f.

[37] Pelzel, *Gelehrte,* 282.

the Faculty of Philosophy, which were in buildings of the former Seminarium S. Wenceslai.[38] Publications on conic sections, the calculus, and an important source on the intellectual history of the region, *Historia matheseos in Bohemia et Moravia cultæ* (written in 1778 at the urging of Count Kinsky), were accompanied by devotional works, a funeral oration on his teacher Stepling, and a collection of Latin epigrams dedicated to his "beloved students." The pinnacle of his professional career came in 1799 when he became *Rector magnificus* of the university. This was followed by two years as the Director des Philosoph-Studiums quoad Mathesim et Physicam.[39] In 1803 Vydra lost his eyesight, and the following year, on January 2, he died in Prague, where he had spent most of his adult life. The philologist Josef Jungmann was among those offering eulogies to the mathematician and humanist.

Vydra, like Cornova, was not only able to bridge the pre- and post-suppression worlds, but he likewise spanned the roles of writer and teacher. If Stepling was more renowned for the originality of his contributions to science and mathematics, Vydra was remembered for the breadth of his interests, his continuing devotion to the Church, and his skill as a teacher. Like many other Jesuits, he left behind disciples who served at the university: his successor in the Chair of Mathematics, Ladislav Jandery, published Vydra's *Origins of Mathematics* after his death. Even more than his writings, his influence on his students assured Vydra a place in the history of the Czech National Awakening.

Yet the part of Vydra's career that concerns us here, namely, before 1773, is harder to decipher. If he and his superiors engaged in any conflicts, there is no trace of them in the records of the Society; and indeed whatever rumors there were may have been distortions or legends that developed later when the Society was being traduced as opposing the Czech National Awakening. The claim that Vydra's mathematical investigations got him into trouble seems even more doubtful, in view of Stepling's successes in this field. As the protégé of the famous and seemingly untouchable Stepling, Vydra should have been able to survive attacks on his own works, none of which were revolutionary in content. Why he began his publishing career relatively late in life is somewhat harder to explain, although parallels are to be found among other Bohemian Jesuits.

There is little of the Baroque in the surviving accounts of Vydra's teaching career or in his scientific publications. The lone exception is the *Oratio funebris,* delivered to a Latin sodality in Prague, which we have already mentioned. No longer under obedience to the Society, Vydra was presumably free to choose to participate in such an event because of his own

---

[38] Tomek, *Geschichte,* 282.

[39] Strahov, D K II 16, Fischer, *Miszellen,* 2:14.

personal convictions. Yet his mathematical and scientific writings were quite unlike the unsystematic works of many Baroque Jesuits. Vydra seems to have been a sincerely devout man primarily interested in the exact sciences and experiencing no tension between these two aspects of his life. This fact in itself says much about the culture of the Bohemian Society and the men who continued to join it in its final decades.

Another Jesuit historian of a very different stamp from Cornova to reach widespread renown during his own lifetime was František Pubitschka. Pubitschka was born in Komotov (Comotov, Kommotau) on August 19, 1722, and entered the Society in 1739.[40] Pubitschka received the usual teaching assignments of rhetoric, Greek, poetics, and grammar, followed by a stint as the *Professor repetentium.* His earliest published works appear to have been conventional devotional works with no particular connection to Czech or Bohemian history.[41] Publitschka did not publish anything of note until he was forty-five years old, and little is known about his formal training or independent reading in history. His first historical treatise, a survey of the history of the Slavs in Bohemia, appeared in 1768 and received considerable attention.[42] A steady stream of publications, in both Latin and German, on early Slavic history followed. In 1770 Pubitshka embarked on an ambitious ten-volume chronological history of Bohemia, to be published, significantly, in German, rather than in Latin, still the customary language of Jesuit scholarly works.[43]

Although Pubitschka did not hold an academic appointment at the university, he did serve from 1767 as the last historian of the Bohemian Province before the suppression. He looked to Austrian Jesuit historians as models, as was understandable, considering the critical success the Austrians experienced and the support they received from the Habsburg court. In Vienna a Chair of History was maintained at the expense of the Society, and even after the suppression former Jesuits continued to be productive scholars.[44] Like Cornova, Pubitschka was able to weather the suppression well: he eventually became the dean of the Faculty of Philosophy at the Prague university in 1796, and continued publishing volumes of his well-received *Chronological History.* Yet, in a more significant way, Pubitschka was far from a success. As early as 1805 his work was being criticized for its "analitische Methode," in contrast to other historians who strove to establish causal

[40] MZAB, Cerroniho sbírka, II, 345, 40.

[41] *Oratio de S. Ioanne Evangelista* (Olomouc, 1756); *De S. Catherina* (Olomouc, 1757).

[42] *Series chronologica rerum Slavo-Bohmeicarum ab ipso inde usque Slavorum in Bohemiam adventu usque ad hæc nostra tempora* (Prague, 1768). See Pelzel, *Gelehrte,* 247.

[43] *Chronologische Geschichte Böhmens unter den Slaven: Erster Theil, welcher das heidnische Böhmen entählt* (Leipzig/Prague, 1770).

[44] Alphons Lhotsky, *Österreichische Historiographie* (Munich: Oldenbourg, 1962), 127.

relationships or develop an original interpretation of the facts.[45] The former Jesuit may have been unduly influenced by the style of the *Litteræ annuæ* and other Jesuit chronicles that presented information in discrete units with no systematic linkages or narrative themes. Gelasius Dobner, and other emerging Czech historians who did not come from the Jesuit tradition, took exception to Pubitschka's interpretation of linguistic evidence.[46] For his part, Pubitschka, under the protection of Prince Karl Egon von Fürstenberg, challenged Dobner's theory that the Czechs had originated as a democratic tribe living somewhere in the Caucasus.[47] Yet it was also charged that the former Jesuit based his own work on Dobner's. Ultimately, Pubitschka's project was only carried as far as White Mountain, and was unfinished at the time of his death in Prague on June 5, 1807, in the Convent of St. Ann.[48] The Bohemian Estates, who had paid in advance for the work, were unable to find another historian to complete it.[49]

Pubitschka was not noted as a teacher and, despite his wide readership, does not appear to have exerted a decisive influence on the younger generation of Prague historians writing in the first half of the nineteenth century. Some contemporaries found his histories pedestrian and derivative, while later, more avowedly nationalist historians were dissatisfied with Pubitschka's use of sources.[50] These reasons, and also his failure to present Bohemian history in such a way as to support the project of the great nineteenth-century Czech historians who sought to reconstruct a coherent national identity for Bohemia, have sent Pubitschka into oblivion today.

While not as renowned individually as Stepling or Cornova, the Azzoni brothers collectively were a well-known, if often absent, element of the Prague Jesuit community. Three brothers entered the Society, of whom

---

[45] L. C. Pfrogner, *Einleitung in die christliche Religions- und Kirchengeschichte* (Prague, 227 f.).

[46] H. Hurter, S.J., *Nomenclator literarius recentioris theologicæ Catholicæ*, 4 vols. (Innsbruck, 1895), 3:642; Arnošt Kraus, *Pražské časopisy 1770–1774* (Prague: České akademie císaře Františka Josefa pro vědy, slovesnost, a umění, 1909), 56; *Hormayr's Archiv für Geschichte, Statistik, Literatur und Kunst* (Vienna, 1810), 420. Pubischka's publications are listed in Sommervogel, *Bibliothèque*, 2:1745.

[47] In this Pubitschka was certainly correct, although Dobner's theory found many adherents among Czech intellectuals seeking to find a historical origin and a linguistic context for their people (Josef Haubelt, "Osvicenská věda—Profil," in Petráň, *Počátky*, 289).

[48] Strahov, D K II 16, Fischer, *Miszellen*, 3, 5.

[49] Zacek, *Palacky*, 11.

[50] Bohemian Jesuit historians of the seventeenth and eighteenth centuries, with the distinguished exception of Bohuslav Balbín, were subjected to the same criticism by later Czech historians (Josef Hanuš, "Mikuláš Adakt Voigt, Český buditel a historík," *Rozpravy české Akademie císăře Františka Josefa pro vědy, slovenost a umění* 3, 32 [1910]: 84 f.).

František achieved the greatest stature.[51] Born in 1717 in Prague, he entered the Society in 1734 and from 1753, until the Society was expelled from the Spanish colonies, taught theology in Quito. Returning to Bohemia, František served as rector of the collegium in Breznice and as master of novices in Brno, a key post in which he could exert influence upon all Jesuits who would later serve as priests in the province. The suppression found him back in Prague, serving as a confessor at the convent of St. Elisabeth of Hungary; there he died two years later.[52] František's brothers Dominik and Petr also became Jesuits, the former teaching in the Faculty of Theology. František's contacts with the "Indies," an experience duplicated by many Bohemian Jesuits, suggests the cosmopolitan nature of the Prague Jesuit community in its last days.

Bohemian Jesuits, as we have seen, had long maintained a connection with belles-lettres. Franz Expedit von Schönfeld was perhaps the last example of the Bohemian Jesuit poet.[53] Schönfeld was born in Prague in 1745, descending from an old family of the nobility. Entering the Society at fifteen as a university student, he took part in public disputations in philosophy and higher mathematics and taught for one year in the Jesuit gymnasium in Nové Město of Prague. At the time of the suppression, Schönfeld had just obtained a doctorate in theology and had been appointed professor of poetics at the Staré Město gymnasium in Prague.[54] He was already gaining renown as a poet: in 1771 he published a poem in German praising Joseph II; in addition, he published numerous orations and other religious works in Latin. Schönfeld's subsequent literary career was among the more remarkable of the former Jesuits. For a few short years, he achieved more recognition among the reading public than any other Bohemian Jesuit historian or educator; uniquely among the Bohemian Jesuits living at the time of the suppression, he was seen as a poet of stature.[55] He was even known to Bohemians who generally paid little attention to literary matters: František Vávak noted in 1779 that P. "František Expedit Schönfeld, ex-Jesuit" had prepared a plan for the decoration of the main altar of the cathedral of St. Vitus.[56]

---

[51] *Český slovník bohovědný,* ed. J. Tumpach and A. Podlaha, 5 vols. (Prague: Cyrillo-Methodějská Knihtiskarna a Nakladatelství, 1912–), 3:819.

[52] Čornejová and Fechtnerová, *Slovník,* 9 f.; Sommervogel, *Bibiliothèque,* 1:742.

[53] Pelzel, *Gelehrte,* 285–88.

[54] *Biographisches Lexikon zur Geschichte der Böhmischen Länder,* ed. Fredinand Seibt, Hans Hemberg, and Helmut Slapnicka, 12 vols. (Munich: Oldenbourg, 1974–), 3, 6, 735.

[55] Schönfeld is the only Bohemian former Jesuit to appear in contemporary or modern reference works on belles-lettres; for example, Elisabeth Friedrichs, *Literarisches Lokalgroßen 1700–1900: Verzeichnis der in regionalen Lexika und Sammmelwerke aufgeführten Schriftsteller* (Stuttgart: J. B. Metzler'sche Verlagsbuchhandlung, 1967), 291.

[56] Vávak, *Paměti,* vol. 1, fasc. 1, p. 123.

According to one account, Schönfeld died on August 26, 1807, in Reichstadt, having spent much of his later life in Hungary.[57] During his Hungarian period, he served as *Hofrath* to the ruling count of Zweibrücken and to Prince Christian of Waldeck; but by that time he had long since ceased to publish.[58] His declining literary production and obscure death, especially considering his promising debut, make him one of the more tragic figures to emerge from the suppression. Unlike many of the other former Jesuits who faded into obscurity after 1773, Schönfeld had shown a great interest in the evolving political and social programs of Maria Theresia and Joseph II. His interest in the latter's promotion of tolerance and his ability to address a wide range of secular topics might have made him one of the important intellectuals of Bohemia in the 1780s and a personality with considerable potential. For reasons not evident in his surviving writings, Schönfeld did not become part of the milieu in which Born and Cornova moved, and did not remain at the Prague university or at any other school within the Habsburg realms. His gradual disappearance from public life will remain one of the most notable mysteries to emerge from the annals of the Bohemian Province.

Conclusion

The handful of Bohemian Jesuits whose careers are briefly detailed here do not constitute the full spectrum of the members of the Society who contributed to the scholarly and educational climate of Prague in the last years of the pre-suppression Society.[59] Yet the variety of their interests and the widely differing experiences that were theirs after the Society had been suppressed provide some clues to the culture of the Society itself during these years.[60] First, despite the flaws in the Jesuit educational system and the decline in the vitality of intellectual life at the Prague university, the Jesuits were still able to recruit and retain talented young men into their order

---

[57] Strahov, D K II 16, Fischer, *Miszellen,* 3:10 f.; the year given for his death is confirmed in Karl Goedeke, *Grundriß der deutschen Dichtung aus den Quellen,* 18 vols. (Nedlen, Liechtenstein: Kraus Reprint, 1975), 6:718.

[58] This information appears only in Goedeke, *Grundriß,* 6:718–20.

[59] There were, in addition to the short list of Jesuits just discussed, many others who were active as scholars and teachers but about whom little is known. One such Jesuit is František Demuth (1730–ca. 1800), who published works on Chaldean (Syriac) and Arabic (Pelzel, *Gelehrte,* 265). The collective presence of such men in Prague undoubtedly influenced the overall climate of the Jesuit community, perhaps providing a countervailing conservative force in opposition to the more innovative or controversial writings of Dobrovský, Cornova, and Schönfeld.

[60] Josef Dobrovský, arguably the most influential of all Bohemian former Jesuits, has not been treated here because virtually his entire career unfolded after the suppression. His relationship to matters of concern to the Society during its final years will be addressed in chapter 10 below.

right up until the suppression. These young men sometimes came from poor families, but others were the sons of prosperous parents or even the lesser nobility. The religious orders that were rivals to the Jesuits also produced intellectuals who played key roles in the 1780s (Gelasius Dobner, Karel Rafael Ungar, who left the Premonstratensians, and the Benedictine abbot F. Š. Rautenstrauch are only three examples); evidently, the Bohemian Society did not enjoy a monopoly on talent.[61] But the reputation and prestige of the Society continued to draw exceptional men to it.

Given the number of highly talented and trained men in the Society, it is no surprise that many would continue to be visible after 1773. What is remarkable is the lack of similarity in their pursuits, and even in their modes of enquiry and expression. If the eighteenth-century Society was, as its detractors claimed, a vast conspiracy sworn to clandestine coordinated efforts to advance its influence and power, the activities of its former members show how ineffective this coordinated effort was. The individualism of the careers of the most prominent Jesuits of Bohemia is in part a reflection of the independence built into the culture of the pre-suppression Society, although this alone is not a sufficient explanation of the distance that men like Dobrovský and Conova placed between their later careers and the fundamental goals of the Society.

In addition to the evangelical and educational modes of operation already proposed, the presence of Jesuits whose subsequent work would betray a restless curiosity and desire to experiment with new forms and ideas suggests that the Society also functioned as a magnet for innovative intellectuals even as its reputation as an institution unreceptive to innovation was spreading. As an institution, the Bohemian Society had no established procedure for dealing with such men; each case had to be worked out individually, perhaps in secrecy. We must therefore ask to what degree the contributions of a Strnad, a Stepling, or a Cornova can even be credited to the Society of Jesus, or whether the affiliation of these men with the Society is at best incidental to their intellectual or artistic development. Considering the power of the corporate identity of the eighteenth-century Jesuits, the influence of the Society should not be dismissed as negligible. The legitimization of intellectual and literary pursuits that the Jesuit educational process fostered remained a powerful force in the lives of many former Jesuits even decades after the pre-suppression Society had vanished. And thus this process indirectly extended its influence to the disciplines that these former Jesuits investigated, and thereby to the new literary and historically oriented culture that would shape nineteenth-century Bohemia.

---

[61] Ungar's work in the Prague university library is recounted in Marie Pavlíková "Vznik a vývoj univerzitní knihovny," in Čornejová, *Dějiny,* 2:216–21. For Rautenstrauch's contribution see Hersche, *Der Spätjansenismus in Österreich,* 198 ff.

chapter eight

AFTER THE FALL

How far the radical frame of mind of young revolutionaries in the 1700s was created by the educational chaos that followed the expulsion and dissolution of the Jesuits from Catholic Europe in the 1760s and 1770s remains to be measured. But the effect was surely substantial.

—William Doyle, *Order*

The most talented young people aren't Jesuits, but generally, thanks to the Principia *coming from Göttingen, turn out quite the opposite.*

—Maximillian Franz von Habsburg

The end of the Jesuit era in eighteenth-century Prague was not unexpected, but its consequences were far reaching and may have exceeded even what the Society's opponents had anticipated.[1] The announcement of the suppression, promulgated on October 5, 1773, produced widespread rejoicing and unleashed the singing of derisory lyrics in many quarters.[2] Among those who rejoiced at the downfall of the Jesuits were many who had themselves either been educated by the Society or had profited from the commitment to the status quo that the Jesuits had espoused.[3] The departure of the Society did not, however, call forth much reflection as to who or what would take its place.

[1] Michael Topf, *Die Aufhebung des Jesuitenordens in Österreich, 1773* (dissertation presented at the University of Vienna, 1929).

[2] Because the brief of suppression was made public in Rome on August 16, the feast of St. Roch, a wit produced the following chronograph (itself a typically Baroque art form): Festo sanCtI roChI totVs MVndVs a peste LIberatVs (the upper-case letters add up to the date August 16, 1773) (Strahov, D. K. I. 24, b. 2., A. Fischer, *Geistliches Panorama.)*

[3] R. J. W. Evans, "Introduction," in *State and Society in Early Modern Austria,* ed. Charles Ingrao (West Lafayette, Ind.: Purdue University Press, 1994), 6.

As is well known, Maria Theresia sought to gain control of what had been Jesuit properties and fought to prevent them from passing into the control of some other agency of the Church; ultimately, ordinary citizens were able to purchase some of these holdings.[4] Many Jesuit properties were converted to barracks or state-run schools, and many of the churches served by the Society were placed under the control of a local parish priest or another religious order.[5] The Clementinum itself served briefly as a prison for the ringleaders of the 1775 peasant rebellion.[6] The extensive estates, many of which had been tended by peasants living in villages owned by the Society, were initially taken over by the government, and Raab's agrarian experiments were carried out on two estates confiscated from the Society.[7] Throughout the Habsburg realms, properties that had been controlled by the Society for several centuries were handed over for military, governmental, or other ecclesiastical uses.[8] The actual disposition of rural Jesuit properties took years, and their ownership was occasionally in doubt. In one instance dating from 1781, deserters from Frederick the Great's army settled illegally on rural property in Moravia once owned by the Society.[9]

The considerable amount of money made available through the confiscation and sale of Jesuit properties and the expropriation of Jesuit cash reserves were expended in many different ways.[10] The precise sum of money made available through confiscations following the suppression and the speed with which this money was made available are difficult to determine, although Tomáš Bílek put the total value of properties owned by the

[4] In November 1775 Franz Mraz, a Prague miller, sought to buy a garden adjacent to the Clementinum; although it is not clear whether he actually succeeded in doing so, surviving records suggest that there was no obstacle to the purchase (HKA Acta SJ Fasc. 2, 60, Nr. 13).

[5] The Domus professa and the Collegium ad S. Nicolaum in the Malá Strana were converted into barracks (Pastor, *History of the Popes,* 38:347).

[6] M. Toegel et al. ed., Prameny k nevolnickému povstání v Čechách a na Moravě v roce 1775 (Prague: Academia, 1975), 380.

[7] Wright, *Serf,* 54.

[8] Maria Theresia bestowed the former collegium in Uzhhrod (Ungvár) on the Uniate bishop of Mukachevo (Munkács) (Khevenhüller-Metsch, *Zeit Maria Theresias,* 8:151 [Aug. 31, 1776]).

[9] Promemoria des Ober Directer Boheim Cameral-Herrschaft von Raab, Wienn den 19. Novembris 1781 (HKA Acta S J Fasc 2, Exjes. Fasc. 2 Roter Nr. 14 folios 1224r–1228r).

[10] The confiscation of the properties of the Society revealed that, although it owned vast tracts of land and many enterprises, there were sectors of the economy in which it played no role. For example, the Society was not significantly involved in the Bohemian and Moravian textile industry, which employed 280,000 persons in 1774 (Hermann Freudenberger, "Industrialization in Bohemia and Moravia in the Eighteenth Century," *Journal of Central European Affairs* 29 [1960]: 350).

Society throughout Bohemia at 6,397,914 florins and 32.5 kreutzer.[11] (See Appendix 2 for notes on monetary uses.) The initial stages of a state-supported public-school program for the Habsburg realms began to take shape only a little over a year after the suppression, and Jesuit funds were intended to be used to help maintain it.[12] A sizeable portion of the moneys made available through the suppression of the Society was to be devoted to salaries and pensions for former Jesuits, some of whom would soon be too old to work. These amounts varied considerably. Joseph Stepling, by far the best-known Jesuit intellectual of the province, fared better than most former Jesuits, and as Director studii mathematici was awarded a salary of six hundred florins annually.[13] Educational institutions were likewise funded by moneys from the same source: the Latin school connected with the university in Prague received a grant of thirty-three hundred florins a year.[14]

The *Jesuitenkasse* helped fund projects as diverse as establishing printing presses at normal schools and providing the basic funding for primary schools.[15] The university itself, now largely secularized, acquired possession of what had been a garden formerly belonging to the collegium in the Old Town of Prague; the university was to make it over into a botanical garden.[16] The Jesuits in Bohemia and elsewhere had long been rumored to be vastly wealthy, and the prospect of obtaining some portion of this

---

[11] Tomáš Bílek, *Statky a jmění kolejí jesuitských, klášterů, kostelů bratrstev, a jiných ústavů v království českém od císaře Josefa II. zrušených* (Prague: Academia, 1970), 118 f. While this sum was not as great as some of the more fanciful estimates put forward in the eighteenth century, it still represents a significant portion of the economy of Bohemia.

[12] An *Allgemeine Schulordnung für die deutschen Normal- Haupt- und Trivalschulen* for the Hereditary Lands was promulgated on December 6, 1774; the following year a general school ordinance was established for Bohemia as well (Josef Hanzel, "Nižší školství," in Petráň, *Počátky*, 131 ff.; P. Vavřenec J. Winter, "Český živel ve skolských reformách za Marie Terezie," *Časopis katolického duchovnestva* 73 [1906]: 377–84; Janet Wolf Berls, *The Elementary School Reforms of Maria Theresa* [dissertation presented at Columbia University, 1970]). Some had argued that, although school reforms increased literacy in rural areas, the lack of a strongly literary curriculum in the new schools founded in the 1770s, especially under Joseph II, actually diminished the status of teachers (Kern, *Bohemia*, 348 f.). The removal of as powerful an organization as the Society from the business of education may also have contributed to this decrease in its status, although a distinction should be made between primary- and secondary-school instruction, the latter being generally held in higher esteem.

[13] HKA, Acta SJ, Fasc. 2 12/110, January 20, 1774.

[14] "Wird verordnet, denen Directoribus der vier Facultäten in der Lateinischen Schulen auf der Universität zu Prag die besoldung Jahres 3,300 nach dem beyliegenden Entwurf aus der Jesuiten-Kasse vom 1 Jänner 1775. Wienn, den 8, März 1775" (HKA, Acta SJ, Fasc 2.)

[15] James Van Horn Melton, *Absolutism and the Eighteenth Century Origins of Compulsory Schooling in Prussia and Austria* (New York: Cambridge University Press, 1988), 15 f.; Ernest Wangermann, *Aufklärung und staatsbürgerliche Erziehung, Gottfried van Swieten als Reformator des österreichischen Unterrichtswesens 1781–1791* (Munich: Oldenbourg, 1988), 218.

[16] HKA, Acta S.J., Fasc 2., 4, Wienn, den 12 März 1775.

wealth attracted many requests for support.[17] For years the *Jesuitenfond* received petitions from a wide range of individuals, including the widows of non-Jesuits employed in the Society's schools, libraries, and other enterprises.[18]

The number of former Jesuits diminished as death took its toll, so more money became available for the construction and staffing of schools.[19] According to references found in Vienna archives, these funds were used to defray university expenses, including the salaries of professors at the Prague university, for many years after the suppression.[20] The governmental bureaucracy itself was supported with money from the *Jesuitenfond*: in 1778 the Jesuiten-Güter Administrator Karavinsky, with the approval of Count Blümegen, hired a secretary, Johan Wenzel Rotta, and paid him 223 florins and 33 kreutzer, more than many former Jesuits were receiving as pensions.[21] What is more surprising, the Crown made liberal use of moneys confiscated from the Society by advancing loans to private individuals: Prince Joseph Schwartzenberg alone was loaned a million florins from Austrian-Bohemian funds, and Prince Lobkowitz over half a million.[22] Thus, even in dissolution, the wealth of the Bohemian Society continued to influence the lives of the most powerful princes of the realm.

Meanwhile, with its sometime rival in the field of schooling out of the way, Vienna tightened its control on the education of all clergy within its borders. The number of *Gymnasien,* increased by the addition of former Jesuit collegia, reached forty-three after the suppression, but was then systematically reduced to twenty within a dozen years.[23] The Clementinum

---

[17] The estimates of Jesuit wealth reaches the wildly speculative figure of 400,000,000 florins for the entire Habsburg lands (Denis, *Bohême,* 2:577). There was a legendary account dating back to the seventeenth century of a treasure buried somewhere in the courtyards of the Clementinum; like other rumors of vast caches of Jesuit wealth, it proved unfounded.

[18] For example, the widow of a "Custos Bibliotheks" requested and was granted a pension of 266 fl. 40 kr. annually (HKA, Acta SJ Fasc. 2, Roter Nr. 14, 45, Wien, den 23. August 1781).

[19] Ferdinand Kindermann, bishop of Schulstein, had originally proposed the use of these funds for schools: "So wie die Exjesuiten absterben und die Einkünfte zunehmen, so ware die Zahl der Zöglinge zu vermehren" (quoted in "Anfänge enines staatlich geförderten Schulwesen," by Margret Friedrichs, *Das achtzehnte Jahrhundert und Österreich* 10 [1995]: 38).

[20] Kaspar (Kasspar) Royko, professor of Church History and, even though he was a priest, a noted supporter of increased toleration, is mentioned as a recipient of support from Jesuit funds, December 23, 1782 (HKA, Acta S. J. Fasc. 2, Roter Nr. 15,) 50.

[21] Wienn, den 7ten März 778, C-G 16 (Exjesuitica), 435, F 2/40.

[22] Dickson, *Finance,* 2:334; see also personal loans to the aristocracy mentioned in *Hungary in the Eighteenth Century,* by Henrik Marczali (Cambridge: The University Press, 1910), 125.

[23] Josef Petráň, *Nástin dějin filosofické fakulty Univerzity Karlvoy v Praze (do roku 1948)* (Prague: Univerzita Karlova, 1983), 83.

became the home of the Seminarium generale in 1783, and remained so until 1790, when the next emperor, Leopold, abolished it, along with other seminaries established by his father.[24] The suppression greatly reduced the relationship between Rome and Prague that had been maintained by the Society. A further break with Rome occurred in 1781, when the Collegium Germanicum was declared off-limits to seminary students from Prague.[25] Although it would be wrong to regard the reforming emperor as an implacable enemy of the Society, Joseph's intentions to gain a more secure hold over the education of the clergy had been facilitated once the Jesuits had been eliminated.[26] Everywhere in the Habsburg lands the clergy, both religious and secular, became less visible during the 1780s, and even those symbols that had only a vestigial connection with their former power were frequently eliminated. In 1784 Joseph abolished academic costume for university instructors, and even clergymen now appeared at university functions in the dress of an ordinary subject.[27]

The successors of Joseph II were by no means as innovative or willing to take on existing institutions as he had been, but both Leopold II and his son Francis preserved the Josephinian concept of state control over the clergy, thus preventing the creation of a self-sustaining educational system for priests such as the Society had operated.[28] The return of the Society to Austria after 1814 did nothing to change this, for the government of Metternich had no desire to surrender any of its control over the schools to any organization, even one as loyal to the dynasty as the Society.[29]

---

[24] *Seminaria Ecclesiæ Catholicæ* (Rome: Typis Polyglottis Vaticanis, 1963), 415.

[25] E. Nittner, "Erzbischof und prager Universität in der Zeit vom Regierungsanstritt Maria Theresias bis zum Entconfessionierung der Universität (1740–1873)," *Archiv für Kirchengeschichte von Böhmen-Mähren-Schlesien* 3 (1973): 118.

[26] Joseph's pragmatism often won out over his personal feelings, whatever they might have been, regarding the Society. He had recommended to his mother on April 3, 1773, that Jesuits be allowed to keep their teaching posts until the educational reforms anticipated to follow the suppression were in place (Szabo, *Kaunitz*, 244).

[27] Josef Petráň, *Univerzitní slavnosti v Karolinu: Instalace, promoce, sponse* (Prague: Karolinum, 1991), 30.

[28] Overall, post-suppression Bohemia suffered from a shortage of priests in rural areas. Exact figures are not available, but the decline in enrollment at the university of Alembic, a center for training priests, is suggestive: from more than 1,000 students in 1700, enrollment dropped to 269 by 1785 (Nešpor, *Dějiny*, 54).

[29] A further sign of the break with the educational traditions of the *Ratio* was the strong emphasis given after 1815 to technical education. In this regard the conservative government of Metternich was innovative and did not seek continuity with the schools of the ancien régime (Bérenger, *History*, 144).

The Fates of Former Jesuits

The fates of former members of the Prague Jesuit community were varied and sometimes unhappy. Provided with a modest *Equipirungsbetrag*, former Jesuits were put out of the collegia to find their way in the world.[30] As difficult as such a transition was, these men were probably much better prepared to enter upon a new life than were the members of cloistered and contemplative orders, who a few years later would have to undergo a similar upheaval in their lives. Antonius Preisler, after a teaching career in collegia throughout the Bohemian Province, returned to the town in which he had been born and served there as a parish priest.[31] Yet the experience of the suppression left many former Jesuits without a community or other means of psychological support. Some former Jesuits, who at first worked in parishes and subsisted on pensions grew old and infirm, and were finally unable to discharge their duties. Others tried to adapt to the new career possibilities in education. A former Jesuit, Wenceslaus (Václav) Lenhard, turned up as the catechist of the new government-sponsored Prague Normal School.[32] Former Jesuits sometimes became the objects of complaints or pity.[33] Petrus Janowka, former provincial and rector at the Clementinum and later rector at Mariascheune, along with other former Jesuits, were lodged in the monastery of Osek (Ossegg), where Janowka died on February 19, 1784.[34]

Former Jesuit priests found work as *Weltpriester* in Prague or in the hinterlands, earning between 192 and 300 florins a year.[35] Some gravitated to the metropolis: "Il ex-Jesuita Stöberg" was serving as the chancellor to the archbishop of Prague in February 1778.[36] Franciscus Schirmer, once a teacher of Greek and the historian of the Jesuit community in Brno, found

[30] Each former Jesuit received one hundred florins when he left the collegium and sixteen florins each month thereafter (Alfred Ritter von Arneth, *Geschichte Maria Theresias,* 10 vols. [Vienna: Wilhem Braumüller, 1863–78], 9:105).

[31] Preisler was born September 8, 1720, in Duchov; the date of his death is not known, but he was a parish priest there at least until 1778 (Čorenjová and Fechtenerová, *Slovník,* 352).

[32] Pavlíková, "Josefinská Praha," 98.

[33] A letter to the Prague Archiepiscopal Consistory from a P. Joannes Hirnschal(?) dated November 7, 1786, describes an unnamed former Jesuit whose memory was failing, resulting in "multi errores in Adminstratione Sacramentorum" (SÚA, APA F 1/1 520 unnumbered folio).

[34] Pelzel, *Gelehrte,* 207 f.; Fechnerová, *Rectores,* 1:6; Hermann Hallwich, "Die Jesuiten-residenz Mariascheune," *Mittheilungen des Vereins für das Geschichte der Deutschen in Böhmen* 6 (1868): 89.

[35] SÚA, AAP/E1, unnumbered folio, undated, ca. 1786.

[36] Dell'Orto, *Nunziatura,* and ASV Vienna 28.1.1778, Garampi al cancelliere Stöberg. Copia *Nunziatura Germana* 425, folio 244v, Vienna, 23.11.1778.

a position as a tutor to the powerful Sternberg family.[37] A few former Jesuits remained part of the urban landscape for decades to come: Joannes Holeczek, "exjesuita," was listed as being employed by the archbishop as late as 1809.[38] Johannes Winarsky, who had been a young priest in the collegium attached to the Church of St. Ignatius, haunted the hospitals and prisons as a *Freiprediger,* and managed to hang on to a position at St. Ignatius as a *cooperator* for many years, living in an adjacent house. In 1822 his name still appeared in the *Catalogus* of clergy working in the city.[39] Matthias Linek, who had been *præses Congregationis Latinæ Majoris,* continued to live in Prague, and died there on January 2, 1784.[40]

Jesuits who had served outside the province in Austria or Saxony sometimes did not return home, and in most cases their fates are not easily traced. Some former Jesuit university instructors were able to stay in their positions, despite the very clearly articulated imperial ban on Jesuits retaining these jobs.[41] Kaunitz himself, no friend of the Society, had already seen to it that Jesuits were allowed to continue teaching in Vienna at the Theresianum, where they had shaped the education of noble youths for decades. Peter Chladek in 1774 became *Professor der Physik* at the Prague university, a position in which he continued until 1789.[42] Mathematics instructors seem to have been among the most successful in keeping their positions, perhaps because of the potentially practical value of their studies and the shortage of others trained in the field.[43] Franz Pohl, professor of logic and mathematics at the university in 1773, may have continued teaching there following the suppression; in any case he remained in the community until at least 1817, presumably the year of his death.[44] Franz Biedau, who at the time of the

---

[37] Schirmer, born in 1732 in Cestice, died in Prague on March 13, 1795 (Čornejová and Fechnterová, *Slovník,* 398 f.).

[38] *Catalogus universi cleri archidiocesansi Pragensis* (Prague Old City, 1809), 15. However, Hollecszek is not identified as a former Jesuit in the 1805 edition of this *Catalogus.*

[39] Strahaov, D K II 16, Fischer, *Miszellen,* 3:5.

[40] Born in Prague, July 21, 1722; entered the Society in 1736; served as the prefect of the Church of St. Salvator (Pelzel, *Gelehrte,* 246 f.; MZAB, Cerroniho sbírka II, 345, 83; Strahov, D K II 16, Fischer, *Miszellen,* 3:11).

[41] Former Jesuits were, by order of Maria Theresia, forbidden to hold university chairs of morals, ethics, theology, sacred history, or metaphysics (Protocoll der Sitzung der Hofkanzlei vom 2. Oktober 1773, in *Maria Theresia's letzte Regierungszeit,* by Alfred Ritter von Arneth, 10 vols. [Vienna: Wilhelm Braumüller, 1863–], 3:569 n. 190). But elsewhere Jesuits continued as professors in the sciences. In Würzburg, Nikolaus Burkhäuser, appointed in 1768 to a chair of theoretical physics, held this post until 1803 (Hellyer, "Jesuit Physics," in O'Malley et al., *Jesuits: Cultures,* 545).

[42] Strahov, D K II 16, Fischer, *Miszellen,* 2:14.

[43] Luboš Nový, "Mathematika na pražské unversitě v druhé polovině 18. stoleti," *AUCP-HUC* 1 (1961): 35–57.

[44] Strahov, D K II 16, Fischer, *Mizsellen,* 3:26.

there, died in Prague on March 25, 1780, but little else is known of his activities following 1773.[45]

One former Jesuit who was able to play a leading role in the new educational order was Franz Xavier Nor, who served as the prefect of the *Gymnasium* in the Malá Strana after the suppression, and was later the director of all the *Gymnasien* in Bohemia, a post he held until his death in 1796.[46] Franz Lorenz, a fourth-year theology student at the time of the suppression, was also serving as a catechist at the Italian Hospital, and later joined other former Jesuits in the Malá Strana *Gymnasium.*[47] Ignaz Kuzel likewise taught after 1788 at the old Jesuit school in the Malá Strana, which seems to have functioned as a safe harbor for many former Jesuits.[48] Other Jesuits left the region to take up posts in provincial towns: Karl John, once a professor of moral philosophy in Prague, returned to his hometown of Brüx (the modern-day Most), where his brother, the cathedral canon in Prague, helped him secure a new position.[49] Two deceased Jesuits even returned to the limelight in February 1784, when their bodies were exhumed from a crypt in the Old Town of Prague, and were found, not surprisingly in the eyes of many, to be in a very good state of preservation.[50]

Yet many living Jesuit scholars and teachers now disappear from the records without a trace; even the dates and locations of their deaths are unknown.[51] A few of the younger former Jesuits left the clergy entirely and married, apparently without public censure.[52] The former collegia themselves continued to teach the sons of the privileged and those fortunate enough to be recognized as having academic promise. Unlike the universities and Jesuit-operated seminaries, these schools did not drastically alter the Jesuit curriculum. Ten years after the suppression, the *Gymnasium* in Prague's Old Town was still training its classes in *Humanitas, Grammatices,*

---

[45] MZAB, Cerroniho sbírka, II, 345, folio 29; Pelzel, *Gelehrte,* 212 f.

[46] Strahov, D K II 16, Fischer, *Miszellen,* 1:6.

[47] Lorenz died in 1807 (Strahov, D K II 16, Fischer, *Miszellen,* 3:4).

[48] Ibid., 1, 22. Of another former Jesuit, Georg Münch, Fischer adds, "Ich finde ihn als Professor der Poetik am kleinseiteren Gymnasium im Schematism von 1791 das letztemal" (ibid., 3:10).

[49] Ibid, 1:26. Fischer does not say what John's new post was, but still later John was "Titular-Canonicus" at the cathedral in Hradec Králové (Königgratz), a position that doubtless provided some income if not many responsibilities. His earlier position may well have been of a similar nature.

[50] Josephus Locatelli, *Babylon Bohemiæ ab anno 1780 ad annum 1790* (A. Podlaha ed. [Prague: Sumptibus s. f. metropolitani capituli Pragensis, 1905], 63).

[51] Many such examples might be cited; one was Dr. Joannes Haan, who lived in the *domus professa* in the Malá Strana from 1766 to 1769. The date of his death is known only as "after 1773" (Fechnterová, *Rectores,* 1:190).

[52] For example, Jacobus Stransky, who married in 1781.

Prague's Old Town was still training its classes in *Humanitas, Grammatices,* rhetoric, and classical Greek, with no apparent concessions to the modern Josephinist educational notions.[53] Former Jesuits who were competent teachers remained in demand; as late as 1804, the erstwhile Jesuit Ignaz Kuzel was still listed as a *Titelhabender Professor* at the *Gymnasium* in the Malá Strana.[54] Thaddäus Wollrab also taught in the Old Town *Gymnasium* after the suppression, becoming prefect there in 1794. He remained at this post until his death in 1815.[55] Nicolaus Krebs, dean of the Philosophical Faculty of the Prague university from 1771 to 1772, became director of a school in Jindřichův Hradec, a post he held until 1796.[56]

A few Jesuits' careers seem to have come to a complete and premature halt. Jacob Rohm, who had taught Oriental languages at the Prague university up until the suppression, lived on a number of years in Prague, but left no record of further teaching or indications of further progress on his Syriac dictionary, which he had begun some years earlier.[57] Godefridus Grätzel, although only thirty-seven years old at the time of the suppression, was pensioned and apparently never worked as a teacher again, although he produced a translation of Xenophon in 1783.[58] Likewise, the later careers of Ludwig Holzäpfel and Johann Zahoransky, both former university instructors, are obscure; Holzäpfel "starb . . . als Privatmann in Prag" at some later date, and all details of Zahoransky's subsequent life are missing.[59]

After 1773 the Society permanently lost all institutional control of the Prague university, and a Premonstratensian became the *decanus* of the Faculty of Theology in 1775, although individual former Jesuits continued to play important roles in its governance.[60] The curriculum of the university

[53] *Nomina iuvenum in Gymnasio Regio Vetero-Pragensis* [1783] (SÚA, CG 16 (Exjesuitica), 14, F 2/40, 9/4, 15). See also Helmut Engelbrecht, *Geschichte des österreichischen Bildungwesens: Erziehung und Unterricht auf dem Boden Österreichs,* 3:88 ff.

[54] Kuzel first appears as teacher there in 1788 (Strahov, D K II 16, Fischer, *Miszellen,* 2:22).

[55] Strahov, D K II 16, Fischer, *Miszellen,* 3:4.

[56] Čornejová and Fechtnerová, *Slovník,* 234 f.; Fischer, "Mathematiker," 205.

[57] Čornejová and Fechtnerová, *Slovník,* 373 f.; Pelzel, *Gelehrte,* 276; Sommervogel, *Bibliothèque,* 7:25 f.

[58] Čornejová and Fechtnerová, *Slovník,* 123 f.; Pelzel, *Gelehrte,* 271.

[59] Strahov, D K II 16, Fischer, *Mizsellen,* 3:18; 3:26. Of Zahoransky, Fischer writes, "Seine weiteren Schicksaale sind mir unbekannt." Čornejová and Fechtnerová's exhaustive study can only report that after 1773 Zahoransky was "ill" and lived in the Old Town of Prague (*Slovník,* 531 f.). Considering the relative prominence and visibility of Jesuit university professors, the obscurity into which some plunged is striking, as is the absence of records regarding the Jesuits who served in Vienna.

[60] The last Jesuit to serve as director of studies in the Theological Faculty resigned from that office in 1761, the same year that a non-Jesuit became *Rector magnificus* of the Prague

was steadily secularized, largely through the influence of German professors invited from Saxony.[61] Joannes Diesbach, who was particularly well connected in court circles, served as *Rector magnificus* and director of the Philosophical Faculty *quoad mathesem et physicam* before his death in 1792; and other former members of the Society such as Joannes Tessanek, Stanislav Vydra and Joseph Stepling likewise held active or honorary posts in the 1770s and '80s.[62]

Yet, while Vydra earned a reputation as an inspiring teacher of youth, and Stepling's successor Tessanek carried out a high standard of scientific work, the one-time Jesuits as a group did not leave a cohesive intellectual legacy or a cadre of committed disciples to carry on their mission. This is not to say that former Jesuits did not train students who played a significant role in the intellectual climate of the next century, only that these students did not fit an easily defined mould. One of Vydra's most famous pupils, the philologist Josef Jungmann, (1773–1847) was cut from a different cloth than the last eighteenth-century Jesuits, busying himself with the rehabilitation of the Czech language and with translations of Milton, and having little to do with the post-1814 Jesuits who once again took up the now seriously outdated *Ratio* as their curricular guide.[63] Yet it should be noted that Jungmann delivered an elegy in Czech, subsequently widely circulated, on the death of Vydra in 1804. Closer to the Jesuit traditions of combining the study of mathematics and theology was Bernard Bolzano (1781–1848), another of Vydra's students involved in the National Awakening at its peak, and one of the outstanding personalities of the Prague university in the *Vormärz*.[64]

---

university (Strahov, D K II 16, Fischer, *Miszellen,* 1:1; Fechtnerová and Čornejová, *Slovnik,* 410 f.).

[61] Novák, *Czech Literature,* 122.

[62] Strahov, D K II 16, Fischer, *Miszellen,* 1:5.

[63] Rene Welleck provides a context for Jungmann, one of the greatest figures in the Czech National Awakening (*Essays in Czech Literature* [The Hague: Moulton and Co., 1963]).

[64] Bolzano's work ranged from mathematics to logic to the philosophy of science. Working in an idiom far removed from that of the pre-suppression Jesuits, Bolzano, an ordained priest, was like most early-nineteenth-century Czech writers in that he published many of his books in German, both in order to reach a larger audience and to avail of the larger technical vocabulary to be found in that language. Discharged from his post at the university of Prague in 1820, he nevertheless continued to produce widely read books, even though his writings were subjected to police surveillance. His most ambitious scientific work, *Wissenschaftslehre* (Sulzbach, 1831), attempts a new model of the theory of science (Leo Santifeller, ed., *Österreichisches biographisches Lexikon,* 11 vols. [Graz/Cologne: Verlag Hermann Böhlau's Nachfolger, 1957], 1:100 f.). Bolzano carried on one important Jesuit tradition well into the era of Romanticism and nationalism: With seemingly little difficulty, he combined careers as a mathematician and as a religious thinker (Jan Mukarovský, ed., *Dějiny české literatury,* 3 vols. [Prague : Nakladatelství československé akademie věd, 1960], 2:148).

Dientzenhofer, the son of the renowned architect Kilian Dientzenhofer, was one of the youngest ordained Jesuits at the time of the suppression. Born in 1750 in the Malá Strana, he entered the Society in 1765, studied in Olomouc, and began to teach grammar classes in the collegium in Jihlav in 1771. After the suppression Dientzenhofer, unique among former Bohemian Jesuits, studied law, and in 1782 became *Professor juris* at the Prague university, succeeding the distinguished Joseph von Riegger. Dientzenhofer, like several other former Jesuits, married, and lived until 1805.[65] Heinrich Trottmann, born in Karlovy Vary (Karlsbad) in 1746, entered the Society at fifteen, as did Dientzenhofer. In 1773 he was living in the Clementinum, a student in his third year of theology and not yet ordained. The following year Trottmann earned a doctorate in philosophy and taught for many years in the Gymnasium in the Old Town that had previously been a Jesuit school. It was during these years that he published a strikingly old-fashioned oration in honor of St. Jan Nepomucký, suggesting the lingering strength of Baroque Catholicism in Prague.[66] After a stint in Boleslav as a *Canonicus honorarius,* he returned to Prague in 1799 to succeed Seibt in the Chair of Logic. Appointed dean of the Faculty of Philosophy in 1801, he appears to have died within the year. He was a representative of eighteenth-century culture who survived into the nineteenth.[67] Less varied was the post-suppression career of Leopold Tirsch, a Hebrew scholar who, as we have seen, had served as royal censor of Hebrew books since 1764, and who continued in this capacity at least until 1786, dying on November 30, 1788. By this time the Jews of Prague had been freed from numerous restrictions, and censorship of the press throughout the Habsburg realms had been loosened.[68]

We can only be amazed by the complete lack of continuity between the prosperous, larger, and well-articulated pre-suppression Society and the organization that slowly and with difficulty regained a presence in Prague after 1814.[69] Half a century after the restoration of the Society, the Church of St. Ignatius, which had been inseparably associated with the mission of the Society in eighteenth-century Prague, was still not reoccupied by Jesuits. In Bohemia former Jesuits kept a low profile politically; there is no evidence

---

[65] Strahov, D K II 16, Fischer, *Miszellen,* 3:26.

[66] *Sacerdos sapiens, seu Oratio in honorem St. Ioannis Nepomuceni in Skalka a se habita* (see Pelzel, *Gelehrte,* 289).

[67] Strahov, D K II 16, Fischer, *Miszellen,* 3:5. Fischer does not indicate if "Bunzlau" refers to Stará Boleslav or Mladá Boleslav.

[68] In addition to his Hebrew-German lexicon, Tirsch produced several other related studies (Pelzel, *Gelehrte,* 266 f.; Strahov, D K II 16, Fischer, *Miszellen,* 2:25).

[69] An officially sanctioned registry of Jesuits active after the restoration of the Society contains no names of Jesuits ordained before 1773 (P. Rufo Mendizabel, *Catalogus defunctorum in renata Societate Jesu ab a. 1814 ad a. 1970* [Rome: Archivum Historicum, 1970]).

the Society in eighteenth-century Prague, was still not reoccupied by Jesuits. In Bohemia former Jesuits kept a low profile politically; there is no evidence that they dabbled in such secret organizations as the Bavarian *Illuminati*, led by former Jesuit Adam Weishaupt. During the first years after the suppression, some regarded this organization with great consternation and were taken in by rumors that it constituted a return of the old Society in Enlightenment garb.[70] The "Fathers of the Most Holy Heart of Jesus," sometimes identified as the shadow of the Society in the Habsburg lands during the suppression, could count few if any intellectuals or outstanding personalities among its members, nor can it be considered a strong link between the institutional cultures of the pre- and post-suppression Society.[71] The restored Society was, in fact, despite its reliance on familiar symbols and rituals, an institution with a different relationship to the communities in which it worked, one that often seemed to attract a type of man quite different from those who had entered it before 1773.

The world had changed. Former Jesuits now working as secular clergy were joined by men who had left the Augustinians, the Dominicans, and other orders, and were seeking new careers in the secularized and increasingly tolerant society of the 1780s and '90s.[72] Late-eighteenth-century Habsburg society, which in retrospect may seem less religious at its core, at the time was not generally perceived as such; rather it was seen as moving toward greater toleration of religions, but not toward a negation of the importance of religion. Furthermore, there is no evidence that the narrow religious training and perspective of former Jesuits was per se a liability. This new society had begun to take shape almost immediately after the suppression, for already in 1774 Bohemian Protestants were allowed, under limited conditions, to build unobtrusive chapels and worship as they wished.[73] By 1783 the critical spirit of the Enlightenment, aided perhaps by some genuinely anticlerical feelings, had reached such a level of acceptance

---

[70] Richard van Dülmen, *Der Geheimbund der Illuminaten* (Stuttgart/Bad Canstadt: Frommann-Holzboog, 1975).

[71] However, the Habsburg connection did remain intact: this new order was founded with money provided by the Archduchess Mariane, a sister of Francis I (Koch, *Jesuiten-Lexikon,* 1462; Pastor, *The History of the Popes,* 29:323; *Liber sæcularis historiæ Societatis Jesu ab anno 1814 ad annum 1914* [Rome: Typis polyglottis Vaticanis, 1914], 10 f.; P. Stanislaus Zalenski, *Les Jésuites de la Russe-Blanche,* trans. Alexandre Vivier, 2 vols. [Paris: Lelouzey et Ane, 1886], 2:33).

[72] See Strahov, D K II 16, Fischer, *Miszellen,* vol. 2 passim.

[73] H. Daniel-Rops, *The Church in the Eighteenth Century,* trans. John Warrington (London: J. M. Dent, 1964), 149. Daniel-Rops does not make clear, however, how widespread the founding of Protestant chapels actually was before the groundbreaking Toleration Patents of the early 1780s, especially in communities where local support of Catholicism was genuinely strong and hostility toward Protestants persistent.

that a weekly review of the sermons preached in the city was being published.[74]

Despite the continuing widespread consensus that religious belief was valid, symbols of the old piety came under attack. The practical-minded Joseph II, it was said, removed the jewels from reliquaries and sold them to finance his governmental and military schemes.[75] But the most significant development in many educated Bohemians was the rise of a new overriding concern: The rationalism and skepticism that had so often seemed the greatest adversary of the late-Baroque Society were themselves gradually replaced by the romantic and frankly nationalistic concerns of the new generation of intellectuals, some of them former Jesuits.[76]

Josef Dobrovský, who lived until 1829 and became the sage of Bohemian intellectuals, was typical of the new age in that he distanced himself from the activities and personalities of the restored Society, becoming instead a leader of the predominantly secular National Awakening, concerning himself exclusively with questions of Bohemian and Czech language and history, and addressing the history of the Bohemian Society only in an oblique and often negative fashion.[77] Such a stance was characteristic of the independent-minded Dobrovský, who has been described as the only member of the first generation of Czech "enlighteners" who did not owe a debt to the ideology of J. G. von Herder, the developer of the extremely influential notion of *Volk*.[78] One searches in vain for clear-cut evidence that Dobrovský sought to leave a legacy reflecting the Jesuit tradition from which he had come; in fact, on occasion he directed his sarcasm at the piety of the Society of which he had been a member.[79] Perhaps the closest he came to continuing such a tradition was the role he played as a mentor of Antonín

---

[74] *Wöchentliche Wahrheiten für und über die Prediger in Prag*; cited in *Nábozenské myšlení ceského obrození*, by Jan Milič Lochman (Prague: Komenského Evangelická Fakulta Bohoslovecká, 1952), 218.

[75] F. Mourret, *A History of the Catholic Church*, trans. Newton Thompson, 8 vols. (St. Louis: Herder, 1930–), 6:496.

[76] Josef Petráň, "Učené zdroje obrození," in Petráň, *Počátky*, 305–17.

[77] Eighteenth-century Jesuits receive negative reviews in Dobrovský's *Geschichte der böhmishen Sprache und Literatur* (Prague, 1792), 206 f.; Koniáš in particular is condemned for his destruction of Czech literature.

[78] Peter F. Sugar, "External and Domestic Roots of East European Nationalism," in *Nationalism in Eastern Europe*, ed. Peter F. Sugar and J. Lederer (Seattle: University of Washington Press, 1969), 15.

[79] As early as 1784 Dobrovský even referred to pious Jesuits as "Jesuitenaffen" (Wolny, *Josephinische Toleranz*, 107).

Pišely (1758–1806), a student of his who, like some Jesuits, combined a priestly career with linguistic researches.[80]

Dobrovský's contributions to Czech culture were many and profound, and here it is only possible to allude to several of those that most directly bear on the themes addressed in this volume. In 1791, on the occasion of the coronation of Leopold II as king of Bohemia, Dobrovský delivered an address calling attention to the preponderance of Slavic peoples within the Habsburg realms and the devotion of these peoples to the dynasty.[81] This speech is frequently cited as evidence of an emerging pan-Slavic consciousness, but it might also be seen as the expression of the convictions of a former Jesuit with regard to the dynasty, which had long been the protector of the Society. Yet it would be wrong to make too much of either Dobrovský's conception of what it meant to be a Slav or of the relationship of the Czechs to the Habsburgs. At heart a student of languages, Dobrovský carried his Jesuit training in this field to new territories, but increasingly he was identified with Czech nationalist sentiments that viewed the vernacular with something approaching religious devotion. In southwestern Bohemia the venerable former Jesuit even became the object of a folk legend that outlived him.[82]

The ranks of those who had undergone formation in the pre-suppression Society thinned, and memories of the institutional culture of those times grew dim. Twenty years after the suppression, the *Gymnasien* of Prague were still staffed by several former Jesuits, but a few years later, these men's names vanish from the lists of instructors.[83] The oldest Prague Jesuit who had been ordained a priest before the suppression, Father Karl Khun, died at the age of 93 on June 15, 1829, bringing to a close the immediate connection between the eighteenth-century Society and the Baroque aesthetic that had flourished in it.[84]

The pre-suppression Jesuit presence in Prague had been quintessentially eighteenth-century in that it had combined, if not always integrated, rationalist pursuits, such as the study of classical and Oriental languages and mathematics, with the cultivation and reporting of the miraculous and the unsystematic, and with a commitment to the status quo of the ancien ré-

[80] Dobrovský collaborated with Pišely, who had served as a chaplain in Count Kinsky's regiment, on *Českých přísloví sbírka* (A collection of Czech proverbs) (1804).

[81] Sugar,"Rise of Nationalism," 105; J. Petráň, "Učené zdroje obrozeni," in Petráň *Počátky*, 315.

[82] Novák, *Czech Literature*, 93.

[83] Strahov, D K II 16, Fischer, *Mizsellen*, 2:22; 2:23.

[84] Ibid, 3:4. Dobrovský had died on January 6 of the same year.

gime, as embodied in the undertakings of the Habsburgs and its allies.[85] It had also sought, with varying success, to reach out to the folk culture of Bohemia, drawing upon artistic, literary, and cultural motifs in its attempt to draw the population into the Catholic Church. In doing so, the Jesuits had, through their selective support and destruction of expressions of popular culture, frequently risked alienating the very people whom they wished to convert; yet they had also contributed to the preservation of the distinctive culture of Bohemia through their use of the Czech language and through the training of scholars and apologists for Czech history and language. Dobrovský is not the only example of this scholarly tradition; in lesser ways men such as Pubitschka and Cornova stimulated awareness of the Bohemian past, and thereby helped lay the groundwork for the National Awakening.

The nineteenth-century Society in Bohemia and elsewhere was of a different stripe than its pre-suppression predecessor. The Society after 1814 would be characterized by an unwavering ultramontanism and a tired formalism in its educational projects, and by an increasing distance from the intellectual and political trends that would dominate the century. Not necessarily through its own choice, the restored Society was greatly restricted from fusing service to both high and low with public ritual intended to imbue religious experience with sensuous beauty. The Baroque culture of processions in the streets, pilgrimages to rural shrines, and hermits living in remote forests and mountains was driven to the brink of extinction by Maria Theresia's decrees, and was given its deathblow by Joseph II's directive that peremptorily closed all monasteries and convents except those that engaged in work serving the public good.[86] The reactionary policies of Metternich, Franz I, and the post-Napoleonic papacy brought back none of the deeper religious spirit of the previous century, when the Society of Jesus had been, materially speaking, the most visible and powerful institution in the lands of the Bohemian Crown and while it still laid claim to spiritual credibility.[87] All

[85] The Jesuit emphasis on Latin looks anachronistic today, and may have also seemed less than completely rational or utilitarian to some French *philosophes;* but in the German-speaking world as late as 1780 one in every eleven books was still printed in this language, and command of Latin was not associated with any particular theological or political position. Only after the restoration of the Society and the creation of the political system that followed the Congress of Vienna did Latin become indelibly associated with an ultramontane ideology (Gay, *Enlightenment,* 2:90).

[86] The Emperor's realignment of dioceses in Upper Austria, Passau, Cheb (Eger), Salzburg, Tyrol, and elsewhere not only severed the last ties between the Holy Roman Empire and Austria but also demonstrated to what degree Catholicism was expected to serve the needs of the State before it addressed the desires of subjects still engaged in traditional expressions of piety (Jedin, *History of the Church,* 6:479).

[87] The lessening degree to which ruling elites took formal religion seriously, or at least outwardly subscribed to its importance, is a phenomenon in the eighteenth century far more widespread than anything Josephinism could have brought about alone. The strengthening of authoritarian governmental policy during this period of fading outward religious commitment

these developments were paralleled by a political transformation. The final extinction of the Holy Roman Empire in 1806 brought to a close a process by which the Habsburgs had gradually distanced themselves from their sacral connections with the old Empire, a journey that was well underway when Austria acquired Galicia in 1772.

The continuing commitment of some Jesuits to the closed-world system of Aristotle, which had dominated intellectual life in the fifteenth and sixteenth centuries, placed them out of the mainstream in the nineteenth.[88] Had the post-Napoleonic Habsburgs needed the Jesuits to maintain social control, undoubtedly they would have made use of them; but instead the dynasty turned to other means of carrying out its domestic policies, including the employment of the secret urban police forces that had taken shape during the reigns of Joseph II and his brother Leopold.[89] The desire to control remained, but the approach had a distinctly modernist quality. Even the Catholic Church was eventually deemed not essential as a provider of elementary and secondary schooling, and in 1868 control of these institutions passed to the imperial and royal governments.[90]

Epilogue

Today the Jesuit community in Prague is small but alive, once again inhabiting lodgings adjacent to the Church of St. Ignatius in the New Town.[91] Anyone walking through the quiet halls lined with worn carpets and adorned with nineteenth-century prints of saints cannot easily discern the relationship of this community and others like it in Bohemia to the complex culture of the Society in the eighteenth century. Years of exile and persecu-

---

is a dynamic that the Society, even after it was restored, could only poorly grasp or deal with. Francis I, educated by the former Jesuit Joannes Diesbach, in general was neither deferential toward nor contemptuous of a theologically derived perspective as he pursued his internal and external policies, and this tendency was perpetuated by his successors (Mikoletzky, *Jahrhundert,* no. 331, et passim).

[88] By the end of the seventeenth century, Aristotle was in total eclipse even among those who did not yet accept the Copernican model (*Dictionary of the History of Ideas,* s.v. "Hierarchy and Order," by C. A. Patrides.

[89] Ernst Wangermann asks, "Is it not significant that, like during this period of reaction, the Ministry of Police was given influence over exactly those areas of government from which the Society of Jesus had been removed during the period of reform?" (*Achievement,* 185). The difficulty with drawing this connection too tightly is that it completely ignores the value the Habsburgs themselves placed on the spiritual and pastoral role of the Society, as well as the variety of interests and activities of individual Jesuits.

[90] Ferdinand Seibt, "Kirche und Gesellschaft von den Anfängen bis zum Ende der Monarchie," in F. Seibt, *Bohemia sacra,* 25.

[91] Thanks to Father Josef Čupr, S.J., for the opportunity to visit the Jesuit community of Prague.

tion and the persistent ambivalence of contemporary Czech society toward the Society have made its return following the Velvet Revolution of 1989 a quiet one. The Jesuit community possesses no archives, artifacts, or mementos of the time when it dominated the cultural life of the region. While there is an awareness among the priests and brothers that the history of the Society in Bohemia is completely intertwined with the history of the region, it would seem that the natural heirs to the late-Baroque Society have little access to its legacy.

Anyone seeking this legacy must look instead in the broader avenues of Czech culture to find the heritage of the last generations of Jesuits to work in Bohemia before the suppression. The Jesuits of Bohemia personified several of the most important themes in the history of the region. They were first and foremost true believers, or at least expected in their public personae to appear as such. From the time of the conversion of the first Slavic princes to Christianity through the Hussite wars and the reconquest of the land for the Catholic Church, passionate fidelity to a belief, even to the point of martyrdom, has been held up as a model of faith.[92] The true believer represented a standard against which others were measured. Yet the belief the Jesuits championed was the faith of the dynasty that had conquered the land and transformed its aristocracy into a pliant ally. Catholicism was a religion rejected by many in Bohemia. The Society therefore can never be completely separated from its connections with a foreign dynasty, and the imposition on the Bohemian peoples of a faith they had once rejected.

Yet, as we have seen in the preceding chapters, the intersection of orthodox Catholicism and popular expressions of religion greatly complicated this relationship. Religious expression endorsed and promoted by the Jesuits of Bohemia produced works of art now recognized as important cultural treasures of the Czech lands. Examples of this legacy that still survive are visible in hundreds of villages throughout the Czech Republic, as well as in Prague itself. By contrast, the intellectual contributions of the most gifted Jesuit scholars and scientists of the era are not readily visible; most of their work lies unread in obscure libraries and archives. The physical world, a world in which the Society also worked, tells another story of the contributions of the Jesuits of Bohemia. The statues of saints, the gilt altars, and Baroque effusions of parish churches remain the most lasting material legacy that the Society has bequeathed to Bohemia, and provide the

---

[92] While the facts in the matter are murky, the pious version of the death of Svatý Václav (St. Wenceslaus) is that he was murdered at a church door in Stará Boleslav because of his devotion to the Church (Marvin Cantor, ed., *The Origins of Christianity in Bohemia: Sources and Commentary* [Evanston, Ill.: Northwestern University Press, 1990], 226 ff.).

most telling metaphor for the work of the Bohemian Jesuits, spiritual, educational, and intellectual, in the second half of the eighteenth century. Their achievement, potent but elusive, is based upon values and premises that its modern heirs, like pilgrims striving toward a distant landmark, can only momentarily glimpse from afar.

appendix one

A Note on Proper Names

Bohemia in the eighteenth century was a land where three or more languages were commonly used in public life. Latin was the medium of communication for the Catholic Church and the universities; a good deal of the most official level of governmental affairs was conducted in that language, and the majority of scholarly works were written in it. German was the native tongue (in its Viennese dialect form) of the Habsburg dynasty; but, more important, it was also used by burghers, nobility, and peasants. German is found in many official documents as well. Czech, its low prestige notwithstanding, was the native tongue of the majority of people living in that region, including many Jesuits. It never completely vanished from official usage, and continued to appear in popular literature. In addition, some aristocrats made use of Italian and French in their personal correspondence. Each of these languages rendered Czech proper names in different ways, but for the sake of consistency in this book, we must determine which form of proper names would be the best to adopt.

In the case of place names, I have generally striven to employ the names currently in use in the Czech Republic and its modern neighbors. Thus the reader will find the Ukrainian *Mukachevo* instead of the Hungarian *Munkács*. The most important exception to this rule is Prague, which is much less jarring than the authentically Czech *Praha*. Thus we will use Olomouc and Brno, rather than the somewhat more familiar Olmütz and Brünn, and we will refer to Königgratz (often written Königgrätz) as Hradec Králové. Other Czech and Moravian communities will be identified in a similar way. Wrocław, however, will be rendered in its German form, Breslau, since in the eighteenth century the city was German.

So place names are relatively easy. In the instance of given names of individuals, however, the situation is far more complicated. The names of all priests of the Society of Jesus appear in all its records in their Latin form. Thus Karl John is always written Carolus John. If the setting were monolingual, as in France, it would be an easy matter to convert all Latinized given names to their vernacular equivalent. But in Bohemia it is not always clear to which vernacular one should turn. Should Ignatius Cornova be written "Ignaz" (the German form), "Ignatz" (a German variant), "Ignatius" (which also happens to be the English equivalent), or "Ignac" (the Czech form)?

Thus I have arrived at a compromise that, although it is not perfect, will, I hope, at least not be distracting.

The names of those Jesuits who may be with confidence associated with a Czech ethnicity will be given in their Czech form. In the case of Cornova, his identification with Czech-nationalist issues was the deciding factor. All other proper names will be written in their Latin or German forms, which will never be technically incorrect, even though they might occasionally be awkward. Where the secondary literature (often in Czech) commonly uses the Czech form of a Jesuit's name, this name will appear in parentheses after the Latin form. Jesuits active after the suppression of the Society will be denominated with the Latin, German, or Czech forms of their names that were in most common use at the time. The reader will therefore encounter Franciscus Zeno and Ignac Cornova.

Occasionally family names pose a similar dilemma. Generally I have followed the usage that appears most common in contemporary documents, so that Pubitschka, the Germanized form, has been chosen over the Czech Pubicka. In the case of the names of the Jesuit *coadjutores temporales,* the form that appears in the Society's records will be followed; sometimes this is a vernacular form, and at other times that name will appear in its Latin form.

There remains the question of the correct title to apply to the annual reports of the Society. These are commonly referred to in secondary literature as *Literæ annue*. The actual documents sometimes are entitled *Annales,* and the spelling of *Literæ annue* can also appear in such variant forms as *Litteræ annuæ, Litteræ annue,* and occasionally still others. In this book *Litteræ annuæ* will be used to preserve consistency, but the notes will retain the title and spelling that appear in the original document.

A Note on Monetary Units and Prices

During its last decades of existence, the Holy Roman Empire presented a bewildering confusion of units in which to conduct financial transactions. Not only was there no unified system of currency, but the rate between silver- and gold-based units of currency was not always the same. Paper money was not in common use until the end of the century. In Bohemia the most commonly used unit of currency was the silver florin, in German sources sometimes referred as the gulden and in Czech sources as the zlaty. The florin was divided into sixty kreutzers, which were each in turn divided into four pfennig or eight heller. The florin was estimated in 1792 to be worth about two English shillings or forty-eight United States cents; earlier in the century the florin may have been closer to four shillings in value.[1] The situation was further complicated because neighboring regional currencies bore the same name but had different values. In 1746 it was reported that a Bohemian florin was worth fifty-six "Creutzer," while a Silesian florin was worth twenty "Kayser-Groschen oder 16 Groschen."[2]

The gold ducat, a monetary unit of Venetian origin used throughout Europe, was less commonly employed than the florin for transactions in Bohemia. During the second half of the eighteenth century, silver fell in value compared to gold, so that in 1750 a ducat was worth four florins ten kreutzer, and by 1786 four florins thirty kreutzer. A thaler, a silver coin widely used throughout the empire, was worth two florins in 1793.[3]

As for the actual purchasing power of the florin, one must avoid overgeneralizing from prices recorded by Viennese writers of the period, as these were significantly higher in the *Residenzstadt*. Johann Pezzl observed that a gentleman living in Vienna in the 1780s could do so in reasonable style for about four hundred florins annually.[4] Although the life of the

[1] Wright, *Serf, Seigneur, and Sovereign,* 195.

[2] Rochezang von Isecern [Zschackwitz], *Historische und geographische Beschreibung des Königreichs Böheim, Erster Theil* (Frankfurt/Leipzig, 1746), 152.

[3] Josef Anton Riegger, *Archiv für Geschichte und Statistik, inbesondere von Böhmen,* 3 vols. (Leipzig, 1793), 2:341, 393.

[4] Leslie Bodi, *Tauwetter in Wien* (Frankfurt a/M: Fischer, 1995), 441–44.

nobility was ostentatious in Prague as well, it was generally known that it cost less to live there than in Vienna, and many families no doubt managed comfortably on an income of eighty or one hundred florins a year. Prices for ordinary commodities such as flour, shoes, or beer are occasionally recorded, but should be used cautiously, as a major famine—for example, the one that struck in 1774—would completely disrupt these exchanges.[5] The further one ventured into the countryside, the lower wages were, and a barter economy helped compensate for the shortage of cash.[6] Thus, a rural schoolteacher might earn only sixty-four florins a year, but might also receive food or firewood, and perhaps clothing as well, in addition to his salary. It is worth noting that in the 1780s, the poor who received relief were granted (an admittedly meager) four kreutzer a day.[7]

---

[5] See Paul Shore, "The Suppression of the Society of Jesus in Bohemia," *AHSI* 65, no. 1 (Jan.-June 1996): 141 n. 11.

[6] Jerome Blum, *The End of the Old Order in Rural Europe* (Princeton: Princeton University Press, 1978), 244.

[7] Ludmila Hlavacková, "Chudinská pece a zdravnoství," in *Pocátky ceského národního obrození, 1770–1791,* ed. Josef Petráň (Prague: Academia, 1990), 126.

appendix three

The *Coadjutores Temporales* of the Province of Bohemia

Not all Jesuits working in the Province of Bohemia were priests; many were brothers, or *coadjutores temporales,* a category of Jesuits who played an important role in carrying out the works of the Society. As early as 1546, the brief *Exponi nobis* had approved the admission of lay coadjutors or helpers into the Society, charged with performing a wide variety of tasks.[1] *Coadjutores temporales* (usually translated as lay brothers or Jesuit brothers) were required to take the first three vows of the Society, those of obedience, poverty, and chastity, just as did the *coadjutores spirituales* (usually translated as spiritual coadjutors; these were priests who did not pronounce the fourth vow of obedience to the pope regarding missions).[2] They were then considered members of the Jesuit community. Although many Jesuit lay brothers performed less skilled tasks in the community, for example, doing janitorial work or caring for animals, these men should not be classed with the medieval *conversi* belonging to orders such as the Cistercians from the twelfth century onward.[3] The latter were also illiterate for the most part, and were clearly differentiated from the other members of the community.

The thousands of acres of land owned by the Society and other extensive holdings in the form of vineyards, breweries, and farms all required management and a hard-working labor force. The lay brothers filled this role, in some cases doing work similar to what they had done elsewhere in the Society, even overseas. In many cases brothers had acquired skills before entering the Society. Because these men were generally not directly involved in the educational or sacramental aspects of the mission of the Society, records of their activities are almost always far less complete than those of the spiritual coadjutors. Their story is largely missing from general histories of the Society, as well as from the histories of individual provinces drawn up during the eighteenth century. Yet it is impossible to understand

[1] Ignatius of Loyola, *Constitutions,* no. 6 and n. 19 (p. 71).

[2] Ibid., no. 13 (p. 83).

[3] C. Warren Hollister, *Medieval Europe: A Short History,* 7th ed. (New York: McGraw-Hill, 1994), 203.

either the corporate identity of the Jesuits or the impact that the Society had on the surrounding community without an appreciation of the Jesuit brothers.

The lives of these men are largely shrouded in mystery today. Obituary notices predictably lay stress on the virtues of the departed brother, although occasionally a hint of possible complications and conflicts among the brothers or perhaps between the brothers and the priests can be detected. In the obituary notice of Christophorus Loser, who died on November 12, 1765, we read that "his love of his fellow men, which sometimes among the [lay] brothers is rather rare, was in him most eagerly demonstrated."[4] The obituary of Joseph Thomsa, who died in Prague on March 14, 1772, contains a few brief references to the tasks he had been given during his years in the Society, but like most notices, it says nothing about his own personality.[5] At best we might find the predictable references to a brother's piety.

Records of the Bohemian Province from 1764 provide a glimpse of the range of backgrounds found among the lay brothers. The province catalogs record the language skills of each lay brother, an important consideration in this region, where the ability to function in two or more languages was a great asset. Some lay brothers spoke only one language, but it was not unusual to find brothers who could get along in two or three, a skill they shared with many others in eighteenth-century Bohemia. Carolus Koch, belonging to a professed house at an unidentified location somewhere in the province, was exceptional: he had command of Czech, German, and Latin "supra mediocriter," and even more unusual, he was a lawyer.[6] Most other lay brothers had the skills of artisans; in the same professed house are listed a cook, a tailor, a notary, and two coopers. Each one's level of skill in arithmetic was also noted, along with his ability to read or write; also recorded was a list of the skills that he had already acquired.

Although such lay brothers as Thomas Schwarz had had musical careers earlier in the century, in the years before the suppression there is little evidence of musical or artistic abilities noted among these men. Nor did temporal coadjutors rise beyond their station in the Society. The manifold secular responsibilities of the Jesuit communities were the work of the lay brothers, and the distance in educational attainment between them and the priests of the Society was never breached. Nowhere in the annals of the

---

[4] ". . . illius autem charitas, quæ inter fratres quandoque solet esse rarior, [præstantissima erat]" (NK, 2L23/15F folio 411v. *Annales Prov. Boh. 1765*).

[5] "Natus est Drzebnicii in Bohemia 1709 . . . adscriptus S. J. 1731 . . . formatus 1741" (NK, 23/19, *Litt. An. Collegii Clementini S. J.. 1772*, folio 421r).

[6] *Catalogus personarum et officiorum Provinciæ Bohemiæ Societatis Iesu ad annum 1764*, 28. In the same community was Ignatius Petzel, born in 1727, who was also a lawyer (ibid., 29).

Bohemian Society is there mention of a lay brother who later became a priest. The degree to which this barrier was related to social class is ambiguous, but the gap between university-trained priests and the ordinary brothers possessing less formal education doubtless reinforced class differences that were already present.

The gap between brother and priest did not decrease after the suppression. Former lay brothers did not receive a large share of the *Jesuitenfond* set up after the suppression of the Society. Thomas Slavik, two years after the suppression, was awarded a pension of twelve florins a month, or less than half the typical pension of a priest, and a fourth of what former spiritual coadjutor Joseph Tessanek earned as a university professor.[7] Anton Tentschke, a lay brother who had spent years as a missionary in the Indies, did somewhat better, receiving 192 florins annually, although it appears that since he was forty-nine years old, he would be expected to continue to work.[8] In the upheavals following 1773, elderly former Jesuit brothers varied widely in their fortunes. Matthias Pruha, aged eighty and no longer able to work, was awarded the relatively generous pension of three hundred florins a year.[9] But Johann Petz, also elderly, was simply awarded the right to remain in the collegium in Glogow, Silesia, where he had spent so many years.[10] Many former Jesuit brothers, like some priests, after 1773 disappear from the records without a trace.

The lay brothers possessed skills of great value to the communities in which they lived. The Jesuit community in Prague in 1764 included Andreas Fischer, an "apothecarius" born in 1699, who had worked in that capacity for thirty-two years.[11] He had entered the Society in 1728, suggesting that the decision to do so may have been motivated by the loss of a job or a wife. His knowledge of Latin may also point to training or formal education obtained before entering the Society. Fischer did not complete his formation until the age of about forty, and appears to have worked some years as a porter and at other more menial tasks before being assigned to the pharmacy. That Fischer learned his craft of pharmacy while in the Society cannot be determined with certainty, but seems likely. Thomas Kowarzik, about fifty-seven years old and a pharmacist as well, presents an intriguing picture. He had knowledge of German, Czech, Latin, and Italian, although his

[7] HKA, Exjesuiten Acta Boheim Nr. 13, #23, Acta SJ, Fasc. 2,23; Wienn, den 14 Octobris 1775.

[8] HKA, *Verzeichnis aller Exjesuiten . . . in Böhmen*. Exjesuiten Acten: Inventarium Roter Nummer 155, folios 320v–321r.

[9] Ibid., folios 300v–301r.

[10] Prag, den 7 Januarii 1774 (SÚA C-G 16, [Exjesuitica] 131, F2/40 167, folio 1v).

[11] *Catalogus* (1764), 152.

command of this last language was identified as "infra mediocritatem."[12] Had he traveled to Italy, served as a soldier there, or worked for one of the Italian-speaking diplomats or families of Italian descent residing in Prague? Like Fischer, Kowarzik had entered the Society relatively late, at the age of about twenty-six, and had completed his formation by the time he was about thirty-seven. Franciscus Pursche, another pharmacist, was born in Silesia in 1731 and entered the Society at the age of twenty-two, suggesting that, unlike some of the Jesuit brothers, he had relatively little experience as an adult worker outside the context of the Society.[13]

Many of the other brothers in the "Vetero-Pragensis" community give less indication of other types of training. Antonius Backalarz, about twenty-three years of age, was a cook, although he had some command of German, Czech, and Latin. Ioannes Hawranek, about thirty-seven years old, was a surgeon who had command of Latin, Czech, and German "super mediocr." He too, was a late arrival, entering the Society at about age thirty-five.[14] Josephus Müller was another older Jesuit brother housed in the "Vetero-Pragensis" community. Born in 1704 in Swabia, Mueller had worked as a cooper, a "cellarius," and "excitator," charged with awakening the community in the mornings, as well as a night watchman, a job many brothers are known to have held.[15]

The presence among the lay brothers of men who had passed a significant portion of their lives outside the Society is one of the most significant features of the Bohemian Jesuit communities as a whole and must have had a great impact on the character of individual communities, particularly the smallest ones, where many interactions between members were unavoidable. We must bear in mind that a man at age forty or even thirty-five might well have considered that most of his adult life was already over. Such an individual would have lived as an adult "in the world" (outside the religious life), for two or more decades, forming habits of work and of interaction with others that would not be changed easily. Some men entering the Society would have done so with an already strong faith, but it cannot be assumed that all who undertook formation had such a faith.

Formation itself took a number of years, and a brother often did not complete the process until after the age of forty.[16] Yet, while aspirants to the life of a Jesuit might have considered demands of formation an obstacle,

---

[12] Ibid., 253.

[13] He died on Sept. 29, 1760 (NK, 1416 MS XXIII 105/18, *An. Prov. Boh. 1760*, folio 96r).

[14] *Catalogus* (1764), 165.

[15] Ibid., 252.

[16] For example, Wenceslaus Kerth, born Sept. 23, 1712, completed his formation July 1, 1754, and died August 15, 1765 (NK, 1287 XXIII C105/15, *An. Prov. Boh. 1765*, folio 400r).

many of the men who entered the Society as temporal coadjutors apparently were not deterred by them. In an era before systematic, government-sponsored public assistance, it was not uncommon for a widower or man whose family life had been profoundly disrupted to seek to enter religious life. Men might make such a choice in the best of times; the unsettled economic conditions of midcentury would have contributed to the tendency of older men to live as religious brothers.[17] Of course, entering the Society as a brother did not mean that one's life was to become an isolated and uninteresting existence. The university community itself was staffed with Jesuit brothers. Josef Koprziwa had served as the beadle or "bedellus academicus" for the Faculties of Theology and Philosophy until the suppression, and then sought a pension the following year.[18]

The Jesuit priests who kept the records of the Prague communities devoted little space to their "charissimi" lay colleagues. This bias in part reflects the class divisions of the day, but also is a consequence of the emphasis on formal education that permeated the Society and set it somewhat apart from orders such as the Franciscans or Benedictines. Yet occasionally we catch a glimpse of the activities of a lay brother and of the way in which these men were viewed by Jesuit priests; for example, we have the obituary of "Ch[arissimus]. Augustinus Heintze," who was born in Silesia in 1691, entered the Society at the age of twenty-eight, and died in Prague in 1757. The obituary writer noted, "How often have we seen this excellent brother carrying sheets and blankets? And how often have we seen him in the watches of the night, which would have frightened another, going about his job in good spirits?"[19] Another brother whose responsibilities included care for linens was Joannes Pfeffer, born in Moravia in 1691. Brother Joannes entered the Society at the age of thirty-eight, worked as a sacristan, and was later in charge of bed linens, clothing, and other linens, jobs he held for decades. Pfeffer died July 22, 1757.[20] Bro. Joannes Zalusky, who died in 1761 at the age of seventy-four of "gangrena exteriore et interiore," also earned praise in his obituary notice. Zalusky, "molestus nemini, gratus omnibus," managed the finances of the collegium in the Old Town of Prague, a job of considerable responsibility.[21] Most remarkably, Zalusky is described as being as learned as a priest, rare praise from the priest who presumably wrote the obituary notices that appeared in the *Litteræ*.[22]

---

[17] The "Ivanites," a congregation of religious hermits, attracted numerous followers from among older and sometimes widowed men during this period (Pavel Zahradník, "Antonín Stoy a kongragace ivanitů," *BS* (1996): 69–99.

[18] SÚA, C-G 16 (Exjesuitica), 148, f 2/40, 191, 14 Januarij 1774.

[19] Strahov, FX IV 28, 18 b. Pragæ, 30 June 1757.

[20] Ibid., 18c.

[21] Strahov, D A III 32, *Epitome historiæ Collegii S. J. Vetero Pragæ ad annum 1761,* folio 75r.

[22] NK, 1288 MS XXIII C105/15 *An. Prov. Boh. 1761*, folios 235r.

Generally, however, the virtues of brothers recorded in the Society's annals stressed personal piety and the capacity to perform many different tasks. Brothers might be assigned to the same professed house, but others performed tasks in different settings, especially when the house or collegium was responsible for missions or properties outside the city. Joseph Gorlich and Victor Preibil were both "socii Procuratoris," the former performing his job "extra urbem" and the latter "infra."[23]

By the late 1760s a brother occasionally returned to a community in Bohemia after being expelled, along with his community, from one of the missions in "the Indies." Such an individual would bring back special skills, languages, and experiences little known in Bohemia, but of value to the community in which he settled. Georg Schultz, who died in 1768, had recently returned from a mission in Mexico, where he had served at the College of SS. Peter and Paul until the expulsion of the Jesuits from the Spanish empire.[24]

But "the Indies" might also be a place of great moral danger, as the case of Fr. Franz Xaver Reitenberger, S.J., illustrated all too well. Reitenberger, born in 1707 in Prague, was sent to the Marianas Islands in 1735. In this remote setting, he established a congregation of women in 1757 dedicated to the "Most Holy Mother of Light." Yet it seems that this congregation was also dedicated to other things, as an investigation conducted after Reitenberger's death revealed: apparently sexual orgies had been conducted under the Jesuit's direction.[25] Scandals such as those involving Reitenberger were, of course, an exception to the rule; but the time spent in distant foreign countries undoubtedly had a great impact on many brothers, who may have arrived at their exotic assignments with little experience of life beyond the district in which they had been raised. The experience of arriving in Bohemia on the eve of serious famine and a period of social unrest may have been particularly trying for men who had spent much of their lives in bucolic settings, even though some probably had spent their years abroad longing to return home.

A few Bohemian lay brothers became famous in their own lifetimes. The best-known Bohemian Jesuit brother in the middle of the eighteenth century was Josef Kramolin (also spelled Cramolini, Grammolin, and Kramolini), who achieved considerable renown as a painter.[26] Born in 1730

---

[23] These brothers were assistants to the procurator (treasurer) of the house, one working outside the city, the other, in it ("Coadjutores Domus Pragæ ad S. Nicolaum," *Catalogus pesonarum et officiorum Prov. Boh. Soc Jesu an. 1761,* col. 2).

[24] NK, 23/19 *Lit. An. Boh. Prov. 1768,* folio 130v.

[25] Bernd Hausberger, *Jesuiten aus Mitteleuropa in kolonialem Mexiko: Eine Bio-Bibliographie* (Vienna: Verlag für Geschichte und Politik; Munich: R Oldenbourg, 1995), 280 f.

[26] Strahov, DK III 5, Adolf Fischer, *Miscellanea B.* 1837 N: 136, 6.

in Nymburk, Kramolin entered the Society in 1758. He decorated many Jesuit churches in the regions with his works. An especially skilled portraitist, in 1789 he painted the still extant portrait of the Strahov abbot Wenzel Mayer.[27] The suppression had no apparent effect on his artistic output, for Kramolin continued painting until his death in 1802 in Karlovy Vary (Karlsbad). His brother, Wenzel Kramolin, was also a well-known artist who painted figures in St. Vitus Cathedral in Prague; together the brothers produced the altar panels at St. Clement's Church in Prague.[28] Not as well known as the Kramolins was Ignatius Raab, a Jesuit lay brother born in Nový Bydzov (Bidschau) in 1715 who became a Jesuit at the age of twenty-nine. Raab painted the apostles in the church of the Strahov monastery, and after he died on January 21, 1787, in Moravia, earned mention in Dlabacz's *Künstlerlexikon.*[29] Another brother of great ability was Thomas Schwarz, an organist and organ builder who in 1747 designed the organ of St. Nicholas's Church in the Malá Strana, which is still in use today.[30] Like other brothers who achieved a high degree of skill in music-conscious Prague, Schwarz did not pass into complete obscurity, although we do not know much about his other responsibilities.

Ultimately, very little is known about a large number of Jesuit brothers, and especially about their fate after the suppression. Lacking close family connections and enjoying only meager pensions, many former brothers must have faced dreary prospects. A collection of death notices of former Bohemian Jesuits stretching from 1786 to 1795 provides some names, but we cannot even be entirely sure which of these men might have spent time serving in the communities of Prague.[31]

---

[27] Gottfried Johann Dlabacz, *Allgemeines Künstler-Lexikon für Böhmen* (Prague, 1815), 125 f.

[28] No birth date for the younger Kramolin is reported in the brief biographical entry in Dlabacz, *Künstler-Lexikon,* 126.

[29] Strahov, D K III 5, Fischer, *Miscellanea* B, 7. A Bohemian *coadjutor temporalis* who distinguished himself as an organist was František Horcicka of Opava, who continued his career after the suppression, marrying and living in Frydek (now Frydek-Místek) until his death in 1800 (Jiří Sehnal, "Hudba a jesuité české provincie v 17. a 18. století," in *Morava a Brno na sklonku třicetileté valky,* ed. Jan Skutil [Brno: Magistrát hlavního města Brna, 1995], 164).

[30] Strahov, D K III 5, Fischer *Miscellanea B,* 1837, N: 136, 7.

[31] Twenty-nine names appear during this ten-year period: Franz Hraczek, Jan, 11, 1786; Joseph Petschoch (?), May 29, 1787; Joseph Feiter, Jan. 24, 1788; Joseph Swoboda, Sept. 9, 1788; Karl Gross, in a document dated Dec. 17, 1788; Johann Kindl(?), August 5, 1789; Johann Sur, in a document dated March 11, 1791; Johann Michael Gessel, Dec. 10, 1791; Johann Havranek, April 26, 1791; Johann Busch, May 6, 1791; Franz Pillman(?), in a document dated August 3, 1791; Johann Weiniger, Sept. 1, 1791 (age seventy-seven); Johann Wenzel Horzky, August 27, 1791 (age seventy); Johann v. Wendlingen, Sept. 19, 1791 (age seventy-four); Franciscus Jarosch, March 29, 1792; Anton Mayer, May 24, 1792; Johann Renner, July 16, 1793; Martin Lenke, August 16, 1793 (age fifty-five); Johann Dänemark, Sept. 8, 1793; Anton Kammel, Jan. 8, 1794; Joseph Hlozek, Feb. 18, 1794; Ignatz Striwank(?; a pharmacist), Feb. 16, 1794; Thomas Sotmann, March 9, 1794; Karl Koch, Apr. 8, 1794 (age fifty-six); Franz

Although a small number of Jesuit priests were of noble families, a matter of some pride to the chroniclers of the Society, very few Jesuit brothers could claim such ancestry (but notice "Johann v. Wendlingen," mentioned above). A possible exception was an unnamed Jesuit, blood brother of Ernest de Max, whom Ernest was attempting to reach through the archbishop of Prague in pursuit of some legal or financial claim. The archbishop disclaimed any authority over the Jesuit and suggested that Ernest appeal to his provincial. The Jesuit in question may have been either a priest or a brother, but the letter offers no clarification on this point.[32]

The careers and personalities of the Bohemian lay brothers are in every surviving instance refracted through the sensibilities and literary tropes of the priests who recorded these details. Nothing written by these men themselves has been identified. The circumstances under which obituaries and other records of the lives of the brothers are compiled by no means invalidate these records, but they do pose a challenge to the researcher, who must distinguish among clichés, conventional literary devices, and authentic details about these "helpers."

The case of Carolus Habermann, who died in Prague on March 9, 1770, after having lived a long life in the Society, is typical.[33] Born in 1692 in Moravia, he had entered the Jesuit order at the age of thirty-one and completed his formation at the age of forty-two. His obituary records his devotion to St. Martha, who provided him with relief from discomfort that he felt in his feet. His generosity to those suffering in prison was also noted, a rare detail in the obituaries of brothers.[34] Little else about Haberman's work or life is described, although he had passed almost half a century in the Society.

Breitmüller, June 20, 1794; Thomas Kowarzik, May 26, 1795 (age eighty-eight); Johann Hartl, June 14, 1795; Anton Jarosch, in a document dated August 7, 1795); Gregor Kaysser, Oct. 11, 1795 (SÚA, ČG-Publ. 1786–1795, 85, Fasc. 61–113).

[32] Excellentissime et Reverendissime Domine Domine Colendissime in Causa Domini Ernesti de Max, quam Su. Excellentia nuperrima Epistola mihi commendavit, meam haud queo interponere operam cum ejusdem Domini Ernesti Frater e S. J. pluribus annis extra meam Archi-Diocesim commoratus fuerit, isque temporalium abdicationem in Silesia fecisse, perhibeatur. Proinde eidem Domino Ernesto consulendum censeo, ut is ad patrem Provincialem illius Provinciæ in qua memoratus religiosus S. J. degit utpote ad primam competentem instantiam servato debito juris ordine recursum faciat. Quod reliquum est omni cum cultu, et observantia singulari continuo sum Excellentiæ Suæ, etc. (Anton Peter Przichowsky, archbishop of Prague, to Nuncio Eugenio Visconti, Vienna; Prague, Oct. 29, 1769; ASV Nunziatura di Vienna 145, folio 187r). Max has not been identified in lists of priests in *Catalogi personarum* of the period.

[33] NK, 23/19 *Lit. An. Boh. Prov. 1770*, folio 284v.

[34] "Religiosæ inopiæ amorem divisione rerum sibi oblatarum cum egenis, aut carcere pressis liberaliter ac hilariter coluit" (ibid), indicating that he joyously cultivated his love of religious poverty by sharing whatever he was given with the needy or the imprisoned.

In the largest Jesuit communities in Prague, brothers and priests did not need to be in constant contact with one another, but in smaller communities it seems likely that they worked together closely. Jesuit records are silent about the specifics of relations between the two groups, and disputes that might have arisen would have been excluded from reports sent to Rome. It is safe to say, however, that the world of the Jesuit coadjutors, even those like Zalusky who excelled at more scholarly pursuits, provided them with little encouragement. The case of Johann Neumann, who became a physician after the suppression, seems unique.[35]

The quality and quantity of surviving data on lay brothers is a reminder of how the Bohemian Society chose to represent itself in its own records, and also how deeply it was influenced by the prevailing cultural norms of the day. These norms put a higher value on the presence of a noble's son in a Jesuit school than on the accomplishments and personal characteristics of a "temporal helper." Yet these men enriched the culture of the Society and in more than a few instances made considerable cultural contributions themselves.

---

[35] About eleven years after the suppression, Neumann was described as "M. D., und diente irgendwo in einer Kreise als Phisicus, aber bei einem Spitale angestellt werden" (*Verzeichniss aller Exjesuiten . . . in Böhmen* [HKA, Exjesuiten Acten: Inventarium Roter Nummer 155, folios 327v–328r]).

Bibliography

Abbreviations Used in This Book

AfKvB-M-S	Archiv für Kirchengeschichte von Böhmen- Mähren- Schelsien
AHSI	*Archivum Historicum Societatis Iesu*
AHY	*Austrian History Yearbook*
AUCP—HUC	*Acta Universitatis Carolinae Pragensis—Historia Universitatis Carolinæ*
BS	Bibliotheca Strahoviensis
ČČH	*Český časopis Historický*
ČČNM	Časopis Českého Národního Musea
ČMKČ	Časopis Musea Království Českého
hj	*Historical Journal*
HKA	Hofkammer Archiv
jb	*Judaica Bohemica*
MVGDB	*Mittheilungen des Vereins für Geschichte der Deutschen in Bömen*
MZAB	Moravský zemský Archiv v Brně
NK	Národní Knihovna (National Archives)
PSH	*Pražský Sborník Historický*
SEER	Slavonic and East European Review
SÚA	Státní Úřední Archiv Prague

Primary Sources

Archiv Univerzity Karlové
Matricula Facultatis Medicinæ Pragensis MCDLII

Archivio Segreto Vaticano
Nunziatura Vienna 175

Archivum Romanum Societatis Jesu
Boh. Prov. 194

Arhivele Statului Cluj-Napoca, Fondul Liceal Romano-Catolic

Harvard Business School
C-1 1766–1788
Paar family papers

Hofkammer Archiv Wien
Acta SJ
Fasc. 2
Fasc. 3 Roter Nr. 28, Roter Nr. 155
Acta Exjes.

Fasc. 2 Roter Nr. 14

Moravský Zemský Archiv v Brně
Cerroniho Sbírka, II, 345.

Národní Knihovna Praha: (NK)
Litteræ Annuæ Provinciæ Bohemiæ Societatis Jesu 1750, 1760, 1761, 1766–72
NK 2L/23/15f
NK 23/17
NK 23/19
NK 1281 MS XXIII C 105/15
NK 1287 MS XXIII C 105/16
NK 1416 MS XXIII C105/18

Národní Muzeum Praha
VII A 5
Millauer, M., *Geschichte der theologischen Fakultät der prager Universität*

Státní Úřední Archiv Praha:
České Gubernium 16 (Exjesuitica)
435
F3/1/701a
JS, III-415

Strahov Monastery Prague
D A III 32
Epitome annuarum litterarum Provinciæ Bohmiæ ab anno 1761 ad annum 1763
Epitome Historiæ Collegii S. J. Vetero-Pragæ ad annum 1761
D A III 33
Epitome Historiæ Dom. Prof. ad S. Nicolaum anno 1758, 1759, 1761, 1762
Epitome Historiæ Collegii S. J. ad S. Ignatium Vetero-Pragæ ad annum 1759, 1760, 1761
Epitome Historiæ Collegii Soc. Iesu Reginæ Hradeii Annus 1758, 1760
Epitome Historiæ Provinciæ Bohemiæ Soc. Jesu ad annum 1758, 1759, 1760
Epitome Historiæ Residentiæ Kossumbergensis Societatis Jesu ad annum 1761, '62, et '63
D K I 24
Fischer, Adolf *Geistliches Panorama . . .*
D K II 16
Fischer, Adolf, *Mizsellen über die prager Universität*
D K III 5
F X IV 28
HT I 43

Catalogs of Primary Sources

Švabenský, M. *Jesuité v Brně 1241–1773.* Brno: Inventáře a Katalogy Fondu Státního Archivu v Brně, 1954.

Zemek, Metodej. *Jesuité v Uherském Hradišti 1635–1773.* Brno: Inventáře a Katalogy Fondu Státního Archivu v Brně, 1955.

Primary Printed Sources

Angelo, Don Rotundo Christoforo. *Il neomartire di Boemia; o vero, la conversione e martirio di Simon Abeles descritto in due oratori, per musica.* Strahov, BP VI 5 I c. 80.

Auctorum triennalium in schola rhetorices per Provinciam Bohemiæ Societatis Jesu prælegendorum Quorum syllabum sequens pagella exhibet annus primus. Prague: Typis Universitatis Carlo-Ferdinandeæ in Collegio Soc. IESU ad S. Clementem, anno 1720.

Beschreibung des Auszugs der sämtlichen Prager-Judenschaft aus Prag. . . . Nürnburg: Geyer, 1745.

Catalogus personarum et officiorum Provinciæ Austriæ Societatis Jesus pro anno MDCCLXXIII.

Catalogus personarum et officiorum Provinciæ Bohemiæ Societatis Jesu pro anno MDCCLXVII.

Catalogus personarum et officiorum Provinciæ Bohemiæ Societatis Jesu pro anno MDCCLXI.

Catalogus personarum et officiorum Provinciæ Bohemiæ Societatis Jesu pro anno MDCCLXX.

Catalogus universi cleri archidiocesansi Pragensis. . . . Prague, Old City: Typis Achiepiscopalibus per Josephum Diesbach, 1809.

Cordara, Iulius. *Historia Societatis Iesu pars sexta.* Rome: Ex Typ. Antonii de Rubies, 1750.

Cornova, I. *Unterhaltungen mit jungen Freunden der Vaterlandsgeschichte Böhmens.* 4 vols. Prague: Calve, 1799-1803.

———. *Die Jesuiten als Gymnasiallehrer.* Prague: Calve, 1804.

———. *Der Grosze Böhme Bohuslav von Lobkowitz.* Prague [?], 1808.

Csiba, S. *Dissertatio historico-physica de montibus Hungariæ.* Nagyszaombat: 1714.

Dobrovský, Josef. *Geschichte der böhmische Sprache und Literatur.* Prague, 1792.

Eder, Joannes. *Virilis constantia pueri duodennii Simonis Abeles in odium fidei a judeo parente. . . .* Prague, 1694.

Fabritius, L. *Mrawna naučení na nědele celého roku.* Prague: Typis Sophia Kirchnerianæ Typographicæ Aulicæ, 1760.

Fundamenta virtutum: Thema quatuor meditationum Congregationis Latinæ Majoris monacensis B. Mariæ V. [Munich]: Typis viduæ Johannis Christophoris Mayr, 1768.

Der Getaufte Jude: Weder Jude noch Christ. Vienna: Bei Sebastian Hartl, 1781.

Hammerschmied, J. F. *Prodromus gloriæ Pragæ.* Prague, Old City: Typis et Impensis Wolffgangi Wickart, 1723.

Ioannis Ferrandi Anciensis e Societate Iesu Disquisitio reliquaria. . . . London: Sumptibus Laurentii Anisson, et. Soc., 1647.

Katona, Stephanus. *Historia critica Regni Hungariæ stirpis Austriacæ. . . .* Buda: Typis et Sumptibus Regiæ Universitatis Pestanæ, 1809.

Klausal, Ioannes, S. I., *Curiosa naturæ arcana inclyti Regni Bohemiæ et appertinentium Provinciarum Moraviæ et Silesiæ, quaestionibus philosophicis indagata.* Prague, 1724.

———. *Controversia fidei particularia populari captui accommodata, cum Thesibus ex universa Theologia.* 2 vols. Prague, 1733.

[Koniáš, Antonín], *Clavis hæresim claudens et aperiens. . . .* W Hradci Král., 1749.

Meusel, Johann Georg. *Lexikon der vom Jahre 1750 bis 1800 verstorbenen teutschen Schriftsteller.* 15 vols. Leipzig, 1802–16.

Moretto, Petrus, *De ritu ostensionis reliquiarum. . . .* Rome: Typis Rocchi Bernabo, 1721.

———. *De ritu ostensionis sacrarum reliquiarum.* Rome, 1721.

Neue Kronik von Böhmen vom Jahre 530, bis 1780. Prague: Gedruckt und verlegt von Johann Ferdinand Edlen von Schönfeld, 1780.

Pelzel, Franz Martin. *Abbildungen böhmischer und mährischer Gelehrten und Künstler.* Prague: M. A. Schmadl, 1782.

———. *Böhmische, mährische und schlesische Gelehrte und Schriftsteller aus dem Orden der Jesuiten.* Prague, 1786.

———. *Gelehrte und Schriftsteller aus dem Orden der Jesuiten.* Prague: 1786.

Petráň, Josef, ed. *Počátky českého Národního Obrození, 1770–1791.* Prague: Academia, 1990.

Pfrogner, L. C. *Einleitung in die christliche Religion- und Kirchengeschichte.* Prague: Bey Widtmann, 1805.

Pleiner, Joachim. *Die Glaubens- und Sittenlehre nach dem Evangelien gerichtet, zum Gebrauch der polisch-sächsischen Truppen.* Dresden(?), 1746.

———. *Der in Lebensgefahr begriffene Soldat, durch trostreiche Ermahungen und anmutige Gebeter zu einem Ermangung eines priesterlichen Beystands, zum Trost dem in sächsischen diensten befindlichen Soldaten vorbereitet.* Dresden, 1748.

Processus inquisitorius. . . . Prague: bey Caspar Zacharias Wussin, 1728.

Proprium Societatis Jesu pro Provinciæ Bohemiæ officiis Sanctorum. Prague: Typis Universitatis Carlo-Ferdinandeaa in Collegio Societatis Jesu, 1679.

Ratio atque institutio studiorum Societatis Iesu. Antwerp: Apud Ioannem Meurium, 1685.

Riegger, Josef Anton. *Materialen zur alten u. neuen Statisitk von Böhmen.* 12 vols. Prague und Leipzig: Kaspar Widtmann, 1787.

———. *Archiv für Geschichte und Statistik, inbesondere von Böhmen.* 3 vols. Leipzig: In der Waltherischen Hofbuchhandlung, 1793.

Rochezang von Isecern. *Historische un geographische Beschreibung des Königreichs Böheim, Erster Theil. . . .* Frankfurt and Leipzig, 1746.

Rogalsky, Guilielmus Leopoldus. *Fortissimus Dei miles et martyr invictus sanctus Joannes Nepomucensis S. Metropolitanæ Ecclesiæ Pragensis Canonicus sub annuis. . . .* Prague, Old City: Aula in Regia Literis Archi-Episcopalibus per Jacobum Schweiger Archi-Episcopalem Typographum, 1763.

Romaňák, Andrej. "Reformy armády." In Petráň, *Počátky.*

Schematismus für das Königreich Böheim 1790. Prague: In der Schönfeld-Meißnerschen Buchhandlung, 1790(?).

Schmidl, Joannes. *Historia Provinciæ Bohemiæ S. J.* 4 vols. Prague, 1749–59.

Stepling, Joseph. *Litterarum commercium.* Bratislava, 1782.

Strnad, Antonius. *De divi Joannis Nepomuceni gloria, quam sibi loquendo et jacendo. . . .* Prague: J. A. Hagan, 1781.

Tanner, Mathias. *Societas Jesu usque ad sanguinis et vitæ profusionem militans in Europa, Asia, Praga, America. . . .* Prague: 1678.

Thám, K. I. *Neuestes, ausführliches und vollständiges böhmisch-deutsches Nationallexikon oder Wörterbuch.* Prague: Franz Johann Scholl, 1805.

Über der Unnütz und Schädlichkeit der Juden im Königreich Böhmen, und Mähren. Prague, 1782.

Wiezenek, F., Comes de. *Adhortio ad Senatum populumque academicum dum augusta Iosephi et Mariæ Theresiæ munificentia Iosepho Steplingo monumentum in Bibliotheca Clementina erigitur.* Prague, 1780(?).

Wydra, Stanislaus, *Historia matheseos in Bohemia et Moravia cultæ.* Prague, 1778.

———. *Laudatio funebris J. Stepling.* Prague, 1778.

———. *Oratio ad monumentum a Maria Theresia Augusta Iosepho Steplingo in Bibiliotheca Clementina erectum. . . .* Prague, 1779.

———. *Vita admodum reverendi ac magnifici viri J. Stepling.* Prague, 1779.

Modern Editions of Primary Documents

The Autobiography of St. Ignatius of Loyola with Related Documents. Translated by J. F. O'Callaghan, edited with introduction by J. C. Olin. New York: Harper Torchbooks, 1974.

Balbín, Boheslav. *Dissertatio apologetica pro lingua Slavonica, præcipue bohemica.* Edited by F. M. Pelzel. Prague, 1777.

"Die Berichte der Pastoralvisitationen des Görzer Erzbischofs Karl Michael von Attem in Kärten von 1751 bis 1762." *Fontes rerum Austriacarum diplomatica et acta,* 87 (1993).

Carlen, Claudia, ed. *Papal Encyclicals, 1740–1878.* Raleigh: Consortium, 1973.

Chrysostom, John, St. *Discourses against Judaizing Christians.* Translated by Paul Harkins. Washington, D.C.: CUA Press, 1977.

Divarkar, Parmanandra R., S.J., trans. *A Pilgrim's Testament: The Memoirs of Saint Ignatius of Loyola.* St. Louis: Institute of Jesuit Sources, 1995.

Ignatius of Loyola, *Spiritual Exercises of St. Ignatius.* Translated by Anthony Motola, S.J. New York: Image Books, 1963.

———. *The Constitutions of the Society of Jesus.* Translated and edited by George E. Ganss, S.J. St. Louis: The Institute of Jesuit Sources, 1970.

———. *The Spiritual Exercises (SpEx).* Edited and translated by George E. Ganss, S.J. St. Louis: Institute of Jesuit Sources, 1992.

Khevenhüler-Metsch, Rudolf, and Hanns Schlitter, eds. *Aus der Zeit Maria Theresias: Das Tagebuch des Fürsten Johann Joseph von Khevenhüller-Metsch.* 8 vols. Vienna: A. Holzhausens, 1907–.

Klueting, Harm, ed. *Der Josephinismus: Ausgewählte Quelle zur Geschichte der thesianisch-josephinischen Reformen.* Darmstadt: Wissentschaftliche Buchgesellschaft, 1995.

Kodytek, Antonín. *Kunvadská kronika 1740–1786.* Chocen: Kniznice Orlického muzea, 1970.

Kollmann, I., ed. *Acta Sacræ Congregationis de Propaganda Fide res gestas Bohemicas illustrantia.* Prague: Sumptibus Comitorum Bohemiæ Deputationis—Typis Gregorianis, 1939.

Kosmova Kronika Česká. Přeložili K. Hrdina a M. Blahová. Prague: Svoboda, 1972.

Locatelli, Josephus. *Babylon Bohemiæ ab anno 1780 ad annum 1790.* Edited by A. Podlaha. Prague: Sumptibis f. metropolitani capituli Pragensis, 1905.

Meztler, J., ed. *Sacræ Congregationis de Propaganda Fide memoria rerurm.* Vol. 2, 1700–1815. Rome/Freibug/Vienna: Herder, 1973.

Pelcl, F. M. *Paměti.* Prague: Státní Nákladatelství krásné literatury, hudby a umění, 1956.

Podlaha, Antonius, ed. *Relationes super statu Ecclesiæ et archidiocesis Pragensis ad S. Congregationem Concilii ab Archiepiscopis Pragensibus factæ a. 1759–1781.* Prague: Cyrillo-Methodoejská knihtiskárna V Kotruba. Nákladem vlastním, 1908.

Pubitschka, František. *Chronologische Geschichte Böhmens unter den Slaven.* Leipzig/Prague, 1770.

The Ratio studiorum *of 1599.* Translated by Allan P. Farrell, S.J. Washington, D.C.: Conference of Major Superiors of Jesuits, 1970.

Der Schriftverkehr zwischen dem päpstlichen Staatsekretariat und dem Nuncio am Kaiserhof Antonio Eugenio Visconti 1767–1774. Vienna: Hermann Böhlaus Nachfolger, 1970.

Schulz, Václav, ed. *Korrespondence Jesuitů Provincie České z let 1584–1770 z Archivu Musea Království Českého.* Prague: Nákl. České Akademie císáře Františka Josefa pro vědy, slovesnost a umění, 1900.

Skopec, Jindřich, ed. *Paměti Františka Vaváka souseda a rychtaře Milčeckého.* 5 vols. Prague: Cyrillo-Methodějská Knihtiskárna V. KotrubaNákladem "Dědictví Sv. Nepomuckého, 1907.

Synopsis actorum S. Sedis in causis Societatis Jesu, 1605–1773. Louvain: Ex Typographis J.-B. Istas, 1895.

Šimák, J. V., ed. *Zpovední seznamy Arcidiecese Pražské z r. 1671–1725*. 3 vols. Díl 3, sv. 1: Plzensko a Loketsko. Prague: Nákladem hist. Spolku za pomoci minister. Školství a národní osvěty, zem spravního výboru, nádaní hlavková, České akademie, 1935.

Toegel, M., et al., eds. *Prameny k nevolnickému povstání v Čechách a na Moravě v roce 1775*. Prague: Academia nakladatelství Československé akademie věd, 1979.

Weizäcker, Wilhelm, ed. *Quellenbuch zur Geschichte der Sudetenländer*. Munich: Robert Lerche, 1960.

Wydra, Joannes, S.J., *Zpovední Seznamy Arcidiecese Pražské z r. 1671–1725*. Edited by J. V. Šimák. 3 vols. Díl 3, sv. 1: Plzensko a Loketsko. Prague: Nákladem hist. Spolku za pomoci minister. školství a národní osvěty, zem spravního výboru, nádaní hlavková, České Akademie, 1935.

Reference Works

Atlas zur Kirchengeschichte: Die christlichen Kirchen in Geschichte und Gegenwart. Edited by H. Jedin, K. S. Latourette, and J. Martin. Freiburg/Basel/Rome/Vienna: Herder, 1987.

Biographisches Lexikon des Kaiserthums Österreich. Edited by Constant von Würzbach. 60 vols. Vienna: Wilhelm Braumüller, 1858–60.

Biographisches Lexikon zur Geschichte der Böhmischen Länder. Edited by H. Sturm. 12 vols. Munich: Oldenbourg, 1974–.

Bibliographia dramatica et dramaticorum. Edited by Reinhart Meyer. 13 vols. Tübingen: Max Niemeyer Verlag, 1986–99.

The Book of Saints. Compiled by the Benedictine monks of Ramsgate. London: Adam and Charles Black, 1966.

Breuer, Mordechai, and Michael Granz, eds. *Tradition and Enlightenment, 1600-1780*. Translated by William Templer. Vol. 1 of *German-Jewish History in Modern Times,* edited by Michael A. Meyer. 4 vols. New York: Columbia University Press, 1996.

The Cambridge Economic History of Europe. Edited by M. Postan, C. Colman, and Peter Mathias. 8 vols. Cambridge: Cambridge University Press, 1977.

Catholicism in Early Modern History: A Guide to Research. Edited by John W. O'Malley. St. Louis: Center for Reformation Research, 1988.

Collinge, William J. *Historical Dictionary of Catholicism*. Lanham, Md.: Scarecrow Press, 1997.

Československá vlastvièda. Díl II: Dějiny svazek 1, II. Prague: Orbis, 1963.

Český slovník bohovědný. Edited by J. Trumpach and A. Podlaha. Prague: Cyrillo-Methodějská knihtiskarna a Nakladatelství, 1912–.

Dictionary of the History of Ideas. Edited by Philip Weiner. 5 vols. New York: Charles Scribner's Sons, 1973.

Dictionnaire d'histoire et géographie ecclesiastiques. Edited by A. Baudrillart. 26 vols. Paris: Libraire Letouzey et Ane, 1912–.

Dictionnaire de spiritualité. 17 vols. Paris: Beauchesne, 1937–1995.

Encyclopedia of Religion. 16 vols. New York: Macmillan, 1987.

Encyklopedia jezuicka. www.jezuici.krakow.pl

Handbuch der Geschichte der böhmischen Länder. Edited by Karl Bosl. 4 vols. Stuttgart: A. Hiesemann, 1966–.

Handwörterbuch des deutschen Aberglaubens. Edited by Hanns Bachtold-Stäubli. 10 vols. Berlin/New York: Walter de Gruyter, 1987.

The HarperCollins Encyclopedia of Catholicism. New York: Harper Collins, 1995.

Jewish Encyclopedia, The. 22 vols. New York: Funk and Wagnalls, 1907.

Koch, Ludwig. *Jesuiten-Lexikon.* Paderborn: Verlag Bonifacius Druckerei, 1934.

Lexikon der vom Jahre 1750 bis 1800 verstorbenen teutschen Schriftsteller. Edited by Johann Georg Mesuel. 15 vols. Leipzig, 1802–16.

Marienlexikon. Edited by R. Baumer and L. Scheffczek. 6 vols. St. Ottilien: Eos Verlag, 1988.

Neue deutsche Biographie. 19 vols. Berlin: Duncker und Humblot, 1953–.

The New Catholic Encyclopedia. 19 vols. New York: McGraw-Hill, 1967.

Österreichisches biographisches Lexikon. Edited by Leo Santifeller. 11 vols. Graz/Cologne: Verlag Hermann Böhlaus Nachfolger, 1954–.

Ottův slovník naučný. 28 vols. Prague: Otto, 1894.

Pastor, Ludwig Freiherr von. *History of the Popes.* 40 vols. St Louis: Herder, 1899–1953.

Reiser, H. *Der Geist des Josephinismus und sein Fortleben.* Cited in *The Church in the Age of Absolutism and Enlightenment,* vol. 6 of *History of the Church,* edited by Hubert Jedin, translated by Gunther J. Holst. London: Burns and Oates, 1981.

Sacramentum mundi: An Encyclopedia of Theology. Edited by Karl Rahner. 6 vols. New York: Herder and Herder, 1968–70.

Sommervogel, Carlos. *Bibliothèque de la Compagnie de Jésus.* 11 vols. Brussels: O. Schepens; Paris: A Picard, 1890–1932.

Secondary Works

Adámek, Karel Václav. *Listiny k dějinám lidového hnutí náboženského na českým vychodě v xviii a xix věku: Díl 1. Z lety 1750–1782.* Prague: Historický Archiv České Akademie cisaře Františka Josefa pro vědy, slovesnost, a umění, 1912.

Adel, Kurt. *Das Wiener Jesuitentheater und die europäische Barock-dramatik.* Vienna: Österreichischer Bundesverlag, 1960.

Agnew, Hugh Le Caine. *Origins of the Czech National Renaissance.* Pittsburgh: University of Pittsburgh Press, 1993.

Alden, Dauril. "Tribulations of a Special Relationship: The Society of Jesus vs. the Crown of Portugal, Sixteenth to Eighteenth Centuries." In *Render unto Caesar: The Religious Sphere in World Politics,* edited by Sabrina Petra Ramet and Donald W. Treadgold. Washington, D.C.: American University Press, 1995.

Altschuler, David, ed. *The Precious Legacy: Judaic Treasures from the Czechoslovak State Collections.* New York: Summit, 1983.

Aretin, Karl Otmar Freiherr von. *Reichsverfassung und Staatssouveränität.* 2 vols. Wiesbaden: Franz Steiner Verlag, 1967.

Arneth, Alfred, Ritter von. *Maria Theresias letzte Regierungszeit.* 10 vols. Vienna: Wilhelm Braumüller, 1863–.

———. *Geschichte Maria Theresia's.* 10 vols. Vienna: W. Braumüller, 1863–79.

Arnould, M. A.. *Les Jésuites depuis leur origine jusqu'à nos jours.* 2 vols. Paris: Duterte, 1846.

L'arte del Baroco in Boemia. Milan: Bramante, 1966.

Auty, Robert. "Language and Society in the Czech National Revival." *The Slavonic and East European Review* 35 (1956–57): 240–48.

Aveling, J. C. H. *The Jesuits.* New York: Stein and Day, 1981.

Bach, H. I. *The German Jew: A Synthesis of Judaism and Western Civilization, 1700–1930.* Oxford: Oxford University Press, 1984.

Bachman, Erich. "Plastik." In *Barock in Böhmen.*

Bachmann, Hanns. *Das Mirakelbuch des Wallfahrtskirche Mariastein in Tirol als Quelle der Kulturgeschichte (1678–1742).* Innsbruck: Wagner, 1973.

Bailey, Gauvin Alexander. " 'Le Style jésuite n'existe pas': Jesuit Corporate Culture and the Arts." In *The Jesuits: Cultures, Sciences, and the Arts (1540–1773),* edited by John W. O'Malley, Gauvin Alexander Bailey, Steven J. Harris, and T. Frank Kennedy. Toronto/Buffalo/London: University of Toronto Press, 1999.

Bangert, William. *A History of the Society of Jesus.* 2nd ed. St. Louis: The Institute of Jesuit Sources, 1986.

Barton, Peter. "Der österreichische Barockkatholicismus: eine unerreichte Blütezeit kirchlicher Leben?" In *Horizonte und Perspektiven: Festschrift für Erik Turnwald,* edited by Gerhard Messler. Heidelberg/Vienna: Johannes-Mathesius Verlag, 1979.

Bartoš, F. M., "Dobrovského *Kritische Versuche,*" *ČČNM* 103 (1929): 22–51.

Bauer, Stephen. "Shrines, Curiosities and the Rhetoric of Display." In *Visual Display: Culture beyond Appearances,* edited by Lynne Cooke and Peter Woolen. Seattle: Bay Press, 1995.

Beales, Derek. "The False Joseph II," *hj* 3 (1975): 467–95.

———. *Joseph II.* Cambridge: The University Press, 1987.

———. *Joseph II: In the Shadow of Maria Theresia.* Cambridge: The University Press, 1987.

———. "Joseph II and the Reshaping of the Austrian Church." *hj* 36 (1993): 89–114.

———. "Was Joseph II an Enlightened Despot?" In *The Austrian Enlightenment and Its Aftermath,* edited by Ritchie Robertson and Edward Timms. *Austrian Studies,* no. 2. Edinburgh: Edinburgh University Press, 1991.

———. "Joseph II and the Monasteries of Austria and Hungary." In *Religious Change in Europe, 1650–1914: Essays for John McManners,* edited by Nigel Aston. Oxford: Clarendon Press, 1997.

Bednar, F. *Toleranči patent.* Hradec Králové: Nakladatelství Nedělní Besídky, 1931.

Behrens, Betty. "Government and Society." In *The Economy and Organization of Early Modern Europe,* edited by E. E. Rich and C. H. Wilson. Vol. 5 of *The Cambridge Economic History of Europe,* edited by M. Postan, C. Coleman, and Peter Mathias. 8 vols. Cambridge: Cambridge University Press, 1977.

Bellenger, Dom Aiden. " 'Superstitious Enemies of the Flesh'? The Variety of Benedictine Responses to the Enlightenment." In *Religious Change in Europe, 1650–1914: Essays for John McManners,* edited by Nigel Aston. Oxford: Clarendon Press, 1997.

Bělohlávek, P. V. "Konvikt prazský." In *Dějiny ceských križovníků s červenou hvězdou.* Díl 1, 200; NK, 23/17. Prague: Nákladem Českých Križovníků v Praze, 1930.

Bělohlávek, P. V., and P. J. Hradec. *Dějiny českých Křižovníku s červenou hvězdou.* Prague: Nákladem řádu českých Křižovníků v Praze, 1930.

Benedikt, Heinrich. *Franz Anton Graf von Sporck.* Vienna: Manz Verlag, 1924.

Benetka, Bořivoj. *P. Stanislav Vydra: Učitel kněz a vlastinec.* Olomouc: Vítezové, 1938.

———. *Jesuité v Čechách.* Prague: Nakladatelství Vyšehrad, 1941.

Beránek, Karel. "O počátcích pražské lékařské fakulty, 1348–1622." *AUCP-HUP* 9, no. 2 (1968): 62–69.

———. "Teologická fakulta," in Čornejová, *Dějiny,* 2.

Bérenger, Jean. "The Austrian Church." In *Church and Society in Catholic Europe of the Eighteenth Century,* edited by William J. Callahan and David Higgs. Cambridge: Cambridge University Press, 1979.

———. *A History of the Habsburg Empire, 1700–1918.* Translated by C. A. Simpson. New York: Longman, 1997.

Berls, Janet Wolf. *The Elementary School Reforms of Maria Theresa and Joseph II in Bohemia.* Presented as a doctoral dissertation at Columbia University, 1970.

Bernard, Paul P. *Jesuits and Jacobins.* Urbana/London/Chicago: University of Illinois Press, 1971.

———. "Poverty and Poor Relief in the Eighteenth Century." In *State and Society in Early Modern Austria,* edited by Charles W. Ingrao. West Lafayette, Ind.: Purdue University Press, 1994.

Bílek, Tomáš. "Reformace katolická v Čechách, 1650–1781." *Časopis Musea Království českého* 55 (1881): 56–72.

———. *Dějiny konfiscaci v Čechách po r. 1618.* Prague: V Kommissi u Františka Rivnace, 1883.

———. *Reformace katolická neboli obnovení náboženství katolického v království českém po bitvě bělohorské.* Prague: Bačkovský 1892.

———. *Statky a jměni koljei jesuitsých, klášterů, kostelů braterstev, a jiných ústavův království českém od císare Josefa zrušených.* Prague: Academia, 1970.

Bilý, Jirí. *Jezuita Antonín Koniáš: Osobnost a doba.* Prague: Vyšehrad, 1996.

Binder, Ludwig, "Die evangelische Kirche in Siebenbürgen zur Zeit der Reformen Joseph II. mit besonderer Berücksichtigung des Toleranzpatents." In *Im Lichte der Toleranz: Aufsätze zur Toleranzgesetzgebung des 18. Jahrhunderts in den Reichen Joseph II., ihren Voraussetzungen und ihre Folgen. Studien und Texte zur Kirchengeschichte und Geschichte,* edited by Peter Barton. Band IX. Vienna: Institut für protestantische Kirchengeschichte, 1981.

Bireley, Robert. *The Refashioning of Catholicism, 1450–1700.* Basingstoke: Macmillan, 1999.

Blažíček, Oldrich J., *Pražská sbírka universitních thesí.* Prague: Zvlaštní otisk z Hollar sborníku grafického umení, 1940.

———. *Rokoko a konec Baroku v Čechách.* Prague: Matice Česká-Orbis, 1948.

———. *Iskusstvo cheskogo barokko.* Leingrad: Ministersvo Kulturi SSSR, 1974.

Bloc, Marc. *Les Rois thaumaturgiques: Étude sur le caractère surnaturel attributé á la puissance royale particulièrement en France et en Angleterre.* Paris: Gallimard, 1983.

Bloom, Allan. *The Closing of the American Mind.* New York: Simon and Schuster, 1987.

Blum, Jerome. *The End of the Old Order in Rural Europe.* Princeton: Princeton University Press, 1978.

Blunt, Anthony. *Artistic Theory in Italy.* Oxford: Clarendon Press, 1962.

Bodi, Leslie. *Tauwetter in Wien.* Frankfurt a/M: Fischer, 1995.

Bolzano, Bernard. *Wissenschaftslehre.* Sulzbach, 1831.

Borovy, Klement. *Antonín Brus z Mohelnice, Arcibiskup Pražský.* Prague: Kn. Arcib. Knihtiskárny, 1873.

Brandes, Stanley. "Conclusion: Reflections on the Study of Religious Orthodoxy and Popular Faith in Europe." In *Religious Orthodoxy and Popular Faith in European Society,* edited by Ellen Badine. Princeton: Princeton University Press, 1990.

Brechka, Frank T. *Gerhard van Swieten and His World, 1700–1772.* The Hague: Martinus Nijhoff, 1970.

Briggs, Martin. "Introduction." In Plicka, *City of Baroque and Gothic.*

Brodrick, James. *The Progress of the Jesuits (1555–79).* Chicago: Loyola University Press, 1986.

Brückner, Wolfgang. "Zur Phänomenologie und Nomenklatur des Wallfahrtswesen und seiener Erforscher." In *Volkskultur und Geschichte: Festgabe für Josef Dünniger,* edited by Dieter Harmening. Berlin: E. Schmidt, 1970.

Bruford, W. H. *Germany in the Eighteenth Century: The Social Background of the Literary Revival.* Cambirdge: At the University Press, 1959.

Brzonowski, Mieczysław. "Il mundo della predicazione politica in Europa centro-occidentale dal XVI al XX secolo." In *The Common Christian Roots of the European Nations.* An International Colloquium at the Vatican. Florence: Le Monnier, 1982.

Burian, Jan, Dalibor Kusák, Vladimir Hyhúk, and Miroslav Krob. *Baroko v Čechách a na Moravě.* Prague: Poligraphia, 1993.

Burke, Marcus B. *Jesuit Art and Iconography, 1550–1800: Introductory Essay and Exhibition Catalogue.* Jersey City: St. Peter's College, 1993.

Burke, Peter. "How to Be a Counter-Reformation Saint." In *Religion and Society in Early Modern Europe, 1500–1800,* edited by Kaspar von Greyerz. London: George Allen and Unwin, 1984.

Burns, John V. *Dynamism in the Cosomology of Christian Wolff.* New York: Exposition Press, 1966.

Caballero, Raimundo Diosdado. *Bibliotheca scriptorum Societatis Jesu: Supplementum primum.* Rome, 1814.

Cerný, Václav, ed. *Kéž hori popel můj: Z poesie evropského baroka.* Prague: Mladá Fronta, 1967.

Chadwick, Owen. *The Popes and the European Revolution.* Oxford: Clarendon Press, 1981.

Châtellier, Louis. *The Europe of the Devout: The Catholic Reformation and the Formation of a New Society.* Translated by Jean Birell. Cambridge: Cambridge University Press, 1987.

———. *The Religion of the Poor: Rural Missions in Europe and the Foundation of Modern Catholicism.* Translated by Brian Pearce. Cambridge: Cambridge University Press, 1997.

Clark, Kenneth. *Civilization.* New York: Harper and Row, 1969.

Clebach, William A. *Christianity in European History.* New York: Oxford University Press, 1979.

Cooke, Lynne, and Peter Woolen, eds. *Visual Display: The Culture of Appearances.* Seattle: Bay Press, 1995.

Coreth, Anna. *Österreichische Geschichtsschreibung in der Barockzeit.* Vienna: A Holzhausens, 1950.

———. *Pietas Austriaca.* Munich: Oldenbourg, 1959.

———. "Priesterlicher Wirken im barocken Wien: P. Antonius Khabes 1687–1771." *AHSI* 121 (1992): 71–89.

Cragg, G. R. *The Church and the Age of Reason, 1648–1789.* Harmmonsworth: Penguin, 1960.

Crétineau-Joly, J. *Histoire religieuse, politique et littéraire de la Compagnie de Jésus.* 6 vols. Paris: P. Mellier, 1845–46.

———. *Clement XIV et les Jésuites, ou histoire de la destruction des Jésuites.* 6 vols. Paris: Mellier Frères, 1848.

Croxton, Derek. *Peacemaking in Early Modern Europe: Cardinal Mazarin and the Peace of Westphalia, 1643–1648.* Selinsgrove: Susquehanna University Press, 1999.

Cubitt, Geoffrey. *The Jesuit Myth: Conspiracy Theory and Politics in Nineteenth Century France.* Oxford: Clarendon Press, 1993.

Černý, Václav, ed. *Kéž hoři popel můj: Z poesie evropského baroka.* Prague: Mladá Fronta, 1967.

Čornejová, I., ed. *Dějiny Univerzity Karlovy 2.* Prague: Univerzita Karlova, 1994.

———. *Tovaryšstvo Ježíšovo: Jezuité v Čechách.* Prague: Mladá Fronta, 1995.

———. "Správní a institutionální vývoj pražské univerzity." In *Dějiny Univerzity Karlovy,* vol. 2, edited by I. Čornejnová. 3 vols. Prague: Univerzita Karlova, 1995–98.

Čornejová, I., and A. Fechtnerová. *Životopisný slovník pražské univerzity: Filosofická a teologická fakulta 1654–1773.* Prague: Univerzita Karlova, 1986.

Danielou, Jean, and Herbert Forgrimler, eds. *Sentire cum ecclesia: Das Bewusstsein von der Kirche als gestaltende Kraft der Frömmigkeit.* Freiburg: Herder, 1961.

Daniel-Rops, Henri. *The Church in the Eighteenth Century.* Translated by John Warrington. London: J. B. Dent, 1964.

Darlap, Adolf. "Demons." In the article "Devil," *Sacramentum Mundi: An Encyclopedia of Theology,* ed. Karl Rahner, 6 vols., vol. 2. New York: Herder and Herder, 1968–70.

Daum, Hermann. *Die Verfolgerungen der Evangelisten in Böhmen.* Darmstadt: Eduard Zernin, 1860.

Davis, Natalie. "From 'Popular Religions' to Religious Cultures." In *Reformation Europe: A Guide to Research,* edited by Steven Ozment. St. Louis: Center for Reformation Research, 1982.

dell'Orto, Umberto. *La nunziatura a Vienna di Giuseppi Garampi, 1776–1785.* Vatican City: Archivio Vaticano, 1995.

Delooz, Pierre. "Towards a Sociological Study of Canonized Sainthood in the Catholic Church." Translated by Jane Hodgkin. In *Saints and Their Cults: Studies in Religious Sociology, Folklore, and History,* edited by Stephen Wilson. Cambridge: Cambridge University Press, 1983.

Delumeau, Jean. *Sin and Fear.* Translated by Eric Nicholson. New York: St. Martin's Press, 1990.

Denis, Ernest. *La Bohême depuis la Montagne-Blanche.* 2 vols. Paris: Ernest Leroux, 1903.

Dickson, P. G. M. *Finance and Government under Maria Theresia, 1740–1780.* 2 vols. Oxford: Clarendon Press, 1987.

Dillon, Kenneth J. *King and Estates in the Bohemian Lands, 1526–1564.* Brussels: Les Éditions de la Librairie Encyclopédique, 1976.

Dimler, Richard. "The Bee-Topos in the Jesuit Emblem Book." In *The Emblem in Renaissance and Baroque Europe: Selected Papers of the Glasgow International Emblem Conference, 13–17 August, 1990,* edited by Alison Adams and Anthony Harper. Leiden/New York/London: E. J. Brill, 1992.

Dlabacz, Gottfried Johann. *Allgemeines Künstler-Lexikon für Böhmen.* Prague, 1815.

Donnelly, John Patrick, S.J. "Religious Orders of Men, Especially the Society of Jesus." In *Catholicism in Early Modern History: A Guide to Research,* edited by John W. O'Malley, S.J. St. Louis: Center for Reformation Research, 1988.

Dömötör, Tekla. *Hungarian Folk Beliefs.* Bloomington: Indiana University Press, 1982.

Donat, Heinrich, ed. *Die deutschen Katholiken in der Tschechoslowakischen Republik.* Warnsdorf: Optiz, 1934.

———. "Die Marianischen Congregationen." In *Die deutschen Katholiken in der Tschechoslowakischen Republik,* edited by Heinrich Donat. Warnsdorf: Opitz, 1934.

Donohue, John W. *Jesuit Education: An Essay on the Foundations of an Idea.* New York: Fordham University Press, 1963.

Doueihi, Mihad. *A Perverse History of the Human Heart.* Cambridge: Mass.: Harvard University Press, 1997.

Doyle, William. *The Old European Order, 1600–1800.* Oxford: Oxford University Press, 1978.

The Drawings of Ignacio Tirsch, a Jesuit Missionary in Baja California. Narrative by Doyce B. Nunis, Jr., translated by Elsbeth Schulz-Bischoff. Los Angeles: Dawson's Bookshop, 1972.

Drozd, Kurt Wofgang. *Schul- und Ordenstheater am Collegium S. J. Klagenfurt (1604–1773).* Klagenfurt: Landesmuseum für Kärnten, 1965.

Ducreux, M.-E. "Kniha a kacírsvtí, zpusob cetby a knizní politika v Cechách doby baroka." *Literarní archiv* PNP 27 (1994): 61–89.

———. "Reading unto Death: Books and Readers in Eighteenth-Century Bohemia." In *The Culture of Print: Power and the Uses of Print in Early Modern Europe,* translated by Lydia G Cochrane, edited by Roger Chartier. Princeton: Princeton University Press, 1987.

———. "La 'Question tcheque' exorcisée?" In *Les Religions de l'est,* edited by Patrick Michel. Paris: Les éditions du Cerf, 1992.

Duhr, B. *Jesuiten-Fabeln: Ein Beitrage zur Culturgeschichte.* Freiburg im Breisgau, Herder'sche Verlagshandlung, 1899.

———. *Geschichte der Jesuiten in den Ländern der deutschen Zunge in der ersten Hälfte des XVII. Jahrhunderts.* Freiburg/Regensburg: Herder, 1913.

Dülmen, Richard van. *Der Geheimbund der Illuminaten: Darstellung, Analyse, Dokumentation.* Stuttgart/Bad Canstadt: Frommann-Holzboog, 1975.

Eco, Umberto. *Semiotics and the Philosophy of Language.* London: Macmillan, 1984.

Egglmaier, Herbert. "Am Beispiel Österreich: Die Wissenschaftspolitik eines aufgeklärt-absolutischen Staates." *Mitteilungen der österreischischen Gesellschaft für Wissenschaftsgeschichte* 15 (1995): 101–26.

Elias, Norbert. *The Court Society.* Translated by Edmund Jephcott. New York: Pantheon, 1983.

Fahler, Eberhard, ed. *Emblem und Emblematikrezeption: Vergleichende Studien zur Wirkungsgeschichte vom 16. Bis 20. Jahrhundert.* Darmstadt: Wissenschaftliche Buchgwscellschaft, 1978.

Emerson, Ralph Waldo. *Letters and Social Aims.* Boston/New York: Houghton Mifflin, 1905.

Engel, Johann Christian von. *Geschichte des Ungrischen Reichs.* 5 vols. Vienna: In der Camesinaschen Buchhndlung, 1814.

Engelbrecht, Helmut. *Geschichte des österreichischen Bildungswesens: Erziehung und Unterricht auf dem Boden Österreichs.* 5 vols. Vienna: Österreichischer Bunderverlag, ca. 1982–ca. 1988.

Erben, Karl Jaromir. *Die Primatoren der Königlichen Altstadt Prag.* Prague: Gottlieb Haase Söhne, 1858.

Erman, Wilhelm, and Ewald Horn. *Bibliographie der deutschen Universitäten.* 3 vols. Leipzig/Berlin: Teubner, 1904–5.

Evans, R. J. W. *The Making of the Habsburg Monarchy, 1550–1700.* Oxford: Clarendon Press, 1979.

———. "Comment," AHY 30 (1999): 229–33.

———. "German Universities after the Thirty Years' War." In *Continuity and Change.* Vol. 1 of *History of Universities.* Amersham: Avebury, 1981.

———. "Introduction." In *State and Society in Early Modern Austria,* edited by W. Ingrao. West Lafayette, Ind.: Purdue University Press, 1994.

Eyck, Frank. *Religion and Politics in German History.* New York: St. Martin's 1998.

Faber du Faur, Curt von. *German Baroque Literature.* New Haven: Yale University Press, 1958.

Fallon, Daniel. *The German University: A Heroic Ideal in Conflict with the Modern World.* Boulder: Colorado Associated University Press, 1980.

Farrell, A. P. *The Jesuit Code of Liberal Education.* Milwaukee: Bruce, 1956.

Fechnerová, Anna. "Klementinští kniovnici." *Miscellanea oddělaní rukopisů* 2 (1985): 86–144.

———. "Klemintinští knihovnici od roku 1609 do roku 1773." *Miscellanea oddelení rukopisu a vznacných tisku* 2 (1985): 88.

———. *Rectores collegiorum Societatis Iesu in Bohemia, Moravia, ac Silesia usque ad annum MDCCLXXIII iacentum.* 2 vols. Prague: Národní Knihovna, 1993.

Fehr, Götz. "Höhepunkte der Kunst im Kernland Europas." In *Tausend Jahre Bistum Prag (973–1973).* Munich: Ackermann Gemeinde, 1974.

Fischer, Karl Adolf Franz. "Jesuiten-Mathematiker in der deutschen Assistenz bis 1773." *AHSI* 47 (1978): 159–224.

Florovský, Antonín Vasilejvic. *Čestí Jesuité v Rusí.* Prague: Nakladatelství Vyšehrad, 1944.

Fojtík, Karel, and Oldrich Sirovátka. "Czech Ethology and Folklore: A Short Outline of Their Development." In *Man and Culture II.* Contributions of the Czechoslovak Ethnologists for the VIII International Congress of Ethnologists in Tokyo 1968. Prague: 1968.

Foucault, Michel. *Religion and Culture.* Edited by Jeremy R. Carrette. Manchester: Manchester University Press, 1999.

Fouchier-Magnan, Adrien. *The Small German Courts in the Eighteenth Century.* Translated by Mervyn Savil. London: Methuen, 1958.

Franzel, Emil. *Der Donauraum im Zeitalter des Nationalitätenprinzips.* Bern: Dalp-Taschenbücher, 1958.

Frazer, James George. *The Golden Bough: A Study in Magic and Religion.* One-vol. abridged ed. New York: Macmillan, 1922.

Freist, Dagmar. "Religious Difference and the Experience of Widowhood in Seventeenth- and Eighteenth-Century Germany." In *Widowhood in Medieval and Early Modern Europe,* edited by Sandra Cavallo and Lyndan Warner. Harlow: Longman, 1999.

Freudenberger, Hermann. "The Industrialization of Bohemia and Moravia in the Eighteenth Century." *Journal of Central European Affairs* 4 (1960): 347–56.

Friedirchs, Elisabeth. *Literarische Lokalgrößen 1700–1900: Verzeichnis der in regionalen Lexika und Sammelwerken aufgeführten Schriftsteller.* Stuttgart: J. B. Metzler'sche Verlagsbuchhandlung, 1967.

Friedrichs, Margret. "Anfänge eines staatlich geförderten Schulwesen." *Das achtzehnte Jahrhundert und Österreich* 10 (1995): 38.

Frijhoff, Willem. "What Is an Early Modern University? The Conflict between Leiden and Amsterdam in 1631." In *European Universities in the Age of Reformation and Counter-Reformation,* edited by Helga Robinson-Hammerstein. Dublin: Four Courts Press, 1998.

Frisz, Joseph, and Louis Leger. *La Bohême historique pittoresque et litéraire.* Paris: Libraire Internationale, 1867.

Fulbrook, Mary. *Piety and Politics: Religion and the Rise of Absolutism in England, Württemburg, and Prussia.* Cambridge: Cambridge University Press, 1983.

Gabriel, Astrik. *Garlandia: Studies in the History of the Mediaeval University.* Notre Dame, Ind.: The Mediaeval Institute at the University of Notre Dame, 1969.

Gams, Pius Bonifacius. *Series episcoporum Ecclesiæ Catholicæ.* Graz: Akademische Druck- und Verlaganstalt, 1957.

Gates-Coon, Rebecca. *The Landed Estates of the Esterhazy Princes: Hungary during the Reforms of Maria Theresia and Joseph II.* Baltimore: Johns Hopkins University Press, 1994.

Gay, Peter. *The Enlightenment: An Interpretation.* 2 vols. New York: Alfred Knopf, 1969.

Geremek, Bronislaw. *Poverty: A History.* Oxford: Blackwell, 1994.

Gindely, Antonín. *Geschichte der Gegenreformation in Böhmen.* Leipzig: Duncker und Humblot, 1894.

Ginzburg, Carlo. *The Cheese and the Worms.* Translated by Jon and Anne Tedeschi. Baltimore: Johns Hopkins University Press, 1980.

Goedeke, Karl. *Grundriß der deutschen Dichtung aus den Quellen.* 18 vols. Nedeln, Liechtenstein: Kraus Reprint, 1975.

Goldsmith, Jan ten Brink, J. Patrice Marandel, J. Patrick Donnelly, and J. B. Harley. *Jesuit Art in North American Collections.* Milwaukee: Patrick and Beatrice Haggerty Museum of Art, 1991.

Goodwin, Mary Clare. *The Papal Conflict with Josephinism.* New York: Fordham University Press, 1938.

Grimm, Gerald. *Die Schulreform Maria Theresia's, 1747–1775.* Frankfurt a/M: Peter Lang, 1987.

Grodziski, Stanislaw. "Les Réformes de Marie-Thérèse et de Joseph II en Galicie de 1772 à 1790." In *Unité et diversité de l'Empire Habsbourg à la fin du xviiie siècle,* edited by R. Mortier and Hevré Hasquin. Édition de L'Université de Bruxelles, no. 15 (1988).

Grohmann, Josef Virgil. *Sagen aus Böhmen.* Prague: Verlag der J. G. Calve'schen k. k. Universitäts-Buchhandlung, 1863.

Grulich, Rudolph. "Der Beitrag der böhmischen Länder zur Weltmission des 17. und 18. Jahrhunderts." *AfKvB-M-S* 5 (1978): 375–91.

"Grundungspriveleg Ferdinands I. für das Jesuitenkolleg bei St. Klemens zu Prag 1562." In *Quellenbuch zur Geschichte der Sudentenländer,* edited by Wilhelm Weizäcker. Munich: Robert Lerche, 1960.

Gutkas, Karl, ed. *Österreich zur Zeit Josefs II.* Vienna: Niederösterreichische Landesaussstellung, 1980.

Haas, Robert. *Die Geistliche Haltung der katholische Universitäten Deutschlands im 18. Jahrhunderts.* Freiburg: Herder, 1952.

Habermas, Rebekka. *Wallfahrt und Aufruhr: Zur Gechichte des Wunderglaubens in der früheren Neuzeit.* Frankfurt/New York: Campus, 1991.

Haberzettl, Hermann. *Die Stellung der Exjesuiten in Politik und Kulturleben Österreichs zu Ende des 18. Jahrhunderts.* Dissertation presented at the University of Vienna. Vienna: Verband der wissenschaftlichen Gesellschaften Österreichs, 1973.

Hallwich, Hermann. "Die Jesuitenresidenz Mariascheune." *Mittheilungen des Vereins für das Geschichte der Deutschen in Böhmen* 6 (1868): 89.

Hammerstein, Notker. *Aufklärung und katholisches Reich: Untersuchungen zur Universitätsgeschichte und Politik katholischer Territorien des Heiligen Römischen Reichs deutscher Nation im 18. Jahrhundert.* Berlin: Duncker und Humblot, 1977.

Hamperl, Wolf-Dieter, and P. Aquilas Rohner. *Böhmisch-oberpfälzishe Akanthusaltäre.* Munich/Zürich: Schnell & Steiner, 1984.

Hanák, Peter. "The Alienation of Death in Budapest and Vienna at the Turn of the Century." In *The Mirror of History: Essay in Honor of Fritz Fellner,* edited by S. Wank et al. Santa Barbara/Oxford: ABC-Clio, 1988.

Hanáková, Markéta. "Otázky kolem život a smrti českého misionáře Ignáce Xavera Kellera." *Český lid* 82 (1995): 293–306.

Hantsch, Hugo. "Die Aufklärung in Böhmen." In *Tausend Jahre Bistum Prag (973–1973).* Munich: Ackermann Gemeinde, 1974.

Hanus, Franciscus. *Church and State under Frederick II, 1740–1786*. Texts, Documents, and Studies in Medieval and Modern Church History. Washington, D.C., 1944.

Hanuš, Josef. "Počátky Král. české společnost nauk." *ČČH* 14 (1908): 141–52.

Hanzel, Josef. "Studium zemedelství na pražské university (1775-1844)." *AUCP-HUC* 4 (1963): 144.

———. "Nižší školství." In Petráň, *Počátky*.

Harkins, William E. "The Periodization of Czech Literary History, 1774-1879." In *The Czech Literary Renaissance*, edited by Peter Brock and H. Gordon Skilling. Toronto: University of Toronto Press, 1970.

Hanuš, Josef. "Bohuslava Balbína *Bohemia Docta*." *Český Časopis Historický* 12 (1906).

———. "Mikuláš Adakt Voigt, Český buditel a historík." *Rozpravy české Akademie cisáře Františka Josefa pro vědy, slovenost a umění* 3, 32 (1910): 84 f.

Haubelt, Josef. "Seminarium publicum a Gelasius Dobner." *ČČH* 27 (1979): 76–112.

———. "Osvicenská věda—Profil." In Petráň, *Počátky*.

Hausberger, Bernd. *Jesuiten aus Mitteleuropa in Koloniaalem Mexiko: Eine Bio-Bibliographie*. Vienna: Verlag für Geschichte und Politik; München: Oldenbourg, 1995.

Havránek, Jan, Josef Petráň, and Anna Skybová. *Universitas Carolina*. Prague Univerzita Karlova, 1986.

Hawlik-van de Water, Magdalena. *Der schöne Tod: Zeremonialstrukturen des Wiener Hofes bis Tod und Begräbnis zwischen 1640 und 1740*. Vienna: Herder, 1989.

Häusler, Wolfgang. "Das östereichische Judentum im Zeitalter des josefinischen Toleranz." In *Österreich zur Zeit Josefs II*, edited by Karl Gutkas. Vienna: Amt der Niederösterreichischen Landesregierung, 1980.

Heimbucher, Max Josef. *Die Orden und Congregationen der katholischen Kirche*. Paderborn: Druck und Verlag von Ferdinand Schönigh, 1908.

Hellyer, Marcus. "Jesuit Physics in Eighteenth-Century Germany: Some Important Continuities." In *The Jesuits: Cultures, Sciences and the Arts, 1540–1773*, edited by John W. O'Malley, Gauvin Alexander Bailey, Steven J. Harris, and T. Frank Kennedy. Toronto/Buffalo/London: University of Toronto Press, 1999.

Hemmerle, Josef. "Die prager Universität in der neuen Zeit." In *Bohemia sacra: Das Christentum in Böhmen, 973–1973*, edited by F. Seibt. Düsseldorf: Schwann, 1974.

Hengst, Karl. *Jesuiten an Universitäten und Jesuitenuniversitäten*. Paderborn: Ferdinand Schöningh, 1981.

Henkel, Arthur, and Albrecht Schöne, eds. *Emblemata zur Sinnbildkeit des XVI. und XVII. Jahrhunderts*. 2 vols. Stuttgart: J. B. Metzler, 1967–76.

Heřman, Jan. "Jewish Community Archives from Bohemia and Moravia." *Judaica Bohemica* 7, no. 1 (1971): 4.

Herr, Alfred. "Zur Geschichte des Egerer Gymnasiums." *MVfGDB* 74 (1936): 95–104, 121–57.

Hersche, Peter. *Der Spätjansenismus in Österreich*. Vienna: Verlag der Österreichsichen Akademie der Wissenschaften, 1977.

Hertz, Deborah. "Seductive Conversion in Berlin, 1770–1809." In *Jewish Apostasy*, edited by Todd Endelbaum. New York/London: Holmes and Meier, 1987.

Hertzberg, Arthur. *The French Enlightenment and the Jews*. New York/London: Columbia University Press, 1968.

Herzogenberg, Johanna von. "Heiligtümer, Heiltümer, und Schätze." In *Bohemia sacra: Das Christentum in Böhmen (973–1973)*, edited by F. Seibt. Düsseldorf: Schwann, 1974.

Hets, Aurelian, J. *A jezuiták iskolái Magyarországon a 18. század közepen.* Pannonhalma: Pray Rent, 1938.

Hitchins, Keith. "Religion and Rumanian National Consciousness in Eighteenth Century Transylvania." *SEER* 57 (1979): 214–39.

Hlavacková, Ludmila. "Chudisnká peče a zdravnoství." In *Počátky Českého Národního Obrození,* edited by Josef Petráň. Prague: Academia, 1990.

Hlavacková, Ludmila, and Petr Svobodný, *Dějiny pražských lékařských fakult.* Prague: Univerzita Karlova, 1993.

Hoensbach, Paul von. *Die Jesuitenorden.* 2 vols. Berlin/Leipzig: Paul Haupt, 1926.

Hofer, Philip. *Baroque Book Illustration.* Cambridge, Mass.: Harvard University Press, 1951.

Holas, František Xav. *Dějiny poutního místa marianského Svaté Hory u Příbamě.* U Příbamě: Nakladem Matice Svatohorské, 1929.

Hollis, Christopher. *A History of the Jesuits.* London: Weidenfeld and Nicolson, 1968.

Hollister, C. Warren. *Medieval Europe: A Short History.* 7th ed. New York: McGraw-Hill, 1994.

Hoos, Eva. "At the Crossroads of Ancient and Modern: Reform Projects in Hungary at the End of the 18th Century." Discussion paper no. 36; November 1996, Collegium Budapest/Institute for Advanced Study.

Hojda, Zdeněk, and Ivana Čornejová, "Pražska univerzita a vzdělanost v Českých zemích v 17. a 18. století." In *Dějiny Univerzity Karlovy,* vol. 2, edited by I. Čornejová. 3 vols., Prague: Univerzita Karlova, 1995–98.

Hosp, Eduard. *Zwischen Aufklärung und katholischer Reform.* Vienna: Jakob Frint, 1962.

Hörger, Hermann. "Organizational Forms of Popular Piety in Old Rural Bavaria." In *Religion and Society in Early Modern Europe, 1500–1800,* edited by Kaspar von Greyerz. London: Allene and Unwin, 1984.

Huber, Kurt A. "Der Sudetendeutsche Katholizismus." *AfKB-M-S,* 1 (1967): 45.

———. "Italienische Kultmotive im Barock der böhmischen Länder." *AfKB-M-S* 6 (1982): 103–31.

Hurter, H., S.J. *Nomenclator literarius recentioris theologicæ Catholicæ,* vol. 3. 4 vols. Innsbruck, 1895.

Impey, Oliver, and Arthur Macgregor. *The Origins of Museums: The Cabinet of Curiosities in Sixteenth- and Seventeenth-Century Europe.* Oxford: Clarendon Press, 1985.

Ingrao, Charles W. *The Habsburg Monarchy, 1618–1815.* Oxford: The Clarendon Press, 1994.

Jahreiß, Astrid. *Grammatiken und Orthographielehren aus dem Jesuitenorden: Eine Untersuchung zur Normierung der deutschen Schriftsprache in Unterreichtswerken des 18. Jahrhunderts.* Heidelberg: Carl Winter/Universitätsverlag, 1990.

Janácek, Josef. *Malé dějiny Prahy.* Prague: Panorama, 1983.

———, ed. *Dějiny Prahy.* Prague: Nakladatelství politické literatury, 1961.

Jedin, Hubert, ed. *The Church in the Age of Absolutism and Enlightenment.* Vol. 6 of *History of the Church,* translated by Gunther J. Holst. London: Burns and Oates, 1981.

Jestrábský, Valentin Bernard. In *Dissenting View of a Simple Peasant,* by id. 1710.

Die Jesuiten in Bayern 1549–1773: Ausstellung des bayrischen Hauptstadtsarchivs und der Oberdeutschen Provinz der Gesellschaft Jesu. Weissenhorn: Anton H. Konrad Verlag, 1991.

John, Alois. *Sitten und Brauch im deutschen Westböhmen.* Prague: G. G. Calve'sche K. k. Hof- u.Universitäts Buchhandlung, 1905.

John, Karl. *Institutiones philosophicæ activæ.* Prager gelehrte Nachrichten.

J. Hanuš, "Počátky král. České společnosti nauk." *ČČH* 14 (1908): 152.

Johnson, Trevor. "Blood, Tears and Xavier-Water: Jesuit Missionaries and Popular Religion in the Eighteenth Century Upper Palatinate." In *Popular Religion in Germany and Central Europe, 1400–1800,* edited by Bob Scribner and Trevor Johnson. Basingstoke: Macmillan, 1996.

Jungmann, Josef. *Historie literatury ceské.* Prague: W Komissi Kněhupectwí F. Řiwnace, 1849.

Jutte, Robert. *Poverty and Deviance in Early Modern Europe.* Cambridge: Cambridge University Press, 1994.

Kann, Robert. *A Study in Austrian Intellectual History: Late Baroque to Romanticism.* New York: Praeger, 1960.

———."Aristocracy in the Eighteenth-Century Habsburg Empire." *East European Quarterly* 7, no. 1 (1973): 12.

———. *A History of the Hapsburg Empire.* Berkeley/Los Angeles/London: University of California Press, 1974.

Kantor, Marvin, ed. *Vorlesungen über die Geschichte der Mathematik.* 4 vols. Leipzig: Teubner, 1900–1908.

———, ed. *The Origins of Christianity in Bohemia: Sources and Commentary.* Evanston, Ill.: Northwestern University Press, 1990.

Kapner, G. *Barocker Heiligenkult in Wien und seine Träger.* Munich: Oldenbourg, 1978.

Kapossy, Johann. "Stellung des ungarländischen Barock in der europäischen Kunstentwicklung." *Ungarische Jahrbücher* 11 (1951): 38–55.

Katz, Wilhelm, S.J. "Exjesuiten als Bischöfe." *AHSI* 6 (1937): 200.

Kaufmann, Thomas Da Costa. *Court, Cloister and City: The Art and Culture of Central Europe, 1450–1800.* Chicago: University of Chicago Press, 1995.

———. "Jesuit Art: Central Europe and the Americas." In *The Jesuits: Cultures, Sciences and the Arts (1540–1773),* edited by John W. O'Malley, Gauvin Alexander Bailey, Steven J. Harris, and T. Frank Kennedy. Toronto/Buffalo/London: The University of Toronto Press, 1999.

Kavka, F., J. Polišenský, and F. Kutnar. *Přehled dějin Československa v epoše feudalismu III.* Prague: Státní pedagogické nakladatelství, 1963.

Kazbunda, K., "Dvě kapitoly z dějin 'stolice dějin' na pražské universitě." In *Od pravěku k dnešku: Sborník prací z dějin československých.* Prague: Historický Klub, 1930.

Kern, Edmund M. "An End to the Witch Trials: Reconsidering the Enlightened State." *AHY* 30 (1999): 159–95.

Kerner, Robert. *Bohemia in the Eighteenth Century: A Study in Political, Economic, and Social History with Special Reference to the Reign of Leopold II, 1790–1792.* New York: Macmillan, 1932.

Kieval, Hillel J. "Autonomy and Independence: The Historical Legacy of Czech Jewry." In *The Precious Legacy: Treasures from the Czechoslovak State Collections,* edited by David Altshuler. New York: Summit Books, 1983.

Kink, R. *Geschichte der kaiserlicher Universität zu Wien.* 2 vols. Vienna: Carl Gergold und Sohn, 1854.

Kisbán Emil. *Hell Miksa: A magyar czillagász.* Publicationes ad Historiam S. J. in Hungaria Illustrandam. Budapest, 1942.

Kisch, Egon Erwin. *Prager Pitaval.* Berlin: Erich Reiss, 1931.

Kisch, Guido. *Die Prager Universität und die Juden.* Amsterdam: B. Grüner, 1969.

Klabouch, Jiří. "K počátkum protischolastických proudů pražské university v 18. století." *AUCP—HUC* 2 (1958): 96.

Klaniczay, Gábor. *The Uses of Supernatural Power: The Transformation of Popular Religion in Medieval and Early Modern Europe.* Translated by Susan Singermann, edited by Karen Margolis. Oxford: Polity/Blackwell, 1990.

Klima, Arnošt. *Čechy v období temna.* Prague: Státní pedagogické nakladadelství, 1961.

Kloczowski, Jerzy. "Les Slaves dans la chrétienté aux XIV et XVI siècles." In *The Common Christian Roots of the European Nations.* General Sessions. Florence: Le Monnier, 1982.

Knihopis československých tisků od doby nejstarší az do konce xviii. století. Díl: Tisky z let 1501–1800. Prague: V Komisi Knihupectví F.Topice, 1967.

Kočí, Josef. *Naše národní obrození.* Prague: Státní nakladatelesví politické literatury, 1960.

———. "Protest proti Koniášovou *Klící* v předvečer Tolerančního Patentu." *Pražský sborník historický* 8 (1967–68): 113–29.

———. *Čarodějnické procesy.* Prague: Horizont, 1973.

———. *Česká národní obrození.* Prague: Nakladatelství Svoboda, 1978.

Kollmann, Josef. "Praha v polovině 18. století očima italských cestovatelů." *Pražský Sborník Historický (PSH)* 16 (1983): 119–30.

Kontler, László. *Millennium in Central Europe: A History of Hungary.* Budapest, Atlantasz, 1999.

Kop, František, Václav Bertuňek, and Antonín Novotný. *Praha: Šest let církevní metropol.* Prague: Českomoravské akciové tiskarské a vytavateské podnik v Praze, 1944.

Kosáry, Dominic (Domonkos). "Gabriel Bethlen: Transylvania in the xviith Century." *The Slavonic and East European Review* 17 (1938–39): 162–72.

———. "L'Éducation en Europe Centrale et Orientale a l'âge des Lumières." In *Les Lumières en Hongrie, en Europe Centrale et en Europe Orientale.* Budapest: Akadémia Kiadó, 1984.

Kozak, Bohumir. *Hradčany a Malá Strana.* Prague: Orbis, 1964.

Krejcová, Danuše. "Poznámka k jazykové hranici na mapách v tomto díle." In Petráň, *Počátky.*

Kriss-Rettenbeck, Lenz. *Das Votivbild.* Munich: Verlag Herrman Rinn, 1958.

Kroess, Alois. *Geschichte der Böhmischen Provinz der Gesellschaft Jesu.* 2 vols. Vienna: Ambr. Opitz, etc., 1938.

Kraus, Arnošt. *Pražské časopisy, 1770-1774.* Prague: České akademie cisáře Františka Josefa pro vědy, slovesnost, a umění, 1909.

Kuchařová, Hedvika, "Slavností disputace a grafické listy tezí v arcipiskupském semináři v Praze." *bs* 2 (1996): 137–43.

Kučera, Karel. "K akademickým volbám na pražské universitě v 17. a 18. století." *Acta Universitatis Carolinæ- Philosophica et Historica II Vojtiskuv sborník* (1959).

Kutnár, František. "Život a dílo Ignace Cornovy." *ČČH* 36 (1930): 327-50, 491-519.

Lackner, Franz. *Die Jesuitenprofessoren an der philosophischen Fakultät der wiener Universität (1712–1773).* Dissertation presented at the University of Vienna. Vienna: Verband der wissenschaftlichen Gesellschaften Österreichs, 1976.

Laqueur, Thomas. *Making Sex.* Cambridge, Mass./London: Harvard University Press, 1990.

Lea, Henry Charles. *Materials towards a History of Witchcraft.* Edited by Arthur C. Howland. 3 vols. Philadelphia: University of Pennsylvania Press, 1939.

Lecler, Joseph. "Die Kirchenfrömmigkeit des heiligen Petrus Canisius." In *Sentire cum ecclesia: Das Bewusstsein von der Kirche als gestaltende Kraft der Frömmigkeit,* edited by Jean Danielou and Herbert Vorgrimler. Freiburg: Herder, 1961.

Lecouture, Jean. *Jesuits: A Multibiography*. Translated by Jeremy Leggatt. New York: Counterpoint, 1995.

Lehmann, Hartmut. *Das Zeitalter des Absolutismus*. Stuttgart/Berlin/Cologne/Mainz: Verlag Kohlhammer, 1980.

Lhotsky, Alphons. *Österreichische Historiographie*. Munich: Oldenbourg, 1962.

Liber sæcularis historiæ Societatis Jesu ab anno 1814 ad annum 1914. Rome: Typis Polyglottis Vaticanis, 1914.

Lieben, Salomon Hugo. "Handschriftliches zur Geschichte der Juden in Prag in den Jahren 1744–1754." *Jahrbuch der jüdisch-literarischen Gesellschaft* 2 (1904–5): 267–31; 3 (1905–6): 241–76.

Lignou, Daniel. "Jésuites et Francs Maçons: A propos d'un article de R. P. Riquet." *Dix-huitième siècle* 8 (1976): 273–85.

Ligthart, C. J. *The Return of the Jesuits: The Life of Jan Phillip Roothaan*. London: T. Shand, 1978.

Link, Edith Muir. *The Emancipation of the Austrian Peasant, 1740–1798*. New York: Columbia University Press, 1949.

Lochman, Jan Milič. *Náboženské myšlení českého obrození*. Prague: Komenského Evangelická Fakulta Bohoslovecká, 1952.

———. *Duchovní odkaz obrození*. Prague: Kalich, 1964.

Lorenz, Hellmut. "The Imperial Hofburg: The Theory and Practice of Architectural Representation in Baroque Vienna." In *State and Society in Early Modern Austria*, edited by Charles W. Ingrao. West Lafayette, Ind.: Purdue University Press, 1994.

Lorsky, Grete. *Barocke Embleme in Vorau und anderen Stiften Österreichs*. Graz: Auslieferungsstelle: Buchhandlung Styria, 1962.

Louthan, Howard. *The Quest for Compromise: Peacemakers in Counter-Reformation Vienna*. Cambridge: Cambridge University Press, 1997.

Lumières en Hongrie, en Europe Centrale et en Europe Orientale, Les. Budapest: Akadémia Kiadó, 1984.

Macartney, C. A. *The Habsburg Empire, 1790–1918*. London: Weidenfeld and Nicolson, 1968.

Machilek, Franz. "Reformorden und Ordensreformen in den böhmischen Ländern von 10. bis 18. Jahrhundert." In *Bohemia sacra: Das Christentum in Böhmen 973–1973*, edited by F. Seibt. Düsseldorf: Schwann, 1974.

MacKenzie, John J. *The Roman Catholic Church*. London: Weidenfeld and Nicolson, 1969.

Magocsi, Robert. *Historical Atlas of East Central Europe*. Seattle and London: University of Washington Press, 1993.

Maiwald, V. "Geschichte der öffentlichen Stiftsgymanaisums in Braunau." *Beiträge aus österreichischen Erziehungs- und Schulgeschichte* 12 (1912): 1–288.

Malínský, František. *Otázka svatováclavská v české historii*. Brno: Nákladem svazu osvětových ústředí moravsko-slezských v Brně, 1929.

Mansi, A. A. "Le icone di Maria: Un cammino teologico." In *Liturgia e spiritualità nell' Oriente cristiano*, edited by C. Giraudo. Milano: San Paolo, 1997.

Marczali, Henrik. *Hungary in the Eighteenth Century*. Cambridge: Cambridge University Press, 1910.

Mayr, Otto. *Authority, Liberty, and Automatic Machinery in Early Modern Europe*. Baltimore: Jons Hopkins University Press, 1986.

Masaryk, Tomáš G. *The Meaning of Czech History*. Translated by P. Kussi. Chapel Hill: The University of North Carolina Press, 1974.

McClelland, Charles E. *State, Society, and University in Germany, 1700–1914.* Cambridge/New York: Cambridge University Press, 1980.

McManners, John. *Death and the Enlightenment: Changing Attitudes towards Death among Christians and Unbelievers in Eighteenth Century France.* Oxford: Clarendon Press, 1981; New York: Oxford University Press, 1981.

———, ed. *The Oxford Illustrated History of Christianity.* Oxford: Oxford University Press, 1990.

Megill, Allan. "Aesthetic Theory and Historical Consciousness in the Eighteenth Century." *History and Theory* 17 (1978): 29–62.

Melton, James Van Horn. *Absolutism and the Eighteenth Century Origins of Compulsary Schooling in Prussia and Austria.* New York: Cambridge University Press, 1988.

———. Introduction to *State and Society in Early Modern Austria,* edited by Charles W. Ingrao. West Lafayette, Ind.: Purdue University Press, 1994.

Mendizábal, Rufus. *Catalogus defunctorum in renata Societatis Jesu ab a. 1814 ad a. 1970.* Rome: Archivum Historicum, 1970.

Merz, Gerog. *Die Pädagogik der Jesuiten: Nach den Quellen von der ältesten bis in die neueste Zeit.* Heidelberg: Carl Winter's Universitätsbuchhandlung, 1898.

Meyer, Michael A., ed. *German-Jewish History in Modern Times.* 4 vols. New York: Columbia University Press, 1996–98.

Michalová, Milena Cenaková. "Divadlo na trnavskej universite." In *Trnavská universita v dejinach školstva a vzdelnosti. Zborník referatov vedeckej konferencie konanej v Bratislave dňu 26. Novembra 1985 pri prílezitosti 350 výročia založenia trnavskej university.* Bratislava, 1986.

Midelfort, H. C. H. Erik. "Witch Hunting and the Domino Theory." In *Religion and the People, 800–1700,* edited by James Obelkevich. Chapel Hill: University of North Carolina Press, 1979.

Mikoletzky, Hans Leo. *Österreich: Das grosse Jahrhundert.* Vienna: Austria-Edition, 1967.

Mitrofanov, Paul von. *Joseph II.* Translated by V. von Demelic. Vienna/Leipzig: C. W. Stein, 1910.

Monter, William. *Ritual, Myth, and Magic in Early Modern Europe.* Athens, Ohio: Ohio University Press, 1983.

Moravek, Jan. "Schmidel Balbín a Ware: Příspevek k jesuitiské historiografii v Čechách." *ČČH,* 19 (1913): 69f.

Morgan, David. *Visual Piety: A History and Theory of Popular Religious Images.* Berkeley: University of California Press, 1998.

Morton, A. G. *John Hope, 1725–1786: Scottish Botanist.* Edinburgh: Edinburgh Botanic Garden Trust, 1986.

Mourret, F. *A History of the Catholic Church.* Translated by Newton Thompson. 8 vols. St. Louis: Herder, 1930.

Mukarovský, Jan, ed. *Dějiny české literatury,* vol. 2. 3 vols. Prague: Nakladatelství československé akademie věd, 1960.

Mullett, Michael. *Popular Culture and Popular Protest in Late Medieval and Early Modern Europe.* London: Croom Helm, 1987.

Muneles, Otto. *Bibliografický přehled židovské Prahy.* Prague: Státní zidovské muzeum, 1952.

Müller, Rainer. "The Colleges of the 'Societas Jesu' in the German Empire." In *I collegi universitari tra il xiv e xvii secolo,* edited by Domenico Maffei and Hilde de Ridder-Symoens. Milan: Guiffrè Editore, 1991.

Münch, Hermann. *Böhmische Tragödie: Das Schicksal Mitteleuropas im Lichte der tschechischen Frage.* Braunschweig/Berlin/Hamburg: Georg Westermann Verlag, 1949.

Münch, Paul. *Lebensformen in der frühen Neuzeit.* Frankfurt a/M: Propyläen, 1992.

Myers, W. David. *"Poor, Sinning Folk": Confession and Conscience in Counter-Reformation Germany.* Ithaca: Cornell University Press, 1996.

Myl'nikov, Alexandr Sergejevic. *Vznik národní osvicenské ideologie v českých zemích 18. století.* Prague: Universita Karlova, 1974.

Neck, Rudolf. "The Haus-, Hof-, und Staatsarchiv: Its History, Holdings, and Use." *Austrian History Yearbook* 6–7 (1970–71): 3–16.

Nemec, Ludvík. *Church and State in Czechoslovakia.* New York: Vantage Press, 1955.

Nešpor, Václav. *Dějiny University Olomoucké.* Olomouc: Nákladem Národního výboru hlavního města Olomouc, 1947.

Nicolai, Friedrich. *Barocker Heiligenkult in Wien und seine Träger.* Munich: R. Oldenbourg, 1978.

Nicolson, Harold. *The Age of Reason.* New York: Doubleday, 1961.

Nittner, Ernst. "Erzbistum und Prager Universität in der Zeit von der Neugründung bis zur Entkonfessionalisierung 1654–1873)." In *Tausend Jahre Bistum Prag (973–1973).* Munich: Ackermann Gemeinde, 1974.

Nolan, Mary, and Sydney Nolan, *Christian Pilgrimage in Modern Western Europe.* Chapel Hill: University of North Carolina Press, 1989.

Norman, Edward. "Epilogue: The Changing Role of the Ecclesiastical Historian." In *Religious Change in Europe, 1650–1914: Essays for John McManners,* edited by Nigel Aston. Oxford: Clarendon Press, 1997.

Nosek, Vladimir. *The Spirit of Bohemia: A Survey of Czechoslovak History, Music, and Literature.* London: Allen and Unwin, 1926.

Novák, Arne. *Czech Literature.* Translated by Peter Kussi. Ann Arbor: Michigan Slavic Publications, 1976.

Novák, V. J. "Studenské nepokoje v Praze roku 1767." *ČČH* 15 (1909): 463–46.

Novotný, Antonín. "Pražská sensace A. D. 1694." *Aventinský magazin* 4 (1930): 10–17.

Nový, Luboš. "Mathematika na pražské universtě v druhé polovině 18. století." *AUCP-HUC* 1 (161): 35–57.

Oberkofler, Gerhard, and Peter Goffer. *Geschichte der Universität Innsbruck (1669–1945).* Frankfurt a/M: Peter Lang, 1996.

O'Brien, Charles. "Ideas of Religious Toleration at the Time of Joseph II." *Transactions of the American Philosophical Society.* New ser. 59, pt. 7 (1969).

O'Brien, Conor Cruise. *On the Eve of the Millennium.* Concord, Ontario: House of Anansi Press, 1994.

Odlozik, Otakar. "The Nobility of Bohemia, 1620–1740." *East European Quarterly* 7, no. 1 (1973).

Ogilvy, A. M. *Latin and Greek.* London: Routledge and Paul, 1964.

O'Malley, John W. *The First Jesuits.* Cambridge, Mass.: Harvard University Press, 1993.

———. "The Historiography of the Society of Jesus: Where Does It Stand Today?" In *The Jesuits: Cultures, Sciences, and the Arts (1540–1773),* edited by John W. O'Malley, Gauvin Alexander Bailey, Steven J. Harris, and T. Frank Kennedy. Toronto/Buffalo/London: University of Toronto Press, 1999.

Ornstein, Martha. *The Role of Scientific Societies in the Seventeenth Century.* Chicago: University of Chicago Press, 1928.

Padberg, John W., Martin D. O'Keefe, and John L. McCarthy, eds. *For Matters of Greater Moment: The First Thirty General Congregations: A Brief History and a Translation of the Decrees.* St. Louis: The Institute of Jesuit Sources, 1994.

Palacky, Franz. *Joseph Dobrowsky's Leben und gelehrtes Wirken*. Prague: Gottlieb Haase Söhne, 1835.

Palmer, R. R. *Catholics and Christians in Eighteenth Century France*. New York: Cooper Square Publishers, 1961.

Pammer, Michael. *Glaubensabfall und wahre Andacht: Barokreligiösität, Reformkatholicizmus und Laicizmus in Oberösterreich 1700–1820*. Vienna: Verlag für Geschichte und Politik, 1994.

Pascu, Stefan. *Die Babeş-Bolayi Universität aus Cluj*. Translated by Maria Moiscu. Cluj: Dacia Verlag, 1972.

Passelecq, Geroges, and Bernard Suchecky. *The Hidden Encyclical of Pius XI*. New York: Harcourt, Brace, 1997.

Pastor, Ludwig Freiherr von. *History of the Popes*. Translated by E. F. Peeler. 40 vols. St. Louis: Herder, 1899–1953.

Patzak, B. *Die Jesuitenbauten in Breslau und ihre Architekten*. Straßburg: Heitz, 1918.

Patzak, V. "The Caroline University of Prague." SEER 19 (1940): 83–95.

Paulsen, Friedrich. *Geschichte des gelehrten Unterrichts auf den deutschen Schulen und Universiäten*. 2 vols. Leipzig: Von Veit and Co., 1896.

Pavlík, Ondrej. *The Development of the Czechoslovak School System with Regard to Slovakia*. Bratislava: Comenius University Institute for Studies in Teacher Education, 1969.

Pavlíková, Marie. "K osudu pražské universitní knihovny v 18 století." *Knihovna* 4 (1950): 130 n. 42.

———. "Vznik a vývoj univerzitní knihovny," in Čornejová, *Dějiny*, 2.

———. "Josefinská Praha." In PSH, 85–112. Prague: Orbis, 1968.

Payne, Harry. *The* Philosophe *and the People*. New Haven/London: Yale University Press, 1976.

Pavlíková, Marie. "Vznik a vývoj univerzitní knihovny." In Čornejová, *Dějiny*, 2.

Pekař, Josef. *Z duchovních dějiny Českých*. Prague: Melantrich, 1941.

Pekař, P. "Simon Abeles." *Kalendář česko-židovský* 23 (1912–13): 92–94.

Pěkný, Tomáš. *Historie Zidů v Čechách a na Moravě*. Prague: Sefer, 1993.

Pitrau, P. "Seznam jesuitských misionářů české provincie ze 17. a 18. stol. o. O. o. J."

Petranová, Alena. "Z korespondence Františka Steinského, prvního profesora pomocných ved historických na Karlové Universite." AUCP—HUC 2 (1958): 105 f.

Petráň, Josef. *Nástin dějin filosofické fakulty Univerzity Karlovy v Praze (do roku 1948)*. Prague: Univerzita Karlova, 1983.

———. *Univerzitní slavnosti v Karolinu: Instalace, promoce, sponse*. Prague: Karolinum, 1991.

———. "Učené zdroje obrozeni," in Petráň *Počátky*.

Pick, Richard. *Empress Maria Theresa: The Early Years, 1717–1757*. London: Weidenfeld and Nicolson, 1966.

Plicka, Karel. *City of Baroque and Gothic*. London: Lincolns-Praeger, 1946.

Po-Chia Hsia, R. *Social Discipline during the Reformation: Central Europe, 1550–1750*. New York/London: Routledge, 1989.

———. "Printing, Censorship, and Antisemitism in Reformation Germany." In *The Process of Change in Early Modern Europe: Essays in Honor of Miriam Usher Chrisman*, edited by Phillip N. Bebb and Sherrin Marshall. Athens, O.: Ohio University Press, 1988.

Podlaha, Antonín. "Dodatky a opravy k biografiím starších spisovatelů českých." *Časopis musea Království českého* 69 (1895).

———. ed. *Relationes super statu ecclesiæ et archdiocesis Pragensis ad S. Congregationem Concilii ab Archiepiscopis Pragensibus factæ a. 1759–1781*. Prague: Cyrillo-Methodìjská knihtiskárna V. Kotruba. Nákladem vlastním, 1908.

Pokorný, Jiří. "České literární kultura." In Petráň, *Počátky*.

Polišenský, Josef. "Società e cultura nella Boemia del Barocco." In *L'arte del Barocco in Boemia*. Milan: Bramante, 1966.

Porev, Ivan. *Habsburgs and the Ottomans between Vienna and Belgrade, 1683–1739*. Boulder: East European Monographs, 1994.

Porter, Roy. *A Social History of Madness: Stories of the Insane*. London: Weidenfeld and Nicolson, 1987.

Post, John D. "Nutritional Status and Mortality in Eighteenth Century Europe." In *Hunger in History,* edited by Lucile F. Newman. Oxford: Blackwell, 1990.

Prášek, Justin. *Dějiny Čech a Moravy na počátku národního znovuzrození*. Prague: Praze: Nákladatelství I. L. Kober Knihupectví, 1903.

Pražák, R. "Die böhmische Länder, Belgien und die Reformen von Joseph II." In *Unité et diversité de l'Empire des Habsbourg à la fin du xviiie siècle,* edited by Roland Mortier and Hevré Hasqin. Édition de l'Université de Bruxelles, no. 15 (1988).

Preiss, Pavel. "Malby Karla Palka v klášterech doksanském a strahovském." *bs* 2 (1996): 145–66.

———. "Böhmen und die österreichischen Malerei." In *Österreich im Europa der Aufklärung: Kontinuität, und Zäsur zur Zeit Maria Theresias und Josephs II.* Vienna: Verlag der Österreichischen Akademie der Wissenschaften, 1985.

Prodan, David. *Supplex libellus Vallachorum, or the Political Struggle of the Romanians in Transylvania during the 18th Century.* Translated by Mary Lazarescu. Bucharest: Publishing House of the Socielist Republic of Romania, 1971.

Pynsent, R. B. "The Baroque Continuum of Czech Literature." *SEER* 62 (1984): 321–43.

Raeff, Marc. *The Well-Ordered Police State: Social and Institutional Change through Law in the Germanies and Russia.* New Haven and London: Yale University Press, 1983.

Raková, Ivana. *Katalogy posluchačů Pražské University, 1752–1882: Inventární seznam.* Prague: Universita Karlova, 1984.

———. "Les Essais de réforme à l'Université de Prague dans la première moitié du XVIIIe siècle." In *Les Grandes Réformes des universités europeénes du XVI au XXe siècles: Zeszyty naukowe uniwersytetu Jagiellonskiego. Prace historyczne* 79 (1985): 75–82.

Redlich, Oswald. *Das Werden einer Grossmacht: Österreich von 1700 bis 1740.* Baden bei Wien: Ruldoph Reiner, 1938.

Rice, Louise. "Jesuit Thesis Prints and the Festive Academic Defence at the Collegio Romano." In *The Jesuits: Cultures, Sciences, and the Arts (1540–1773),* edited by John W. O'Malley, Gauvin Alexander Bailey, Steven J. Harris, and T. Frank Kennedy. Toronto/Buffalo/London: University of Toronto Press, 1999.

Robek, Antonín. *Lidové zdroje národního obrození.* Prague: Universita Karlova, 1974.

Roberts, John. *Revolution and Improvement: The Western World, 1775–1847.* Berkeley: The University of California Press, 1976.

Roider, Karl A., Jr. *Austria's Eastern Question, 1700–1790.* Princeton: Princeton University Press, 1982.

Rosten, Leo. *Hooray for Yiddish! A Book about English.* New York: Simon and Schuster, 1982.

Rouleau, F. A. "Maillard de Tournon, Papal Legate at the Court of Peking." *AHSI* 31 (1962): 204–323.

Rousseau, G. S. *Perilous Enlightenment: Pre- and Post-Modern Discourses.* Manchester: Manchester University Press, 1991.

Rowlands, Alison. "Witchcraft and Popular Religion in Early Modern Rothenburg ob der Tauber." In *Popular Religion in Germany and Central Europe, 1400–1800,* edited by Bob Scribner and Trevor Johnson. New York: St. Martins' Press, 1996.

Royt, Jan. *Obraz a kult v Čechách 17. a 18. století.* Prague: Karolinum, 1999.

Rude, George. *Europe in the Eighteenth Century: Aristocracy and the Bourgeois Challenge.* London: Weidenfeld and Nicolson, 1972.

Russo, Carla. *Società, chiesa e vita religiosa nell' "ancien régime."* Naples: Guida Editori, 1978.

Ryneš, Václav. "Los Jesuitas bohemicos trabajando en las misiones de América Latina después de 1620." *Ibero-Americana Pragensia* 5 (1971): 193–201.

Sadek, Vladimír. "From the MSS Collection of the State Jewish Museum MSS of Historical Context," *jb* 9, no. 1 (1973): 19–20.

Saisselin, Remy. *The Enlightenment against the Baroque: Economics and Aesthetics in the Eighteenth Century.* Berkeley: University of California Press, 1992.

Scharfe, Martin. "The Distances between the Lower Classes and Official Religion: Examples from Eighteenth Century Württemberg Protestantism." Translated by Deborah Monroe. In *Religion and Society in Early Modern Europe, 1500–1800,* edited by Kasper von Greyerz. London: George Allen and Unwin, 1984.

Schiller, Gertrude. *Iconography of Christian Art: The Passion of Jesus Christ.* 2 vols. London: Lund Humphries, 1972.

Schlafly, Daniel, Jr. "The *Ratio Studiorum* on Alien Shores: Jesuit Colleges in St. Petersbrug and Georgetown." *Revista Portuguesa de Filosofia* 55, no. 3 (1999): 253–74.

Schleuns, Karl A. *Schooling and Society: The Politics of Education in Prussia and Bavaria, 1750–1900.* Oxford/New York/Munich: Berg, 1989.

Schmidtmeyer, Rudolph. "Beiträge zur Geschichte des Jesuiten-Gymnasiums (Gymnasium Rosense) in Krummau." *Beiträge zur österreichischen Erziehungs- und Schulgeschichte* 13 (1912): 289–334.

Schunemann, Konrad. *Österreichs Bevölkerungspolitik unter Maria Theresia.* Berlin: Deutsche Rundschau, ca. 1943.

Schürer, Oskar. *Prag: Kultur/Kunst/Geschichte.* 2nd ed. Vienna/Leipzig/Prague: Verlag Dr. Rolf Passer, 1935.

Scult, Mel. *Millennial Expectations and Jewish Liberties: A Study of the Efforts to Convert Jews in Britain up to the Mid Nineteenth Century.* Leiden: E. J. Brill, 1978.

Šedinová, Jirina. "The Hebrew Historiography in Moravia at the 18th Century—Abraham Treibitsch (around 1760–1840)." *jb* 10, no. 1 (1974): 51–61.

Sehnal, Jiří. "Hudba a jesuité české provincie v 17. a 18. století." In *Morava a Brno na sklonku tricetileté valky,* edited by Jan Skutil. Brno: Magistrát hlavního města Brna, 1995.

Seibt, Ferdinand. "Kirche und Gesellschaft von den Anfängen bis zum Ende der Monarchie." In *Bohemia sacra: Das Christentum in Böhmen 973–1973,* edited by F. Seibt. Düsseldorf: Schwann, 1974.

Seibt, Fredinand, Hans Hemberg, and Helmut Slapnicka, eds. *Biographisches Lexikon zur Geschichte der Böhmischen Länder.* 12 vols. Munich: Oldenbourg, 1974–.

Seminarium Ecclesiæ Catholicæ. Rome: Typis Polyglottis Vaticanis, 1963.

Seavoy, Ronald E. *Famine in Peasant Societies.* New York: Greenwood Press, 1986.

Seydl, Otto. "Z nejstarších dějin pražské hvězdárny." *ČČH* 44 (1938): 499.

———. *Knihovna astronoma Antonína Strnada ředetele pražské hvězdárny.* Prague: Tiskárna "Prometheus," 1939.

Seton-Watson, R. W. *A History of the Czechs and Slovaks.* Hamden, Conn.: Archon, 1965.

Sheehan, James J. *German History, 1770–1866.* Oxford: Oxford University Press, 1989.

Shore, Paul. "The Suppression of the Society of Jesus in Bohemia." *AHSI* 65 (1996): 138–56.

———. "Loving the Souls, Hating the Bodies: Jesuit-Jewish Relations in Bohemia during the Eighteenth Century." *Proceedings of the Fifth Biennial Conference on Christianity and the Holocaust.* Princeton, N.J., October 18–19, 1998.

———. "The *Vita Christi* of Ludolph of Saxony and Its Influence on the *Spiritual Exercises* of Ignatius of Loyola." *Studies in the Spirituality of Jesuits* 30 (1998): 1–32.

———. "The Society of Jesus and the Culture of the Late Baroque in Bohemia." *East European Quarterly* 34, no. 1 (2000): 8.

———. "Jewish Students at the University of Prague, 1782-1822," *AUCP-HUC* (awaiting publication).

———. "Missions and Schools of the Jesuits in Transylvania and Eastern Hungary, 1700–1773." In *Lesestoffe und kulturelles Niveau des niedrigen Klerus: Jesuiten und die nationalen Kulturverhältnisse,* edited by I. Monok and P. Ötvös. Szeged: ScriptumRT, 2001.

Sierra, Vicente. *Los Jesuitas Germanos en la Conquista espiritual de Hispano-America, Siglos XVII-XVIII.* Buenos Aires: Faculdades de Filosofia y Teologia, 1944.

Silvio, Enea. *Historia Bohemica (Historie česká).* Translated by Dana Martinková, Alena Hadraková, and Jiří Matl. Prague: KLP, 1998.

Simmons, Alison. "Jesuit Aristotelian Education: The *De Anima* Commentaries." In *The Jesuits: Cultures, Sciences, and the Arts (1540–1773),* edited by John W. O'Malley, Gauvin Alexander Bailey, Steven J. Harris, and T. Frank Kennedy. Toronto/Buffalo/London: University of Toronto Press, 1999.

Skutil, Jan, ed. *Morava a Brno na sklonku třicetileté valky.* Brno: Magistrát hlavního města Brna, 1995.

Slavík, F. A. *Dějiny českého studentstva.* Prague: Nakladem vlaštním, 1973.

Smith, Sydney. "The Bullying of Clement XIV." *The Month* 465 (1903): 259–77; 466 (1903): 383–403.

Sobatová, Magdalena. "Příbamští tiskaři v 18. století." *Středoceský sborník historický* 10 (1975): 223–35.

Soergel, Philip M. *Wondrous in His Saints: Counter-Reformation Propaganda in Bavaria.* Berkeley: University of California Press, 1993.

Sommer, Ernest. *Into Exile: A History of the Counter-Reformation in Bohemia.* Translated by Victor Grove. London: New Europe, 1943.

Sorkin, David. "Reform Catholicism and Religious Enlightenment." *Austrian History Yearbook* 30 (1999): 187–219.

Sousedík, Stanislav. "Böhmische Barorockphilosophie." In *Bohemia sacra: Das Christentum in Böhmen (1973–1973),* edited by F. Seibt. Düsseldorf: Schwann, 1974.

Sox, David. *Relics and Shrines.* London: Allen and Unwin, 1985.

Stahl, Anton, S.J. "Der deutsche Priester- und Ordensnachwuchs in der Tschechoslowakei." In *Die deutschen Katoliken in der Tschechoslovakischen Republik,* edited by Heinrich Donat. Warnsdorf: Verlag A. Opitz, 1934.

Stein, A. *Die Geschichte der Juden in Böhmen.* Brünn: Jüdischer Buch- und Kunstverlag, 1904.

Stichweg, Rudolf. *Die frühmodern Staat und die europäische Universität: Zur Interaktion vom Politik und Erziehungssystem im Prozess ihrer Ausdifferenzierung.* Frankfurt a/M: Suhrkamp, 1999.

Stöger, Johann Nepomuk. *Scriptores Provinciæ Austriacæ Societatis Jesu.* Ratisbon: Manz, 1855.

Strakosch, Henry E. *State Absolutism and the Rule of Law: The Struggle for Codification of Civil Law in Austria, 1753–1811.* Sydney: Sydney University Press, 1967.

Stranka, Cyril. "Reforma pražských zednarských lozí r. 1778," *ČČH* 31 (1925), 129f.

Sugar, Peter F. "The Nature of Non-Germanic Societies under Habsburg Rule." *Slavic Review* 22 (1963): 1–30.

———. "The Rise of Nationalism in the Habsburg Empire." *Austrian History Yearbook* 3 (1967): 91–120.

———. "External and Domestic Roots of East European Nationalism." In *Nationalism in Eastern Europe,* edited by Peter F. Sugar and J. Lederer. Seattle: University of Washington Press, 1969.

Svátek, Josef. *Dějiny Českého Národa od roku 1705 do roku 1780.* Prague: I. L. Kober, 1898.

Svatoš, Martin. "Antonín Koniáš S. J. von seinen Ordensbrüdern dargestellt." *Humanistica Lovaniensia* 43 (1994): 411–24.

———. Antonín Koniáš—sluzebník Bozi či Dáblův?" *Dějiny a soucastnost* 2 (1996): 15–19.

Svatoš, Michal, and Jan Havránek. "University Colleges at Prague from the Fourteenth to the Eighteenth Centuries." In *I collegi universitari in Europa tra il xiv e il xvii secolo,* edited by Domenico Maffei and Hilde de Ridder-Symoens. Milan: Guiffrè Editore, 1991.

Svoboda, George J. "The Odd Alliance: The Underprivileged Population of Bohemia and the Habsburg Court, 1765–1790." In *The Czech and Slovak Experience: Selected Papers from the Fourth World Congress for Soviet and East European Studies, Harrogate, 1990,* edited by John Morison. New York: St. Martin's Press, 1992.

Svoboda, Jiří, *Protifeudalní a socialní hnutí v Čechách na konci doba temna (1750–1774).* Acta Universitatis Carolinæ: Philosophica et historica monographia, no. 17. Prague: Universita Karlova, 1967.

Svobodný, Petr, and Ludmila Hlavačková. "Lékařská fakulta." In Čornejová, *Dějiny,* 2.

Sw. Stanisław Kostka. Warsaw: Nakladem XX. Jezuitow w Warszawie, 1928.

Szabo, Franz A. J. *Kaunitz and Enlightened Absolutism.* Cambridge: The University Press, 1994.

Szilas, Ladislaus (László). "Die österreichische Jesuitenprovinz im Jahre 1773: Eine historische-statistische Untersuchung." *AHSI* 47 (1978): 97–158; 297–349.

Szilas, László (Ladislaus). "La Compagnia di Gesù e la politica eccelsiastica dell' Imperio Asburgo nei secoli xvii e xviii." In *I Gesuiti e gli Asburgo: Presenza della Compagnia di Gesù nell' area meridionale dell' Imperio Asburgo nei secoli xvii-xviii.* Trieste: Lint, 1995.

Štemberková, Marie. *Universitas Carolina Pragensis.* Prague: Charles Unversity, 1995.

Tanner, Marie. *The Last Descendant of Aeneas.* New Haven: Yale University Press, 1992.

Tapié, Victor-Lucien. *The Rise and Fall of the Habsburg Monarchy.* Translated by Stephen Hardman. London: Pall Mall Press, 1971.

———. *L'Europe de Marie-Thérèse.* Paris: Fayard, 1973.

Teich, Mikuláš. "The Royal Bohemian Society of Sciences and the First Phase of Organized Scientific Advance in Bohemia." *Historica* 2 (1960): 161–81.

Tetlow, Joseph. *Ignatius Loyola: Spiritual Excercises.* New York: Crossroad, 1992.

Teuber, Oskar. *Geschichte des prager Theaters.* 2 vols. Prague: A Hasse, 1883.

Thomson, S. Harrison. *Czechoslovakia in European History.* Princeton: Princeton University Press, 1943.

Thorndike, Lynn. *A History of Magic and Experimental Science.* 8 vols. New York: Columbia University Press, 1923–58.

Till, Nicolas. *Mozart and the Enlightenment.* London: Faber and Faber, 1992.

Tocanel, Petru. "Attestamento delle Missioni in Bulgaria, Valachia, Transilvania, e Moldavia." In *Sacræ Congregationis de Propaganda Fide Memoria rerum*, vol. 2 (1700–1815), edited by J. Metzler. Rome/Freiburg/Vienna: Herder, 1973.

Tomek, E. *Kirchengeschichte Österreichs*. 3 vols. Insbruck: Tyrolia, 1935–.

Tomek, W. W. *Geschichte der Prager Universität*. Osnabrück: Biblio Verlag, 1969.

Topf, Michael. *De Aufhebung des Jesuitenordens in Österreich, 1773*. Dissertation presented at the University of Vienna, 1929.

Trevor-Roper, Hugh. *The European Witch-Craze of the Sixteenth and Seventeenth Centuries, and Other Essays*. New York: Harper Torchbooks, 1967.

Trexler, Richard C. "Reverence and Profanity in the Study of Early Modern Religion." In *Religion and Society in Early Modern Europe, 1500–1800*, edited by Kaspar von Greyerz. London: George Allen and Unwin, 1984.

Tumpach, J., and A. Podlaha, ed. *Český slovník bohovědný*. 5 vols. Prague: Cyrillo-Methodějská Knihtiskarna a Nakladatelství, 1912–.

Umbach, Maiken. "Visual Culture, Scientific Image, and German Small-State Politics in the Enlightenment." *Past and Present* 158 (1998): 11–145.

Vocelka, Karel, Walter Pohl, and Brigitta Vacha. *Die Habsburger*. Verfasst von und. Graz: Styria Verlag, 1993.

Vajdako, György M. *Wien und die Literaturen in der Donaumonarchie: Zur Kulturgeschichte Mitteleuropas*. Vienna: Bohlau Verlag, 1994.

Valley, Eli. *The Great Jewish Cities of Central and Eastern Europe*. Northvale, N.J./Jerusalem: Jason Aronson, 1999.

Veit, Andreas, and Ludwig Lenhart. *Kirche und Volksfrömmigkeit im Zeitalter des Barock*. Freiburg: Herder, 1956.

Vernard, Marc. "Popular Religion in the Eighteenth Century." In *Church and Society in Catholic Europe of the Eighteenth Century*, edited by William J. Callahan and David Higgs. Cambridge: Cambridge University Pres, 1979.

Vicenzi, Otto. *Das Gymnasium: Eine Chance für Europa*. Vienna: Hermann Böhlaus Nachfolger, 1983.

Vlček, Emanuel. *Sv. Jan Nepomucký: Jeho život umučení a slavné působení ve světle současné historie a antropologie*. Prague: Vesmír, 1993.

Vlček, Jaroslav. *Dějiny české literatury*. 3 vols. 3rd edition. Prague: Nakladatel L. Mazac, 1931.

Vodička, Felix, ed. *Dějiny české literatury: II. Literatura Národního Obrození*. Prague: Nakladadelství československé akademie věd, 1960.

Voigt, Petr. *Pražské Klementinum*. Prague: Národní Knihovna, 1990.

Voigtländer, Lutz, *Die preussische Kriegsgefangenen der Reichsarmee, 1760/1763*. Duisburg: Gilles and Franke Verlag, 1995.

Volf, Josef. "Domněly pokus svob. zednářů o vzpouru v Praze 16. V. 1766." *ČČNM* 109 (1935): 78–99.

Vovelle, Michel. *Pieté baroque et déchristianisation en Provence au xviiie siècle*. Paris: Plon, 1973.

Vrchotka, Jaroslav. "Vědecké knihovny a muzejní sbírky." In Petráň, *Počátky*.

"Vydra, Stanislav," *Ottův Slovník naučný*.

Výdrová, J. *Pražské baroko: K vystaní umění v Čechách sedmnácteho až osmnácteho století*. Prague: Tiskla Prota, 1938.

Walf, Knut. "Kirchliche Aufklärung." In *Bohemia sacra: Das Christentum in Böhmen (973–1973)*, edited by F. Seibt. Düsseldorf: Schwann, 1974.

Walker, Mark. *The Salzburg Transaction: Expulsion and Redemption in Eighteenth Century Germany*. Ithaca/London: Cornell University Press, 1992.

Wandruszka, Adam. "Die Historiographie der thersianisch-josephinischen Reformzeit." In *Ungarn und Österreich unter Maria Theresia und Joseph II*, edited by A. M. Drabek, R. G. Plascka, and A Wabndruszka. Vienna: Verlag der österreichischen Akademie der Wissenschaften, 1982.

Wangermann, Ernst. *The Austrian Achievement, 1700–1800*. London: Thames and Hudson, 1973.

———. *Aufklärung und staatsbürgerliche Erziehung: Gottfried van Swieten als Reformator des österreichischen Unterrichtswesens, 1781–1791*. Munich: Oldenbourg, 1988.

Ward, W. R. *Christianity under the* Ancien Régime. Cambridge: Cambridge University Press, 1999.

Weber-Kellermann, Ingeborg. "Problems of Inter-Ethnic Research in Southeast Europe: A Consideration of Method." In *German* Volkskunde: *A Decade of Theoretical Confrontation, Debate, and Reorientation (1967–1977)*, translated and edited by James R. Dow and H. Lixfeld. Bloomington, Ind.: Indiana University Press, 1986.

Weckowicz, Helen Liebel. "Auf der Suche nach neuer Autorität: Raison d'état in der Verwaltungs -und Rechtsreformer Maria Theresias und Josephs II." In *Österreich im Europa der Aufklärung*. Vienna: Verlag der Österreichischen Akademie der Wissenschaften, 1985.

Weinzierl-Fischer, Erika. "Die Bekämpfung der Hungersnot in Böhmen 1770–1772 durch Maria Theresia und Joseph II." *Mitteilungen des Österreichischen Staatsarchivs* 7 (1954): 478–514.

Weizäcker, Wilhelm, ed. *Quellenbuch zur Geschichte der Sudentenländer*. Munich: Robert Lerche, 1960.

Welleck, René. *Essays in Czech Literaure*. The Hague: Mouton, 1963.

Wentzlaff-Eggebert, F. W. *Deutsche Mystik zwischen Mittelalter und Neuzeit*. Berlin: Walter de Gruyter, 1969.

Werstadt, Jaroslav. "Politické dějepisectví devatenáctého století a jeho čeští představitelé." *ČČH* 26 (1920): 1–93.

Whaley, Joachim. "Austria, 'Germany,' and the Dissolution of the Holy Roman Empire." In *The Habsburg Legacy: National Identity in Historical Perspective*, edited by Ritchie Robertson and Edward Timms. Edinburgh: Edinburgh University Press, 1994.

Wieser, Merry. "Paternalism in Practice: The Control of Servants and Prostitutes in Early Modern German Cities." In *The Process of Change in Early Modern Europe: Essays in Honor of Miriam Usher Chrisman*, edited by Phillip N. Bebb and Sherrin Marshall. Athens, Oh.: Ohio University Press, 1988.

Winter, Eduard. *Tausend Jahre Geisteskampf in Sudetenraum: Das religiöse Ringen zweier Völker*. Salzburg/Leipzig: Verlegt bei Otto Müller, 1938.

———. *Der Josephinismus: Die Geschichte des österreichischen Reformkatholizicismus, 1740–1848*. Berlin: Rütten und Loening, 1962.

———. *Barock, Absolutismus und Aufklärung in der Donaumonarchie*. Vienna: Europa Verlag, 1971.

Winter, F. *Tabulæ exhibentes sedes antiquæ Societatis Jesu: Missionum stationes et collegia, 1556–1773: Provinciæ Bohemiæ et Silesiæ*. Vienna: Sumptibus Monasterium Societatis Jesu, 1899.

Winter, Vavřenec J. "Český živel ve školských reformách za Marie Terezie." *Časopis katolického duchovnstva* 73 (1906): 377–84.

Witkowska, Alexandra. "The Cult of the Virgin Mary in Polish Religiousness from the 15th to the 17th century." In *Common Christian Roots: Written Contributions to the Twelve Carrefours.* Florence: LeMonnier 1982.

Witteschek, Helmut. "Absolutismus und Josephinismus." In *Bohemia sacra: Das Christentum in Böhmen (973–1973),* edited by F. Seibt. Düsseldorf: Schwann, 1974.

Wittkower, Rudolph, and Irma Jaffe, ed. *Baroque Art: The Jesuit Contribution.* New York: Fordham University Press, 1972.

Wiskemann, Elizabeth. *Czechs and Germans: A Study of the Struggle in the Historic Provinces of Bohemia and Moravia.* Oxford: The University Press, 1938.

Wolf, Gerson. *Das Unterriechtswesen in Österreich unter Kaiser Josef II.* Vienna: A Holder, 1880.

Wolf, Josef. "Z dějin tiskárny v Hradci Královĕ v. 18. století." *ČČNM* 104 (1930): 74–79.

Wolfsgruber, Cölestin. *Christoph Anton Kardinal Migazzi: Fürstenbishof von Wien.* Saulgau: Hermann Kitz, 1890.

Wolny, Reinhold J. *Josephinische Toleranz unter besonderer Berücksichtigung ihres geistlichen Wegbereiters Johann Leopold Hay.* Munich: Verlag Robert Lerche, 1973.

Wölfflin, Heinrich. *Renaissance and Baroque.* Translated by Katharine Simon. Ithaca: Cornell University Press, 1964.

Wright, William E. *Serf, Seigneur and Sovereign: Agrarian Reform in Eighteenth Century Bohemia.* Minneapolis: University of Minnesota Press, 1966.

Wyklicky, Helmuth. *Das Josephinum.* Vienna/Munich: Christian Brandstetter, 1985.

Zacek, J. F. *Palacky: The Historian as Scholar and Nationalist.* The Hague: Mouton, 1970.

Zahradník, Pavel. "Antonín Stoy a kongragace ivanitů." *bs* (1996): 69-99.

Zalenski, Stanislaus. *Les Jésuites de la Russie-Blanche.* Translated by Alexandre Vivier. 2 vols. Paris: Letouzey et Ané, 1886.

Zborowski, Mark, and Elizabeth Herzog. *Life Is with People: The Jewish Little-Town of Eastern Europe.* New York: International Universities Press, 1952.

Zuber, Rudolf. *Osudy moravské církve v 18. století 1695–1777: VI. Díl. Dějiny olomoucké arcidiecéze.* Prague: České katolická Charita v Ústředním církevním nakladatelství, 1987.

———. "Die marianischen Wallfahrten im 18. Jahrhundert." *AfKvB-M-S* 10 (1989): 89–94.

Zwischen Andacht und Andenken: Kleinodien religiöser Kunst und Wallfahrtsandenken aus trierer Sammlung: Ein Katalog zur Gemeinschaftsausstellung des bischöflichen Dom- und Diözesanmuseums Trier und des Städtischen Museums Simeonstift Trier von 16. Oktober 1992 bis 17. Januar 1993. Trier: 1992.

Index